FROM PONTEFRACT
TO PICARDY

And when the summons in our ears was shrill
Unshaken in our trust we rose, and then
Flung but a backward glance, and care-free still
Went strongly forth to do the work of men.

W.N. Hodgson
(Last verse of the poem 'The Call')

Lieutenant William Noël Hodgson MC, of the 9th Battalion
Devonshire Regiment, was killed in action at the age of 23 on
1 July 1916, near the village of Mametz, on the Somme.

FROM PONTEFRACT TO PICARDY

TO PICARDY

THE 9TH KING'S OWN YORKSHIRE LIGHT INFANTRY IN THE FIRST WORLD WAR

DEREK CLAYTON

TEMPUS

This history is dedicated to the men of the 9th KOYLI
who died in the service of their country.

First published 2004

Tempus Publishing Ltd
The Mill, Brimscombe Port
Stroud, Gloucestershire GL5 2QG
www.tempus-publishing.com

British Library Cataloguing in Publication Data.
A catalogue record for this book is available from the British Library.

ISBN 0 7524 3165 X

Typesetting and origination by Tempus Publishing.
Printed and bound in Great Britain.

CONTENTS

ACKNOWLEDGEMENTS

The successful completion of this project would simply not have been possible without the help of many people and organisations. So many have shown interest and encouraged me over the seven years it has taken me to research and write the book, and to all of them I express my grateful thanks.

Particular mention must, however, go to the following, who appear in no particular order: to the staff at the Public Record Office in Kew where I spent many days poring over War Diaries, maps and other documents. Their help in tracking down the documents has been invaluable. To the staff in the Department of Printed Documents at the Imperial War Museum who found for me the letters and papers of Brigadier Ellenberger and Captain Yeo. To Major Deedes, Secretary of the KOYLI Association, and his predecessor Colonel Cowley, for allowing me access to various documents, papers, letters, maps and so on, held at their offices in Pontefract.

To Julie and Michael Renshaw of Auchonvillers, France, for their hospitality on many visits to the Western Front battlefields. To David Tattersfield, author of *A Village Goes to War*, for allowing me to use several photographs of 9th KOYLI men from his book, and for ploughing through archives of the *Dewsbury Reporter* and *Huddersfield Examiner* on my behalf. To David and his wife, Dawn, my thanks for their constant encouragement and interest.

To Thierry Boulet, of Louviers, France, for his encouragement, and for his help in researching the *Chemin des Dames* battle of May 1918.

To Paul Reed, of Courcelette, France, for sending me a copy of the photograph of 9th KOYLI officers which appears in his book, *Walking the Somme*, and for allowing me to reproduce it in mine. To the staff of the Commonwealth War Graves Commission in Maidenhead who, patiently and courteously, dealt with my numerous requests for information in pre-website days.

To Mrs Hermione Parker for graciously allowing me to quote extensively from the papers of her late father, Brigadier G.F. Ellenberger. To Mr Mark Cornwall Jones for allowing me to quote from the letters of Colonel H.E. Yeo, and to Peter Yeo, the Colonel's son, for permission to publish his photograph of the 9th KOYLI Football team of 1914.

To Jenny, for uncomplainingly following me across the battlefields of France and Belgium over the years, and for understanding when the project occasionally reached the levels of an obsession.

D.C.
January 2004

INTRODUCTION

Sunday 28 June 1914 was a sunny day in the Bosnian capital of Sarajevo. Archduke Franz Ferdinand, heir to the throne of the Austro-Hungarian Empire, arrived with his wife Sophie on the royal train at ten minutes to ten that morning, their wedding anniversary. They were driven from the station in an open car to the Filipovitch parade ground, where they inspected the 15th and 16th Corps of the Austrian Army, in Sarajevo on their annual manoeuvres. Within half an hour they were on their way to the Town Hall, where an official welcome awaited them.

Recent Balkan history had been turbulent. Quarrels over the Slav states had been going on for generations: Austria-Hungary, Turkey and Imperial Russia had long struggled for dominance, and each sought to exert its influence over the confusing array of nation-states during the late nineteenth and early twentieth centuries. Many nations were demanding that the lines on the maps of Eastern Europe be re-drawn. The two Balkan Wars of 1912-13 had done nothing to encourage stability. Bosnia-Herzegovina was a recent Hapsburg acquisition, being annexed only in 1908. The inhabitants, Muslims, Serbs and Croats, resented the Austrian presence, and agitation for a political union with the neighbouring state of Serbia was growing. The Archduke's visit in his official capacity of Inspector General to the Austrian Armed Forces was to go some way towards reminding the people of the region just who was in charge.

A handful of young assassins were in Sarajevo that day, planning to kill the Archduke in an attempt to further their cause. They succeeded more by luck than by dint of careful preparation. The first would-be assassin froze into inaction as the Archduke's car swept past him. Another threw a bomb at the car as it made its way to the Town Hall. The bomb missed, wrecking the following car and injuring some twenty spectators.

The Archduke insisted that the agenda should go ahead as planned and duly made his speech at the Town Hall. On the advice of his aides, he was, for security reasons, to take a different return route, offering the opportunity to visit the hospital where the injured from the earlier failed assassination attempt had been taken. He was never to reach the hospital. His chauffeur took a wrong turning, realised his mistake and stopped the car. Fate decreed that the car should come to a halt within feet of eighteen-year-old Gavrilo Princip, one of the conspirators, who stepped onto the running-board and shot the Archduke and his wife. They died almost immediately, the time: 11.00 a.m.

The 'fatal spark was struck',[1] as Basil Liddell Hart saw it. It was the excuse Austria needed to put Serbia in its place once and for all. Serbia, in turn, greeted the event with unconcealed pleasure.

Emperor Franz Josef of Austria-Hungary saw a chance to isolate Serbia and to limit, if not indeed to reverse, its expansion. He was not going to move, however, before receiving assurances from Germany that it would support him if his actions were to precipitate Russian involvement on the Serbian side. Kaiser Wilhelm II of Germany gave the hoped-for safeguards, believing that Russia was not ready for war. With this support confirmed officially on 6 July, and despite a distinct lack of evidence that the Serbian government was implicated in the assassinations, the Austro-Hungarian government issued an ultimatum to the Serbs on 23 July. The ultimatum was worded so as to be a direct violation of, and threat to, Serbian independence. The Serbs were also only given forty-eight hours in which to reply. The Serbian answer, handed to the Austrian Ambassador two minutes before the expiration of the ultimatum, acceded to all but two of the Austrian demands, those requiring that Austrian troops be allowed to enter Serbia to search for conspirators.

Serbia had already mobilised her forces as a precautionary measure, and, three hours later, orders for Austria's partial mobilisation were also sent out. Preparatory measures for mobilisation in Germany and Russia were almost simultaneous.

On 28 July at 11.00 a.m., Austria's declaration of war was delivered to the Serbian government. The document, signed by the Emperor Franz Josef, contained a sentence confirming that Serbian forces had already attacked Austrian troops. This was fantasy, a pretext to get the Emperor to sign, and the offending phrase was removed prior to its despatch.

Europe's Generals now appeared to put their weight behind the lumbering juggernaut that was early twentieth-century diplomacy. None wished to be caught at a disadvantage by delaying mobilisation for too long.

Logistics required that Austria-Hungary mobilise fully: the huge numbers of men involved and complex railway timetabling allowed no other course of action. Increased Austro-Hungarian hegemony in the Balkans threatened Russia's trade route through the Black Sea, and as protector of Serbia, and of its own economic interests, Russia had no choice but to declare general mobilisation on 30 July.

Germany was a relatively young country. It had enjoyed unification only in 1871, under Prussian dominance, after a victorious war against France. Its first Chancellor, Otto von Bismarck, dominated European diplomacy and cemented in place a complex structure of alliances which had kept the peace between the major powers, amongst whose number Germany now counted itself, until this point. Under Kaiser Wilhelm II, who came to the throne in 1888, and once Bismarck had been removed from the scene, the delicate balance of power had tipped and rocked alarmingly through a series of crises: the system of alliances had polarised Europe into two main camps; Britain, France and Russia on the one side, Germany and Austria-Hungary on the other.

Germany's promise to support Austria-Hungary against Russia, and Russia's subsequent mobilisation, meant that Germany was now running out of options. A German demand for Russian demobilisation within twelve hours (impossible to achieve within such time restraints even with Russia's acquiescence) was refused, and on 1 August Germany declared war on Russia.

The German military plan to defeat Russia had been named after the Chief of Staff who had devised it in 1892, Alfred von Schlieffen. Fearful of a war on two fronts, and mindful of the time required for Russia to complete its extensive and complex mobilisation, calculated in weeks rather than in days, the Schlieffen Plan required Germany to deliver a quick knock-out blow to France, thus allowing her to turn her undivided attention, and her undivided Armies, eastwards in time to face the ponderous Russian military machine. The plan had been prepared with minute attention to detail and to a rigorous timetable, and had not been fundamentally altered since its inception.

Left: *Memorial plaque in the KOYLI Chapel at York Minster.*

Right: *26925 Private Hubert Battye, great-uncle of the author.*

Unwilling or unable to improvise, the German General Staff's implementation of this plan meant that Germany, without pretext or warning, declared war on France on 3 August.

The Schlieffen Plan was put into force, its strict timetable requiring the fall of Paris in thirty-nine days. One and a half million men crossed the Rhine, three-quarters of them ready to outflank France's border fortifications to the north by attacking through neutral Belgium. They would brush the English Channel with their right flank and then swing southward in a huge arc to defeat the French Army and capture Paris. The loss of the capital would surely induce surrender.

A German request on 2 August to be allowed free passage for their troops through Belgian territory was refused the following day. On 4 August, at 8.30 a.m., German cavalry entered Belgium, the German Chancellor announcing in the Reichstag that: 'necessity has no law… we must hack our way through.'[2]

The only remaining question to be answered was whether Britain would be drawn into the war. The Belgians opposed the German advance as best they could and appealed to Britain, France and Russia for assistance. Britain and Germany had been naval rivals for some time, and a threat to the dominance of the Royal Navy was a threat to the Empire, but the British government fell back on a treaty signed in 1839, requiring them to guarantee Belgian neutrality, and sent an ultimatum to Germany.

Assurances were required by midnight (11.00 p.m. GMT) 4 August that the neutrality of Belgium would be respected. At 4.00 p.m. the British government gave orders for the mobilisation of the Army. No assurances were forthcoming, and with the following announcement, issued at 12.15 a.m. on the morning of 5 August 1914, Britain found itself at war:

Owing to the summary rejection by the German Government of the request made by His Majesty's Government for assurances that the neutrality of Belgium will be respected, His Majesty's Ambassador at Berlin has received his passports and His Majesty's Government have declared to the German Government that a state of war exists between Great Britain and Germany as from 11.00 p.m. on the 4 August.[3]

1

NEW ARMIES

On Sunday 9 August, the fifth day of mobilisation, the first troops of the British Expeditionary Force (BEF), two corps strong and totalling some 100,000 men, officially landed in France. The bulk of the troops arrived there between the 12th and the 17th, landing at Boulogne, Rouen and Le Havre, mostly at night.

Field Marshal Sir John French, the sixty-two-year-old Commander-in-Chief, left London on 14 August, arriving in Amiens that same evening. The BEF was to move northwards and form the extreme left of the French line of advance, to the left of the French 5th Army, in order to assist in the advance against the invading German forces. First contact by British troops with the enemy was made on 22 August at dawn, by a patrol from 'C' Squadron of the 4th Dragoon Guards (2nd Cavalry Brigade) firing upon German troops near Soignies. These were the first hostile shots fired by British troops on the continent of Western Europe for ninety-nine years.

Many were inclined to believe that the war would not be a long-drawn-out affair. Indeed, the German plan, if it were to succeed, depended wholly on this premise, and on the Allied side, the over-used phrase 'over by Christmas' was taken seriously by a significant number of people.

One man who did not share this view was the recently made Earl, Field Marshal Lord Kitchener. On 3 August 1914, he was in England, preparing to return to Egypt where he was Consul General, when Colonel Repington, military correspondent to *The Times*, suggested that he would be the best choice for the newly created and, as yet, unfilled post of Secretary of State for War. That day, Kitchener had got as far as Dover, and was waiting for his boat to depart, when he was suddenly recalled to London by the Prime Minister, Herbert Asquith. On 5 August, Kitchener was persuaded to take the post. He was not keen at first, but accepted that it was his duty in this time of crisis for the country. To the majority of the people in Britain, however, the appointment of this non-political figure, the hero of Sudan and South Africa, was exactly what was needed to unify and inspire the nation.

Kitchener differed from most of the military leaders of the time in believing that the war would last for some considerable time after Christmas. His estimate was a minimum of three years, and predicted that Britain's full military strength could not be put into the field until 1917 at the earliest.

With that in mind, on 6 August, he sought parliamentary approval for the expansion of the Army by half a million men, volunteers all. The following day, the newspapers published Kitchener's preliminary call to arms: 'The addition of 100,000 men to His

Majesty's Regular Army is immediately necessary in the present grave National Emergency. Lord Kitchener is confident that this appeal will be at once responded to by all those who have the safety of our Empire at heart.'

The appeal was for men between nineteen and thirty years of age, five feet three inches tall and upwards, who were willing to enlist for three years, or 'until the war is concluded'. Pay was to be between 1s 3d and 10s 6d a day, 'according to Branch of Service and qualifications'.

The Army Council agreed the details of the organisation of the 'First New Army' on 11 August. The standard Division was to be made up of three brigades, each of four battalions. At this time, a battalion consisted of approximately 1,000 men, under the command of a lieutenant-colonel. Simple arithmetic allows us to calculate the strength of a brigade to be 4,000 men, and a Division 12,000. Once Divisional artillery, a Pioneer battalion and other ancillaries are added, the total is somewhat higher.

The Division was the largest self-contained unit that moved around as a single entity. Men identified to some extent with their Division, but the nearest thing to a 'family' on which to nail their loyalty was the battalion. The make-up of a Division could change, a brigade was known occasionally to alter, but the battalion itself remained inviolate. It was at this level that a soldier could really 'belong'.

Smaller units existed within the framework of the battalion. Four companies of 250 men, commanded by a captain and these further sub-divided into platoons of approximately sixty, a lieutenant or second-lieutenant at its head, and the smallest, a section, with a corporal or lance-corporal in charge. It will be seen later that the exigencies of war and their attendant shortages often meant that the outline pattern outlined above could not be maintained. Companies commanded by second-lieutenants, battalions by majors or captains were not uncommon.

The flow of volunteers into the pre-war British Army had been around the 30,000 a year mark from the entire United Kingdom, or an average of fewer than 100 per day. Between 4 and 8 August 1914, the total number attested was 8,193 – about 1,640 daily. These figures were still seen as slightly less than encouraging, but in reality the actual numbers of those attested in no way represented the numbers who turned up to recruiting stations in their hundreds and thousands, only to be turned away at the end of a day's fruitless queuing. The system in place simply could not cope.

The number of recruiting stations was duly increased, some towns and cities making their town halls available: large numbers of clerks and doctors were drafted in to augment the incumbent recruiting staffs, and during the second week of the war the recruiting campaign began to gather some momentum, with 45,354 men enlisting between 9 and 15 August. The following week's figure was 49,982.

The early rate of acceleration in recruiting was not maintained, however, and reasons for this were quite diverse. Many married men were keen to ensure that their families were well cared for before they joined the Army: some required assurances that their jobs would still be there for them on their return. A patchy recruitment policy meant that in some areas, numbers were disappointing; in others, recruiting regulations were being applied rigorously, turning down men for trivial reasons that would not have prevented them joining up elsewhere in the country. Some held back thinking that 100,000 was all that was needed.

Indeed, that figure was reached on 25 August, the day on which the first reports of the Battle of Mons reached the British public. The newspapers spoke of a battle that had not gone too well for the Allies, and with the BEF subsequently forced into retreat, an upsurge of patriotism seemed to sweep the nation. The recruiting figures for that day, at

10,019, were the highest for any single day so far, and the final figure for that week stood at an impressive 63,000.

On 28 August, Kitchener's appeal for a second 100,000 appeared in the press. The upper age limit was extended to thirty-five for new recruits, forty-five for ex-soldiers and fifty for certain ex-non-commissioned officers, with the need for the last of these becoming pressing. Further press reports of the BEF's 'glorious retreat', their 'terrible losses', and the need for 'more and more men' encouraged yet another upturn in the recruiting figures, the end of August and the beginning of September seeing a kind of 'recruiting fever'.[1]

Even before this boom, on 21 August the first six Divisions of Kitchener's Army officially came into being. These were numbered 9th to 14th, and became known as 'K1', the 'First New Army', denoting that these Divisions came from Kitchener's first 100,000. Such was now the rush to the recruiting stations that the second 100,000 was raised in under a week. The second series of Divisions, numbered 15th to 20th, was authorised on 1 September, and 'K2' came into being officially on the 11th of that month.

By 4 September, Prime Minister Asquith stated that Kitchener's appeal had already produced between 200,000 and 300,000 men. The Third Army, 'K3', was to be raised immediately, being made up of the 21st to 26th Divisions, and was officially created on 13 September 1914.

The 9th (Service) Battalion King's Own Yorkshire Light Infantry came into being at this time as part of the 64th Brigade, 21st Division.

The history of the King's Own Light Infantry Regiment goes back to long before it bore that name. Its direct ancestor, if one may speak in genealogical terms, was the 53rd of Foot, formed in 1755, its recruits coming chiefly from the Leeds area. Its designation was changed the following year to the 51st and it first saw action in 1757 during the Seven Years' War.

In 1759, during the same conflict, 'the regiment won what was perhaps its greatest Battle Honour'.[2] The Battle of Minden took place on 1 August 1759, with 41,500 British and Hanoverians facing a French force of 52,000. The 51st of Foot formed part of the reserve force and, as too often in war, a misinterpreted order sent the reserves forward by mistake to face frightening odds: on this occasion a mass of French cavalry and sixty heavy cannon.

Over a distance of two hundred yards it calmly advanced through a storm of shot, the ranks steadily closing together as men were killed and wounded. Eleven squadrons of French cavalry hurled themselves against that 'astonishing infantry', but the column, remaining quiet until the horses were only ten paces off received them with volley and bayonet. The cavalry were beaten off.[3]

When ordered repeatedly to do so, the British cavalry would not move in their support, and 'once more the French cavalry charged upon the British column. Again they were met with perfect coolness and determination, and again – this time finally – they were driven off the field... and the battle was won.'[4]

It is said that as they advanced, the soldiers of the 51st plucked flowers and stuck them in their tunics. From that time, the regiment celebrated Minden Day on 1 August and the white rose of Yorkshire was worn by all ranks in their caps.

After time spent in Ireland and Spain, the 51st became a Light Infantry Corps and at Waterloo held the extreme right of the British line. Renamed the 51st King's Own Light Infantry (Second Yorkshire West Riding Regiment) in 1821, they fought in the Second

Burma War some thirty years later. Meanwhile, the 2nd Battalion had evolved from the Second Madras European Regiment, formed in 1839. From this branch of the 'family' came the regimental motto, *Cede Nullis*.

The reorganisation of the Army in 1871 finally brought the two units together as the 1st and 2nd Battalions King's Own Light Infantry (South Yorkshire Regiment), and these became the KOYLI in 1887.

On the outbreak of the First World War, the 1st Battalion was in Singapore. It received orders to mobilise and immediately sailed for England, arriving in November 1914. The 2nd Battalion was already in England and crossed the Channel with the British Expeditionary Force, playing an important role in the Battle of Le Cateau on 26 August, facing the advance of von Kluck's IV Corps. 'That night the 2nd KOYLI mustered only eight officers and 320 rank and file but it had held up the Germans at the only point where they had penetrated into the British position, and thus gave the rest of the 5th Division a clear start in their retirement'.[5]

The KOYLI had traditionally recruited from the industrial West Riding of Yorkshire, and when Kitchener's call came, the young men of the region were not slow to come forward. The *Dewsbury Reporter* of 22 August 1914 wrote:

BRISK RECRUITING IN DEWSBURY
NIGHTLY SCENE IN THE MARKET PLACE

Every evening this week about 5 o'clock there has been a scene in the Dewsbury Market Place which has stirred the emotions and appealed strongly to the imagination of the onlookers – we refer to the departure of the batches of recruits for Lord Kitchener's New Army. So far, Dewsbury's response to that fine soldier's appeal has been simply splendid – far ahead of any other similar district. Up to last Saturday no less than 153 recruits had been sent to the Pontefract depot since the day of mobilisation. There has been no fuss or undue demonstration. The men have walked to the front of the Town Hall, taken their seats in the cars and with a smile on their faces have waved a cheery goodbye to their friends as the cars sped away. In many cases their womenfolk have joined in the send off, and not until the car has passed out of sight did they turn away to wipe the tears from their eyes with the corner of their shawls or aprons. On the whole a good class of recruit has been obtained. They are taken to Pontefract for general service, to be drafted as required, but most of them have signified a wish to join the Yorkshire Light Infantry or the Artillery.[6]

One week later, the same newspaper printed an appeal under the title: 'WANTED: MORE MEN. MAJOR WALKER'S ROUSING APPEAL'. Maj. Walker wrote:

Sir, – It has been my privilege during the last few weeks to swear into Lord Kitchener's New Army a great many men from this town and district, and I am proud to say that the hard-working men of the district are responding splendidly to the appeal of the government and War Minister for more men for the Army. I should like to take this opportunity of emphasising the fact that unless men come voluntarily forward in larger numbers the Government will be bound to bring in a measure to compel them to join the Army... What has struck me during the last few days is: where are the better-educated young men of this town? Surely, in the various tennis, cricket, football and even golf clubs there must be many who feel they are not doing their duty for King and Country... In conclusion, let me say that a group of young fellows who know each other well and who would join a regiment together would find soldiering a far finer recreation than cricket, tennis or golf.[7]

Recruiting Drive by the KOYLI at Dewsbury Town Hall.

An appeal from the Mayor of Dewsbury in the same edition echoes this sentiment, asking why the 'sons of working men' should bear the brunt. Ominously, on the same page, an early and therefore understandably imprecise report from the front announces heavy British casualties:

Fighting continues all over Europe, but little detailed news comes from the Armies. The British on their retreat from Mons in Southern Belgium after the fighting of Sunday, suffered 2,000 casualties. Sir John French, reporting the losses says the troops, in spite of hard marching and fighting, are in the best of spirits.

By the time Kitchener's famous recruiting poster appeared in late September, pointing its inescapable finger at every young man in the country, recruiting was again in decline. The design, incorporating the slogan 'Your Country Needs You', had first appeared on Saturday 5 September in the magazine *London Opinion*. The *Dewsbury Reporter* of that day proudly broadcast:

Remarkable and unprecedented scenes have been witnessed in Dewsbury this week, in connection with the recruiting for Lord Kitchener's Army. Whether or not it is the result of the stirring speeches at Crown Flatts last Saturday, there has certainly been a splendid response this week, nearly 400 men having been sent to Pontefract from Monday to Thursday, making the total since the outbreak of hostilities into close on 500.

The scenes at the Market Place and the Lancashire and Yorkshire Railway station on Tuesday evening, when 127 were sent away, were without parallel in the history of the borough. A vast concourse gathered in the Market Square, the Dewsbury Borough public band played patriotic selections, and as the train steamed out, to the accompaniment of ringing cheers and the discharge of numerous fog signals, there were not many who were left unaffected.

Addressing the men, Major Walker V.D., JP, who has evinced the keenest interest in the recruiting, said that most of them were going to join one of the most famous regiments in the world, the King's Own Yorkshire Light Infantry. (Cheers) The Commanding Officer of the 2nd Battalion, Lieut-Col. Bond, who has been killed in action, was a gentleman for whom he entertained the highest esteem and affection. They were going to avenge his death – (Cheers) – and they would no doubt cover themselves with glory. (A Voice: 'We'll try, sir').

Lusty cheers were then given for the Mayor, Major Walker, and the KOYLI. The men were presented with packets of cigarettes, and a big crowd, which overflowed the platforms on to the lines, waited patiently until the train steamed out in order to give a last cheer to the men going out into the unknown. The total number of men sent off from Dewsbury since the commencement of the war is 779.[8]

Scenes such as these would have been repeated on varying scales all over the West Riding, throughout Yorkshire as a whole, and indeed nation-wide as the depots filled with eager recruits. It had been decided by this time that Pontefract would now only receive men destined for the KOYLI or Yorks & Lancs Regiments.

The depots, in actual fact, had been filled to overflowing some time ago. The sheer number of men to be processed had long since outstripped the Army's ability to cope with any real measure of efficiency. 'On every side there were acute shortages of accommodation, uniform, weapons, personal equipment, blankets, bedding and even rations.'[9]

The men who converged on Pontefract had all undergone the same procedure of enlistment. They had answered a dozen or so questions as set out on the attestation form, ranging from name and age to admitting any previous record of imprisonment or previous military service; they had passed a fairly rudimentary medical examination, had taken an oath of allegiance and had been given the King's shilling (one day's pay).

Two differing accounts will serve to shed some light on the conditions 'endured' by the new recruits, who though certainly 'in the Army', had not yet learned to which battalion they were about to be attached.

George Eskritt, who was to become a private in the 9th KOYLI, wrote to a former officer of the battalion some sixty-five years later, describing what had happened to him. Complaining of a lack of food, and being short of money, he simply sauntered out of the depot in Pontefract and walked home to Leeds with a friend, a distance of some fifteen miles:

We had to take the chaff that we had come home for our Sunday dinner. Our mothers said we would get shot for desertion. Well, we went back by train the following Wednesday and in the field before you came to the barracks there were crowds of volunteers, so we mingled amongst them and then ambled down to the railway station and were taken to Tring in Hertfordshire.[10]

A no-doubt carefully chosen letter was printed in the *Dewsbury Reporter* of the 26 September under the heading: 'Life in Pontefract Camp – Silly Rumours Contradicted – Letters from Batley Soldiers'. The article continued:

Many rumours have been circulated in the district regarding the conditions under which our local soldiers are housed at Pontefract and the treatment they have received with regard to food etc. The following letter has come to hand this week, and we trust that it will put an end to the ridiculous tales: To the Editor of the Reporter, Sir, – Having heard that there have been many rumours about that the Pontefract camp is in a filthy condition and that there is not enough to eat for the soldiers, we, the undersigned, wish to contradict these rumours. We are all Batley chaps who have been at Pontefract for three weeks, and we are all in the pink of condition and ready for anything. The camp is cleared up and disinfected every day, and as for eating, we have enough and to spare. For breakfast we have bread and butter – not margarine – and jam or cheese: to dinner we have boiled beef, fresh every day, along with cabbage and carrots; and for tea we get bread and butter, tinned salmon and tinned herrings or potted beef: so you will see whether we are pined or not.
–Yours etc.,

A. Pickles, T.W. Hirst, J.W. Thompson, T.H. Marsden, J. Collinson, T. Peel, J. Bairstow, G.H. Mitchell, J. Nutton, J. Fitzpatrick, T. Freeman, W. Wilson.

Each man who passed through Pontefract, at varying times, at varying rates, would have his own version of events, based on comparisons with his home life, each from his own particular personal standpoint. Suffice it to say that the situation in this and many other depots was at worst difficult, at best interesting, and for the great many recruits for whom this would have been their first time away from home, an adventure.

As it is, our story now moves southwards along with the recruits from Pontefract, as they collected at Berkhamsted, and were formed into two sister battalions, the 9th and 10th KOYLI. They were placed, as previously noted, in the 64th Infantry Brigade, along with the 14th and 15th Durham Light Infantry.

The new Divisions were not short of men: it was a very different story where officers were concerned. Every battalion commander in the 21st Division at this time had come back from retirement to take up the post. Indeed, 'only fourteen officers in the entire

Division had any previous experience in the Regular Army. The remainder, over 400 in number, had all been granted commissions since the war began and were mostly without officer training.'[11]

The Army List (Public Record Office, Ref: 1363a) lists the officers of the 9th KOYLI in October 1914 as: Lt-Col. G.L. Holland (In command); 2nd-Lts H. Yeo, E. Cambie, L.D. Spicer, B.L. Gordon, G. Haswell, N.L. Alexander, E.F. Graham, L.D. Head, C. Jones, H.A. Telfer, T. Brearley.

Second-Lieutenant Spicer, in his book *Letters from France*, describes Lt-Col. Holland as a 'pleasant enough old boy', but was of the opinion that he was a 'little behind the times'. By November, Capts F.C. Phillips, A. Hine and T. Trad, along with Lt R.E. Graham-Clarke, 2nd-Lt P.J.O. Morris and Lt C.K. Butler as Adjutant had been added to the numbers.

It was not only the depots that were by now full to capacity: accommodation in barracks was only available for 262,000 men – not enough for the first two New Armies. New, previously unused sites had to be found for the Third New Army. The 21st Division was to be stationed at Halton Park, between Tring and Wendover, on land owned by Lord Rothschild. Prior to that, they were placed in billets in nearby towns; the 9th KOYLI found themselves in Aylesbury.

The men of the Brigade were practically all Yorkshire and Durham miners, and the north country accent was heard everywhere in the streets of Aylesbury. They were of course still dressed in civilian attire, and the only feature that marked them down as soldiers was an arm-band with the name of the Regiment stamped on it.[12]

The stay at Aylesbury was a short one. The camp at Halton Park was soon ready to receive them:

The march to Halton Park was not more than four miles, but it was our first march, and a notable one. It must have taken us about two and a half hours to accomplish! We paraded in the Market Place at Aylesbury preparatory to marching off, and although we had scarcely been in the town ten days, we appeared to have already acquired a large number of friends and admirers. At least I judged this from the very enthusiastic crowd that came to see us off, and from the number and variety of free drinks which some of us had obviously had, and of which some of us were still partaking.

With the exception of most of the officers, and a few NCO's, who were old Regulars, there were no uniforms to be seen, and consequently the parade did not have a very military appearance. We didn't march to Halton, we walked! Anyhow, we eventually got there, which was what mattered most at the time.[13]

Accommodation at Halton Park consisted of fifteen- to twenty-man tents in a field described as 'pleasant enough', but almost incessant rain from mid-October reduced the whole area to a sea of knee-deep mud. Conditions became very unpleasant. 'The tents had no tent-boards, we had no waterproof sheets and the blanket ration did not then allow of more than one per man.'[14]

The limits of endurance of these north-country men were stretched further one morning when the supply of bacon for breakfast fell woefully short of the required amount per man. Late-comers received none at all, and, taking exception to this, the men failed to turn up for the next parade, and a number of them set off for the station, grumbling about their 'rights'. Just how this situation was resolved is not recorded!

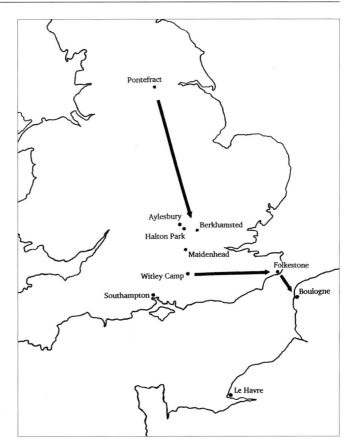

Training. Movements, September 1914–September 1915.

Training began almost at once. The programme, however, lacked imagination. From 6.30 to 8.30 a.m. was physical exercise, the men being instructed in this by their own officers, none of whom was a trained gymnastic instructor. One hour was then set aside for breakfast, followed from 9.00 a.m. to 1.00 p.m. and from 2.00 to 5.00 p.m. by Squad Drill, this to be performed with no rifles as there were none to be had! This pattern endured for three weeks, any variation on the scheme being strictly forbidden. At first the programme ran for six days a week, only Sunday being free. It was not long, however, before Saturday afternoon also became free time.

'If boredom could kill, we should all have died within two days.'[15] The unnamed chronicler and a fellow officer showed some initiative, concocting a scheme to allow some variation for the men under their command.

We had both been in the OTC at school and at Cambridge, and had therefore a very fair smattering of infantry movements. We were both in the same company and were the only officers in it. We agreed that for one hour he should take half the company into a remote corner of the large field, which was our parade ground, and unobserved, should carry out any small scheme that he might invent. At that time I, with the other half of the company, should 'carry on' Squad Drill, marching up and down in front of his corner, the better to obscure his movements. Also of course, I should be able to give timely warning of the approach of any senior officer. At the end of the hour we were to change over. This manoeuvre was successfully carried out on more than one occasion, and pleased the men immensely.[16]

The equipment shortage was being felt by the men of the 9th KOYLI at this time: no uniforms had yet been issued, and Drill and PT alike were undertaken in civilian dress. The men's own clothes were simply not strong enough to withstand this kind of treatment and were beginning to wear out. The opportunity to miss parade arose once a recruit could claim that his clothes had worn out to such an extent that decency was compromised. The downside to this was that these men were also confined to camp, as their clothes, by their own admission, were not suitable for 'walking out' in the evening or at weekends. The need to try and keep clothes in a serviceable condition was soon appreciated by many!

One quaint, but useless sergeant was very perturbed at having no uniform. He was only a sergeant because at some time or another, probably in a previous existence, he had been in the Army, and consequently knew the words of command. His dress consisted of a bowler hat (which was not in the heyday of youth), a starched collar (the only one he had, and after three weeks it was looking a trifle tired), a dickey, but no tie, a black waistcoat and a black tailcoat, a pair of nondescript trousers and an ancient pair of brown boots. He had a sandy moustache, a pink nose, a mottled complexion... and a husky voice. It was no wonder that (as he complained to me), the men did not realise his position. 'But', he whispered confidentially, 'it will be all right, Sir, as soon as I get my stripes up.' But it wasn't, and he had to come down to private.[17]

It was at about this time that, in the absence of sufficient khaki cloth to clothe the entire Army, uniforms of blue serge began to be issued. This was obviously a great improvement on the current situation: at least all the men would now be dressed alike, and a parade would look more of an authentic military occasion. The blue uniforms were not greeted with universal or unqualified approval by the men, however, some being of the opinion that they looked more like postmen than soldiers.

As November began, the battalion moved into huts in another part of Halton Park. The standard hutment measured sixty feet by twenty feet. Tables and benches took up the space down the centre of the hut, leaving room for thirty beds down the sides. The hutments consisted of a wooden framework, with corrugated iron roof and walls. Unfortunately, the huts at Halton were unfinished, and within a fortnight of moving in, the battalion had moved out again, this time into billets in nearby Maidenhead.

The time spent in billets was reasonably uneventful, with training progressing slowly. One aspect of this training was simulated trench life. Trenches were dug and men were obliged to inhabit them for certain periods of time. On one occasion, 'A' and 'B' Companies were occupying facing trenches, each playing the part of the other's enemy. The night exercise developed into an unofficial battle between the rival companies, using such weapons as over-ripe tomatoes, eggs, home-made stink bombs, sticks, fists, pepper, squibs and bad language. On another occasion, this time whilst digging trenches on a wet and dismal day, a voice suddenly rose clearly from one: 'Are we downhearted?' to be answered from another with 'Yes, I should bloody well think we are!', this followed by roars of appreciative laughter.

In February 1915, the weather once more did its worst, and floods prevented one company from leaving its billets for four consecutive days. The beginning of April saw the battalion move back into the now completed hutments of Halton Park. This coincided with the resignation due to ill health of Lt-Gen. Sir Edmund Hutton, Commanding Officer 21st Division. His replacement was Maj.-Gen G.T. Forrestier-Walker.

Forrestier-Walker had already seen service in France since the start of the war as Chief of Staff to General Sir Horace Smith-Dorrien (GOC II Corps), and had some knowledge of the kind of war the Division would be expected to fight. With his arrival, the pace of training quickened. He was a great believer in route-marching, so they marched and marched and marched. March discipline improved quickly: at first each brigade could expect between thirty and forty men to fall out on a twelve-mile march. Within a couple of months, after two or three route-marches per week, seventeen miles carrying full pack would result in three or four 'casualties'. The men would often sing on the march, and well-known hymns were re-written to match the feeling of the times. A popular one amongst the KOYLIs was to the tune of 'We are but little children meek', and, surprisingly free from obscenities, their version ran:

> *We are but little soldiers meek,*
> *And only get three bob a week.*
> *The more we work the more we may,*
> *It makes no difference to our pay.*

It was also at about this time that the battalion received proper khaki uniforms, finally allowing them to really look the part. The webbing equipment to accompany them, belts, pouches, pack and so on, did not arrive until June.

Just before Christmas 1914, an invasion scare had prompted the delivery of fifty serviceable rifles to the battalion, and some training in their use was thus possible. For drill purposes, the men had to make do with wooden substitutes until the real thing became available.

At the outbreak of war, the country possessed 795,000 rifles and had a standing Army of 725,000 men. Seventy thousand spares meant that there were not enough to equip even the first New Army. War Office instructions to arms factories saw output rise: by the middle of 1915, the Birmingham Small Arms factory alone was producing almost 8,000 rifles per week. It was at the end of June that year that the 9th KOYLI received a complete issue of rifles. The ammunition caught up with them two weeks later on 15 July, and a general course of musketry commenced at once.

Firing went on at the range at Halton continuously from 4.30 a.m. to 8.30 p.m. A prompt start in the morning was seen as vital, so as not to waste any daylight. The range was about twenty minutes' walk from the camp, and preparations could take up to an hour, meaning that the poor musketry officer for that day had to get up at about 2.30 a.m. No staff officer ever made it to the range by 4.30 a.m., but rumour had it that the General set his alarm clock to wake him at 4.25 a.m., allowing him to hear the first shots being fired. A volley was therefore routinely fired at the appointed time, regardless of whether everything was ready or not.

The musketry course was completed early in August, and on the 9th the Division marched off from Halton for the last time, arriving at Witley Camp, Surrey, four days later. Training continued, including the inevitable route-marches, but, so intense had the training become, and so short was the time left to them, that at one point, bayonet practice had to be fitted in at night, by moonlight.

As September began, and the battalion approached the first anniversary of its inception, orders were received to go to France. Our unnamed officer continues the story:

We were to start almost at once. We had of course guessed for the past week or two that we should not be long, but somehow or other, when the actual orders did come, to me at any rate it was a shock. In a peculiar way the incident struck me as dramatic. We were assembled together in the

*9th KOYLI Battalion
Football Team.
Maidenhead, 1914.*

Mess Ante-Room just after mess on the night when the Colonel made the announcement. He was brief and to the point. 'Gentlemen, you will be glad to hear that the Divisional Commander told me today that the Division has received orders to proceed overseas, it is understood to France. We shall start in about ten days. 'This is of course confidential'. There was dead silence for a space of about five seconds, the air was charged with electricity, then in a moment we were talking again and very soon we passed on to the closing of mess accounts and so forth… We should all go to France together, but how many of us would come back?

On 10 September, the battalion paraded at Witley Camp and then marched to Milford railway station. No music accompanied the march or the farewells; the battalion band had been forbidden to take their instruments to France.

The officers of the 9th Battalion leaving for France were: Lieutenant-Colonel C.W.D. Lynch; Majors A.E. Fitzgerald and F. Brewis; Captains H. Greenwood, W. Walker, G. Haswell and G.E. Griffin; Lieutenants D.J. Bethell, B.W. Cook, L.D. Head, E.M.B. Cambie, A.N. Richardson, B.L. Gordon, H.E. Yeo, L.D. Spicer and C.D. Jones; Second-Lieutenants N.L. Alexander, E.F.S. Graham, H.A. Telfer, F.G. Morris, C.W. Howlett, J.J.F. Oldershaw, W.F. Keay, A.G. Spark, C.A.C.J. Hendricks, E.R. Nott, G.L. Sly, H.F. Kingston, F.N. Smith, J.C. Sayers, J.P. Stevens, H.M. Green, W.R. Stokes, F.J. Powell, A.E. Day, R.A. Stokes, T.H. Ibbetson and A. Stephenson. Adjutant: Captain C.K. Butler. Quartermaster: Lt W.K. Pethed.

The Transport Section, Machine Gun Section and HQ Personnel were to sail from Southampton to Le Havre and meet up with the rest of the battalion in France.

At Folkestone, the battalion embarked on the boat that was to take them to France. The *St Seriol* was ninety-five feet long, built in 1886 at the Swan Hunter yard at Wallsend, Newcastle, and named after a sixth-century Welsh saint. It was a dark night with no moon, and the troops were not allowed to show any lights. Once they were all on board there was very little room to spare, the men standing shoulder to shoulder on deck. Each man was supposed to have a life belt, but the crowding made effective distribution impossible, and many had to do without. The submarine threat was a real one, but the crossing was without incident and the *St Seriol* docked safely in Boulogne at about 1.00 a.m. on the morning of 11 September 1915.

2

BAPTISM

We had a splendid crossing and I thoroughly enjoyed the trip. Today is splendid and we've played cricket and washed at intervals... Quite an ideal existence.[1]

Thus wrote Lieutenant Harold Yeo as part of a two-page letter home to his parents on 12 September 1915, the day after the 9th KOYLI's arrival in France. They were at this time in the rest camp at Ostove on the outskirts of Boulogne. Lt Yeo had been a law student at Trinity College, Cambridge at the outbreak of war and had volunteered immediately for service. He sent home almost 300 letters during the course of the war, and as we shall see, displayed an almost unwavering sense of optimism and enthusiasm.

That same night, the battalion marched the short distance to Pont de Briques station, entrained at 1.00 a.m. the following morning, and in doing so, met up with those of the battalion who had previously crossed to Le Havre. Complete once more, they set off north-eastwards through the night. They disembarked at 4.30 a.m. and moved into billets at Zutkerque, near Ardres, where they remained and trained for the next week. 'Life is really quite interesting out here, though of course as usual very strenuous'[2] wrote Lt Spicer on 16 September. On the previous day, twenty officers of 64th Brigade had been sent forward to Westoutre, just over the Belgian border, to spend twenty-four hours in the trenches with the 28th Division. Harold Yeo was one of them. On 19 September he wrote home in his usual style: 'Incidentally we had great fun in the trenches. I sniped most of the day and had the immense joy of seeing a Bosche bowled over.'[3] Whether the 9th KOYLI had claimed its first victim, or whether Yeo's enthusiasm had got the better of him remains open to speculation.

Many letters sent home during this time contained requests for items of food, clothing and, above all, cigarettes. Some of the officers often did their best to supplement their men's supply: 'Sometime, if you could, send me a large cake for them as I know it would be very popular'[4] (Spicer), 'You can't imagine how the men appreciate cigarettes – they are absolutely lost without them'[5] (Yeo). Not all of the officers' good intentions were appreciated by the men under their command. The Commanding Officer, Lt-Col. Colmer William Lynch, a strict disciplinarian, instigated the first of a series of measures which were to make him extremely unpopular, not least amongst his own officers. Soon after arriving in France, he ordered the entire battalion to have its heads shaved: he had seen a report that a number of head wounds had proved fatal due to infection from hair having entered the wound. (It should be noted here that the British soldier did not wear a helmet at this time. This part of his equipment did not become standard issue until early 1916.)

On 20 September the Division left the Zutkerque area, marching as ever at night, covering some twenty kilometres to arrive at Arques, just east of St Omer, by the early hours of the following day. They bivouacked in a field off the St Omer–Arques road. By moving at night and resting by day, it was hoped to avoid detection by enemy aircraft reconnaissance patrols: Divisional orders required the men to bivouac near hedges on the perimeter of fields, or, if no hedges were present, to 'Bivouac in brown fields rather than green.'[6] So that the column would not lose its way along the unfamiliar lanes, cyclists would go out ahead and mark the route, and at difficult points would block the wrong roads. They could be recognised in the darkness by the white paper with which they were instructed to cover their caps.

Their stay at Arques was a short one. At 9.00 p.m. that same evening they marched off to Fontes, and went into billets, their march having taken them this time in a southerly direction. Fontes, too, was a mere staging-post, as unusually, they set off on a daytime march, still southerly, to Amettes on the 22nd. The sequence of one-night stays continued, however, the battalion moving on once more on the 24th, reaching Four-au-Chaux at 2.00 a.m. on the 25th, where the entire 64th Brigade camped in one large field.

The march was a tedious one, chiefly owing to delays at the level crossings at Marles les Mines and Place à Bruay due to railway traffic; most of the Infantry were in their areas by 3.00 a.m. on the 25th, but the tail of the Division not until some hours later.[7]

They were required to advance along narrow roads, forcing their way past motorised and horse-drawn vehicles coming in the opposite direction. 'It was like trying to push the Lord Mayor's procession through the streets of London without clearing the route and holding up the traffic.'[8]

At one level crossing the 64th Brigade was held up for over an hour and a half due to an accident to a train. Soon after midnight, just to add to the misery, it had started to rain. Four and a half hours later, not far to the east, a misty dawn saw the British Army launch a massive attack near the mining town of Loos.

The General Staff of the French Army had had plans for a final offensive in 1915 which were nearing completion back in early June of that year. The German Army was occupying a huge salient, bulging forward from its line, the French town of Noyon near its furthest point of south-westerly extension. The plans were to render the Noyon salient untenable through the implementation of two flanking attacks, one by the French Army in a northerly direction from their positions in the Champagne region, the other eastwards from Artois. The German 1st, 2nd and 7th Armies, consisting of some 30,000 men, would be encircled, isolated and defeated.

A draft scheme was sent to French GHQ on 4 June, and the BEF was asked to help in two ways. They were to take over twenty-two miles of the French front line south of Arras, thus freeing up French troops for the Champagne attack, and participate in the Artois offensive by attacking either north of Lens or across the Somme uplands south of Arras.

Sir John French agreed to this participation, hoping plans would be complete by mid-July. He intended to take the first attacking option, namely an advance north of Lens, using units of his First Army. Its commander, General Douglas Haig, was asked on 19 June to submit a detailed report on the feasibility of such an attack. This he did four days later, and wrote that:

*after a personal reconnaissance of the area south of the [La Bassée] canal, he was forced to the conclu-
sion – which proved only too well founded – that it was not a favourable one for an attack. The
German defences were so strong that until a greatly increased establishment of heavy artillery was
provided, they could only be taken by siege methods; that is by a series of progressive attacks from trench
to trench which would involve hand-to-hand fighting and bombing. The ground, for the most part bare
and open, would be so swept by machine-gun and rifle fire both from the German front trenches and
the numerous fortified villages immediately behind them, that a rapid advance would be impossible.*[9]

His recommendation was for subsidiary attacks only to the south of the La Bassée canal,
with the main advance taking place astride and to the north of it, adding that the present
shortage of heavy artillery and ammunition was an additional factor of overriding importance. Continued pressure from General Joffre, however, meant that the offensive was
ordered to go ahead as originally planned.

Allied commanders discussed the proposed autumn attack at Sir John French's headquarters at St Omer on 11 July. Joffre, without saying why, expressed the opinion that the BEF
would find the ground between Lens and the La Bassée canal 'particularly favourable'.[10]

Throughout July, the Germans had been strengthening their positions on this very
ground, constructing a second line of defence, including strong points, redoubts and
emplacements for machine guns, all fronted by barbed wire entanglements fifteen feet in
breadth. This line was positioned so as to be out of range of British artillery so long as
the front line held. Any subsequent attack on the second line could only take place after
a pause in which the British guns, along with fresh troops, were brought forward. This
allowed time for German reserves to be introduced to the battlefield.

The existence of this new system of defences had become known to the British,
strengthening Haig's opinion of the poor ground over which the attack was to take place,
and an attack further north near Aubers Ridge became the next British suggestion.

General Foch would not be diverted from his original plan, however, and the situation
on the Eastern Front was such that action was needed to take pressure off the Russian
Armies, whose predicament was becoming perilous, having just lost Warsaw and been
forced onto the retreat.

Lord Kitchener visited French GHQ by invitation of General Joffre on 16 August and
had prolonged discussions. On hearing of a further setback on the Eastern Front (the loss
by the Russians of the fortress of Novo Georgievsk on the Vistula), on his return to
London, he telegraphed Sir John French on 21 August telling him to 'take the offensive
and act vigorously.'[11]

The *Official History* sums up the situation:

*Under pressure from Lord Kitchener at home due to the general position of the Allies, and from
Generals Joffre and Foch in France, due to the local situation in France, the British Commander-
in-Chief was therefore compelled to undertake operations before he was ready, over ground that was
most unfavourable, against the better judgment of himself and General Haig.*

The date for the attack was agreed originally as 8 September, four days before the arrival
of the 9th KOYLI in France. Two postponements at Joffre's insistence pushed this date
back to the 25th.

The final detailed plans involved the British attacking with six Divisions on a frontage
of six miles between Grenay and the La Bassée canal. Three Divisions were to be held in
general reserve, along with the Cavalry Corps, in readiness to exploit any breakthrough.

Due to the extent of the line to be attacked, all available troops were needed for the preliminary assault. (Four experienced Divisions had been moved from the area to help form the new Third Army taking over the French trench lines north of the Somme.) This meant that Sir John French was left with no choice but to earmark the newly formed XI Corps under Gen. R.C.B. Haking as general reserve. This corps comprised the 21st and 24th Divisions, who would be held in a state of readiness to act as and when appropriate. Supporting these two forces would be the also newly formed Guards Division. It may well be the fact that the two Kitchener Divisions were inexperienced that led Sir John French to retain this general reserve under his own personal command. He would only release them to Haig when he saw fit. It was envisaged in any case that their role would be a relatively easy one: 'little more was required than a long march in pursuit of an already retiring and demoralised enemy... in no conceivable circumstances would the 21st and 24th Divisions be put in unless and until the Germans were absolutely smashed and retiring in disorder.'[12] This was the impression gained by Maj.-Gens Forrestier-Walker (21st Division) and Ramsay (24th Division) when they received their orders a few days prior to the battle.

The artillery bombardment, no doubt heard by the men of the 9th KOYLI as they arrived and bivouacked in the Four-au-Chaux area, was put down by 951 guns of all calibres, using 535,000 rounds of ammunition, two-thirds of those being fired in the four-day preliminary bombardment which had commenced on 21 September. Neither the weight nor the intensity of such a bombardment was enough to damage German trenches or dugouts to any great extent. Nor was it capable of cutting the wire in front of the German positions sufficiently well to allow the British troops an unhindered line of advance. In any case, the German second line was beyond the range of the British wire-cutting guns.

The British commanders knew this, and their answer was to supplement the final bombardment with chlorine gas, a weapon used so effectively by the Germans earlier that year at Ypres. This was to be released from cylinders in the British front line and allowed to drift across no man's land into the German trenches and dugouts. It was calculated that the German gas masks of the time were effective for only thirty minutes: a discharge of gas commencing forty minutes before the infantry assault was therefore deemed ample to allow them to meet German troops suffering from the effect of this gas for some ten minutes, their resistance and fighting spirit broken.

The efficacy of this plan was not to be tested, however. Miscalculations over the rate of gas discharge from the cylinders and problems with the manufacture and supply of sufficient quantities of the gas itself meant that a compromise solution had to be reached. It was just not possible to release the chlorine gas for an uninterrupted period of forty minutes, so it was decided that it would be supplemented by smoke. Gas would be released for twelve minutes, followed by eight minutes of smoke, twelve more minutes of gas, and a final eight of smoke. Twenty-four minutes of poison gas would barely test the effectiveness of German masks.

There remains one additional vital factor relating to the effective use of poison gas and smoke; a factor over which the British generals had absolutely no control: a breeze of six to eight miles per hour towards the German trenches (anywhere between north-west and south-west would do!) was a prerequisite. The weather forecast at 9.45 p.m. on 24 September seemed favourable, and orders for the gas attack were confirmed. During the next few hours, however, the direction of the wind varied between west and south-east, and it dropped at one point to almost dead calm. Haig's final decision was based on an ambiguous forecast made at 3.00 a.m. on the 25th that the wind would probably be stronger just after dawn: the gas would be released from 5.50 a.m., the infantry would attack at 6.30 a.m.

From right to left along the British line, from Lens to La Bassée, the attacking Divisions were deployed as follows: 47th, 15th, 1st, 7th, 9th and 2nd. The final intensive artillery bombardment began at 5.50 a.m., along with the gas and smoke. In front of the 47th, 15th and 9th Divisions, a thirty- to fifty-feet-high dense cloud of gas carried well over to the German trenches. Further north, however, on the 2nd Division front, the gas hung around the British trenches and began to drift along the British front line from right to left. This prompted the 2nd Division commanders to discontinue the discharge almost immediately. On the 1st Division front, the wind was light, and the clouds of gas persisted over no man's land. Amidst ground mist, poison gas and acrid smoke, the infantry rose from their trenches at 6.30 a.m. precisely and advanced, in many cases blindly, towards the waiting German defenders.

The advance of the 47th and 15th Divisions went well, the town of Loos being mostly in British hands by 8.00 a.m. Units of 15th Division had overrun Hill 70 but thereafter wheeled to the right, coming up against the unbroken German second line: heavy machine-gun fire halted the advance and German counter-attacks had retaken the crest of the hill by 1.00 p.m.

The 1st Division advancing choking, through their own gas clouds met with mixed fortune. Their right-hand brigade found the wire in front of the German trenches relatively intact and withdrew to their original positions. On the left, the German line was overwhelmed and British troops were digging in in front of the German second line facing the town of Hulluch.

The 7th Division also took the German front line, but their advance on Hulluch was held up by heavy machine-gun fire. The 9th Division made some headway, but the failure of the 2nd Division to their north to make any gains forced them to withdraw some advanced units to form a defensive flank. Those German troops holding out in their front line facing the 2nd Brigade of the 1st Division found themselves outflanked on both sides and finally surrendered, giving up the unequal struggle at around 2.30 p.m.

The *Official History* describes 25 September as a day of 'initial success': 'Only the units of the 2nd Division, owing to extremely adverse conditions, had failed in their operations and had been obliged to return to their original trenches; all the other Divisions had gained possession of the German front positions and advanced beyond it.'[13] They had indeed advanced beyond it, only to come up against the strongly fortified second line, untouched by the British artillery bombardment. And at what cost? The *Official History* continues:

When night fell, the First Army, instead of being in old-established continuous trenches covered by wire, was in extemporised positions broken by gaps. Worse than this, it was much exhausted by fighting and had suffered very heavy casualties, amounting in total to 470 officers and 15,000 other ranks, nearly a sixth of its forces engaged.[14]

When the first reports of a breakthrough filtered back to General Haig's headquarters at about 7.00 a.m. on 25 September, Haig sent a staff officer by car to inform Sir John French of the successes and to urge him to place the XI Corps at Haig's disposal, ready to be pushed forward at once. French finally gave his consent at 9.30 a.m. Such was the difficulty where the flow of information was concerned, that his decision had to be taken

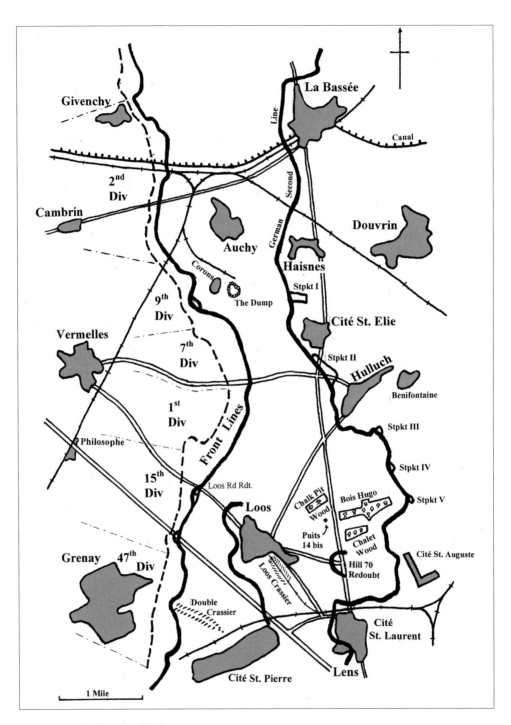

Loos: Dawn, 25 September 1915.

based on reports already over two hours old, and the troops required to act on it were still scattered in bivouacs up to six miles behind the front.

It was nearly 11.15 a.m. by the time the first brigades were on the march to their assembly positions. The 64th Brigade were on the move by about midday, the order having been delayed in reaching them, but were halted almost immediately to let an artillery ammunition column cross its route. As a result of this and numerous other delays of a similar nature, they did not reach their positions at Mazingarbe, a distance of only seven miles, until 4.00 p.m.

Initial optimism on the part of General Haig had meant that among the first orders received by 21st Division from General Haking, Officer Commanding XI Corps, was one requiring the Division to advance between Loos village and the Vermelles–Hulluch road to secure crossings over the Haute Deule canal at Loison sous Lens, Harnes and Pont à Vendin. At that point in time, these objectives lay some three miles behind the unbroken German second line of defence. Subsequent orders became less ambitious!

However, the receipt of such an order led Maj.-Gen. Forrestier-Walker, Officer Commanding 21st Division, to believe that the enemy were defeated, demoralised and retiring, and that all that was required was the long march previously mentioned. With this in mind, the order went out that greatcoats and extra rations were to be carried.

At 5.45 p.m., 21st Division Order O.O. No.8 required the 64th Brigade, more realistically this time, to 'form up on a front 1,000 yards west of deployment of 63 Inf Brigade, i.e. line G26 centre-G20 centre and will follow 63 Brigade at approx that distance ready to support it.'[15]

The starting point at Mazingarbe was very congested, and the brigade did not actually move off until 7.00 p.m., by which time it was raining hard. The orders had assumed that the move would be made in daylight. Now that night had fallen, no need for any modification to these orders was deemed necessary. The infantry would move across country (transport units only would use the roads), on a compass bearing, in the dark, over unfamiliar territory. Speedy progress seemed unlikely.

On passing Divisional HQ in Vermelles, 64th Brigade was able to receive further instructions from the Divisional Commander, filling in information contained in several messages which had hitherto failed to reach it. Apparently, 63rd Brigade was required to 'make good time' in its advance between 24th Division and Hill 70, that is to the Lens–Hulluch road, as first objective, and then on to the town of Annay (still behind German lines!). The 62nd Brigade had been lent to the 15th Division and was already supporting that embattled unit's attempts to hold on to its hard-fought gains between Hill 70 and Puits 14 bis.

The 64th Brigade reached the northern end of its line of deployment on the Béthune–Lens road just south-east of Philosophe at about 9.00 p.m. Once there, it took three hours to deploy the brigade as required. Machine guns, ammunition, bombs and tools had to be unloaded, and only then could the troops begin to take up their required positions. Any reconnaissance of the line of advance was impossible, and it was decided to move off on a compass bearing once more. During the forming up period, an officer sent forward to establish contact with 63rd Brigade, whom they were to follow, discovered from its Brigade Commander, Brig.-Gen. Nickalls, that it had moved off around 9.00 p.m. 'They therefore had a long start of us' affirms the writer of the 64th Brigade Diary.

With the 14th and 15th Durham Light Infantry side by side in the lead, 9th and 10th KOYLI following as best they could, each battalion in four columns, each of one company, the whole formation, thus eight columns wide, moved off into the darkness at

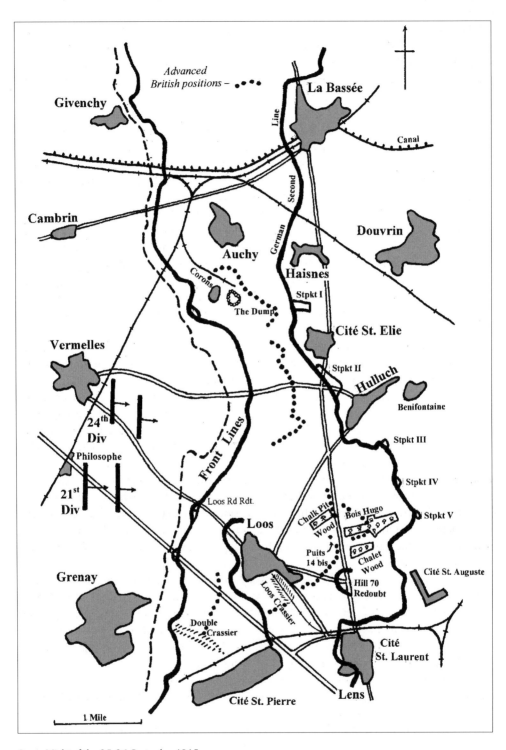

Loos: Night of the 25-26 September 1915.

about midnight, over unfamiliar ground, following, as they still believed, a demoralised enemy.

The original British front-line trenches were crossed at around 1.00 a.m., near the Loos Road redoubt. This manoeuvre slowed progress even more. Some trenches could be jumped, while others had had narrow causeways filled in across them. Some had planks placed across them. All this necessitated long delays to allow troops to file over each trench system and then reform the marching columns before encountering the next obstacle.

The rain had by now stopped, and in the moonlight a column of wagons was seen to the north moving parallel to them. Afterwards it was discovered that there were cookers and water carts of IV Corps unit moving up to join them in Loos. Later, the 64th Brigade struck the track the wagons had been using, realising too late that if they had known of this track before setting out, they could have probably halved their marching time.

2.00 a.m. saw the brigade negotiating the German trench systems, held up additionally this time by the German wire, where in some places there were only narrow gaps. They were also being shelled at this point: a terrifying baptism of fire for these inexperienced troops. Luckily, many of the shells dropping close by failed to explode. It is extremely unlikely that the brigade had been targeted specifically. The German gunners would have known the location of their own front line to the inch and would have sent shells over sporadically during the night with the aim of frustrating British attempts to send up reserves.

An hour later the brigade was successfully collected and reformed just to the east of the original German front-line positions. Patrols were sent out at this time to attempt to establish contact with the 63rd Brigade, but they returned without finding them.

As daylight approached, a single line of abandoned German trench was found along the Loos–La Bassée road, and the brigade faced a difficult dilemma: to advance or stay put.

Had the 63rd Brigade mistaken its direction in the night leaving nothing between the 64th and the enemy? If so, it was too late to push on to the Loos–Hulluch road. The occupation and consolidation of these trenches was best done under the cover of darkness, and the risk of stumbling across an entrenched enemy whilst out in the open on ground offering no cover, in daylight, with no contact with neighbouring units, was too great. On the other hand, if the 63rd Brigade was indeed ahead of them and had consolidated the trenches on the Loos–Hulluch road as required, the 64th Brigade was now in exactly the right place from which to support them. Such impeccable reasoning removed the dilemma.

It was decided to make use of the cover they had found, to await daylight proper, and then to establish contact with troops right and left of them. The 9th and 10th KOYLI were placed in this trench and the 14th and 15th DLI were sent forward to occupy other trenches reported to be ahead. One company of the 15th DLI had to be sent back to occupy the ground to the right of the 10th KOYLI, as there was not enough room for them in the advanced positions held by their comrades.

The men of the 21st Division had finally arrived on the field of battle. They now waited, wet, hungry, exhausted, apprehensive and no doubt in some cases excited, to see what their commanders would ask of them.

The British High Command had actually decided by that time that the continuation of the attack on 26 September was their preferred option. Haig resolved that the main thrust should be renewed between Hulluch and Loos, and that the 21st and 24th Divisions would play a major role.

The Germans had not been idle overnight, however, and reinforcements had been brought forward to strengthen the still intact second line, and to facilitate limited counter-attacks. 'Thus, in all, twenty-two additional battalions were moved into the battle area, and by daylight on the 26th, the second position was more strongly held than the first had been at the time of the British assault.'[16]

So the British Divisions, either exhausted and depleted from the previous day's fighting, or new to the battlefield, were to be asked to attack a strongly held and rein-forced position without the benefit of extended artillery support, and without the cover of smoke or gas. The prospect was daunting, at the very least. The orders for a renewed attack were sent out from First Army Headquarters. There was to be a general assault at 11.00 a.m., with the 21st and 24th Divisions advancing on the German second line between Hill 70 and Hulluch. The danger was that with the Germans still in possession of both of the above-mentioned locations, they would be able to overlook the planned assault and enfilade the advancing troops from both right and left.

In an attempt to eliminate this problem, the 1st Division, having failed the previous day, was to launch another attack and capture the village of Hulluch; the 15th Division, with the 62nd Brigade still 'on loan' from the 21st Division in close support, was to retake Hill 70. The attack on Hill 70 was timed to begin at 9.00 a.m. At the appointed time, there was low cloud, mist and rain; little or no help was available from the air, and artillery support limited. 'A number of shells fell along the British front line, which the batteries had been informed would be temporarily evacuated.'[17]

The orders to do so had not reached all units, and those left in their original positions suffered casualties. The mist cleared just before 9.00 a.m. and the troops went forward into a redoubt strengthened overnight and forewarned of the attack by the bombardment. The redoubt itself was partially captured after a severe hand-to-hand struggle, but any advance past its flanks proved impossible. In exhorting their men to greater efforts, many of the officers fell wounded or killed. By 10.00 a.m., among the units of the 62nd Brigade, it having added its weight to the assault with little success, many of the attackers were falling back to their jumping-off positions on the western slopes of the hill. A German artillery bombardment at 11.00 a.m. precipitated a further withdrawal, leaving a thin, broken line of determined troops clinging on to their trenches. Hill 70 remained stubbornly in German hands.

Obstinacy prevailed at Headquarters:

The failure to capture Hill 70 and the fact that the village of Hulluch was still in enemy hands did not cause General Haking to change his plan for the attack by the 21st and 24th Divisions between these two localities. He had the reasonable expectation that the 1st Division would secure Hulluch and that, if the German second position were broken through between Bois Hugo and Hulluch, the Hill 70 position could readily be outflanked and enveloped, and the whole of that sector of the front carried.[18]

The 21st Division attack was to be directed at the German second line, by now complete and protected by barbed wire entanglements four feet high and between fifteen and twenty feet broad, between Bois Hugo on the right and Stutzpunkt IV on the left. The 24th would attack the remaining line to the north between this strongpoint and Hulluch.

The one hour-long artillery bombardment, beginning at 10.00 a.m., was disap-pointing. The batteries had received their orders in many cases very late; moving to their new positions in darkness and mist proved almost impossible, and by daylight they found

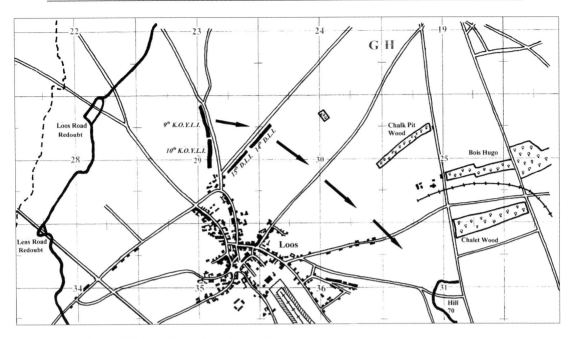

Loos: Advance of 9th KOYLI, 26 September 1915.

themselves 1,000 yards in the rear of their designated areas, and in full view of the German batteries who immediately began counter-shelling. The British bombardment was 'spasmodic and unsystematic; little more than a few ranging shots being fired by the field artillery, and no great amount by the heavy artillery.'[19]

The late hour of the attack also gave the Germans the opportunity to pre-empt it. Advanced parties had been sent up from Cité Auguste during the night into Bois Hugo and Chalet Wood, and these were reinforced during the early morning by larger units of infantry. As soon as the mist cleared, these troops attacked the precarious British positions in front of them. The 63rd Brigade south of Bois Hugo suffered heavy losses and began to fall back. The 10th Yorks & Lancs sent up to rescue the position misunderstood their orders, entered the woods themselves and incurred very heavy losses. Brig.-Gen. Nickalls, at 8.53 a.m., wrote a very hurried note to Brig.-Gen. Gloster in command of the 64th Brigade asking for reinforcements. The 14th Durham Light Infantry was sent forward. A further German advance to the north of the woods at about 10.30 a.m. was halted by rifle fire, but it had distracted the British troops from the main thrust through Bois Hugo, and enfilade fire from this position caused heavy British casualties and prompted a general withdrawal. It was at about this time that Brig.-Gen. Nickalls was killed. The loss of his leadership at such a critical moment proved decisive, with many other units joining in the rearward movement.

The 14th DLI arrived just as the retreat gathered momentum, and, mistaking the retreating men for Germans, opened fire on them. The mistake was quickly recognised, and the Durhams continued their advance through the retreating lines and on towards the woods. Machine-gun fire from the trees accounted for seventeen officers, including their CO Lt-Col. Hamilton, and 220 Other Ranks, driving them back.

In accordance with their orders for the general assault, their sister battalion, the 15th DLI, arrived on the scene and continued the attack. Advancing through retreating comrades, in the confusion of battle, they lost direction and advanced not against the intended section of German line, but veered to the right towards the slopes of Hill 70. The battalion attacked the only manned positions it could see: in trenches believed to have been evacuated by the British, they saw troops in long greatcoats and gas helmets on the slopes of the hill. Taking them to be German, they turned to the south-east, leaving their flanks exposed to the real danger contained in Bois Hugo. (The supposed enemy were in reality remnants of the British 45th, 46th and 62nd Brigades, still clinging on to their hard-won positions.) Enfilade machine-gun fire from the wood halted the Durhams' advance, forcing them to retreat back down the slope.

To the north, at the appointed hour, the troops of the 24th Division began their advance. The sight of these units moving forward with almost parade ground precision had the effect of steadying the retreating men on their right, some turning and rejoining the assault. In reality, the units were by now so mixed up, so lacking in leadership – many of their officers having become casualties – that their participation in the attack added little to its chances of success.

The 24th advanced bravely, passing Bois Hugo to the north, but they came up against the German second line with its barbed wire, strong points and machine guns. By this point they were also being fired upon from their rear. German troops in Hulluch, which the 1st Division had again failed to capture, and Bois Hugo directed everything they could against them. The attack was repulsed, their retreat coinciding with that of the remnants of the 21st Division to the south.

The 9th and 10th KOYLI at this point were still being held in reserve, positioned as they had been since dawn, under intermittent shell fire, in trenches along the Grenay–Hulluch road. The Durhams were retreating towards them, and both of their commanding officers, (Lt-Col. Lynch of the 9th and Lt-Col. Pollock of the 10th) were

Left: *Loos–Vermelles Road. (IWM Q17379)*

Right: *Captured German trenches near Loos. (IWM Q28982)*

at 64th Brigade HQ, having been summoned there to receive orders. Brig.-Gen. Gloster, realising that the two battalions were his sole remaining uncommitted troops, was of the mind to consolidate the position they held and await the arrival of reinforcements. Before he could issue such orders, events overtook him. As the retreating troops approached the KOYLI positions, the front line of the 9th KOYLI, urged on by a never-to-be identified staff officer, climbed out of their trenches and advanced. They were soon beyond recall, and all that Brigade could do was to order the 10th KOYLI to advance in support, hurriedly adding that none of the troops should advance beyond the Loos–Hulluch road, but were to occupy and consolidate trenches there. There was nothing left for Lt-Col. Lynch to do but run after his battalion. The orders limiting the advance never reached the 9th KOYLI; indeed only two companies of the 10th received them and acted upon them. In their forward movement, many of the retreating troops rallied, turned and joined in their advance. Urged on by their company commanders, the 9th KOYLI and their attached remnants crossed the Loos–Hulluch road, and, making the same error as the Durhams had earlier, presumed the greatcoat-clad men on Hill 70 to be their enemy, and advanced upon them.

The German machine gunners in Bois Hugo and Chalet Wood would scarcely have been able to believe their luck. Once again escaping a frontal assault, they poured withering fire into the flanks of the Yorkshiremen advancing over the open country in front of them. They were joined by German troops in the Hill 70 redoubt, and the KOYLIs were therefore receiving fire from both front and left, with little or no chance for reply. The *Official History* gives us the German viewpoint:

The account of this attack from the German side is of interest: 'Near 12 noon (British time) masses of infantry, estimated at about a Division, began to advance in about twenty waves on a front between Loos and Chalk Pit Wood, moving in a southerly direction towards Hill 70... The advancing masses were... taken under fire by the machine guns and rifles in the Hill 70 redoubt and effectively enfiladed by those of the 153rd Regiment and a company of the 106th Reserve Regiment which had advanced during the morning through the woods east of Puits 14 bis and occupied the line of the Lens–La Bassée road, between Hill 70 and Puits 14 bis. The effect of this fire from two sides was very considerable, whole lines being mown down by the machine guns... Later he attacked again in a similar manner against Hill 70 and against the 153rd Regiment in position along the Loos–La Bassée road. He was easily and completely repulsed, his advance being again taken under concentric fire from Hill 70 redoubt and from the Lens road.[20]

The inevitable retreat ensued, the KOYLIs returning to their original trenches, here being rallied by the 64th Brigade staff and their own reserve companies. Lieutenant Harold Yeo took part in this ill-fated attack, and in a letter to his father dated 7 November 1915, gave his own personal account:

As the mist cleared off on Sunday morning we looked around us. Just to our right was Loos in front, and beyond we could see the attack going up Hill 70 and hear a tremendous amount of firing. In our trench were done-in Bosches, pickelhaubes and all kinds of kit. The place had lots of dead about it of course. In the dugouts there were tins of food and clothing etc.

About 10 o'clock the people on the hill got driven in, but went up again. About an hour later back they came and then we expected a big advance against us, as their guns suddenly got tremendously busy on us. The men were extraordinarily cool and joked the whole time, though it was their first experience of that sort of thing. Our battalion was in reserve all this time. From some unknown

Left: *16550 Lance-Corporal Fred Smith.*

Right: *16955 Private Alfred Gardiner.*

source we suddenly got orders to advance and we clambered out and tore along in the direction of where we supposed the enemy to be shelling from. It was decidedly better to be moving on than sitting in a trench being shelled, but exactly why we went up I don't know. Apparently the orders didn't reach one of the companies, who were in a position where they couldn't see us advance. Anyway we went ahead in a sort of line with everyone just where they happened to be when the forward impulse came. I was nowhere near my platoon, nor was anyone else, but one merely had to get up each time and call out to come on, irrespective of who they belonged to. Eventually, after several such rushes I found myself with a following of men of an altogether different Division and about half a dozen of our own. A machine gun (or rather several ditto) was making progress rather difficult and I was just lying down thinking of how to shut them up or get them shut up when the CO of my new hearties sent orders to retire. Thinking he must be mistaken or have developed chilly feet I told such as I could make hear to stay with me. There was a devilish row going on, and I found that my crew had diminished from forty to six, among whom I found Morris, who was as surprised to see me as I to see him. A sniper neatly bagged one of the party at once, and we decided that we could hardly carry on to much effect as we were, so we decided to stay and await eventualities. After two hours (during which time we passed round pills to the wounded and shot at whatever might hold Germans in front in turns) it seemed as though our winter would be spent in making sausages on a black bread diet if we didn't get a move on. Therefore we trotted back and on the way called in a small house in Loos, and there found about twenty wounded all over the place, and a French woman giving them coffee and hot milk. We patched up that lot and distributed such cigarettes and grub as we had as we had to push off to find the battalion, which had meanwhile been withdrawn. As it was just getting dark we found the main body and we all eventually occupied a line of trench running in front of the one we had been in the night before. The night was spent securing our position, and although we heard attacks on our flanks at odd times, nothing much came our way.[21]

The majority of the men had regained their original positions long before Harold Yeo returned. Maj.-Gen. Forrestier-Walker sent the following message to XI Corps during the afternoon:

Situation two forty-five p.m. as follows: I am with General Gloster in German Support Trench in G23 d 2.0. General Gloster believes that practically the whole of his brigade are in this trench and a similar trench 200 yards to east of it. This brigade (64th) holds the above mentioned trenches roughly from the figure 9 in square G29 to an unknown distance northwards. 63 Brigade position cannot be definitely ascertained.[22]

The men remained in these trenches for the rest of the day, being severely shelled for two to three hours and suffering additional casualties. A further message from Forrestier-Walker timed at 5.52 p.m. reported that 'the men are considerably demoralised.'[23]

By this time, arrangements for the relief of the remnants of the 21st Division were underway. Sir John French had placed the Guards Division at the disposal of General Haig, and they were moving forward from their positions near Noeux les Mines. The 64th Brigade received news to this effect just after 8.00 p.m. The Guards' march towards the front was beset by the same kind of problems encountered by the 21st and 24th Divisions a day earlier, and as a result, the relief of the 9th and 10th KOYLI was not begun until after midnight, and it was 3.45 a.m. before the survivors were withdrawn into bivouacs between Noyelles les Vermelles and Sailly la Bourse.

Casualties had been heavy. The 21st Division had suffered 3,853 casualties.

The 9th KOYLI came out with these figures:

	KILLED	WOUNDED	MISSING
OFFICERS	0	2	0
OTHER RANKS	13	167	34

Reference to Appendix I will show that the final number of fatalities for the 9th KOYLI from this engagement was forty-seven. The two officers wounded were Capt. C.K. Butler and 2nd-Lt E.R. Nott, and Lieutenant Powell was reported to be suffering from the effects of gas and shock. Nott, for his part in this action, was awarded the Military Cross, 'for conspicuous gallantry and determination during operation at Hill 70 on Sept 25/26. Although twice wounded, he continued to advance, leading and encouraging his men.'

Much has been made of the failure of the 21st and 24th Divisions at Loos; some criticise and condemn, others excuse. Brig.-Gen. Gloster's report not surprisingly attempts to defend his men:

The march to the front being carried out over heavy plough in necessarily irksome fashion by compass bearing. Absence of all transport necessitated the man-handling of machine guns with their ammunition, also 1,000 bombs per battalion and an additional fifty rounds per man. After two days and nights under arms on the march, it is not too much to say that the men arrived on the battlefield in an exhausted state. Nevertheless there was never a word of complaint, and the élan with which the advances were made was nothing short of astonishing... That the attack failed was no fault of the men's or of their training.[24]

The *Official History*'s verdict is not so forgiving, but neither is it devoid of understanding:

It was as 'old campaigners' that the Divisions failed, and this, seeing how few experienced men they contained, can be no reproach to them... The 21st and 24th Divisions failed because the direction of large bodies of troops is an art which cannot be acquired in a year of hard training. Rank and file, if of good will, can be taught the elements of their duty – to march, shoot and obey – in a few months. Soldiers may thus be created in a short time, but not officers; still less Divisions, which, composed of all arms, require not only that individuals and units should be fully trained, but also a knowledge of staff work and team work which takes much experience and long practice to acquire.[25]

What cannot be challenged is the fact that the repercussions were felt at the very highest level of command. The details of this aftermath do not lie within the remit of this narrative, but suffice it to say that the misuse of the XI Corps was a significant factor in the subsequent resignation of Sir John French as Commander-in-Chief on 17 December 1915 and his replacement by Sir Douglas Haig.

The battle of Loos dragged on into the middle of October; no further substantial gains were achieved. The German second line remained unbroken.

3

ARMENTIÈRES
WINTER 1915

On the evening of Monday 27 September 1915, the 9th KOYLI were safely out of the firing line in their tents between Vermelles and Noeux les Mines. It poured with rain, was very cold, and Lt Spicer noted that no-one got a great deal of sleep. Before the attack on the previous day, the men had been ordered to remove their packs. They never saw them again.

The following evening, at about 9.00 p.m., they marched, in the rain, without water-proofs or greatcoats (which were still with their packs, stacked neatly somewhere on the battlefield), to the railway station in Noeux les Mines. They stood outside getting wetter and more and more miserable for five hours, before finally boarding a train, which two hours later deposited them in Berguettes, a further three hours' march from their billets in Ligny-les-Aire. Here they remained for three days. The battalion received fresh kit, equipment and drafts of men. All their losses were to be made good.

The beginning of October saw them on the move again, ending up in billets in the town of Bailleul on the 8th. The following day, by 6.30 p.m., one platoon of each company was in the trenches again, this time in support of the front line at the strangely named 'Piggeries' in Ploegsteert Wood, south of Ypres. Over the next few days, companies took their turns in the trenches, becoming acclimatised to the routine, the system of reliefs and the day to day life in, or just to the rear of, the front line. From the 14th to the 18th, the entire battalion, *for the first time*, occupied a stretch of ordinary front-line trench. The War Diary describes the five-day tour of duty here with the words 'Situation Quiet', but adds that one 'Other Rank' was killed. This was 19046 Pte Horace Shaw. How he was killed is not recorded, but it is likely to have been as a result of shell fire. He is buried in Ploegsteert Wood Military Cemetery, close to where he fell. He was to be the only fatal casualty suffered by the 9th KOYLI during their time in this relatively quiet part of the line.

Relieved by the 14th Durham Light Infantry on the 19th October, the battalion moved back out of the line. A draft of fifty-one men arrived that day, along with the news that 18946 Lance-Corporal A. McKelvey had been awarded the DCM for gallantry displayed in the recent action at Hill 70.

The families of the men would not, as a rule, have known precisely where their menfolk were: Harold Yeo wrote to his mother on 24 October, using a trick which, it would appear, consistently fooled the censors;[1] the first letter of each sentence spelt out the word 'BAILLEUL'. A letter of a week earlier had hinted at the conditions in

Grave of Private Horace Shaw, Ploegsteert Wood Military Cemetery.

'Plugstreet' Wood: 'This night I have walked slap into a trench full of slush up to the knee – it is nearly dry now, but looks like plaster of Paris round my legs.'[2]

Further correspondence, written in November, describes another incident in Ploegsteert Wood:

Last time I went shooting was in a big wood, where we were in the trenches. We were waiting behind, ready to go in and Spicer and I saw a big pheasant. So off we went with my pistol to shoot him. We were stalking the thing and Spicer went into the wood to drive him out, while I waited to shoot him as he came. All of a sudden there was the rush of a shell and a terrific 'voom', and a German six-inch landed in the field, about 60 yards from where we stood. Lots of bits of earth go all over the place always from those things, but beyond being earth-spattered and rather astonished, we were none the worse. That was about a month ago... and I expect that old pheasant still hops about.[3]

Towards the end of October, the battalion was chosen to take part in an inspection of the Corps by King George V, east of Bailleul, this to be on the 27th. 'Clean, smart, well-behaved men only to be selected', insisted the 21st Division War Diary. The *Daily Mail* reported the gathering as follows:

It was an unforgettable experience to have seen the King in the midst of his Army in the field. The last inspection of the day was held on a pleasant stretch of greensward running up at the back to a low brown knoll... The very greenness of the grass gave the weather-beaten khaki of the troops, drawn up in four battalions, an olive tint. Beside a white flagstaff at which the old Union Jack was fluttering a line of Generals in red-bound staff caps was drawn up.

... Trench warfare leaves little time for the formalities of the parade ground. The more credit, therefore, to the troops, many of whom had only come out of the trenches in the rain of last night, that their march past was admirably executed. Many of them were still plastered with the yellow mud of the trenches, and the Burberrys of the officers were old and stained; but however unpolished their appearance, the men's alignment was excellent, and the whole body presented an appearance of soldierly efficiency which reflected great credit on their famous corps... It did one's heart good to hear the splendid British cheers that greeted the King as he drove away in his motor car.[4]

Harold Yeo's letter of that date was less effusive: 'A certain number of men and officers... represented each battalion at a sort of review today, where the King, Sir John French, and all kinds of other blokes were present.'[5] The 9th KOYLI War Diary was matter-of-fact: 'Representative Divisional Battalion paraded before King.'[6]

A fortnight of route-marches, parades, drills, inspections and working parties followed. When they were supposed to be away from the rigours of the front-line trenches, it was common for 'working parties' from 'resting' battalions to be used to dig or repair trenches and their wire, to carry food, equipment or ammunition up to the line, or to engage in the thousand and one other activities required to keep an Army in the field, which included repairing roads, building railways and filling sandbags.

The 12 November had the battalion on the move again, but the journey was a short one. For the next few months, 'home' for the 9th KOYLI was to be the trenches and rear areas around Houplines, a north-eastern suburb of Armentières. Battalion Headquarters was set up in the suburb in the Rue de l'Egalité. On the 15th, at 9.30 a.m., fourteen German shells landed in and around this house, including three direct hits through the roof. There were casualties, but the 9th KOYLI escaped any fatalities: the Sergeant Shoemaker and his men were very lucky in that only five of them were wounded when a shell landed and exploded in the room where they were busy mending boots. Battalion HQ was shortly afterwards moved back some distance to the Rue Nationale in Armentières itself.

The battalion first went into the trenches that were to become very familiar to them on 18 November and set to in trying to improve the conditions. Yeo describes the state of the trenches in a letter begun the previous day: 'Life goes on in the ordinary (!) way... The trenches here are very muddy and it's difficult to get along in places... one almost has to swim.'[7]

The following day he wrote: 'Richardson, our MG officer, got stuck in the mud in a narrow trench and, having tremendous feet, had to be evacuated as he simply couldn't move.'[8]

The 9th KOYLI came out of the front line six days later, having been relieved by the 14th DLI, and having suffered two fatalities, the latter being 22209 Pte Clayton Gilberthorpe, who was wounded just as the relief was being completed. He subsequently died of his wounds.

In and out of the trenches throughout the month of December, the KOYLIs watched the conditions worsen in the generally unkind weather. Water had to be pumped out of the trenches almost continuously, trenches 81-84 being reported as having eighteen inches of water in them on 11 December. As if the elements were not enough to contend with, the Diary of that day also states that an enemy sniper was active the afternoon. This kind of harassment was not one-sided, however, the Diary asserting on the 23rd that 'one of our snipers in trench 82 reported killing an enemy sniper.'

The enemy was not, however, top of the ordinary soldier's list of nuisances. On 21 December, 2nd-Lt George Fothergill Ellenberger, who had been with the 9th

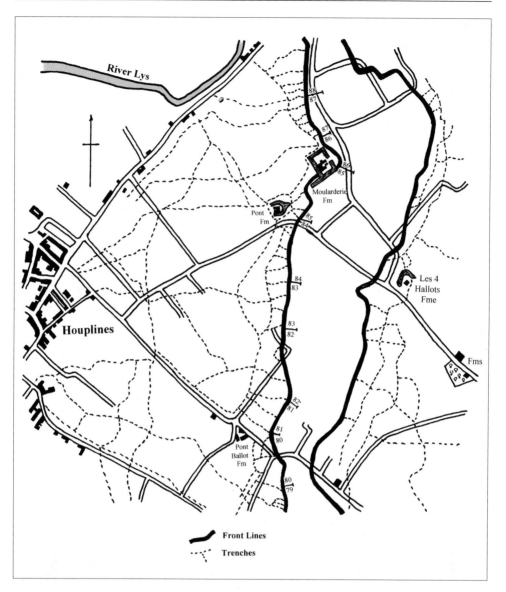

Houplines Sector, winter 1915-16.

during its training in England in 1915, but had missed the embarkation to France and the Loos fighting (owing to his attending an officers' course), rejoined the battalion. His first letter home brought trench conditions squarely to the fore: 'I came up to the trenches yesterday morning – I was attached to B. Coy. We wear India-rubber waders up to our thighs, as there is a lot of water and mud about... there are lots of rats in the trenches. Rats and rain are the worst things.'[9] (Ellenberger was transferred to C Company almost immediately to make way for Lt Telfer, who came back to join his old company).

Out of the trenches, the officers enjoyed some comforts: Lt Spicer described the town of Houplines thus:

A few shops still keep going, but large numbers are closed. There is one place for which we are all grateful, in the shape of a small tea shop, which is a very nice place, and always crowded every afternoon… The cakes and drinkables are excellent, everything is nicely served, and the room is comfortable… it has a good piano in it and someone can usually be found to play – it is also not expensive. So as you can see it is a tremendous boon. There is also a restaurant, at which you can get an excellent lunch or dinner, but that is more expensive, and personally I don't like it so much – tho' I'm going to dine there this evening.[10]

Ellenberger's letter home on the 27 December described the grimmer side of warfare:

I saw this morning the first 'casualty' I've seen – they were bringing the man down the communication trench on a stretcher as we were going up to work: he had been hit in the head by a bullet, and I think he was most probably dead – it wasn't a pleasant sight, but you told me to tell you the nasty things as well as the nice!! And besides I must get used to that sort of thing. I've never seen a dead person before.[11]

Christmas Day seemed to have passed by almost unnoticed in an area where the previous year there had been much fraternisation between the British and German troops. The War Diary reported a Church Parade in the morning (the 9th KOYLI had had the fortune to be relieved in the trenches by the 14th DLI on Christmas Eve) but work parties had been required by the Royal Engineers for the remainder of the day. These work parties toiled in the trenches held by the 1st East Yorks for four days before the battalion moved in and took them over on 30 December. The 1st East Yorks had joined the 64th Brigade, replacing the 14th DLI on 26 November. The East Yorks was a regular battalion:

Waterlogged British trench near Houplines. (IWM Q50560)

it was thought that the Brigade needed 'stiffening' after its performance at Loos. As 1916 dawned, the 64th Brigade consisted of: 9th KOYLI, 10th KOYLI, 15th DLI, and 1st East Yorks.

New Year's Eve did not slip by so easily. In a letter written two days later, Harold Yeo describes the events: 'It is a strange thing in the trenches to think that the Huns are an hour faster than we are in time. On New Year's Eve at 11.00 p.m., I was in the front line and suddenly heard shouts from over the way and sort of *'feu de joies'* being fired by them. Then I realised that 300 yards away it was 1916 already. What exactly there is to shout about I don't know, but still they are funny devils altogether.'[12]

The routine of time spent in the front line, or in support, or in reserve continued into the New Year, with casualties remaining low. Two fatalities on 11 January could possibly have been avoided, however. Our artillery had fired on the Pont Ballot salient, cutting a lane through the enemy wire entanglements and destroying part of their trench parapet, prior to a raid by the battalion on the 9th KOYLI's right. Houplines received fifty-one heavy and thirty lighter shells in reply. One of these heavy shells killed Ptes Thomas Birch and George Dodds, battalion grenadiers, and wounded four of their comrades. 'These men were, contrary to orders, out of cellars.'[13] They are buried side by side in the Cité Bonjean Military Cemetery. The reason for their untimely excursion is not known.

Five days later, another man was killed whilst in the open. This time, however, L/Cpl Thomas Bevan was working over the parapet, presumably involved in the very dangerous job of repairing the battalion's own wire. Avoiding exposure to enemy fire whilst thus occupied was all but impossible.

On 25 January, a party from the 10th KOYLI embarked on a trench raid at 9.55 p.m., entering the German trenches opposite Trench 88, only to find it evacuated and barricaded. This type of trench raid was a regular feature of life in the front line. It was part of the British strategy to attempt to dominate no man's land, not being content with remaining purely on the defensive.

The German reply to this particular raid involved three days of heavy retaliatory shelling on and behind the British front line, costing the 9th KOYLI eleven dead, though this number was described as 'light' by the battalion diarist, considering the intensity and strength of the bombardment. The battalion was relieved by the 1st East Yorks the following day, 29 January. The early part of this bout of shelling was described by 2nd-Lt Ellenberger in a letter dated 27 January 1916:

Our company has no casualties although there were a certain number of nasty fragments flying over – they go two to three hundred yards from the explosion of a big thing like that. One piece fell literally between my feet where I was standing in the trench and buried itself in the mud between the floorboards so that I could not get it out – looking back at it, it really was a narrow shave (it would have been a 'Blighty' – England – alright if it had hit me in the foot!)... 'though it all happens before you realise it and it doesn't disturb you at all. D Company had to leave their trenches and come along and take refuge in ours. They had about eight to ten casualties – four or five men were suffocated in a dug-out which fell in on top of them – pretty beastly being buried alive. I think I'd prefer anything to that.[14]

This group is also buried together in Cité Bonjean Military Cemetery.

Just over a week later, a 'tremendous explosion'[15] from a *Minenwerfer* (literally 'mine-launcher') cost them another six men killed. Ellenberger had written home two days

Right: *Grave of Private Thomas Birch.*

Below: *9th KOYLI graves in Cité Bonjean Military Cemetery, Armentières.*

earlier complaining that the blame for some of the bombardments suffered by the 9th KOYLI lay at the door of others:

What did annoy me... was the way our Trench Mortar people go on. They come up here, set up their machine in our trenches, fire a few inferior bomb-things into the Germans, then when the Huns retaliate with 'sausages', instead of staying and giving them three for every one, our Trench Mortar people gather up their skirts and hare off down the communication trench leaving us to face the music they've called for! They're not exactly popular with our lads!!![16]

He was, no doubt, himself a cause of annoyance to the Germans opposite when he took part in a patrol a few days later: '... it's quite an exciting game. It consists of getting out of our trench (by night of course) and wandering about between the trenches in no man's land.'[17]

During the next 'rest' period, over 300 men were supplied each night for working parties, just as the weather turned cold, clear and frosty. Within days the front line area was covered by a blanket of snow. Keeping warm became a major concern. Lt Spicer listed what he considered to be the normal winter garb: 'shirt, pants, socks, boots, tunic, trousers, furskin coat, overcoat, waterproof cape, mackintosh sheet and leather jerkin' adding that 'passing in a communication trench is a tricky business'.

The snow persisted well into March, but the routine of trench life changed little, if at all. Shelled while in the front line, used as pack mules in working parties while out of it, the men simply put up with the conditions, particularly difficult once the thaw did finally set in, and with the moods of their own CO:

... C Coy on our right were less fortunate; the water there came over the top of their boots and they were literally standing in water for four days and nights. All the time we were pumping hard and by the end of the third day had reduced the depth of the water considerably, indeed in parts of the trench it was only ankle deep. The last night we were there it rained hard and all the field drains poured the water back into the trenches, and C Coy in particular were back where they started. Lynch was furious. He had been very sarcastic about the conditions in which the trenches had been handed over to us, and was waiting to receive praise from Brigade HQ as to what he had been able to do. That proud prospect was over. He appeared to have no sympathy for the men and the conditions which they had endured. He said it was their fault – he apologised to the incoming troops and to Brigade HQ for the inefficiency of his men, and said that as a punishment they would be sent up to the line that night to pump for the incoming company. So the wretched men of C Coy came out of the line in the morning, having had no sleep for four days and four nights, were out for about eight hours and then were sent back to the line to another eight hours pumping for the troops who had relieved them. C Coy very nearly refused to go, which would have been mutiny, but the company officers, who were themselves indignant at the orders, persuaded them not to disobey.[18]

2nd-Lt Ellenberger, also of C Company, tried to paint a less severe picture for the benefit of his family back home: 'I hope you aren't getting the idea that the cold, rats and lack of sleep are intolerable – they're not as bad as all that. The trenches are jolly good ones, and I've only seen one rat, though I believe there are more'.[19] He described a more harrowing scene in a letter dated 28 February:

Last night... I tied up a wounded man. It was rather awkward as it was almost pitch dark, and I could not show a light as we were in the open, but I managed somehow or other and as it was a clean wound slick through his leg just beneath the knee – about as easy a place to bandage as any I suppose – I daresay my very unprofessional method of dressing the wound didn't at any rate make matters worse.[20]

The man concerned was from Ellenberger's own platoon, and was wounded while putting up wire in front of the British trenches. He was less than three yards from Ellenberger when he was hit, along with another who was more seriously wounded.

The routine of early March was punctuated by three noteworthy events. On the 7th, the battalion was paraded to witness the promulgation of sentences set by a Court Martial held two days earlier. On the 17th, the Corps Commander, Sir Charles Ferguson presented ribbons to Capt. Arthur Stephenson (MC) and to 12565 L/Cpl Richmond (a stretcher-bearer) and 13596 Pte Unwin (both DCM), these awarded for gallantry under shell fire on the first day of the month. Ellenberger mentioned the incident in a letter, saying how they had together tried, 'under heavy shell-fire, to save a man who'd been pretty well blown to bits – the explosion had blown him right up onto the parapet.'[21] The ceremony took place at 63rd Brigade HQ and the Guard of Honour was provided by the 9th and 10th KOYLI.

Along with the 1st East Yorks, the battalion was drawn up alongside the Bailleul–Outtersteen road on the 25th, there to be inspected by General Haig, by this time, of course, Commander-in-Chief. Lieutenant Spicer, in the absence of his Company Commander, Griffin, had the ceremonial duties fall upon him:

We were lined up at the side of the road, and as he came along, each company had to present arms – then slope them – and then the Company Commander had to fall out and be introduced to the C-in-C, and walk alongside him down the length of his company while he asked the usual inane questions... You trot up to him, salute him, then shake hands. His first remark to me was: 'Well, this is a great responsibility on your young shoulders, isn't it?' I feel the correct reply would have been either; 1) 'What about yourself?', or 2) 'You can't talk!' As it was I merely murmured 'Yes, Sir' and let him carry on.[22]

Second-Lieutenant Ellenberger appeared equally unimpressed by the whole event when he wrote home two days later: 'I suppose it will eventually find its way down into battalion orders how the GOC in C expressed his great satisfaction and so on – they're always complimentary on these occasions. It's 'not done' to be anything else.'[23]

Two days later the Division received orders to join XIII Corps, and on 30 March, an advanced party of the battalion under Lt Richardson left for Godeswaersvelde, six miles to the north-west of Bailleul, at 4.00 a.m. 'A' Company and the Transport Section followed at 7.45 a.m., the rest of the battalion moving off in pursuit two hours later. A train holding the entire battalion left the station at 1.40 p.m., and travelled through the following night, arriving at Longeau, just to the south-west of Amiens, at 3.40 a.m. From here, the battalion marched to La Neuville, arriving at 10.10 a.m. on the last day of the month, before moving into billets. There, they were met by Lt C.W. Ellis, joining from the 5th Entrenching Battalion.

On 1 April 1916, the battalion remained in billets. All leave was cancelled until further notice. Longeau and the smaller La Neuville lie in the valley of the River Somme. They had left fifty-eight of their comrades in the cemeteries around Bailleul and Armentières. The Somme was to reap a far greater harvest.

4

SOMME
PART ONE

On 29 December 1915, General Haig, at Joffre's invitation, attended a conference at Chantilly; also present were the French Prime Minister, the Minister of War, and several Army commanders. The next day, following the discussions, Joffre sent a letter to Haig proposing a massive combined Franco-British offensive on a sixty-mile front straddling the River Somme, this to take place in the spring or summer of 1916. The newly appointed British Commander-in-Chief was also asked to take over the part of the line south of Arras at that time held by the French Tenth Army. The acquisition of this sector would mean that the British Army held an unbroken line of trenches from Ypres in the north to the Somme in the south. The French line extended from here south and east to the Swiss border.

The plan as originally intended was never put into practice. Preparations were pre-empted by the German attack on the French positions at Verdun on 21 February. This battle grew into an attritional struggle on a scale not yet seen during the war. Seventy-eight French Divisions were eventually drawn into this maelstrom of a battle, losing 315,000 casualties.

On the 27th, Joffre and Castelnau came to Montreuil for a conference with Haig and Sir William Robertson (CIGS). They informed the British commanders that fifty of their Divisions had already passed through the battle raging at Verdun, some of these more than once, and that two-thirds of their available reserves were already engaged. They were fighting for their survival; Verdun had become a cause of almost holy proportions to the French. With *Ils ne passeront pas* as their maxim, the French Army was bleeding to death. It was possible that if the British did not act soon in their support, the Allies could lose the war that year.

Haig promised that the newly formed Fourth Army under General Sir Henry Rawlinson would be ready to attack north of the Somme by 20 June. He did add that he would have preferred to wait until mid-August to allow a greater number of troops to be assembled. Joffre replied that 'the British would not be called on for their effort until 'about the 1 July'.[1]

The *Official History* continues:

It had become apparent to the Commander-in-Chief and the C.I.G.S. during the discussions that the French government... expected the British to make the great effort of the year... The Verdun battle was gradually depriving them of the power of making any important contribution, indeed it was becoming doubtful whether they would make any at all.[2]

On 29 May Haig informed Rawlinson that he might have to attack alone. Following a high-level French conference two days later, Joffre was able to assure Haig that the French would play a role in the forthcoming offensive, but on a much smaller scale than was originally envisaged. The French involvement was to be limited to a front of eight miles, as opposed to the original twenty-five. It would be a supporting role, no more. Although the offensive was now to be largely British, it was the French who had chosen the ground, (Haig had favoured an attack in Flanders that year), and with the situation at Verdun becoming even more critical, they effectively also chose the date. On 16 June, Joffre requested that the attack should commence on the 29th of that month. Haig agreed. He did actually veto a subsequent request for a two-day postponement, citing the increased risk of discovery by the Germans of the troop concentrations then building on the Somme. With 29 June finally agreed upon, Foch and Rawlinson were nevertheless given the power to postpone, by mutual agreement, on a day to day basis, if the weather proved unsuitable.

The actual plan of attack had necessarily gone through various stages of proposal, discussion and amendment. Rawlinson had anticipated a limited attack, which would, after an artillery bombardment of four to five days, occupy the German front-line positions; a pause of two to three days would be used to bring up artillery and reserves before attacking the second position. The lessons of Loos were evidently not being totally ignored. Briefly, this would involve an advance of between one and one-and-a-half miles on a front of 20,000 yards by ten Divisions.

General Haig was more optimistic. He saw the chance of a breakthrough and an opportunity to use his cavalry in open warfare once more. 'Should the enemy's resistance breakdown, the advance was to be 'pressed eastwards far enough to enable our cavalry to push through into the open country beyond the enemy's prepared lines of defence. Our object then will be to turn northwards, taking the enemy's line in flank and reverse.'[3]

Haig also preferred a short, intense artillery bombardment as a prelude to the great assault, stating also that 'much larger steps could be taken with much shorter intervals between them.'[4] He envisaged the capture of the first two German lines in quick succession.

The eventual plan was something of a compromise. The 'hurricane' bombardment was just not possible given the number of artillery pieces available to the Fourth Army. The first objectives finally decided upon were somewhat more ambitious than Rawlinson's first thoughts would have suggested, but neither was Haig able to play his full hand. They included the part of the German second line where it was nearest to the front line, that is, opposite the northern half of the attack frontage, north of the Albert–Bapaume road (see map). 'South of the road the German [second] line lay further back and, as the French on his right were only planning a small advance on the first day, to push on too far would leave Rawlinson's right flank open.'[5] The five-day preliminary bombardment was to go ahead as per Rawlinson's plan.

The British front line here roughly formed the shape of a capital 'L', with the fortified town of Fricourt at the apex of the salient. The main attack was to take place between the town of Serre in the north and Montauban in the south. Fricourt itself was not to be attacked frontally, but outflanked on both sides, quickly rendering its position untenable. To the north of Serre, a diversionary attack was to be directed by Third Army units against the town of Gommecourt. The Somme area had seen only limited fighting up to the summer of 1916; indeed it was regarded by the ordinary soldiers as something of a 'cushy number'. The German units, largely unmolested here, had had plenty of time to organise their defences. Their line had been positioned most carefully.

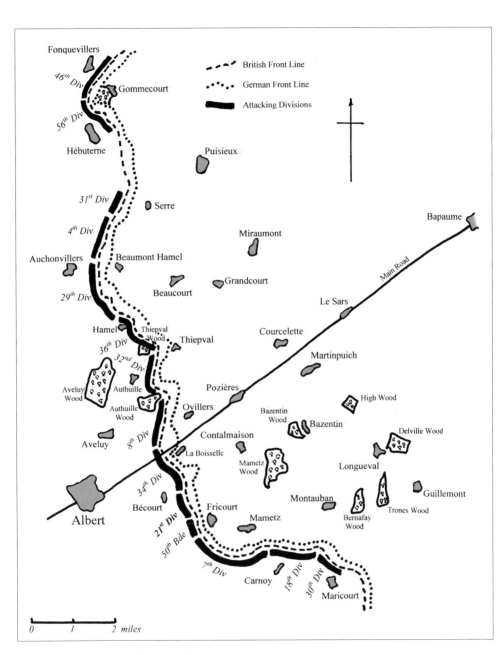

Somme: 1 July 1916. Overall Attack frontage.

Here giving up a stretch of low-lying ground, there withdrawing from a steep river valley, they had backed off to build a line that hugged the high spurs and contours of the chalky downland, so that every slope, every natural ravine, each natural declivity, every wood and hilltop could be turned to maximum advantage for observation, for concealment, for defence.[6]

For nearly two years the German military engineers had been burrowing extensively beneath the trenches, creating tunnels and galleries deep beneath the surface where troops could live unobserved and in far greater comfort than their British counterparts, but, more importantly, safe from all but a direct hit by the largest of artillery shells. Some of these dugouts within the fortified towns just behind the German lines were of a two-storey construction, with proper furniture and beds and often electricity. Lyn Macdonald sums up: 'By the summer of 1916, every hilltop was a redoubt, every wood an arsenal, every farm a stronghold, every village a fortress.'[7]

The War Diary of the 9th KOYLI usually describes the battalion's journeys across the French countryside in a matter-of-fact manner. Their arrival on the Somme at the end of March 1916 was no exception. Lieutenant Ellenberger, however, fills in a few details and is not above passing comment on the arrangements: the battalion started some sixty miles from its destination as the crow flies. 'Not being crows, we marched eight miles in the opposite direction, then fourteen hours on a train around three sides of a quadri-lateral.'[8]

They arrived at Longeau, east of Amiens, at 3.00 a.m. on 1 April. Ellenberger was feeling 'well April-fooled' as they were faced with another march of ten miles. Ellenberger continues the story:

We fell in on the road and moved off. It was almost dawn and gradually through the damp mist we could make out what nature of country it was to which we had come. The poplar-lined pavés straight-stretching across the continuous plains of the North were a thing of the past; the road on which we were wound up and down following the valley on our left, on the other side of which the country rose again in delightful hills; in the bottom of the valley flowed the Somme; the land we were traversing recalled the downs of Hampshire, its chalky slopes undulating and covered with coarse grass, and here and there dotted with dark copses and small woods. It was a sumptuous new world in the morning mist, seeming almost as if it were home to which we had come from the flat mud of Flanders.[9]

The battalion was billeted in the small town of La Neuville, just to the north-west of Corbie, where the River Ancre joins the meandering Somme. Ellenberger describes the billeting arrangements:

... although these houses were in a street, (almost each of them had a farmyard of its own) almost next door to one another; that is to say men were billeted in large outhouses and barns belonging to the farms, while Coy HQ was in one of the farmhouses. There were four officers in the company, and we had two rooms in the house, one used as a company office, and we slept on straw palliasses on the floor in the other one. It was one of the best billets we ever had: Madame was very nice and hospitable. Indeed we were to find all the inhabitants down here were kindly disposed to us. We soon found she baked excellent bread and had some home-brewed beer, which was better than most French beer. To celebrate our arrival in this new part of the world we bought two barrels from her and had a beer parade – the most popular parade the company ever attended![10]

From 'C' Company Headquarters Lt Ellenberger looked out over the garden and the River Ancre itself, which was about twelve feet wide and three to four feet deep at this point; excellent for bathing. He and his men took advantage of this over the next few days of beautiful weather. La Neuville was separated from Corbie only by a level-crossing, and in the larger settlement were estaminets for the men and a shop where English newspapers, only one day old, could be bought.

The idyllic lifestyle was brought to a halt on the morning of 6 April, when the battalion were on the move again, once more eastwards: they did not know where they were going, but the rumours were that it was not just for a change of air and scenery. They were confident that they were not going to be left out in the next big push. 'Perhaps we viewed the country here in much the same spirit as a visiting team views the ground on which the match of the season is to be played', added Ellenberger. The march took them along the path of the River Ancre to the town of Ville, where they halted for three hours for dinner. Onwards from there they reached Méaulte and by 6.30 p.m. were settled into their new billets. The very next day they went into the trenches, relieving the 8th Devonshires. They were welcomed into the new sector by an enemy who launched a large number of rifle grenades onto their new trench.

The 9th KOYLI remained in the trenches for a further week, rifle grenades and mortar fire accounting for the death of four members of the battalion. The 16 April was a Sunday: Church Parade was held at 9.30 a.m., and at 5.00 p.m. the officers of the battalion were photographed by Madame G. David of Corbie (the photograph is reproduced in this book).

Monday was a working day, as ever, as 400 men formed a working party. Second-Lieutenant Stokes reported back from leave, but the battalion was obviously eager to have all its officers present and wired 2nd-Lt Ellenberger, who was still enjoying leave, to return at once. Ellenberger set off straight away, via Southampton. He sailed at 1.00 a.m. It was a rough crossing and he spent the night on deck, though not as seasick as he had at first expected to be. Dry land was a welcome relief as they docked in France at about 8.00 a.m., whereupon Ellenberger met up by chance with his captain (presumably Capt. Walker) on the train. They finally found the battalion at 10.00 p.m.; 'C' Company was feeling very sorry for itself having just received inoculations. Ellenberger could see no apparent reason for his recall from leave one day early and when he next put pen to paper left no-one in doubt of his feelings on the matter: 'The recalling was pretty general and I hear on pretty reliable authority that it was a mistake on the part of some b——— fool of a staff officer.'[11]

Working parties of up to 600 men were the order of the day for the next few weeks. To assemble the troops necessary for the coming attack, along with all the food, supplies and ammunition required, was no mean task. Existing roads had to be maintained, new ones built, along with miles of narrow-gauge railway track to allow trains and lorries to keep the flow of equipment coming; too often, lorries and trains were not sufficient, or at least the infrastructure was lacking, and working parties turned into carrying parties as thousands of men sweated under the weight of gas cylinders, water containers, petrol cans, duckboards, shells and a hundred other items essential to war. The Royal Engineers expressed their satisfaction with the way the men of the 9th KOYLI went about these tasks. The thoughts of the men on the same subject were not recorded. Sometimes things did not go according to plan, however. Writing home on 24 April, 2nd-Lt Ellenberger described one such outing of which he was in charge. The working party marched six miles to where it was to commence work, only to find that there were no tools. The men sunbathed, lunched, and before long 100 tools arrived for the 500 men. They worked for about half an hour and set off to march the six miles back 'home'.

On 26 April, Lt-Col. Lynch was to take another decision that did nothing to improve his relationship with the other officers of the battalion. He promoted Capt. Stephenson to Temporary Second-in-Command of the battalion. (Maj. Greenwood had gone sick and been sent to hospital some days earlier). Captain Stephenson was a personal friend of the CO, and this move catapulted him from mere Second-in-Command of his company, thus passing over all the existing company commanders. Lt Spicer saw this as 'a piece of extraordinary impertinence.'[12]

On 2 May, as Spicer wrote home again, the situation had come to a head:

Griffin (captain commanding 'C' Company, Stephenson's company) and the CO have been having a big row, and things generally were pretty uncomfortable, and I was heartily wishing to be out of it all. At that moment, to be exact on Thursday evening, a chit came round asking for officers for Balloon Observation work. Here seemed an opportunity thrust into my hand, and tho' I did not care tuppence about Balloon Observation I did want to get away and so I put my name down. So did other officers of the company, three in all. I knew when I did so that Lynch would probably want to know why I was putting in for it, and if he asked me I was prepared to tell him why. Two days later, i.e. Saturday, Lynch summoned in all officers. At the time Lynch was (and still is) Acting Brigadier owing to the Brigadier being away on leave. He first of all started fairly reasonably by justifying himself in promoting Stephenson… in his absence to command the battalion, laying stress on the fact that he was entitled to do exactly what he liked by General Routine Orders. He then praised Griffin's work and generally soft-soaped him, and said that it was no slur to him that he was being passed over. Having said all this he then asked Griffin to leave the room, the ostensible reason being that he wished to tell us that he had not promoted Griffin because of his 'not being a gentleman'. As a matter of fact, from this moment onwards he became purely insulting – so insulting that it was quite unbelievable, and his insults were all directed at me! He told us that he was now addressing the officers of 'D' Company (my company). He then stated the facts as to our applying for this balloon job and said that in the first place it showed that we were insubordinate, and secondly it showed cowardice. The latter charge he dwelt on for some time.[13]

The situation simmered on, but Lynch took no further action apart from blocking the transfer requests. Indeed, he put Spicer in temporary command of 'C' Company while Capt. Walker was ill in hospital. Walker returned briefly before taking some leave, and Spicer pens some personal portraits of his fellow officers in a letter dated 15 May:

My present Company Commander is a Captain Walker – a nervous and very reserved Scotsman – a thorough gentleman, but never meant to be a soldier… personally, I like him, but to work with, well I find him a little trying… The other officers in the company at present are: 1) 2nd Lt Oldershaw, a heavily built and heavily minded youth of some twenty-four summers, well-meaning, but as heavy as a lump of lead. I don't dislike him, but no-one bores me to tears more than he does, 2) 2nd Lt Ellenberger, a loquacious and argumentative young gentleman (so, as I am told, am I, I believe!) who possessed sufficient brain to get a scholarship to Winchester and also New College, Oxford, which shows a fair amount of brains – but owing to the war, only completed one term there; and who therefore has all the self-satisfaction produced by having been at Oxford, but who was not there long enough to reap any of the benefits.[14]

Right: *16698 Private Fred Holmes. Killed in action,
1 July 1916.*

Below: *Fred Holmes' name on the Thiepval Memorial.*

['Ellen' became a close friend of Spicer, a friendship that lasted until the former's death in 1975. Ellenberger became a regular soldier after the war and attained the rank of Brigadier.]

The 2 May saw the battalion on the move once again, though this time not far: they paraded at 5.45 a.m. and marched to Méaulte, arriving four hours later, having been thoroughly drenched by a thunderstorm on the way. The following day they relieved the 1st Lincolns and took over from them 298 steel helmets and quantities of Mills bombs, (grenades). Shelling caused two slight casualties in 'D' Company, but no fatalities. On the 10th, the Divisional Commanding Officer notified Lynch that the GOC-in-Chief had awarded the Military Medal to Sgt Ellis of 'B' Company.

The battalion moved out of the trenches once more on the 12th, being relieved by the 10th Yorks & Lancs, and marched off, each company at twenty-minute intervals through Ville, Méricourt and Treux back to La Neuville, the rearmost troops arriving at 3.30 a.m. The following day was, not surprisingly, a rest day. They were allotted baths at the 63rd Field Ambulance, and 'A' and 'B' Companies' rifles were overhauled by the 1st East Yorks Armourer Sergeant. There was a Church of England parade the following morning: the entire brigade formed square and the service was taken by the Revd Capt. Lester.

Two days later, 2nd-Lts W.W. Shepherd and D. Williams reported for duty and were posted respectively to 'A' and 'B' Companies. That same day, the battalion had taken part in trench manoeuvres at the Grenade School.

On the 17th, they formed up on ground especially chosen for its similarity to that over which they were destined to attack in six weeks' time. They stood in imaginary assembly trenches, marked on the ground by flags and tapes, awaiting the order to advance on similarly marked out enemy positions. At 10.45 a.m., eight flares went up, and the

British trench near Fricourt. (IWM Q17489)

Wrecked German trench near Fricourt. (IWM C0230)

battalion advanced, 'C' Company on the left, 'A' on the right, with 'D' and 'B' respectively in support. The 15th Durham Light Infantry came on behind in support. The 10th KOYLI headed the attack on the left, and bombers brought up the rear. Lewis Gun teams, newly formed, were attached to the leading platoons. Once the first objectives were 'gained', they consolidated the line and set up outposts. By 12.30 p.m., the telephone message to return had been received. No casualties were reported, but units were able to inflict damage of a more tangible kind on each other two days later when the Brigade Boxing Competition took place

The practice attack was repeated on the 21st, this time accompanied by airplane observation and support, and a bombing competition rounded off the day.

The next ten days were taken up by the inevitable working parties, and the battalion adopted Ville as its home once more. On the 31st, Lt-Col. Lynch inspected the 10th Yorks & Lancs' trenches opposite Fricourt prior to taking over. Also on this day, Lt Spark left for leave prior to his attachment to 62nd Brigade HQ for training in staff duties. He was to miss the Big Push. Second-Lieutenant Keay took over as Adjutant.

During May, a significant change had taken place in the higher echelons of command. Major-General D.G.M. Campbell had taken over command of 21st Division. 'Soarer' Campbell had earned his nickname by riding a horse of that name to victory in the 1896 Grand National. He was a cavalryman and had led his men in a charge near Mons in 1914. He proved to be an excellent Divisional Commander who embraced and understood the new mechanised war being fought by his men. He may well have been wounded by a German lance in 1914, but by 1918 he was personally making aeroplane reconnaissance flights as Observer, often requesting his pilot to attack targets of opportunity which may have presented themselves, including, on one occasion, an enemy aircraft. He adopted the code name 'Barbara', and often the hurried message sent down the chain of command of 'Barbara on the loose' warned subordinates to expect an otherwise unannounced visit.

On 1 June, the battalion took over the front line from the 10th Yorks & Lancs. At 10.30 p.m. on the 4th, notification was received of a DSO for Lt-Col. Lynch. The battalion War Diary records the congratulations from brigade and staff and all ranks of the battalion. A planned raid for later that night failed to materialise: our preparatory bombardment provoked an enemy retaliation of such intensity that our troops were unable to leave the front-line trenches. Lt Ellenberger described being caught in this bombardment in a letter written home three days later: 'Last Sunday [I] lay out in a ravine in front of the trenches with nine men during a bombardment from both sides. Every other shell seemed to be bursting on my tin hat.'[15] The Battalion War Diary records casualties for this stint in the front line as five 'Other Ranks' (OR) killed, three OR died of wounds, one officer wounded (2nd-Lt Kingston) and thirty-four OR wounded.

The next few days involved the battalion supplying wiring parties and other working parties as required. On the 7th, 2nd-Lts Maconachie and Kemp reported for duty, 2nd-Lt Stokes and Lt Hendricks coming back from leave the following day. On the 11th, the 10th Yorks & Lancs took over the battalion's scattered positions, allowing them to gather in the tented camp near Bray. Captain Walker assumed command of the battalion, and 2nd-Lt Ibbetson returned from leave.

On the 14th, the battalion was back on familiar ground at La Neuville, practising the forthcoming attack. That same evening, Lynch, now back with the battalion, gave a lecture to all subalterns. 2nd-Lt Kingston's return from hospital coincided with the introduction of 'Daylight Saving' later that evening when all clocks were set on one hour at 11.00 p.m. The following day saw the brigade practising the attack once more. Later the same day, a carrying party of seven officers and 300 men delivered gas cylinders up to the trenches from Corbie. They did not return until 6.00 a.m. the following morning, leaving behind one man killed, 16864 Pte Harry Bolton. The battalion paraded on the 16th, allowing their gas helmets to be inspected by the Chemical Advisor. At 6.30 p.m., Lynch gave another lecture, this time to all the officers.

Preparations were beginning to gain momentum and the next two days saw seven new officers report for duty: 2nd-Lts. Hardman, Sutcliffe, Golding, Jenkins, Franklin, Vassie and Beattie.

By the 24th, the battalion was back in Ville, and this day was designated a rest day: there were no parades and only small working parties were required. Also on this day, the artillery bombardment in preparation for the attack began along the whole front. The countdown had now begun. The following day, the Commanding Officer, Lt-Col. Lynch, issued Order No.36. This was a fifteen-page document detailing the forthcoming attack: map references gave the exact location of jumping-off trenches, battalion boundaries left and right and position of objectives. Assembly instructions ensured that all the men could reach their positions prior to the attack with the minimum of fuss and confusion. The attacking formations were described in exhaustive detail; ten waves moving forward at not more than 100 yards distance, with about four to five paces between men.

The actual method of advance was not pre-ordained by High Command, it was to some extent left to brigade and even individual battalion commanders. Some deemed that their men would walk across no man's land from their front trenches, expecting to meet no resistance from smashed German positions.[16]

Parallel to, and in front of the 9th and 10th KOYLI positions, a Russian Sap had been dug, that is, to all intents and purposes, a trench with a thin layer of soil left in place as a roof, thus disguising it from enemy observation. This was to be opened up the night before the attack and filled with first-wave troops. This cut the distance to be covered in the open to reach the German front-line trenches from 300 to 180 yards. To reduce this distance even further, troops were to leave this sap just before Zero hour and crawl forwards into no man's land as far as the artillery barrage would allow. 'The advance will be made in quick time,'[17] asserted the order under heading '9', 'Method of Advance'.

The men would not be able to run too quickly, however. Order No.36 also contained a list of equipment to be carried by each man: a steel helmet; equipment in fighting order, haversack on back containing complete iron rations and unused rations – bread, cheese, chocolate; a water bottle, full (cold tea or coffee recommended); gas helmets and goggles; waterproof sheet, securely rolled, eighteen feet long; 220 rounds SAA; two Mills bombs, detonated; two sandbags; entrenching tool and haft; wire cutters, as detailed; field dressings and iodine ampoules; paper and pencil for writing messages if necessary; full oil bottles and pull-through flares.[18]

With this making up a total weight of between sixty-five and seventy pounds, the men would be sure not to outrun the barrage! Later in the document, under 'Discipline', the continuation of the advance, once begun, was assured:

The use of the word 'retire' is absolutely forbidden in this Division. All ranks are distinctly to understand that if such an order is given, it is either a device of the enemy, or is given by some person who has lost his head. In any case this order is never to be obeyed.[19]

Any orders to withdraw had to be given and received in writing, and must contain co-ordinates of the position to be assumed by the unit concerned. Artillery support for the advancing infantry had evolved since the start of the war. The proper 'creeping barrage' was nowhere near perfection by this stage, but a version of it was to be used ahead of the KOYLI troops, the shells gradually lifting from one predetermined line to the next at set intervals. It was up to the infantry to keep pace. Once the battle had opened, it would be impossible to contact the artillery in order to modify the timetable as local situations demanded. The sooner the troops reached a line of trenches after the barrage had lifted from it, the less chance its defenders had to man the parapet and set up machine guns. Division sent down the following message: 'Barrages will lift gradually, covering all the ground to be passed over. Follow burst of shells as closely as possible.'[20] This was a risky business, as it was common for shells to fall short and wreak havoc amongst those they were meant to protect.

On 27 June, the entire battalion was paraded at Buire at 2.30 p.m. and was addressed by Lt-Col. Lynch, who gave some last words of advice and instruction. At 9.35 p.m. that evening, the 9th KOYLI moved up into the trenches, a march of about six or seven miles as the crow flies, but actually much longer, the last part being through winding communications trenches, and once there relieved the 1st Lincolns. Rations were picked up on the way from a dump to the north-east of Méaulte. The War Diary noted: 'All the men were in excellent spirits.' It was nearly four o'clock the following morning by the time everyone was settled in, 'A' and 'C' Companies in the front line, 'B' and 'D' in support, just as during the practices back at La Neuville. Despite some rain and the noise of the bombardment, many of the men managed to sleep during the day.

Officers of the 9th KOYLI. Photograph taken 16 April 1916.

Key:

1 Capt. Revd A. Bouchier
  (Chaplain)
2 Capt. G. Haswell
3 Capt. L.D. Head
4 Maj. H. Greenwood
5 Lt-Col. C.W.D. Lynch (C.O.)

6 Lt A.G. Spark
7 Capt. W. Walker
8 Capt. G.E. Griffin
9 Lt-QM W.K. Pethed
10 Capt. A. Stephenson
11 Lt H.A. Telfer

12 2nd-Lt E.R. Nott
13 Lt J. Buckley
14 Lt L.D. Spicer
15 Lt A. Malseed RAMC (M.O.)
16 2nd-Lt C.W. Ellis

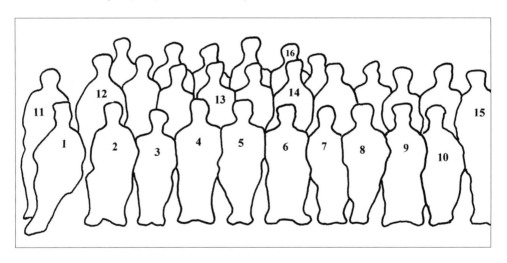

That afternoon the message was received that the attack had been postponed for forty-eight hours. Weather conditions for artillery-spotting and observation had proved less than ideal; only one day out of five since the beginning of the bombardment been fine. Low cloud, mist and rain had hampered operations to such an extent that Rawlinson decided that the attack would now go in on 1 July.

It was something of an anti-climax for the men in the trenches. They were 'all dressed up and no place to go'.[21] 'A' and 'C' Companies swapped places with 'B' and 'D', and the latter sent out patrols that evening into no man's land to find that the enemy wire entanglements had been extensively destroyed by the artillery bombardment.

Earlier the same evening, at about 6.00 p.m., all the officers received a summons to Battalion HQ. When they got there, a glass was put in their hands; there was to be a final drink together before the big attack. The atmosphere was slightly strained as they drank quietly to each other, wishing each other luck, and, no doubt nervously, arranging tentative reunions for after the battle. Lt-Col. Lynch came into the room and was given a glass. In the absence of the Second-in-Command and the Adjutant, Acting Adj. W.F. Keay was in charge of proceedings. At this point he went up to Haswell, the senior captain present, and suggested quietly that he propose a toast to the CO's health. 'I'm damned if I will,' replied Haswell, adding, 'I don't wish him good health and am not prepared to be insincere on this occasion.' Keay insisted, however, and after several seconds of restrained argument, Haswell reluctantly stepped forward and raised his glass, saying, 'Gentlemen, I give you the toast of the King's Own Yorkshire Light Infantry, and in particular the 9th Battalion of that Regiment.' During a slight pause here he recalled a phrase which occurred repeatedly in the written orders for the attack 'Gentlemen, when the barrage lifts.' His brother officers emptied their glasses in silence. An unpleasant scene had been avoided.[22]

The artillery bombardment continued through 29 July. It was another wet day and the 9th Battalion crouched miserably, cold and hungry in their sodden trenches. They were in 'fighting order', with no change of clothes, no blankets, no greatcoats. Luckily, any counter-barrage by the Germans was minimal. The 30th passed in similar vein. There was nothing to do but wait for darkness, when final preparations could begin. Men's thoughts would inevitably turn to home, to family, friends and sweethearts at such times. Many would have written home in the previous days and weeks, knowing that it was possibly the last letter they would ever write, and the content often mirrored this realisation. 2nd-Lt Ellenberger, aged twenty-one at this time, had written one such letter on 25 June, the second day of the bombardment. He sent it to his Aunt Nellie, with instructions that it was only to be given to his mother in the event of his death:

My very, very dearest Mother,
I feel I ought to write you all something in the nature of a farewell in case I should not return to you from this war. You'll understand the difficulty I have in writing a letter that you will not read till I am no more, and that though there is so much that I should like to say, it is exceedingly hard to say it. I will begin by trying to explain what have been my feelings ever since I came out here, but more pronounced now than ever before. I believe I do not fear death – at least I hope not and tell myself I do not; but I am a coward for I do fear pain. I will not dwell on the idea of receiving some horrible wound; but worse than all, I fear causing you to suffer pain – pain which I know would be mental rather than physical, and for that reason the greater. So if there is any afterlife in which we can still take notice of and interest in the things that happen in this world, nothing would cause me greater trouble than to see you, after my death, stricken down by grief. Of course I know

the measure of your sorrow would be the measure of your love for me – and so I do not ask that you should not grieve for me, only that you should not be overcome and dominated by your grief.

All I can do myself is assure you that I have gone into this great adventure loving you with all my heart and with all my soul, further that the great love which I have for you has kept me straight – has almost been my God. I cannot tell you what my feelings are on religion – I do not yet know myself – all I can say is that I am not a Christian in the true sense of the word, but I am also not an atheist. I believe in some good God – more I cannot say, or, at any rate, write. I know nothing – what mortal really knows anything? – of a future life; but I trust that we shall in some state hereafter all meet again… I will not speak of patriotism and sacrifice except to say this: I am sure that if I had hung back when our country said it needed all its youth, I should have disappointed you, though I realise that your sacrifice is greater than mine: I am only offering my life, you have offered your love: and while I have been so busied, and even pleasantly busied and to have little time for cares, it has been your lot – the harder one – to sit at home and suffer anxiety in silence.

[He added a PPS]: *If I die in this war, I did so knowing that I can do no better thing – and what finer consummation of all that I have been brought up to think good and noble can I wish for?*[23]

Under cover of darkness on the night of the 30th, large parties of men were occupied out in no man's land with wire cutters, removing their own wire entanglements as completely as possible. (The men of the KOYLI would not have to bunch up as they passed through 'lanes' in their own wire, giving the German machine-gunners irresistible targets.) Perhaps surprisingly there was no shelling by the Germans, and their machine guns remained silent. The task was accomplished without casualties, and completed before midnight.

There was now nothing to do but wait. Along the entire attack front, eighteen Divisions waited, 234 battalions – almost 520,000 men. Sixty per cent of these were New Army Divisions; every man was a volunteer. It was common practice for a battalion about to go into battle to designate a percentage of its officers as reserve and then to keep them out of the first waves of the attack. This was for two reasons: firstly, it allowed these officers to be ready to go up after the attack, if required, to replace losses incurred. It also ensured that if the worst happened, the battalion would have a core of original officers around which to rebuild. Order No.36 concluded by listing the officers that would take part in the initial attack, and those who would not:

List of officers who will accompany the battalion into action

Headquarters	Lt-Col. C.W.D. LYNCH D.S.O., 2nd-Lt R.A. STOKES
'A' Company	Captain L.D. HEAD, 2nd-Lt C.W. HOWLETT, 2nd-Lt N.L. ALEXANDER, 2nd-Lt A. HARDMAN, 2nd-Lt C.E. VASSIE
'B' Company	Captain G. HASWELL, Lt B.L. GORDON, 2nd-Lt C.W. ELLIS, 2nd-Lt D. WILLIAMS, 2nd-Lt G.A. KEMP
'C' Company	Captain W. WALKER, 2nd-Lt J.J.F. OLDERSHAW, 2nd-Lt G.F. ELLENBERGER, 2nd-Lt A.D. MACONACHIE, 2nd-Lt F.W. GOLDING

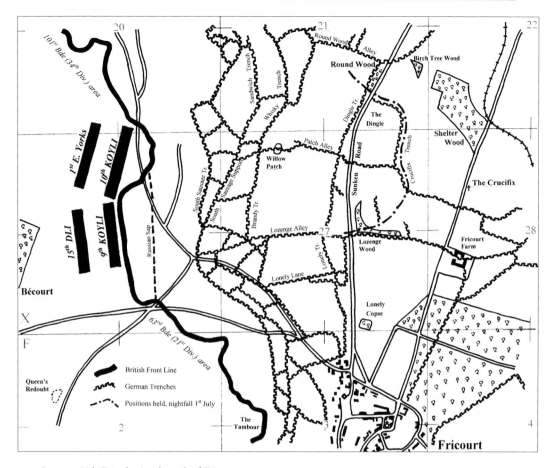

Somme: 64th Brigade Attack north of Fricourt.

'D' Company   Captain G.E. GRIFFIN, 2nd-Lt A.E. DAY, 2nd-Lt W.R. STOKES★, 2nd-Lt R.F. FRAZER, 2nd-Lt J.R. WOOD

Bombing Officer   2nd-Lt F.G. MORRIS
Signalling Officer   2nd-Lt G.H. FEATHERSTONE
Scout Officer   2nd-Lt E.R. NOTT

★ 2nd-Lt W.R. Stokes left the battalion on the evening of 30 June to proceed to England as Training Officer.
Those to be left behind on Day Zero were:
Major A. Stephenson (HQ), Lts C.A.C.J. Hendricks (A Coy), L.D. Spicer (C Coy) and B.H.L. Hart (D Coy); 2nd-Lts W.F. Keay (HQ), W.W. Shepherd (A Coy), H.F. Kingston (B Coy), K.W. Sutcliffe (B Coy), A.M.L. Beattie (C Coy) and E.G.J. Jenkins (D Coy)

Over the seven days of artillery bombardment, 1,437 guns had fired 1,508,652 shells. At 6.25 a.m. on 1 July, a day that was to turn out bright, sunny and hot, the barrage suddenly intensified. Lieutenant Gordon, in the 9th KOYLI front-line trenches with his men, described it as 'more violent than anything I have ever heard, its intensity was terrific.'[24]

Three hundred yards in front of him, below the German front line, troops of the 111th Reserve Regiment sheltered in their deep dugouts, praying that the bombardment they had suffered for seven days would soon be over. Trenches, observation posts and shallow dugouts had all been almost completely destroyed, and those men still alive in the deepest dugouts had often been unable to receive rations since 24 June. They had not much longer to wait. At 7.22 a.m., the intensity of the barrage suddenly grew even further, with Stokes mortars joining in the cacophony.

The rum ration had arrived earlier that morning and the men were ready to go. In front of them the ground rose steadily for some 500 yards. The convex nature of the slope meant that the actual German front line was just out of sight. Once over the spur, the ground fell away for another 5-600 yards as far as a sunken road heading due north from the town of Fricourt, visible from the highest point of the spur a mile away to the southeast. Beyond the sunken road lay Shelter Wood and Fricourt Farm. The 9th KOYLI were to advance beyond these, outflanking Fricourt to the north. The 7th Division were to advance northwards, bypassing the town to the east, capturing Mametz as they did so: Fricourt would be cut off, and despite not suffering a direct frontal assault, would be forced to capitulate.

The 64th Brigade formation had the 9th KOYLI in the front line, the 10th KOYLI to their left. Behind them, in support, respectively, were the 15th DLI and the 1st East Yorks. The left of the 10th KOYLI formed the Divisional boundary. To the north was the 101st Brigade, part of 34th Division, consisting of the 15th & 16th Royal Scots and the Tyneside Scottish battalions, who were to advance up 'Sausage Valley' in the direction of Contalmaison. It was to be an ill-fated attack.

The Sunken Road, north of Fricourt, looking north. (present day)

The remains of Fricourt village. (IWM Q854)

To the right of the 9th KOYLI was the 63rd Brigade, with, left to right, the 8th Somerset LI, 4th Middlesex and 10th West Yorks in the front line.

At 7.25 a.m., the men of 'A' and 'C' Companies, 9th KOYLI, climbed out of the Russian Sap and began to crawl towards the German front-line trench, No.1 Platoon, 'A' Company under 2nd-Lt Alexander and No.9 Platoon, 'C' Company under 2nd-Lt Oldershaw leading the way. The enemy responded with a shrapnel barrage, and machine-gun and rifle fire began from the German trenches; the German troops had left their dugouts despite the intensity of the British artillery fire to man their parapet. Some of the machine-gun fire was coming from German trenches on higher ground near La Boisselle, to the north of the KOYLI advance. Their position allowed the gunners to enfilade these exposed troops with deadly effect.

At 7.28 a.m. two mines were detonated under the German front line, one at the 'Tambour' in front of the 10th West Yorks, and one closer to the 9th KOYLI, in their left rear near La Boisselle, in front of the 34th Division. It is unlikely that the latter, the bigger of the two explosions, went completely unnoticed by the Yorkshiremen, but by now they had other things on their minds.

At 7.29 a.m., Lt Gordon led his men forward from the original front-line trenches into the dense smoke produced by the exploding shells.

The advance was by crawling and by rushes from shell-hole to shell-hole. The noise was deafening and the German machine-gun fire was terrible. Just before reaching the Russian Sap I was struck on the chin by a bit of shrapnel. When I reached the sap I lay down and looked into it. I saw Colonel Lynch, who said: 'Hullo, Gordon, are you hit?' I put my hand to my chin and found it was covered with blood. The Colonel then began to get out of the Sap. He was killed by a shell almost immediately afterwards.[25]

Ahead of him, with 'C' Company, 2nd-Lt Ellenberger reported that his company was greeted by a hail of machine-gun and rifle bullets some twenty yards into no man's land. As they advanced further, they had also to contend with German stick-grenades. His Company Commander, Capt. Walker, was already dead, killed by machine-gun fire. Gordon, coming up behind, passed close enough to the body to recognise him. Gordon continues his story:

By this time our waves were jumbled together and, owing to the smoke, it was difficult to keep direction... after a few more minutes, which seemed ages, I reached the German front trenches. Several 'B' Company men joined me, and I sat in a shell-hole while one of them bandaged my chin, which was cut and bruised, and bleeding freely.[26]

The German front line had been 'frightfully ploughed up' according to Ellenberger, and the KOYLIs reached it within minutes, and in the words of the War Diary, 'in spite of heavy losses carried the front line with little delay.'

The losses were indeed heavy. The battalion suffered the majority of its casualties that day as it crossed no man's land. Of the twenty-four officers who left the trenches, only five succeeded in crossing the German front-line trench. They were Lt Gordon, and 2nd-Lts. Ellenberger, Day, Frazer and Featherstone. 'A' Company had already lost all of its officers. Ellenberger was the only 'C' Company officer left. Eighteen-year-old 2nd-Lt Frank Golding, who had joined the battalion only twelve days before, lay dead in no man's land. Gordon's account continues:

Although our bombardment had failed to knock out the enemy machine guns, its effect on their trenches had been great. For the most part they were entirely knocked in, one long succession of shell-holes, brown craters mainly, for the soil is thick. Now and then one came to an enormous white crater, caused, I believe, by our trench mortars. These were 15 or 20 feet deep and as many yards across.[27]

By this time the 15th DLI had commenced its advance, and in some cases had caught up with the first wave of attackers. Lieutenant Gordon's party had lost direction somewhat in the smoke and the confusion. He realised that he was too far to the south, near to Fricourt, and with his group, which now consisted of some remnants of 'B' Company, some Somersets and a Durham private, began crossing German trench lines, all the time veering to their left to maintain the correct line of advance:

While we were moving to our left we suddenly came upon about a dozen Germans, about ten or twelve yards off. They fired at us with rifles. I whipped out my revolver and fired several rounds, and some of my men also fired. One of the Germans dropped and suddenly my 'Faithful Durham' rushed forward shouting: 'Come on, boys, the b———s are on the run.' The enemy would not face the bayonet. We captured the wounded man and one other, who threw down his rifle and held up his hands. The rest fled.[28]

Ellenberger also recalled the attitude to hand-to-hand fighting prevalent amongst their opponents as, once over the crest of the spur, the battle turned into a series of running fights:

Grave of Second-Lieutenant C.W. Ellis, former pupil of Batley Grammar School. Gordon Dump Cemetery, Somme.

The whole thing was so very fast and it was such hot work that you hadn't time to sit and think over the horrors, but just went on and on, pursued by a decided but unexpressed feeling that you would sooner be anywhere but there. The Hun ran, and we took a lot of prisoners; he has a very unsporting idea about fighting, has the Hun. He'll poop away his machine gun at you, and he'll snipe at you, and he'll throw bombs at you, but as soon as you get to close quarters, with the bayonet, he puts up his hands... I saw a lot of Huns, and a lot of Hun rifles, and it's an absolute fact that none of them had a fixed bayonet – when it came to bayonet work they put up their hands; the bayonets we found afterwards down in their dugouts.[29]

One member of Ellenberger's platoon, Sgt Wigglesworth, was wounded during the advance, and the Sergeant later wrote to the Second-Lieutenant from his hospital bed in London describing the incident. (The spelling and punctuation are Wigglesworth's.)

I will try to explain how I got my Blighty. it was when we got to the second trench i was firing away at the Boches who were only about 20 yards off and i can safely account for knocking six over (without any boast) as i was in a splendid shell hole and was blazing away like hell. We were just getting out when they set their M G on us. the men who was with me in our Pltn was L/C Foster, Duwick, Woaton and a few stragglers out of other Coys just as i got out i felt a sharp hot burn which brought me down again and i found i had received a bullet wound straight through the left hip just missing the bone. i bandaged it up and told the others to push on and wished them good luck... i went to the dressing station and passed from one place to another until i got to Le Havre on the Tuesday night 4th and arrived here on the 5th.[30]

The brigade, by now hopelessly mixed up, fought its way down the reverse slope and into the sunken road, reaching it by about 8.00 a.m. Lieutenant Gordon's party had grown in number, and on these slopes he had met up with the only other brother officer he could find, 2nd-Lt Ellenberger, and they pressed on together. They rushed the last two hundred yards over open country under violent shell fire but made it safely to the comparative shelter of the road, which has steep banks up to ten feet high on both sides.

Just in front of the Sunken Road, which is about 1,100 yards in front of the original British fire trench, was a German subsidiary line of trenches. Here I found many of our own men and others from different battalions in our brigade, but no senior officers except Colonel Fitzgerald of the Durham's. After a short time I realised what had happened, took command of my battalion and reported myself to Colonel Fitzgerald.

About 3 or 400 yards in front of the Sunken Road there is a trench called Crucifix Trench by the British, because just above it there is a crucifix standing between three tall trees [there still is a crucifix standing at this point]. This trench was the ultimate objective of our battalion. I asked Colonel Fitzgerald if I should lead my men to it, but he instructed me not to do so at that time, as owing to the rapid advance of our brigade, both our flanks were exposed. Indeed the Sunken Road itself was being continuously enfiladed by enemy machine-guns firing from the direction of Fricourt on our right and from Birch Tree Wood on our left. I instructed my men to dig themselves in on the line of the Sunken Road, which they began to do, gradually improving the cover against the machine-gun fire, but not before we had sustained further losses.[31]

Whilst in the Sunken Road, Lt Gordon came across a large German dugout, which had been a German Battalion Headquarters, excavated into the forward bank of the road. It was some twenty-five feet deep, consisting of several rooms, both for living and sleeping, with a large oven installed. Gordon also found some cigarettes, and more importantly a substantial store of seltzer water, which he immediately began to distribute to the men who were extremely thirsty: the day was turning into a very hot one indeed. The water was particularly appreciated by the wounded.

At about this time, 19970 Pte J. Kearford of 'B' Company was given the very risky job of trying to make contact with the 4th Middlesex on their right. To do this he had to proceed down the Sunken Road in the direction of Fricourt, not knowing whether his first contact would be with friend or foe. Luckily it turned out to be the former, and his good work earned him a rare (for a private) mention in the Battalion War Diary.

The Brigade Commander himself, Brig.-Gen. Headlam, had reached the Sunken Road briefly, but had been forced to return to our own lines. He had left orders with Lt-Col. Fitzgerald that he was not to advance to Crucifix Trench without first obtaining instructions from Brigade HQ. Unknown to any of the officers left in the Sunken Road at that time, a mixed force from all the battalions in the brigade, under 2nd-Lt A.E. Day of 9th KOYLI, was already there. 2nd-Lt Day had been wounded in the leg by shrapnel whilst crossing no man's land, but had continued to lead the advance, obviously reaching the Sunken Road before any of the others, and, pressing on, had found Crucifix Trench unoccupied. It was around noon before he succeeded in getting a message back to Gordon informing him of the situation. At 1.30 p.m. orders finally arrived from Brigade to advance from the Sunken Road and take Crucifix Trench. The trench was of course in our hands, and had been so for several hours, but it badly needed reinforcing and consolidating. The advance across the two hundred yards or so of open ground was undertaken in three waves under the three remaining officers of 9th KOYLI, Lt Gordon

Gravestones of 9th KOYLI officers killed in action, 1 July 1916.

and 2nd-Lts. Ellenberger and Frazer. The men advanced at the double under heavy machine-gun fire, and arrived to find a trench which, only being a subsidiary line, had never been very deep and which had been badly knocked about by the British artillery bombardment. Consolidation began at once; bombing squads and machine guns were sent out to cover both flanks, and Gordon established a headquarters quite close to the crucifix itself. The position was very exposed; the Germans still held Shelter Wood, Birch Tree Wood and Fricourt Farm. There were no dugouts in the trench and they had to suffer an artillery bombardment during the afternoon.

Second-Lieutenant Day's wound was by this time getting worse and threatening to totally incapacitate him if he did not receive proper treatment. He refused to go back, however, until directly ordered to do so by Lt Gordon. At about 5.00 p.m., Captain Santer of the 10th KOYLI, himself wounded in the chest, arrived from the left and took command of Crucifix Trench. He sent several messages back to the Sunken Road, but got no answer. During this time also, 2nd-Lt Frazer received a shrapnel wound in the head and was forced to go out. At approximately 8.00 p.m., Santer ordered Gordon back to the Sunken Road to find out what was going on, as Crucifix Trench was, by this time, in dire need of reinforcement. On reaching the Sunken Road, Gordon discovered that Lt-Col. Fitzgerald had been wounded in the leg, a wound from which he died a few days later. To his great joy he also discovered that messages had arrived signalling that 62nd Brigade was to advance and relieve the 64th in Crucifix Trench.

The officers of 'Echelon B', those left behind at the start of proceedings, had spent a long, trying and rather frustrating day. They had been unable to observe the attack properly due to the amount of smoke on the battlefield, and had had to rely on infrequent and often inaccurate messages coming back from the fray.

At about 3.30 p.m., Spicer received an order to report to the old Brigade Headquarters at Méaulte at once, bringing four other officers with him. He in turn ordered Keay, Kingston, Shepherd and Hart to get ready and they set off together at about 4.15 p.m., accompanied by Stancliffe and O'Connell, servants respectively of himself and Hart. They set off to walk the three miles from Ville to Méaulte, but hitched a lift for half of the way on a horse ambulance. On arrival they were told to report at once (!) to Brigade HQ in the trenches. It was by then 5.45 p.m. and it took a further hour and three quarters to reach their destination. There, Brig.-Gen. Headlam, looking worn out and tired, told Spicer and his group to head off over to the Sunken Road, and to be prepared to reorganise the battalion, being of the opinion that Spicer would find few, if any, officers there. Once the reserve brigade, the 62nd, had arrived, the remnants of the 64th were to pull back to South Sausage Support, a trench in the German front-line system, the 9th and 10th KOYLI holding that line.

He and his group got as far as the Russian Sap when the German artillery chose to put down a barrage on their own former front line. Spicer decided that to hurry on through this and risk not arriving at all was not in anyone's best interests and so ordered his group to sit tight and wait for the storm to blow over. Within half an hour, the barrage had petered out, and at 8.30 p.m. they clambered out of the Sap and continued on their way. He was forced to give a difficult order to his fellow officers at this point. Despite the cries and groans for help from the many wounded still lying out there, he decided that they must press on and forbade his comrades to stop and render assistance. He did not feel good about this, but 'there was more important work in hand.'[32]

Like Lt Gordon earlier, they lost direction somewhat, veering similarly to the right, ending up, so they feared, in Lozenge Alley, a communication trench leading to the

AYLOR I.
AYLOR P.
AYLOR T. J.
AYLOR V. J. W.
IOMAS F.
IOMPSON J.
IOMPSON J. H.
IORP W.
KNER F.
EY B. H.
CHENER R. J.
OMEY G. D.
VNER F. J.
VNSEND G. A.
VNSEND W.
E A.G.
DD W. P.
SCOTT F.C.
EY D.J.
LETT H.W.
VER C.
VER W. H.
S I.
RHILL H.J.
IER V.
W. A.
FIELD C. G.
F.
ORD C.
ING J.
CE W.
URY S.
G.
N R.
GTON W.J.
IAN P.
V A.
V H.C.
V I. E.
T

WALKER J. N
SECOND LIEUT.
ADAMS T.
ARCHER E.T.
ARMSTRONG C. M
BAKER A.W.
BENTALL W. D.
BLAKEY G.
BOSWELL P. G.
CARTER S. R E
EVERSFIELD C. J.
FEATHERSTONE
          G. H.
FORRYAN D.
GROSS H.G.
HARPLEY R. A.
HOTSON H.C.
JACKSON A. S.
JUBB J.C.
KEMP F.
MILLS S.
MORRISH D. B.
MOUNTAIN A. J.
OLDERSHAW J.J.I
RHODES W. M
ROBINSON P. B. P.
ROYLE W.
SHARP L. F.
SIMPSON A. R. F
SKEVINGTON A V
SMITH L. T.
SMITH R.
STEPHENSON O S
SUTCLIFFE K W.
WALKER H. G.
WATTS A. E.
WILKINSON G. F
WINKWORTH C H.

BEAN R.
BEAUMON
BYRON H.
CHAPPELL
CONWAY
CROOKES
DAVIS G.
DAVISON
FOWLER I
FOX A.
GARSIDE
GEE J.
GEE W. F
GILL J.D
HARRIS
HARTLE
HEATON
HEPWOF
HIRST G
HOLLAN
HOYLE
JACKSOI
KING A
LAW S.
MAJOR
MANN
MARRI(
MASON
MAXFII
MORTC
MOULI
NICHC
PENTE
PICKEI
ROLLII
SALTE
SCHOI
SHAW
SIMPS
CLAINI

Names of KOYLI officers on the Thiepval Memorial.

Sunken Road, but outside the southern flank of the battalion boundary. A meeting with units of the 62nd Brigade, Lincolns and Green Howards, confirmed their location, but they hurried along Lozenge Alley to where it met the Sunken Road. In fact it did not quite reach the road; a sap was being dug to connect them, but a short distance had still to be covered over the top. One man who was digging warned that they should be careful. A sniper in Fricourt Farm would be likely to take a pot at anyone crossing this short stretch in the open. Left with no choice, Spicer went first, scrambled out of the communication trench and dived for the road. By the time he heard the ping of the sniper's bullet he was already safe under the embankment on the far side of the road. The rest of the party were equally fortunate. They began to move northwards along the road by now crowded with British troops. Spicer stumbled upon CSM Warren, who was busy digging himself in the side of the bank. He asked the sergeant if he was aware of any officers being in the vicinity. The answer came in the negative, and, leaving Kingston and Shepherd in charge of that section of road, he and Keay proceeded further. Enquiries led Spicer to the large German dugout, where, he was told, Gordon was still going and had established a Battalion Headquarters.

This was approached by a covered entrance, which had been converted into a temporary dressing station. It was very difficult to get in without treading on the wounded... standing on top of the stairs, I called down to Gordon. A long white figure rose from halfway down the steps, and uttered in fervent tones: 'Is that you, Spicer, is that you? Thank God, thank God.'[33]

Spicer told Gordon of the orders he had received from the Brigadier, only to find that he, Gordon, had just received them himself. A runner was sent forward to Crucifix Trench, telling Ellenberger of Spicer's arrival. Ellenberger, leaving RSM Crossland in charge, came back to the Sunken Road himself to receive orders. He was told of the imminent relief and that his men could fall back. Hart was promptly despatched to fetch them.

The slow process of gathering the men of the battalion together commenced, but it was not until midnight that the operation was anything like complete. About 150 Other Ranks could be mustered. At about this time, Gordon, exhausted and requiring attention to his wound, handed over command to Spicer and made his way back to the Regimental First Aid Post. It was after 3.00 a.m. when he finally reached it, a long eerie walk over the corpse-strewn battlefield. The doctor cleaned up his wound, gave him an enormous whisky and soda and told him to get some sleep. Gordon found a space on the floor and was content to do as he had been told.

Back in the Sunken Road, Spicer and what was left of the battalion were about ready to move, but he had lost Shepherd, Kingston, CSM Warren and his party. He presumed they had already set out for South Sausage Support and was about to give the order for the rest of the battalion to move out when the Commanding Officer of the Lincolns, Colonel Grant, suddenly gave orders that the 64th Brigade were to stay put until the whole of the incoming 62nd were in place.

They were still there at seven the following morning.

GOC Reserve Brigade came up to the Sunken Road and after consultation with the CO 1st Lincolns, we were allowed to move out. We had been detained there all night because two and a half companies of the 12th Northumberland Fusiliers had never arrived. Permission having now been granted, we all filed down Patch Alley and took up our positions in South Sausage Support. We established a Battalion HQ in a 'dugout' at the junction of South Sausage Support and the front line. Though tired, the men could not yet rest. The trench had to be 'reversed' and made defendable.[34]

It was not until the afternoon that Spicer allowed his men a rest period, believing they had 'made quite a reasonable show'. Some food and tea managed to make its way up from Queen's Redoubt, both of which were very welcome. Amazingly, sitting in what had been enemy trenches only the day before, the men also received letters from home.

On 3 July, orders were received that the Division was taking up a new line of support, with the 9th KOYLI occupying a small section to the left of the junction of Patch Alley and South Sausage Support. On arriving, they immediately set to, consolidating this new part of the line. They were shelled for their troubles between 3.00 p.m. and 4.20 p.m., which annoyed them considerably, but caused no casualties, the worst of the shells dropping well short. The War Diary completes the story:

6.00 p.m. Orders received to proceed at once to Dernancourt and bivouac for the night. The battalion accordingly moved from trenches in small parties, and assembled at Bécourt Valley, where remainder of battalion which was in Queen's Redoubt [this was CSM Warren's party], also assembled. The battalion marched from Bécourt Valley through Méaulte to Dernancourt railway siding, arriving at bivouac at about 2.00 a.m. 2nd-Lt. D. Forryan KSLI reported arrival and attached to Btn.[35]

Basil Liddell Hart gives us a clue as to how the men were feeling as they marched:

As soon as we got out on the road, near Méaulte, it was unforgettable to see the way in which the men pulled themselves together and marched through that village singing 'Pack up your Troubles in your Old Kit Bag' – just as the full battalion had sung it on their march up to the trenches four days before. It brought a lump to our throats and we thought of the scores of good comrades who had sung it then and would never sing it again.[36]

The advances gained on either side of the fortress town of Fricourt on 1 July were further extended on the following day, resulting in the town's surrender. By this time it was little more than a pile of ruins. The Battalion War Diary detailed the cost of this pile of ruins: fifteen officers killed and seven wounded out of the twenty-four who went over the parapet. 'Casualties in other ranks number 475 of which about 145 were killed.'[37]

The overall casualty figure may be a slight over-estimate. The *Official History* lists the 64th Brigade casualties for the day as follows:

	OFFICERS	OTHER RANKS
9 KOYLI	21	383
10 KOYLI	21	428
15 DLI	15	373
1 East Yorks	21	478
Total	78	1,662

The 21st Division casualties amounted to a total of 4,256, the seventh highest Divisional figures for the day.

Figures are likely to be inaccurate: it is difficult to assess the number of wounded, and those initially classed as missing may remain so, may be confirmed as killed, or may find their way back to their unit at a later date. Appendix I confirms the 9th KOYLI fatal casualties of 1 July as 178, the Battalion's highest single day losses for the entire war.

5

SOMME
PART TWO

On 4 July, the battalion was moved by train to Ailly-sur-Somme, arriving at about 1.00 p.m., from whence they undertook a two-hour march to find billets in Picquigny, a town on the southern bank of the River Somme, but well away from the battlefields, some seven or so miles to the west of Amiens. Here, Lt Gordon caught up with the battalion and, being senior officer, took command.

The following morning at 8.30 a.m., the entire battalion, or what was left of it, paraded outside its billets, which were in fact the town cinema down by the river, and was addressed by GOC 64th Brigade, Brig. Headlam. Congratulations on their efforts came thick and fast: the very next day, the 6th, the men were marched to Divisional HQ at the Château in Belloy-sur-Somme, a little over a mile away across the river, paraded together with the rest of the brigade in the grounds and listened to the compliments paid them by the GOC 21st Division, Maj.-Gen. D.C.M. Campbell. A march past to the accompaniment of the Regimental March, played by the 21st Divisional Band ensued and the 9th KOYLI returned to Picquigny to reflect on their successes and their losses.

Individuals were trying to piece together and remember exactly what had happened to friends and colleagues in the heat and confusion of the battlefield. Ellenberger described the battalion as 'a weary remnant, reduced by two-thirds of our numbers, almost all our officers gone, but unshaken in spirit.'[1] Some stories, often no more than hearsay or rumour, survive: Griffin had borrowed a riding crop from Hart prior to the battle and tried to convince the latter of his own immunity. His instinct betrayed him. The CO, it was said, was killed by a whizz bang ten yards from his own parapet (compare Gordon's account in Chapter 4). Vassie was killed by machine-gun fire as he was getting over the parapet. The exact fate of countless others will never be known; any witnesses to their deaths, swift and painless or slow and agonising, were either subsequently killed themselves, or were possessed of memories so confused or unbiddable, that their accounts were never told.

It was the sad duty of surviving officers to write to the families of those who had not come through the ordeal. Good form dictated that any such letter should attempt to soften the blow; a wife, mother or father may have been able to draw some comfort from being told that their loved one had fought bravely and had not suffered unduly. Ellenberger wrote one such letter to the parents of young Frank Golding, who had joined the battalion less than two weeks prior to the battle. Frank's father, Alfred, had indeed written to Ellenberger asking for details of his son's death. The nature of Ellenberger's account can be deduced from the further reply it prompted:

I am greatly obliged by your kind letter, which I especially appreciate as you wrote in busy times and thank you for giving me the details on Frank. I am very pleased to learn that he was liked by his fellow officers. He told me he liked his new fellows very much. I am also glad to hear that he faced the fire bravely. I thank you also for promising to ask his platoon sergeant to write me and I am also writing him as you suggest.

If at any time you were able to discover further particulars from anyone I should feel grateful if you would kindly let me know. I hope you will continue to be fortunate.

England owes a lot to her sons in France.

Yours Faithfully,

Alfred Golding[2]

Captain Walker's mother, in what was also her second letter to Ellenberger, expressed similar sentiments: 'I am thankful, (if William had to die), that it was instantaneous.'[3]

Harold Yeo wrote in typical style to Lt Frederick Morris, wounded in the mouth on 1 July:

The brigade did tophole and this Division has got a deuce of a name for itself… I am afraid a lot of good people went west. Of our friends we have to mourn the loss of Col. Lynch, Head, Howlett, Alexander, Griffin, Haswell, Walker, Ellis, Vassie, Featherstone, Huntriss, Col. Stow, Bosanquet, Eames, Ely and some others. All the bn. grenadier officers got wounded. Barker had his leg broken almost up on the road. The other two CO's were wounded. No end of Huns were slain; the brigade got about 200 prisoners and Spark's crew got 1,100… All the battalion did well – in fact the kudos gained is widespread. So much so that we've already started getting those doubtful compliments paid us that you will understand the nature of.[4]

A move to Riencourt on 7 July allowed for parades the following morning under company arrangements, and to its new commander, Ellenberger, fell the duty of calling 'C' Company's roll. On 30 June, the company numbered 258 Other Ranks. One hundred and thirty-one were able to answer their names that day. On the 9th, the first Sunday out of the trenches since the attack, a memorial service was held in an orchard in memory of all those of the battalion who had fallen in the recent offensive. Hymns were played by the Divisional Band and a short address was given by Revd Capt. Lester, in the presence of Brig. Headlam. The same day, Maj. A.G. McClintock reported his arrival and assumed command of the battalion.

Monday saw the battalion move back to and bivouac in Ailly-sur-Somme. They were met by a draft of 237 Other Ranks. The job of bringing the 9th KOYLI back up to strength had begun. The majority of these new men came from the Northumberland Fusiliers, a scattering from elsewhere, but very few from within the regiment. By midnight, a train journey and a march found the battalion back on familiar ground, in billets in Ville. There, a further draft of 329 arrived, again only a few of them belonging to the KOYLI.

It was time to begin to look forward again. The battalion had come through its biggest day, mourned its losses and gathered its spirit once more. Reorganisation could begin. Under the newly appointed company commanders, Gordon, Spicer, Ellenberger and Hart, and their 'cavalryman' CO, Bombing Squads and Lewis Gun teams were formed, 'completely equipping for "Fighting Order"'.[5] The Battle of the Somme had continued in the 9th KOYLI's absence. The line had inched forward some two miles on the XV Corps front. Mametz Wood had finally fallen at great cost and plans for the next major assault had been on the table since 8 July. Rawlinson designated five Divisions to attack the German second line and capture the two Bazentin villages and their similarly named woods, along with Longueval and Delville Wood. The attack was to be made under the cover of darkness, early on the morning of 14 July, following a preliminary artillery bombardment of three days, this concentrating almost solely on the German front trench system and its wire entanglements, and a final five-minute hurricane bombardment. The plan, meant to surprise the Germans with the rapidity of the bombardment and attack, did not at first meet with Haig's approval. Acquiescence came in time for the assault to go ahead as Rawlinson had intended. The 21st Division was once more to be in the thick of it. This time, however, the front-line honours fell to 110th Brigade (6th, 7th, 8th and 9th Leicesters) with the 62nd Brigade in support and the 64th in reserve. [The 110th Brigade, formerly 37th Division, had swapped Divisions with the 63rd]. The 9th KOYLI were to reinforce the attack if the need arose.

On the 13th the battalion marched off by companies from Ville at 3.00 p.m., halting at Méaulte to pick up ammunition and bombs. Re-assembly of the battalion took place in a field north of Bécordel. Even at this late stage, at about 4.00 p.m., a further draft of 100 other ranks arrived.

At 7.45 p.m., the battalion proceeded, by platoons, to march through Fricourt and Fricourt Wood in order to take up their positions near Bottom Wood. They dug in to the east and west of the wood and awaited developments. Brigade HQ was set up in Fricourt Château – little was left of it above ground, but it had been a German HQ a fortnight earlier, and Yeo described it another letter to Morris written on the 20th:

You would have loved to see the place – the Huns had a regimental HQ there and it had the mess in the cellar, the office one storey down below, and a lower storey still contained the signal office and the bedroom of OC 111. The whole lot was panelled with white wood and lit by electric light.[6]

The 110th Brigade attacked the German line in Bazentin-le-Petit Wood at 3.25 a.m. on 14 July. They found the front trenches completely destroyed, nothing more than shell holes, the wire entirely swept away. They quickly captured their second objective to the west of the wood, and despite a minor hold up caused by machine-gun fire, they had captured most of the wood by 4.00 a.m. The north-west corner was finally wrested from the enemy's grasp by 7.00 p.m. that evening.

The 9th KOYLI sat tight. News of the success of the attack filtered back to them, and they experienced the sight of cavalry riding forward. The success of the assault has been attributed by many to the element of surprise and the hour of the attack. These factors were important, but Rawlinson himself remarked that the efficacy of the artillery bombardment in removing the enemy wire and smashing the German trench lines was absolutely vital.

Next morning, the battalion was ordered to move forward. The conditions they found were far from pleasant. Lt Hart continues the story:

… we lay on the edge of Mametz Wood under a hot sun amid rows of the decaying and strong-smelling corpses of men who had fallen in capturing it in the previous week. On pushing into the wood I found the dead still thicker, with Briton and German often locked in a death-grapple, while horribly battered by subsequent shelling. A fatherly old Army grave digger advised me to keep out if I wanted to keep up my spirits for further action![7]

Once more the 9th KOYLI remained inactive and orders received at 9.00 p.m. sent them back to their original positions astride Bottom Wood. It was during this day that Lt Gordon suffered what Spicer later described as a breakdown, brought on by his experiences on 1 July and perhaps triggered by the gruesome sights in Mametz Wood. The War Diary is less specific, recounting simply that Gordon reported sick and left the battalion. Also on that day, Capt. Harold Yeo narrowly missed serious injury or even death when a shell landed and exploded only five yards away from him as he was moving up through Bazentin-le-Petit Wood. He wrote home relating the incident, quickly dismissing the perilous nature of the incident, bemoaning instead the material damage the splinters had caused.

... a bit going tremendously hard hit the top of my Orilux lamp, smashed through, hit my whistle in my left breast pocket, made two rifts in that, went through and smashed my Swan pen in its steel pocket, and then made a scratch on the top of my tummy where the muscles are, and subsequently I found it in my breeks with bits of tunic stuck on the sharp edges of the fragment... said lamp was sent back to J.H. Steward Ltd of the Strand, who sent a replacement, hoping it would do as good a 'Yeo'man service as the old one, apologising in advance for the pun... Part of the pen was kept by Mabie, Todd & Co. Ltd (High Holborn) as a shop window exhibit – a new pen was of course also sent out.[8]

On the 16th, the main part of the battalion remained once more where it was. 'C' Company, however, under Lt B.H.L. Hart, was sent up at 8.00 p.m. to occupy an old German trench immediately behind the southern end of Bazentin-le-Petit Wood. Hart takes up the story once more:

The enemy's harassing fire was all the more unpleasant here because the shells often hit branches of trees and exploded with a shower of descending splinters. On the way I had got a puncture in my right hand, but after having it bandaged had carried on, as only one other officer was left, and he was too inexperienced to take over. When two companies of another battalion eventually came up to relieve us, [the following day – the 17th] my company was withdrawn, and moved back to rejoin our own battalion. As we were passing through Mametz Wood in the dark we heard a lot of shells hitting the ground around us, but only with a faint 'plop' which suggested they had failed to explode. In a few moments there was a pervasive smell of gas. It was our first intimation that the Germans had started to use a lethal gas-shell filled with a new kind of gas, phosgene, more deadly although less painful than the chlorine gas first used in the war the year before... I was coughing violently but stayed on the spot to warn and direct the platoons that were following, and then hurried on to catch the leading platoon at the rallying point, and lead them all back to the battalion bivouac.[9]

The rest of 9th Battalion was by this time bivouacked in a field by the Bécordel-Méaulte road. There, they were joined by a number of officer reinforcements: Capt. W.N. Tempest, Capt. R.J. McCullin, 2nd-Lts V.H. Wells-Cole, H.O. Tomkins, J.R. Caldwell, H.N. Teaz and J.E.N. Fligg.

Hart went to the nearest field ambulance during the morning to have the wound in his right hand properly dressed. He was not feeling too well, and the doctors insisted on examining his chest. They immediately put him onto a stretcher, and via the casualty clearing station at Corbie, he was taken to the Duchess of Westminster's Hospital at Le Touquet, and soon after found himself in King Edward VII's in London. His convalescence was to last into 1917 and he never rejoined his old battalion.

The battalion left their bivouac at 5.30 p.m. on 18 July and marched to Bécourt Valley, occupying dugouts there and in Queen's Redoubt. It was here that two messages were received. One announced a number of promotions: Lt Spicer was to become Captain; 2nd-Lts Ibbetson and Ellenberger were promoted to full Lieutenant. The other, from Maj.-Gen. Campbell, was at once congratulatory and ominous:

Special Order by Maj.-Gen. Campbell 21 Div.
I cannot too strongly express to all ranks my intense admiration for their splendid gallantry in actually breaking through the German first and second lines. No Division has a finer performance to its credit. Until, however, the high ground north of the German Second Line has been seized and consolidated we cannot consider our work complete. Although I fully recognise the tremendous strain which has been imposed on all ranks, I am confident, after their previous magnificent performances, that I can absolutely rely on them to answer any call that may be made upon them until they have wrested their final objective from the enemy.
    David G.M.Campbell
    Major-General
    18.7.16, Commanding 21 Div.[10]

Four days later, having been relieved in Bécourt Valley by the Argyll and Sutherland Highlanders, the battalion was once again in Ailly-sur-Somme, resting and cleaning up prior to a move northwards to the Arras sector. It was now Rawlinson's turn to purvey his compliments to a Division he was about to lose:

I regret that the 21st Division is leaving the Fourth Army, but they performed their part in this great battle in a manner that has filled me with admiration, and I trust that at some future time I may again have the honour of finding them under my command.
    H.Rawlinson
    General, Commanding 4th Army
    HQ Fourth Army
    21 July 1916[11]

At 8.30 a.m. on 23 July, the 9th KOYLI marched through Amiens to Longeau, entraining at 3.20 p.m., and arriving at Le Petit Houvin, west of Arras, that evening. Early the following day they marched the few miles to Berlencourt and went into billets. The entire battalion paraded the next day, the 25th, and was inspected by the CO, now Lt-Col. McClintock and Lt and Adj. W.F. Keay.

The battalion was to be back in the trenches on the 29th. The usual preparations preceded the move: the CO and his company commanders were taken up by motor bus on the 26th to the 41st Brigade HQ in Arras, from where they went forward to reconnoitre the position they were to take over. The same day, 2nd-Lts. J. Hindley, F.W. Lillie and A. Simpson reported their arrival and were taken on the strength of the battalion. News was also received that the following NCOs and men had been awarded the Military Medal: 16840 Sgt J.E. Webster, 17551 Cpl H. Coates, 19970 Pte J. Kearford, 16847 Pte J. Hall and 14856 Pte A. Bullock.

At 3.30 p.m. on 28 July, the entire battalion proceeded by motor bus from Berlencourt to Wanquetin, arriving about 5.00 p.m., where they bivouacked briefly for tea. Two hours later they were on the march, heading for Arras. Progress was slow, hampered as they were by the heavy traffic on the roads. It was after midnight when they reached their billets in the town.

Work parties were the order of the day as August 1916 began. The 1st being Minden Day, the battalion wore white roses, and 2nd-Lt A.E. Day was awarded the Military Cross for conspicuous gallantry displayed exactly one month earlier.

On the 4th, the battalion was together again as it relieved the 1st East Yorks in the trenches on the left of the brigade front to the north of Arras. The front line, support line and the linking communication trenches were heavily bombarded by the enemy artillery during the night 5/6 August. Large numbers of German troops were also spotted in the open before being dispersed by shell fire from our own artillery. Had plans for an enemy raid been thwarted? The 9th KOYLI did suffer casualties that night: the CO himself, Lt-Col. McClintock was slightly wounded, along with a handful of men. Two were killed; 15583 Pte Thomas Rhodes and 12568 Sgt Ernest Radford now lie close together in the Faubourg d'Amiens Cemetery.

Divisional Routine Orders of two days later congratulated the men of 9th KOYLI for the 'soldierly qualities displayed... during the heavy bombardment on their trench on the night 5th/6th August. The Major-General congratulates Lt-Col. McClintock and the officers, NCOs and men of the battalion.'[12]

The 9th KOYLI and 1st East Yorks traded places on a regular basis for the rest of the month and into the next, the KOYLIs being unlucky to be in the front line on 29 August when a heavy thunderstorm badly flooded their trenches. The minds of some of the longer-serving members of the battalion must surely have gone back to the previous winter and the awful conditions they had suffered in the trenches near Armentières.

On 3 September, the fact that the CO and company commanders of the 18th Highland Light Infantry, a unit of an alien brigade, made a tour of the battalion's trenches was a sure sign that a major move was once more imminent. Relief duly arrived in kilts on the 4th and the KOYLIs were soon back in Duislans, only to march a further five miles westwards the day after to take over billets in Manin. Training ensued: physical drill, bayonet fighting, the use of smoke bombs and practice for Lewis Gun teams kept the men busy.

On the 10th, a Sunday, the battalion, together with the 1st East Yorks, paraded at Manin, and was addressed by Maj.-Gen. Campbell, GOC 21st Division. The General announced to the assembled men that the Division would shortly be moving back to the Somme area, and hoped that they would continue to uphold the proud traditions of their unit. There was no Church Parade that day: it may have been inappropriate to give thanks to God for the prospect of a return to Hell! Instead, a rugby match was organised for that afternoon.

The following day, Lt-Col. Heathcote arrived and assumed command of the battalion. He was a regular soldier and a KOYLI, his previous command being that of the regiment's 1st Battalion. By twelve noon on the 13th, the men were back on what for some of them was familiar ground: a train journey from Frévent to Méricourt and a march of some three miles saw them in billets in Dernancourt, just south of Albert. Those of the battalion for whom the Somme was a new experience must have had some idea as to what to expect; if for no other reason than having had to listen to the undoubtedly exaggerated tales told them by the old sweats. If their sense of foreboding needed any deepening, all they had to do was listen – the preliminary bombardment for the next major assault had begun the day before their arrival.

The assault timed for 6.20 a.m. on 15 September involved nine Infantry Divisions of the Fourth Army carrying out the initial attack between Martinpuich and Combles; on

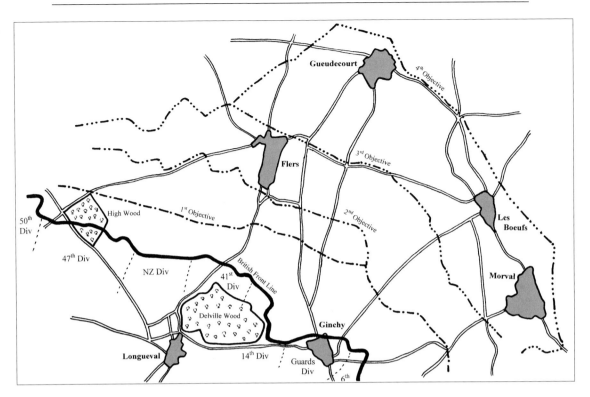

Flers: objectives, 15 September 1916.

their left, the Canadians would attack Courcelette, and on the right, the French Sixth Army would advance between Combles and the River Somme. The III Corps, under Pulteney, were on the left, comprising the 15th, 50th and 47th Divisions (left to right). The New Zealand Division, with the 41st and 14th Divisions, making up Horne's XV Corps, had the middle ground opposite Flers. The line continued south-eastwards with the Guards, 6th and 56th Divisions forming the XIV Corps under Cavan.

For the first time, the advancing infantry would be supported by Britain's new and revolutionary weapon of war, the tank. Forty-eight of these unwieldy monsters were to be available for the attack. Unfortunately, mechanical reliability was not their strong suit and many failed even to arrive at the jumping-off points. On the right, the attack of the 6th and 56th Divisions broke down, and only two of the fifteen allocated tanks went into action. The Guards made some ground, capturing the German front-line trenches but their attempts to advance further ran out of steam in front of Les Boeufs. On the left, tanks assisted the 15th Division in their capture of Martinpuich. In front of High Wood, however, things went badly wrong. The tanks sent in bogged down in the unsuitable terrain (fallen trees, tree stumps, trenches and shell holes combined to make perfect tank obstacles), and the advancing infantry, devoid of artillery support, were cut down as they attempted to move forward. Only heavy trench mortar bombardment and its outflanking by the New Zealanders on the right and the 50th Division on the left enabled the wood to be finally captured and occupied.

The only significant progress of the day was made in the centre. The village of Flers and some trenches further on were overrun. It was here that the tanks had proved most effective. Twelve of them went into action, seven of their number arriving at the German front line just ahead of the infantry. The Germans' first sight of these apparently invincible leviathans led many of them to surrender or flee. The infantry leapfrogged the tanks but were held up on the wire south of Flers. They waited for the tanks to deal with the wire and then followed them into the village, watching them crush several machine-gun nests on the way.

Newspapers were to latch onto a story which had a tank lumbering up the main street in Flers, closely followed by cheering troops. Truth, as ever in war, was slightly different. One tank, D17, 'Dinnaken', did reach the centre of Flers, but had by then advanced into its own artillery bombardment, and with engine trouble as an additional problem, it was decided that D17 should withdraw. Some 300 men of 122nd Brigade, 41st Division, pushed forward into Flers at this point, but they too, conscious of their own shells falling, were not on the heels of D17, but rather spread amongst the houses east and west of the main street, somewhat to the rear of the tank. By 10.00 a.m., however, Flers was in British hands. Some ground north of the village was also taken, but Gueudecourt remained stubbornly out of reach, as did Gird Trench in front of it.

By 3.00 p.m., Rawlinson realised that the attack had lost impetus, and that he would have to rely on reserves to renew the advance the following day.

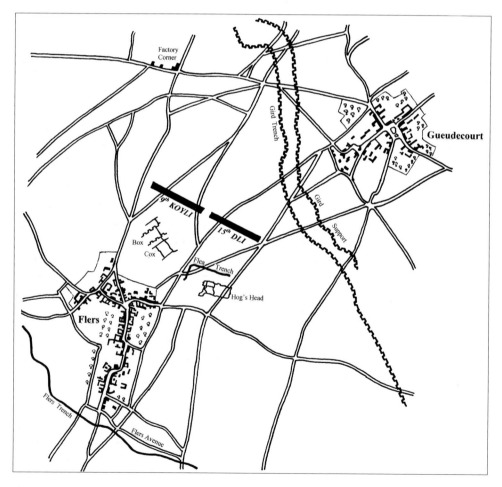

Flers/Gueudecourt: Attack of 64th Brigade, 16 September 1916.

The XV Corps were to take the village of Gueudecourt and then advance beyond the Gueudecourt–Eaucourt l'Abbaye road and link up with III Corps. First objectives would be the two trench lines in front of the village, Gird Trench and Gird Support.

At 8.30 p.m., Maj.-Gen. Lawford, 41st Division, telephoned to say that he only had one battalion available for the forthcoming attack; casualties had been very heavy, this Division having lost about half its strength. Lt-Gen. Horne placed at his disposal the 64th Brigade from 21st Division. The 9th KOYLI were to be catapulted into the action at very short notice.

The day's assaults had captured 9,000 yards of the German front line and some 4,000 yards of the second line around Flers: the cost was just over 29,000 killed, wounded or missing.

On 15 September, as the first assaults were happening, the 9th KOYLI marched firstly to Fricourt Camp and then during the afternoon to Pommiers Redoubt. Brig.-Gen. Headlam, commanding 64th Bigade, was not informed what was required of his men on the following day until he was able to attend a meeting at Divisional HQ near Albert at 11.30 p.m. He then had to return to his own HQ to brief his battalion commanders. 'It was not until 1.30 a.m. that these commanders left brigade HQ in order to issue detailed instructions to their own officers, none of whom had ever seen the ground before.'[13]

The brigade left Pommiers Redoubt at 2.10 a.m. and began their march to the battle zone. They advanced in steady rain over the shell-shattered rear areas already clogged with traffic. Headlam, in the meantime, had received what turned out to be a false report saying that our front-line troops beyond Flers had withdrawn from the 'Box' and 'Cox' trench complexes to new positions south of the Bulls Road (see map).

A hurried message to this effect reached the battalion on the march along with accompanying instructions to improvise as best they could by preparing assault positions on the 'new front line'.

By the time they reached the area to the south of Flers it was already daylight and they were forced to take cover in Flers Avenue, Flers Trench and in shell holes to their rear. Zero hour was 9.20 a.m., but by the time the previous errors had been sorted out, it meant that the men were too far back to benefit from the artillery bombardment, and also that they had to set out some twenty-five to thirty minutes before Zero in order to reach the jumping-off positions for which they had originally set out.

They advanced over open ground to the east of the village and into the shallow valley north of Flers under enemy machine-gun and artillery fire, only to find British troops already dug in. The 9th KOYLI shifted slightly to the left to allow the 15th DLI to come up on their right, the 10th KOYLI and the 1st East Yorks in close support.

The advance went ahead. Gird Trench was on the rise to the right-front of the 64th Brigade troops, the village of Gueudecourt all but invisible over the ridge behind it. The 9th advanced behind one of the tanks, D9, but this was knocked out well short of the German front line. Lt Ellenberger takes up the story:

… we had about 1,000 yards to go before reaching the German trench under heavy fire, especially MG's all the way; however, we started off and pushed on though nobody knew exactly where we had to go, and we seemed to have no supports, and in fact it was very badly organised altogether, and by the time some of us had got within 100 yards of the Hun trench, the attack had collapsed – there was no more control – I don't mean that we ran away. For [we] certainly didn't, but we were scattered about in shell holes and could do nothing except wait for support which never came. Nobody

Looking south-west towards Flers from the approximate position of Gird Trench.

Looking towards Gueudecourt from near the 9th KOYLI jumping-off positions.

behind knew what had happened to us, nor apparently made any efforts to find out. We had a 'Caterpillar' ('tanks' as the papers call them) in front of us, but when it reached the German trenches it just sat there, ceased fire, belched forth columns of black smoke and burst into flames. [This could well have been tank D14 which reached the German front line to the right of the KOYLI advance, there to be destroyed by shell fire]. You only had to show the slightest signs of movement to get a bullet over: that was how I first got pipped. I looked up and saw a Bosche in their trench wearing one of our steel helmets. I bent down to tell this to the fellow with me and just as I was bringing my head down, 'ping' went my steel helmet and fell off and I felt a nasty knock at the side of my head and blood poured forth in torrents. It was a very lucky shot for me: made a hole clear through the brim of my helmet and the top of my left ear and grazed my head!

Later in the morning I tried to get back to let people behind know what was happening but it was no good. I got a bullet through my haversack, knocking a piece of tin into my back, and shortly afterwards a bullet in the top of my left leg, it went in at the side of my leg and on its way out hit some ammunition in my trouser pocket, bent it all about and made a fairly big hole, about one inch by one-and-a-half inches in my leg. I then had to lie in a very shallow scoop in the ground, not a proper shell hole, for about eight hours till it was dark. There was another fellow there and we found we were lying each one's head by the other one's feet, but we couldn't move about and had to lie in almost the same position the whole time. A third man was just getting into the same hole when he got a bullet through the brain and so kept us company as a corpse for the rest of the day. In the afternoon we were shelled by the Bosche, and later equally heavily by our own artillery: it was a marvel I wasn't hit: the man with me was killed about six o'clock.[14]

Both front battalions had been halted and pinned down in shell holes. The attack, ill-prepared as it was, had failed. All four battalions of 64th Brigade had advanced bravely, but with little chance of success. Once darkness had fallen, the remnants were able to make their way back and rally on the line of Bulls Road. Ellenberger continues his story:

At last it got dark and at 6.00 p.m. I crawled back about half a mile (it took an hour) to our own people; there got tied up by the doctor, got some food and some cold sleep: about 3.00 a.m. on Sunday morning stretcher bearers arrived and I was taken off; by stretcher bearer, horse ambulance, motor ambulance, train and boat. I was taken from dressing station to dressing station, hospital to hospital till I reached here about 6 o'clock on Wednesday evening, very glad to get all of my travels ended.[15]

Ellenberger had in fact been taken to No. 36 Casualty Clearing Station at Heilly, from where he had managed to get off a postcard to his sister:

Was wounded yesterday in head, back and thigh – the former very slight, and the latter the worst but none at all dangerous. Am now on my way to England and looking forward to Blighty. Sorry I haven't written to you before. Don't be alarmed.
    Love
    Fothergill.[16]

From there, a hospital train took him to Rouen, a move confirmed by the official War Office telegram: 'Beg to inform you report just received states Lt G.F. Ellenberger, Yorks LI admitted 8 General Hospital Rouen, Sept 19th with gunshot wounds leg and back. Slight.'[17]

    Casualties had been heavy. The 9th KOYLI War Diary reports them as follows:

The casualties incurred during the action were:

	KILLED	WOUNDED	MISSING
OFFICERS	4	6	3
OTHER RANKS	43	180	153

Officers killed: Lt and Adj. F.W. Keay, 2nd-Lt K.W. Sutcliffe, 2nd-Lt A.S. Jackson.
Officers wounded: 2nd-Lt L.D. Spicer, Capt. W.C. Woollett, Lt G.F. Ellenberger, 2nd-Lt
A. Simpson, 2nd-Lt S. Wilkinson, 2nd-Lt T.H. Leason (died of wounds later).
Officers missing: 2nd-Lt D. Forryan, 2nd-Lt G. Blakey, 2nd-Lt H.G. Gross.[18]

Appendix I confirms that the three missing officers were later confirmed killed, and of
those wounded, Capt. Woollett also succumbed to his wounds. Total fatal casualties for
the battalion were finalised at 121. Such was the nature of the battle that only fifteen of
those were able to be given the honour of a recognised place of burial. The rest are
commemorated on the Thiepval Memorial.

The Spicer family also received official notification of their wounded son:

POST OFFICE TELEGRAMS

OHMS *War Office*   *Handed in*   *21 September 1916.*
London   *at 10.25 a.m.*   *Received here at*
                                               11.20 a.m.

To: Sir A. Spicer, Bart., 10, Lancaster Gate, W.
Regret to inform you that Capt. L.D. Spicer, KOYLI, was admitted to 1 Red Cross Hospital Le
Touquet Sept 18 with severe bomb wound left arm and chest will report further news.
Sec. War Office.[19]

Spicer's chest wound was a mere graze, but the one to his arm was more serious: a splinter
had gone through his left arm, entering just above the elbow and exiting just below the
shoulder. No bones were broken, but the wound was septic by the time he arrived in Le
Touquet, and an operation to clean out the wound delayed his return to England.

The battalion was relieved at twelve noon on 17 September by the King's Own
Liverpool Regiment and was able to march back to Pommiers Redoubt. By 3.00 p.m.
on the 18th, they were once more in Fricourt Camp. Four days of reorganisation, training
and inspections followed, during which time Capt. R.J. McMullin returned from hospital
and Lt V.H. Wells-Cole returned to duty with the battalion from brigade headquarters.
There was a brief stint in the trenches near Delville Wood before the 64th Brigade was
again involved in another attack designed to capture the village of Gueudecourt.

The attack went in on 25 September, the 10th KOYLI and 1st East Yorks this time
leading the assault on Gird Trench. Both battalions were held up by uncut wire. Again,
survivors were forced to take cover in shell holes until nightfall permitted a withdrawal.
The following morning the assault was renewed, this time with the help of a tank. It
advanced up Pilgrim's Way and upon reaching Gird Trench, turned right and pushed the
by now fleeing Germans into the mouths of the waiting Lewis Guns of the Guards
Division.

The 15th DLI, the 10th KOYLI and the 9th KOYLI followed up this advance and by
9.00 a.m., the 15th DLI had successfully occupied Gird Trench. Later, the 9th KOYLI

were ordered up to occupy Gird Support Trench, but found it totally obliterated by our own guns. At around 2.00 p.m., the men started to dig a new line, connecting up shell holes. They were leapfrogged once more at 3.00 p.m. by the Durhams who occupied the Gueudecourt–Les Boeufs road; three hours later the 9th KOYLI were on the same road to the right of the 15th DLI, in touch with the Welch Guards on their right. They were relieved that evening by the 12th Northumberland Fusiliers, marched back to transport lines and bivouacked between Trones Wood and Bernafay Wood.

The 9th had suffered casualties again: Maj. W.N. Tempest was killed and Capt. G.A. Gamble, 2nd-Lts. V.H. Wells-Cole, J. Caldwell and G. Panton were wounded. Four Other Ranks were reported as killed (the final number was eight), with sixty-six wounded and twenty-seven missing.

By 3 October, the battalion was turning its back on the battle area once again and heading by train westwards from Méricourt to Longpré, arriving there just after midnight. They immediately marched to Buigny l'Abbé and went into billets in this small, quiet town well away from the noise, the mud, and the suffering of the front. The nearest large town was Abbeville, still on the River Somme, but by the time the waters reach this point, they have only ten more miles to go to reach the English Channel.

6

WINTER 1916-1917

On 4 October, the day the 9th KOYLI arrived in Buigny l'Abbé, Lt Ellenberger wrote to his father from his hospital bed: 'I see in the *Morning Post*'s unofficial list of casualties a Major Tempest killed on 25 Sept: he was in our battalion: surely they weren't still on again in the push on that date!'[1]

The battle of the Somme dragged on officially until 18 November, the last ground taken being an almost unrecognisable stretch of mud through which oozed, somewhere, the River Ancre. The mud was by this time beginning to freeze, and the men, having advanced through the falling snow, pushed the front line just beyond the village of Beaucourt. The total number of casualties for the whole four-and-a-half months of fighting, for the British, French and German Armies, has been calculated at 1,300,000; of these 95,675 British were killed or missing.

The battalion's stay at Buigny l'Abbé was not to be a long one. Maj. C.A. Millward arrived there to take command of the battalion and Capt. R.J. McMullin was appointed Second-in-Command. Some thirty per cent of the men were granted leave at this time, the rest had to make do with physical drill, bombing training and gas helmet drill. By 8 October, the battalion had moved north and east once more and was billeted in Allouagne, west of Béthune, and was able to enjoy the luxury of baths. Officers were also arriving to make up for the battalion's recent losses, and by 11 October, seven had been taken on the strength: 2nd-Lts R.A. Stokes, G.H.L. Cox, E.J. Joels, S. Harvey, R.R. Ackrill-Jones, W. Leggott and L.H. Higgit. That day, the battalion paraded in full marching order, marched to Beuvry and went into billets. They were on familiar ground: to the east of Béthune, a short march north-west of the Loos battlefield.

The day after their arrival, the CO, his Second-in-Command and six other officers went into the trenches to organise the relief by the 9th KOYLI of the 16th Highland Light Infantry, who were holding the line in the Cambrin sector. That same day, notice was received that the GOC had remitted the sentence of seven years' penal servitude passed on 164131 Pte G. Thorpe on 16 April 1916. The sentence had originally been commuted to two years' hard labour, but was remitted in recognition of Thorpe's 'conspicuous courage and devotion to duty during period 1 July–16 Sept 1916.'[2] The War Diary does not mention Thorpe's original misdemeanour.

Two days later, on 14 October, the 9th KOYLI went back into the trenches, setting off at 7.45 a.m. to relieve the Highlanders. The process was complete by 12.30 p.m. and the rest of the day passed quietly. The next day, the Germans welcomed the new arrivals with the dubious gift of fifteen artillery shells fired into the vicinity of Maison Rouge Alley. There were no casualties, however.

During the next thirteen days, the battalion once more became accustomed to the routine of trench life. They spent some time in support before going back to the front line. The trenches were at times knocked about by trench mortar fire and enemy and friendly artillery batteries exchanged fire over their heads. In the meantime, six officers were transferred to the battalion from 10th KOYLI. They were Lt C.D. Jones, 2nd-Lts C.T. Inkpen (who transferred back four days later), G.R. Brierley, J.P. Shaw, T.B. Little and L.J.V. Way.

On his eleventh day with the 9th KOYLI, Lt Jones was in an Infantry Post in the front line when a heavy trench mortar bomb scored a direct hit on it, killing him and five other men. 34977 Cpl Crompton, 31037 Pte Hartley, 26931 Pte Paulson, 14551 Pte Skelton and 13546 Pte Storey now lie together with their officer in Cambrin Churchyard extension.

Routine set in once more. Once more in the front line on 16 November, the battalion received a dummy camouflaged corpse from Brigade HQ, to be used 'for future operations'.

At 10.45 p.m. the following night, a patrol under the command of 2nd-Lt Teaz left the trenches and advanced across no man's land as far as Saxon Crater. The object of the exercise was to enter the enemy front-line trenches in order to learn the identity of the German unit facing them. Stokes guns opened up a short bombardment in support of the men, but their shells fell amongst the patrol, killing one man and wounding another. The men were disorientated and dazed by this: they did not in the end enter the enemy trench and became separated, each man making his own way back to the safety of the British line. As pre-arranged, the camouflaged 'corpse' had been taken out and left about fifty yards from the German wire.

A patrol of one unnamed officer and fourteen men was sent out the following evening, the 18th, at around 5.30 p.m. and made for the 'corpse'. It was so dark, however, that they could not find it. A second patrol sent out later to relieve them apparently located it, but were forced to report that no Germans had come anywhere near it. For the third night in a row a patrol went out to observe the 'corpse'. This foray proved equally fruitless and they returned at 6.00 a.m., this time with the dummy. The ruse had been a complete failure and had cost the life of 16153 L/Cpl Arthur Seed, killed, albeit inadvertently, by his own comrades.

The battalion was in and out of the trenches again over the next few days, swapping places at fairly regular intervals with the 1st East Yorks. On the 25th, Capt. N.R. Daniell was taken on the strength of the battalion and appointed Second-in-Command with the temporary rank of Major. He took over overall command the following day when Lt-Col. McMullin went on leave. Patrols and counter patrols continued as each side vied for dominance of no man's land, and on the 25th, unusually during the day, at about 10.00 a.m., several German soldiers appeared, apparently carrying neither rifles nor other equipment, in front of the 9th KOYLI trench. One of them got into conversation with a member of the battalion in a forward post, saying that he was tired of the war. They did not give themselves up, however, and disappeared back toward their own lines. Their purpose in taking such a risky action must remain a mystery.

December greeted the battalion out of the line, firstly in Béthune, and by the 6th at Philosophe on the road to Lens, where they were gainfully occupied in excavating dugouts for the next nine days.

Graves of Lieutenant Charles Jones and his five men, killed by a trench mortar round on 28 October 1916.

On 18 December, a bombing practice using live grenades produced tragic conse-
quences. Captain Frank William Lillie was in charge of the exercise and was killed when
a grenade exploded prematurely. Lt Ellenberger's servant, Duffield, wrote to his officer
early in the New Year describing the incident:

Mr Lillie, my last officer, got killed while we were in support, it was an accident. He was bombing
officer and one chap was just throwing a bomb when it exploded in his hand and blew it off and got
Mr Lillie all across the stomach.
    He did not live very long. The worst part of it was he was just going on leave in about seven
days' time, it was jolly hard lines.
    Duffield.[3]

Apparently, just before the accident, Lillie had been due to go on leave anyway, but had
asked that it be postponed, presumably so that he could be at home over the Christmas
period.

Christmas Day 1916 came and went almost unnoticed for the 9th KOYLI. The
Battalion War Diary for the day was matter-of-fact, recording merely that thirty rounds of
77mm high explosive, landing in the vicinity of Sap 8, caused no damage. The enemy
trench mortar bombardment later in the day was equally unsuccessful. The 26th followed
a similar pattern, considerable numbers of trench mortar bombs landing on 'A' Company
trench and causing slight damage. At midnight, a sentry out in Lincoln St Post reported
movement out in no man's land. Corporal Pyatt and three men were sent out to investigate. They worked their way along in the darkness towards a disused trench. Seven yards
from this trench they were greeted by grenades thrown by the group of Germans presently
occupying it. Pyatt and his small group retaliated in like manner, succeeding in bombing
the ten or so enemy soldiers out of their lair and forcing them to retreat to their own lines.

The 27th saw the Germans continue the bombardment of the KOYLI trenches with
trench mortars, and some gas shells landed near Annequin. These again caused considerable nuisance, but nothing more. On their last full day in the trenches of the year,
however, the 9th KOYLI did suffer one fatality: 38252 Pte George Frederick Reed was
killed by an enemy sniper.

Relieved by the 1st Battalion, The Buffs, at midday the following day, the battalion
marched into billets in Noeux-les-Mines. Here, kit and equipment was cleaned and deficiencies checked and wherever possible rectified. A draft of 123 Other Ranks also
appeared from the 85th Training Reserve Battalion. Parades under company arrangements saw out what was left of 1916.

More reinforcements arrived on New Year's Day 1917: 111 Other Ranks reported, but
were described by the War Diary as being only 'partly trained'. On the same day, the
London Gazette announced the award of the Military Cross to Lt G.F. Ellenberger,
presently recovering from his wounds in England.

On 5 January, Sgt Wigglesworth, himself still in England, at Rugeley Camp, Stafford,
wrote a congratulatory letter to his old Company Commander: 'Dear Sir, I hope these
few lines will find you recovering from your wounds, but not too quick. Let me congratulate you on your well earned honour in receiving the MC which you fully deserve and
I hope you will live long to wear it.'[4]

Company commanders were busy training their men, integrating the new arrivals into
'the family'. This continued for the greater part of January. On the 8th, the routine was
punctuated by the Battalion Boxing Competition: sadly, no results are recorded. The

brigade competition followed on the 22nd, taking place at Béthune. On this day also, the 'untrained' men of the battalion proceeded to Ferfay to undergo a musketry course.

On the 25th, the Battalion Marathon Race took place. It is unlikely that the 'marathon' was run over the regulation Olympic distance, since it was recorded that the race began at 8.30 a.m., but that by 10.30 a.m., the whole battalion was marching off to the nearby baths. Owing to weather conditions, however (and one can only imagine the comments made by the men at this time) no-one bathed until the afternoon: on their arrival, the water was frozen!

The end of January saw the battalion on the move yet again. On the 28th it entrained at Noeux-les-Mines station at 1.30 p.m., and headed north. By 5.00 p.m., it had detrained at Esquelbecq and was marching to Ledringhem, where it was soon in billets. More training was to follow, interspersed by route-marches and practice alarms. Work Parties were also an inevitable part of the routine, with over 300 men working on the railway west of Poperinghe in Belgium. Even away from the front line, the battalion could not escape tragedy: on 8 February, 2nd-Lt J.H. Blackburn died from pneumonia in No.10 Casualty Clearing Station.

On 10 February, the battalion was inspected by the Divisional Commander, prior to its return to the Béthune area the following day. By the 13th, the 64th Brigade was back in the trenches near Annequin with the 9th KOYLI in reserve. On the 19th they relieved the 1st East Yorks in the right of the left subsector, commencing at 9.00 a.m. 'B' Company suffered five casualties during the completion of the relief at about 1.00 p.m., three men being killed and a further two wounded.

The next few days were to prove very difficult for the battalion. The winter of 1916-17 was a very severe one, with frost and snow almost permanent companions. On 20 February, a severe thaw set in and trench walls, as solid as rock for the previous months, turned to liquid mud. The trenches were almost impassable for the next few days: carrying parties faced almost insurmountable difficulties, some men becoming stuck fast in the mud for hours before being rescued. Communication with the front line became extremely difficult; ration parties arrived either late or not at all, and on the left of the line, where the flooding was at its worst, all attempts to get hot food forward to the two platoons of 'A' Company failed.

Captain Yeo, now on the Staff, recorded events in a letter written home shortly afterwards:

The frost and the following thaw made the trenches impassable for a few days – men were often stuck for six hours and in the end had to leave their gumboots and go on bare footed after being pulled out by ropes. It did not personally affect me very much as I don't go up every day as I used to. In fact, I sometimes have to go up and persuade myself afresh that there is really a war in fact as well as on paper.[5]

Yeo had joined the Staff of 64th Brigade on 18 February, and, in a letter written to his parents from Brig. Headlam, his CO said that 'as Staff Captain he will be about 90% safer than he was as bombing officer (both in and out of battle).[6]

The relative safety enjoyed by Yeo inspired him to commit to paper the first two of his rules for the Army: 1. The easier the work, the easier the promotion. 2. The less the danger, the greater the pay.[7]

Back in the trenches the men's suffering continued. Inter-Company relief was attempted on 22 February. 'B' and 'C' Companies managed to swap positions successfully on the right, but 'D' Company, on its way up to relieve 'A' Company on the left, became well and truly stuck in the ever-present cloying slime. No.2 Platoon of 'A' Company was not relieved until 7.00 p.m. Unfortunately, during this relief, Capt. Stanford,[8] commanding 'A' Company, was killed by a stray bullet.

Two days later, the battalion suffered another officer casualty. The battalion was relieved by the 1st East Yorks, the difficult process beginning at 9.00 p.m. At about 10.30 p.m., Lt R.A. Stokes was killed by enemy machine-gun fire in Railway Trench. The relief was completed by 1.00 a.m.

Battalion casualties for this tour were recorded in the War Diary: two officers and four Other Ranks killed, nine Other Ranks wounded and eighteen cases of Trench Foot.

Training for Lewis Gunners, Snipers and Bombers was undertaken before the battalion was back in the trenches once more on 2 March. The tour was thankfully short and quiet. They were relieved by the 1st Bedfordshires three days later and came out of the line having suffered no further casualties. They marched to Béthune, their uniforms no doubt still plastered with accumulated layers of filth, and must have been mightily grateful to find that fresh uniforms were waiting for them there.

A series of marches over the next few days via Robecq, Ecquedecques, Hestrus and Séricourt, in a huge anti-clockwise semi-circle course finally led the battalion to the small town of Lucheux, north-east of Doullens, on 13 March. Initially in hutments, they moved into billets in the village on the 14th. Two days later they were in the brigade training area practising for the forthcoming attack. This was repeated on the 19th, 22nd and 24th. Between these dates, the inevitable working parties, sometimes up to 500 strong, were sent out to help the Royal Engineers in Robermont Wood. On 18 March, Lt-Col. Millward left the battalion for India. They were to be led over the top by Lt-Col. Daniell.

On 25 March, Church Parade was followed by a rest day – a real one, with no work parties detailed. The next morning, Lt A.E. Day rejoined the battalion, finally recovered from his 1 July wounds. Training in the Pommera area, followed by a move to billets in Berles-au-Bois continued the unit's inexorable creep towards the front line.

Training and preparations intensified as the date of the attack drew near. On the last day of the month the battalion practised consolidating 'captured' enemy trenches in front of Monchy, and April Fools Day saw them march to Adinfer, arriving around noon. On 3 April they moved eastwards again, this time to Boisleux-au-Mont, to relieve 10th KOYLI. The following night a work party of 500 was digging assault trenches in front of Henin-sur-Cojeul. 'D' Company, in Boiry Becquerelle, suffered six casualties, all wounded, from enemy shelling.

Whilst in bivouacs in Boiry-au-Mont on 5 April, three officers and eighty-two Other Ranks were selected to be left behind when the battalion went into the attack, and they marched back into Adinfer, no doubt with mixed feelings. Yet another practice attack was undertaken on the 7th, and at Church Parade on the 8th, the battalion was addressed by the Brigade Commander. That evening, seventeen officers and 614 Other Ranks marched to the front-line trenches and took up their positions ready to attack on the morrow.

7

ARRAS

APRIL 1917

On 18 November 1916 Allied Commanders-in-Chief met at Chantilly for the purpose of long-term planning for the following spring. Preliminary ideas were for a combined, if not simultaneous attack: the British Fourth and Fifth Armies would resume the Somme Offensive, while the Third Army under Allenby would strike from the north of Arras in a south-easterly direction across the Cojeul and Sensée valleys. Further north still, the First Army would form a defensive flank to protect Allenby's left and rear. A limited French attack south of the River Somme would accompany the British efforts. All this would prepare the ground for a massive French assault in the Champagne region some three weeks later.

Several factors led to the gradual dissolving of this plan. Liddell Hart lists them neatly as 'French action, British hesitation and German anticipation'.[1] To take these singly, the French action centred on the dismissal of their commander, Joffre, and his replacement with General Robert Nivelle. At the outbreak of the war, Robert Nivelle was a sixty-one-year-old artillery officer. Once appointed Commander of the French Armies, he envisaged a more spectacular role for the French in the 1917 offensives. His plan for what became known as the 'Nivelle Offensive' promised rapid victory with no great loss of Allied lives. The French would attack with three full Armies, over twenty-seven Divisions. Collecting this kind of manpower in one area would require the British to take over even more of the line occupied at that time by the French: some extra twenty miles were to be added to the British right flank, this move to be completed by 20 January of the new year. (It was actually completed by 26 February.) Haig had no real objections to the French taking the major role in the following spring. He had been wanting to implement his own pet scheme of attacking along the Belgian coast at Ypres for some time, and saw the summer of 1917 as the perfect time to do it. A subsidiary role in a limited-duration offensive suited him: a long attritional battle would not allow him to deploy troops northwards in time, as they would be required to 'occupy' German troops on the French flank to try to limit German reinforcement of the critical area.

David Lloyd George, the British Prime Minister, was by this time an avid opponent of Western Front 'myopia'. He was willing to countenance attacks almost anywhere else in order to avoid major sacrifice of lives in France and Belgium, and made life very difficult for Haig and his Generals who all appeared to him to be suffering from the aforementioned ocular deficiency. He did, however, allow himself to be beguiled by the eloquent English-speaking General Nivelle, whose mother was British, and became an equally avid supporter of the French General's extravagant plan. The plan was meant to end the war in 1917 and involved breaking through the German lines near Arras – this to be the British role in the affair – and in the Champagne region – the French assault – thus destroying the huge salient between the two points of attack.

The Germans, however, had plans of their own. As far back as September 1916 they had begun the construction of new defence positions well behind the existing front line. Their name for it was the 'Siegfried Stellung': the allies were to come to know it as the 'Hindenburg Line'. It ran from Neuville St Vaast by Vimy, north-east of Arras, south-wards to Soissons. It would shorten the overall German line by some twenty-five miles, thus requiring approximately fourteen *fewer* Divisions to man it. It was a system like no other on the Western Front: the concept of defence in depth meant:

a system of strongpoints and wide – sometimes hundreds of yards wide – belts of wire, covered by an interlocking field of machine guns and artillery fire, trenches and strong points equipped with deep dugouts: to all this were added well-concealed observation posts on higher ground, deeply dug communications and telephone lines, and adequate supplies of food, water and ammunition.[2]

Secret orders for 'Operation Alberich' (named after the malicious dwarf of the 'Niebelungenlied'), the code name for the German withdrawal to the Hindenburg Line, were issued on 4 February 1917, and preparations were begun at once. As early as 22 February, some German troops pulled out of the Ancre valley, but the main retirement began on 16 March, when some thirty-five Divisions melted away. Three days later they were safely behind their new positions. British troops were faced with mostly empty trenches: their subsequent advance in pursuit was, perhaps understandably, slow and careful. It was the Germans' intention to leave behind them an *ausgesogenes* land (simple and direct translation of the phrase is difficult, but it meant that the countryside over which the Germans retreated was to be stripped of anything useful, or where this was not practicable, what was left should be destroyed, leaving a wasteland). Villages were destroyed, water supplies were poisoned, bridges and crossroads blown up. The British advanced across a wilderness.

Even before the withdrawal began, the Allies had been bickering amongst themselves. At the Calais Conference of 26 February 1917, Nivelle, with, it must be said, the connivance of Lloyd George, introduced a plan whereby he would take over effective command of British Armies in France for all matters concerning the conduct of operations, including plans for offensives and the strength and boundaries of troop deployments. Even Lloyd George was taken aback by the scope of the proposal and, threatened with Robertson's resignation, was forced to say that he thought the French plan went too far. The proposals were subsequently scaled down so that Haig would only in effect be under Nivelle's command for the duration of the coming offensive. Another conference in London ensued and final details of what became known as the 'Calais Agreement' were drawn up. British Armies would remain under British command, but the British Commander-in-Chief would be required to report directly to his French counterpart.

Time-wasting arguments such as these and the subsequent withdrawal of the German forces to the Hindenburg Line necessitated drastic modifications to the original plan of attack. The main role in the British sector of the attack would now fall to the Third Army. The recommencement of the Somme offensive further south was made redundant by the German withdrawals: the Bapaume salient no longer existed.

Between the right wing of the Third Army and the left of the proposed French assault was a distance of sixty miles as the crow flies. The front-line troops here, including the

British Fourth and Fifth Armies, attempting to construct lines of communication over a devastated hinterland abandoned by their enemy, would scarcely be able to occupy their opponents in such a way as to tie down their reserves, let alone envisage a full-scale attack. The two prongs of the attack would now by necessity be further apart, and support from intervening forces would be minimal.

The Third Army would now be required to break through the old defences just north of the Hindenburg Line and then be able to take the new defensive works in the flank and rear, 'rolling it up' from north to south. Even with this breakthrough in mind, it is useful to remind oneself at this point that in the overall scheme of things, the British role was still a subsidiary one. The *Official History* states that 'The object of these operations would be... to pin down the enemy, draw his reserves, and thus facilitate the task of the main French attack.'[3]

Allenby, in command of the Third Army, proposed a two-day artillery bombardment prior to the assault in order to maintain at least some element of surprise. He was overruled, however: a four-day bombardment would be preceded by three weeks of 'wire-cutting'. Over 2,800 guns, over a thousand of them 'heavy', would take part in the bombardment, a gun to every nine yards of front.

The attack was to be delivered by the Canadian Corps of the First Army on the extreme left, and by XVII, VI and VII Corps of the Third Army, listed north to south. Byng's Canadian Corps was to assault Vimy Ridge and thus cover the left flank of the Third Army's advance.

Ferguson's XVII Corps would form the left wing of the Third Army assault, being positioned to the north of the marshy Scarpe valley, with the 51st, 34th and 9th Divisions attacking north of Arras, the 4th Division leapfrogging through the 9th on the corps' right.

VI Corps under Haldane would have the narrowest front, adjacent to and just south of Arras, with 15th, 12th and 3rd Divisions in the front line, the 37th behind them ready to leapfrog into the town of Monchy-le-Preux.

On the extreme right, Snow's VII Corps had the 14th, 56th, 30th and 21st Divisions in the line, north to south. Lines of trenches to be taken were designated 'Black', 'Red', 'Blue', 'Brown' and finally 'Green' (see map).

Towards the right flank of the British attack front, the line turned to the south-east and briefly due east. This meant that the first targeted line in front of the 21st Division was the Brown Line. Zero hour on Zero day was 5.30 a.m., but the planned capture of the Brown Line was not until Zero plus eight hours, that is 1.30 p.m., followed by a further two-hour delay before advancing on the Green Line. Snow decided to stagger the times of attack of his Divisions, the 14th on the left going in first. This meant that the units of the 21st Division ear-marked for the attack would not be required to advance until approximately 4.00 p.m., and even then only if the attacks of the 30th Division on their left had succeeded in making ground.

The preliminary artillery barrage began as planned on 20 March, the main bombardment commencing fifteen days later at 6.30 a.m. on 4 April. On the following day, after a meeting with Nivelle at Montdidier, Douglas Haig decided that the attack would have to be delayed by one day; the French were not ready, and the weather was awful, falls of snow having hindered artillery observers. The troops would go over the top on 9 April, Easter Monday. Rumour had it that the assault was delayed in order to preserve the sanctity of Easter Sunday. The dissemination of this version of events was not discouraged.

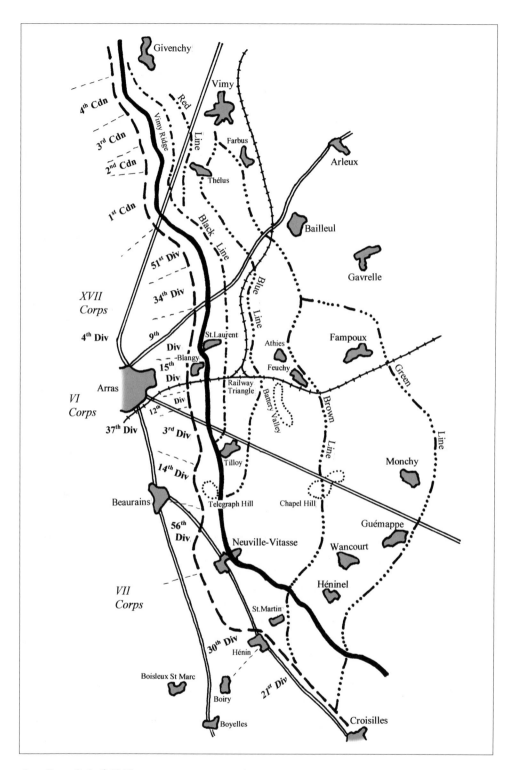

Arras Front, 9 April 1917.

The artillery barrage which fell on the German wire, front lines and artillery batteries was technically a vast improvement on that which had rained down on the Somme the previous summer. Firstly, there were simply more guns available. Their accuracy, range and reliability had all improved greatly in the intervening months. Sound-ranging and flash-spotting were being developed to facilitate the location and subsequent destruction of German batteries. The creeping barrage, in its infancy on the Somme, had come of age: up to six successive lines of shells, lifting in unison, could cover an area up to 2,000 yards deep in front of the advancing infantry. That, at least, was the theory...

Those Divisions advancing directly to the east and north of Arras, that is those of VI Corps, enjoyed another advantage. The inhabitants of Arras had been excavating tunnels, caves and galleries under their town for centuries and had used them for many purposes, from shelter during times of conflict and sanctuary during times of religious intolerance to the more mundane wine cellars and refuse dumps of more peaceful times. Work on extending these subways was taken on by British and New Zealand troops back in October 1916. Tunnels were lengthened, galleries were enlarged, sewage systems were linked: by the time the advance was imminent, just over 11,000 yards of extra tunnels had been completed, along with galleries sufficient to house 24,500 troops in safety, water and electricity supplied. These tunnels extended eastwards from the town, allowing troops to reach their front-line trenches without recourse to an overland march under the inevitable enemy artillery fire.

As previously noted, Zero hour was 5.30 a.m. on 9 April. It was envisaged that the Black line would be in British hands by Zero plus thirty minutes. A one-and-a-half-hour halt would see the attack on the Blue line commence at 7.30 a.m.: it was to be captured by 8.14 a.m. The advance on the Brown line was to be at 12.10 p.m., its seizure, if all went to plan, to be complete by 1.30 p.m. Another halt, this time of two hours, would mean that the men would assault the Green line at 3.30 p.m. At its deepest point, this meant a total advance of four and a half miles in eight hours, with the town of Monchy-le-Preux in British hands by nightfall.

Fifteen Divisions waited in their assembly trenches in the early hours of that Easter Monday. The cavalry, as ever, waited in the rear, ready to exploit the expected break-through. It was bitterly cold, with a strong westerly wind blowing. The ground was very wet and it was beginning to snow again. The eighteen-pounder guns were poised, ready to launch the creeping barrage, fifty per cent high explosive and fifty per cent shrapnel, which would advance at a rate of 100 yards every four minutes during each stage of the attack. Sixty-pounders would pummel each objective line until the creeping barrage reached it, whereupon it would lift to the next. Livens Projectors firing gas shells and Stokes mortars would add their weight to the already unprecedented efforts of the artillery. The extra day's bombardment had proved valuable: the 8th was a sunny day and improved observation allowed 'a great deal to be accomplished that day. It was felt that the artillery preparation had done all that could be expected of it.'[4] This was true of the Black and Blue lines, but the position pertaining to the Brown line was far from satisfactory. It had proved very difficult indeed to cut the wire in front of the right flank of VII Corps. Their eighteen-pounder guns and two-inch mortars, which were largely responsible for this task, could not be brought up into range until 2 April. These two weapons were, therefore, only used to a 'limited extent.'[5] The troops of the 64th Brigade advancing late in the day would find themselves quite literally up against it.

'Easter Monday of the year 1917 must be accounted from the British point of view one of the great days of the war.'[6] Thus begins the account of the battle in the *Official History*:

going against tradition for purely chronological reasons, let us examine the progress of this 'great' day's events from left to right of the Allied line.

To the north of Arras, on the left of the line, troops of the four Canadian Divisions left their trenches, accompanied by a spring snowstorm, and advanced up the slopes of Vimy Ridge.

The 1st Division, with the 2nd on their left, reached and overran the Black Line, the first German defensive position, within half an hour, and by 10.45 a.m. the town of Thélus was in Canadian hands. By 1.00 p.m., the far side of the ridge had been reached and the troops were able to enjoy the panoramic view eastwards over the Douai plain. The 3rd Division were able to take the German front-line trenches in quick time; the passing of the creeping barrage had given the defenders no time to man their positions before the Canadians arrived on top of them. By 8.00 a.m. the far crest of the ridge had been taken and the troops were digging in. The 3rd Division found, however, that their left-hand battalion were being enfiladed by machine gun and small-arms fire from Hill 145, the highest point on the ridge. Although the rest of the Division pressed on towards Petit Vimy and Vimy, a defensive flank had to be thrown back on the left: the 4th Division attack had run into serious trouble.

An hour after the assault had begun, the 4th Division were still facing three untaken strong points; the German second trench, Hill 145 and, on the far left, a knoll known as 'The Pimple'. Hill 145 was finally taken that day by the Nova Scotia Highlanders, but the Pimple was to remain stubbornly in German hands for another three days.

The taking of Vimy Ridge remains the proudest day in Canadian military history. The cost had been high, over 10,000 casualties, 3,598 of them killed.

On the left of Allenby's Third Army were the 51st Division. They ended the day several hundred yards short of their final objectives. On their right, the 34th Division fared somewhat better. Their objectives lay 2,000 yards from their jumping-off positions. The capture of the Blue Line went pretty much to time; subsequently the right-hand brigades secured their final goal, almost on the Green Line, with those in the centre almost matching their achievements. On the left, machine-gun fire meant troops were stranded on the Blue Line.

The advance of the 9th Division was a complete success. The 4th Division passed through the captured position as planned and reached Fampoux. This turned out to be the longest advance of the day – three and a half miles.

The men of the 12th and 15th Divisions were to attack directly east from the town of Arras. It had been their good fortune to be able to spend the five days prior to the assault safe and dry in the tunnels under the town. By 8.45 a.m., the town of Blangy was in British hands. Railway Triangle proved difficult to take, but eventually fell, as did Battery Valley. The 12th Division attacked with their right flank on the Cambrai road. Their advance was finally held up on the Wancourt–Feuchy line.

Third Division finished the day level with their northern neighbours having seized the town of Tilloy. The proposed leapfrogging of the 9th Division onto Monchy-le-Preux came too late in the day and their advance petered out in the gathering gloom of evening.

On the right flank of the attacking forces was Lt-Gen. Snow's VII Corps consisting, north to south, of the 14th, 56th, 30th and 21st Divisions.

The right flank supporting operation was intended to assist the central attack by preventing the Germans from reinforcing the gap – but it was the hardest task of the day. Directly facing these Divisions was a new section of the Hindenburg Line, which began at the Harp just north of

Neuville-Vitasse, cut through the village, then swung south-east in front of Héninel and Fontaine-les-Croisilles. If any success was to be achieved at all, the enemy line had to be broken here.[7]

As previously mentioned, the Corps Commander had decided to stagger the start times of each Division. The 14th would start at 7.30 a.m., the 56th at 7.45 a.m., the 30th Division would send in one Brigade at 12.55 p.m., the other two at 4.15 p.m. to coincide with the advance of the 21st Division. This was due in part to the distances they would have to advance, but due also to the fact the success of each Division's attack would depend largely on the unit to its left's ability to take its objective thereby covering its neighbour's flank. If the 14th and 56th Divisions did not break through the Hindenburg Line and begin to 'roll it up' from the right rear, the attacks further south would be little short of suicidal.

The attack by the 14th Division was executed by the 42nd and 43rd Brigades, on the left and right respectively. The 42nd had the Blue Line in its possession by 8.45 a.m. The 43rd captured some of its objectives, including part of the Hindenburg Line, but the second phase of the assault was forced back by machine-gun fire shortly after midday.

The task facing the 56th Division appeared, on paper, to be relatively straightforward. They were only required to advance as far as the Brown Line and this on a front of only 350 yards. Directly in front of them, however, lay the heavily fortified town of Neuville-Vitasse. If they managed to overcome this first obstacle, they would find, directly behind it, the Hindenburg Line, here a triple trench system. Then they would be required to advance over open ground for nearly a mile prior to taking the heavily wired Wancourt–Feuchy trench system.

Neuville-Vitasse finally fell, but uncut wire and determined resistance by the defenders meant that the Blue Line here was not reached until 4.00 p.m. The attack on the Hindenburg Line went ahead regardless: all three lines were initially overrun, but the 14th Londons eventually fell back to a position in the first. The final assault on the Wancourt–Feuchy line was to be made by the 7th Middlesex, but they found the London battalions held up. Two attacks on the support trench, made in the face of heavy machine-gun fire, were to no avail. The advance would go no further that day: the 56th Division had moved their lines forward 2,000 yards and captured over 600 prisoners, all for a miserly 881 casualties.

The timetable of the 30th Division required the left-hand brigade, the 21st, to go forward in time to be in the Hindenburg Line by 12.55 p.m., this providing the 56th Division on their left had taken Neuville-Vitasse and reached the Blue Line. The 2nd Wiltshires and 18th King's battalions duly went forward at 11.38 a.m. but were beset by problems almost from the outset. Moving out from the sunken Hénin–Neuville road they were met by very heavy machine-gun fire and an enemy artillery barrage. Both battalions suffered heavy casualties, and by the time they had reached the enemy wire, the momentum had gone, and the survivors fell back to the St Martin–Neuville road, joined here by the 19th Manchesters, and they began to dig in. The Hindenburg Line remained in German hands.

On the Division's right front, the 89th Brigade were required to go forward simultaneously with the 64th Brigade on their right at 4.15 p.m. They attacked with the 20th King's Liverpool on the left and their sister battalion, the 19th, on the right. After taking the Hindenburg Line, the latter were to continue the advance and capture the village of Héninel. Both battalions moved forward and had reached St Martin by 3.30 p.m. almost unmolested. From this point things went badly wrong. The wire in front of the first trench of the Hindenburg complex was found to be virtually intact and the attack 'was everywhere held up by terrific machine-gun fire.'[8] Having suffered over 400 casualties between them, the two battalions tried to establish a position in shell holes at the limit of their advance: they were ordered to withdraw under the cover of darkness to positions in the northern outskirts of St Martin.

The 21st Division occupied a frontage of 4500 yards, from the Cojeul River at Hénin to the Sensée at Croisilles. The right-hand brigade, the 110th, was to stand fast, and only on a front of 2,700 yards would they be required to attack (the 110th Brigade would in fact form a defensive flank to protect the right flank of the attacking troops). The task of promulgating the attack fell to the 64th Brigade. In the front line, left to right, were the 9th KOYLI, 15th Durham Light Infantry and 1st East Yorks. The 10th KOYLI would be in reserve.

The first objectives of the attack were the first and second trench lines of the Hindenburg Line system. The brigade's third objective, as can be seen from the map, would form a defensive flank along the ridge to the south-east of Héninel, protecting the town from counter-attack from the side and rear. (As we have already seen, however, the town, the objective of the 19th King's Liverpool Regiment, was not captured.)

The attacking battalions of the 64th Brigade went forward into their jumping-off trenches the evening before the attack. The 9th KOYLI and the 1st East Yorks were there by 10.00 p.m. The 15th DLI took their places between them at midnight. These trenches, totalling 2,400 yards, were situated both sides of a road running south-east from the village of St Martin sur Cojeul and had been dug during the hours of darkness over the three nights prior to the assault. Along the 9th KOYLI front, this road was sunken, with

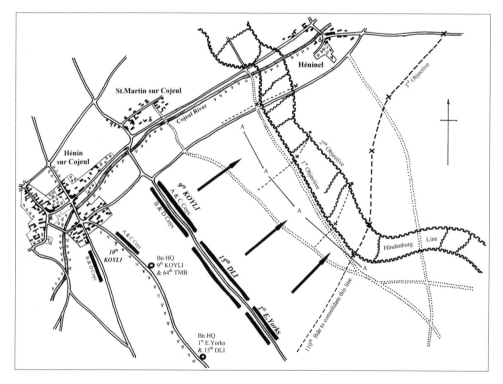

64th Brigade Attack at Cojeul, 9 April 1917.

banks either side varying from six to ten feet high in places; it also climbs gently away from the river valley before levelling out on the 15th DLI front. Some of the KOYLIs, faced with an eighteen-hour wait in what were actually described by the diarist as 'fairly comfortable' trenches, preferred to wait out their time in the sunken road between the two prepared lines. Supplies had been brought forward to these positions from the 64th Brigade dump near the church in Boiry St Rictrude: 2,000 bombs, 500 tins of water, 800 rifle grenades and 500 Stokes mortar bombs along with thousands of .303 rounds.

The advance would be over gently undulating open countryside, sloping right to left down to the river valley, the last few dozen yards to the enemy wire being uphill. The undulations were sufficient to give cover from view and therefore direct fire now and again.

The artillery arrangements were, as ever, strictly regulated, and were as follows: at Zero minus twenty-two minutes, a barrage of eighteen-pounders would be put down south-west of the German wire (marked A——A——A on the map). At twelve minutes before Zero, the barrage would begin to creep forward to the wire. Four minutes later it would reach the enemy's front trench. At Zero minus one, the barrage would leave the front trench, creep forward again and form a standing barrage some 200 yards beyond it, remaining there until Zero plus thirty minutes. It would then creep forwards at its standard rate of fifty yards per minute over the second-line trench and form a similar standing barrage on the far side of it. Over the previous week, the artillery had been trying to cut lanes 100 feet wide in the enemy's wire through which the advancing infantry could pass. The report of the 21st Division 'Daily Summary of Operations' for 5 April was less than hopeful, however; 'Wire from T4 b 8.6 to N34 c 9.6 [directly in front of the 15th DLI] examined and found very thick. Seven rows iron screw pickets about 2 feet apart and wire about 5 feet high so thickly entangled as to resemble a thorn fence'.[9]

Twelve officers and 550 Other Ranks of the 9th KOYLI waited nervously and no doubt impatiently all through the day: indeed, a failure on the VI Corps front to their left would have meant a cancellation of the assault. Wind, rain and snow conspired to make conditions as uncomfortable as possible. They were in fighting order, their jerkin in their haversacks and ground sheet worn behind the belt. Their greatcoats had been stored neatly some distance back from the front line. The elements could do their worst. Each carried 120 rounds, one bandolier and a grenade in each breast pocket. In addition they had their rifle, bayonet, entrenching tool, full water bottle, two days' rations and three empty sandbags. Somehow, between them, they also had to transport sixty eight shovels and thirty-two pickaxes as far as the Hindenburg Line. With flares and wire-cutters to share out too, an unlucky, slightly built man could have ended up carrying half his own weight in equipment into battle.

With 1,000 yards to cover, and a creeping barrage which lifted off the front-line German trench at Zero minus one minute, it would be necessary for the men of 64th Brigade to leave their trenches before Zero with enough time in hand to arrive at the German lines tight on the heels of their artillery support.

No cancellation orders were received and 'A' and 'C' Companies, left and right respec-tively, of 9th KOYLI climbed out of their by now thoroughly sodden trenches at 3.52 p.m., Zero minus twenty-three minutes. They formed up in half-platoon columns and moved in file, with approximately thirty yards between each column. This formation was adopted and held right up to the German wire as it was suspected that gaps would be few and far between. Two hundred yards behind them, in similar formation, came the second wave, comprising 'B' and 'D' Companies. 'A' and 'C' Companies were entrusted with

The sunken road where the men of 9th KOYLI sheltered the night before the attack on the Hindenburg Line near Hénin-sur-Cojeul. (present day)

the task of capturing and consolidating the front-line German trench. 'B' and 'D' Companies were to leapfrog them and do likewise to the second line trench. The Hindenburg Line, if all went to plan, would be in British hands within the hour.

At first, the battalion advanced with little in the way of reply from the Germans. Their retaliatory artillery bombardment was 'prompt but weak'[10] and covering traversing fire from a machine-gun section which had been pushed forward during the night to a portion of the sunken St Martin–Fontaine road seemed to keep the defenders' heads down. Very few casualties were suffered until they came within 150 yards of the enemy wire.

Arriving at the wire, some troops were able to pass quite easily through the gaps; others were held up for some time. It was purely the luck of the draw as to whether a column stumbled onto a suitable gap or onto impenetrable entanglements. Detachments of Stokes mortars were following the first wave troops and these immediately went into action in an attempt to cut more of the wire. 'The Stokes on the right were very promptly brought into action against an advanced concrete-protected post and knocked it out. Captain Piza, the very gallant officer who directed this work was killed shortly afterwards.'[11] (This was Acting Captain Daniel Piza of 64th Trench Mortar Battalion.)

In quick time, the leading companies of the 15th DLI and 1st East Yorks were in their first objective trenches. Flares were promptly sent up to announce the fact and the second wave troops passed through only to find the wire between the first and second German lines uncut and for all practical purposes impregnable. Troops were forced to lie up in shell holes and make their way back to the first line as and when they were able.

Six KOYLI graves at Cojeul British Cemetery.

The 9th KOYLIs on the brigade left had a worse time of it. The men were able to make it through the first belt of wire but were held up by an intact second belt still short of their first objective. 'Heavy losses were incurred in trying to find gaps through this wire, or in endeavouring to cut the wire with wire breakers. The losses were inflicted by machine gun and rifle fire, our barrage having passed over the enemy front-line trench.'[12]

In effect, the KOYLIs were stuck out in the open, between two belts of barbed wire, doing their best to find a way through the second one and the Germans were able to direct withering machine-gun and rifle fire onto them. It is no surprise that the attack broke down here, with most men laying down and taking cover where they could in shell holes. 'B' and 'D' Companies, in the second wave, 'pushed forward under the impression that the leading wave had established a footing in the German front-line trench.'[13] A similar fate to that of the leading companies awaited them.

To their right, the 15th DLI had consolidated their position in the German front-line trench and a party from their left-hand company started bombing their way northward down the trench in an attempt to give what assistance they could to the embattled KOYLIs. They bravely fought on and made some 300 yards progress before running out of bombs and being forced back. Indeed, the Germans pushed on and retook some of the captured trench from the Durhams, but further similar enemy bombing raids on both flanks were successfully beaten off.

At about 5.25 p.m., the CO of 9th KOYLI, Lt-Col. Daniell, sent forward 2nd-Lt R.H. Box with instructions to find out what he could about the battalion's situation. An impatient Daniell went forward himself half an hour later once Box had made his report and found out firsthand that his men were established in shell holes mostly between the two belts of German wire. He realised that it was useless to try to reorganise before dark.

At 7.10 p.m., two companies of the 10th KOYLI moved up in support of their sister battalion, while the rest took up positions in the road in front of the enemy's lines and began to dig in. Daniell observed this advance shortly after dusk and decided that the 9th Battalion should withdraw and form up to the left of the 10th and dig themselves in too. Orders to this effect were given at 7.52 p.m. As many wounded as possible were also collected from amongst the wire entanglements under the supervision of 2nd-Lt Box: this was particularly essential as it was understood that the enemy's position would be subject to artillery bombardment the next day. Rations arrived at about 11.30 p.m. and the men were pleased to receive tea, cold meat, biscuits and rum. It became clear that the men of 9th KOYLI were still in a very exposed position and 'too tired to dig effectively.'[14] They were accordingly ordered at 4.47 a.m. to withdraw to a position behind the sunken road from which 'B' and 'D' Companies of 10th KOYLI had originally advanced (see map).

The 10 April saw the Germans counter-attack from their second-line trench. In repulsing one of these attacks at a block in the captured trench, Pte Horace Waller of 10th KOYLI held his position, eventually single-handed, for an hour, holding back several determined assaults. He repeated his act of bravery in defending against a further attack some time later, but was this time mortally wounded. For his valiant efforts that day he was awarded a posthumous Victoria Cross. Pte Waller, a former pupil of Batley Grammar School, is buried in Cojeul British Cemetery close to where he fell.

The counter-attacks eventually proved successful. The 1st East Yorks were driven out of the German front-line trench and the rest of the brigade was 'forced to conform to its retirement.'[15] By 9.30 that evening, all the attacking British troops on the 64th Brigade front had been forced back to their original assembly trenches. Before this, the exhausted

9th KOYLI had been ordered to withdraw to Boiry St Martin at dusk. The following day was spent resting in bivouacs in Boiry: the War Diary records that the battalion's total strength was twenty-four officers and 751 Other Ranks, and that there was a snow storm from 5.00 p.m. until 9.00 p.m. that evening. The official report on the attack penned four days after the event puts the casualty figures at seven officers and 176 Other Ranks killed, wounded or missing. Appendix I concludes that the final figure for fatalities that day is seventy-two. One of those killed, Cpl Sydney James, earned a special mention in the *Huddersfield Examiner* of 27 April:

News is at hand that Corporal Sydney James, KOYLI, who played centre half-back for Huddersfield Town before joining the forces last year, was killed in action in France on April 9th. James, who hails from Sheffield, played for the Tinsley Church and Bird-in-Hand Clubs in that town previous to coming to Huddersfield Town, who secured him as a centre-forward. A stylish and clever player, he had scarcely the physique necessary to achieve a big result in that position, and later he was moved to centre-half, an experiment which was attended with great success. His work was consistently good, and when called up he promised to be one of the finest centre half-backs in the Second Division of the English League. The news of his death was received yesterday by his mother, who lives at Tinsley, and many players and lovers of football will read the announcement with regret.[16]

Refitting and reorganising began the next day: working parties were sent back up to the Hindenburg Line, which had in the meantime been evacuated by the Germans, to recover salvage and act as burial parties. Several wounded men of the 64th Brigade were found in German dugouts in the abandoned trenches. They had been captured during the German counter-attacks on 10 April and had apparently been treated well in the meantime. Similar activities took up the subsequent two days before the battalion moved via Ficheux to Blairville and were billeted in German underground passages leading from the village to the old front line.

Company training became the main activity of the next week. All the men in the battalion had the opportunity to take a bath, and on 17 April, Maj. Greenwood, who had gone to England sick in April 1916, rejoined the battalion. Three days later, 2nd-Lt Shaw, who had been wounded on the 9th, came back from the casualty clearing station and reported for duty.

A move to Mercatel on the 23rd saw the battalion attached to the 50th Division. This was to be very short-lived; arriving at 4.00 p.m., they immediately received orders for a move to Boyelles and a subsequent attachment to 30th Division. The 64th Brigade would join 19th Brigade the following afternoon, the 25th, in the old Hindenburg front and support lines. They relieved the 1st Cameronians and suffered shelling on the front line during the process. 'A' Company suffered a few casualties, including Lt A.E. Day and 2nd-Lt S.G. Richards wounded. Five Other Ranks were killed. Two more days in these positions passed relatively quietly.

The opposing sides here were in the unusual position of holding adjacent sections of the same trench-line systems. The 9th KOYLI were approximately one and a half miles to the south-east of the section of Hindenburg Line they had previously attacked. They received orders on 27 April to attack in a south-easterly direction along the trench system as far as the road which bisected it running from Croisilles to Cherisy, parallel and a few hundred yards to the north of the River Sensée.

Zero hour was 3.00 a.m. on 28 April. An artillery barrage would begin five minutes later. The advance began on time, but on the right of the attack front, four shells fell short, landing in the middle of the attacking party. This, not surprisingly, disorganised them considerably. They gathered themselves together once more and continued their advance for a further 200 yards where they were held up by a German block. Their efforts to storm the block were in vain and they constructed one of their own in front of it instead. On the left, men were advancing in the open to the north-east of the old second-line trench. They too met with considerable opposition and were forced to take to the trench to find cover. The party continued down the trench but was confronted by another solidly built German block about twelve feet high and approximately 250 yards short of their objective. A stiff bombing fight ensued, lasting several hours, and although the Germans eventually gave up throwing bombs, the KOYLIs found it impossible to rush the block, despite help from two Stokes mortars which had been brought up in support.

The attack had gained only about fifty yards of trench and had cost the battalion fifty casualties, including 2nd-Lts. Teaz and Brierley wounded. Seven Other Ranks, among them CSM Ervine, were killed. A German counter-attack the following morning cancelled out all their gains.

The month ended with a quiet day. The War Diary noted that it was very welcome to all ranks who were feeling in need of a rest.

'One of the great days of the war' was how the *Official History* had described 9 April 1917. Taking the wider view, this may still be the subject of debate, but even despite congratulatory letters from Brigadier.-Gen. J. Burnett Stuart, General Staff, VII Corps and from Maj.-Gen. Campbell, Officer Commanding 21st Division, containing such words and phrases as 'great loyalty and courage', 'tenacity' and 'admiration of their conduct', the men of the 9th KOYLI , whilst having done nothing to damage their impressive reputation amongst their commanders, could not have been expected to view recent events in such positive light. Sombre pride may well have been the best that could have been hoped.

8

SUMMER 1917

The 64th Brigade had one more small part to play in the Battle of Arras before it drew to a conclusion on 17 May 1917. On the 3rd, the brigade took part in an assault: the 110th Brigade was called upon to bear the brunt of the action, crossing the Sensée River, an advance of some 1,400 yards, and then taking the village of Fontaine. The 64th Brigade objectives were part of the Hindenburg Line front and support trenches to the west of Fontaine – almost a repeat, in fact, of their ill-fated advance of five days earlier. The 15th DLI were to attack with 10th KOYLI in support. 1st East Yorks and 9th KOYLI were held in brigade reserve, the latter being detailed for carrying work. Zero hour was 3.45 a.m., but the attack failed to get beyond its starting point. The 15th DLI was relieved by the 1st East Yorks at 8.00 p.m. Lent to this East Yorks force were four bombing squads of 9th KOYLI, two squads each from 'B' & 'D' Companies, totalling forty men in all. Meanwhile, fifty others became carrying parties, ferrying trench mortar and Stokes shells forward. Despite playing no part in the original attack, the 9th KOYLI suffered one fatal casualty that day: 424971 Acting Sgt Nicholas Henry White was reported killed in action.

The following evening the 9th KOYLI relieved its sister battalion in its position of close support to the East Yorks. A patrol was sent out and found the enemy occupying York Trench, but otherwise the night passed quietly. The next two days were spent 'firestepping' the old Hindenburg support-line trench, in effect reversing it to face north–east, and in the unpleasant task of burying the dead from previous assaults.

Orders came on 9 May for the move to Basseux. Battalion strength was 595 Other Ranks and, including the MO and the interpreter, eighteen officers. On 11 May, the Germans sent twenty-five shells over to the camp to serve as a going-away present. The shelling lasted fifteen minutes and caused fourteen casualties in 'A' Company. One of those casualties was fatal – 29966 Pte H. Appleyard is buried in nearby Boyelles Communal Cemetery.

At 1.00 p.m. the battalion marched off in very hot weather conditions to the rest area, some eight miles to the west, finding both comfortable accommodation and their packs on their arrival. A rest day followed, and after Church Parade on Sunday, the battalion began to construct a rifle range. This work was completed the following day, Monday the 14th, allowing musketry training to commence. 'A' and 'B' Companies were first on the range, spending a day each perfecting their marksmanship. 'C' Company had to wait until the Friday for target practice, however; Battalion Sports took precedence on the Thursday as competitors for Saturday's Brigade Sports had to be selected. This event took place at Bailleulval, Basseux's very close neighbour. No outright victories can be reported for the

9th KOYLI contingent, but they were content with a 2nd place in the Relay race, a 3rd in the Quarter Mile and a 2nd in the Officers' Sack Race.

At Church Parade the following day, the GOC 64th Brigade presented Military Medal ribbons to Adj.-Cpl Penty and Lt-Cpl Sutton. The CO, Lt-Col. Daniell went on leave: six days in Paris.

It was also on this day, 20 May, that the much-vaunted Nivelle Offensive was closed down. The Chemin des Dames attacks had been a disaster. The French suffered over 96,000 casualties in the first week, 15,589 being reported killed. The German defences refused to crumble; the morale of the French Army collapsed. Mutinies became widespread and some troops refused to go up to the line: those in the line would hold their positions, but any further attacks were out of the question. Nivelle was ousted and replaced by General Philippe Pétain.

'D' Company finally got a chance to polish their skills with a Lee Enfield .303 on Monday 21 May. Their day on the range coincided with the arrival of reinforcements: seventeen Other Ranks, along with 2nd-Lts F.C. de M. Logsdon, C. Roberts, F.J. Nock, V.R. Gregg, C.D. Quarmby and S. Cundall.

Musketry training continued for the rest of the week and Lt-Col. Daniell returned just in time for an inspection by the CO of VII Corps, Lt-Gen. Sir Thomas d'O Snow, on the Saturday. Another thirty-five Other Ranks reported for duty, as did 2nd-Lts. Jacques and Clarice.

This day, 26 May, also saw the return of a familiar face. Lt Ellenberger returned from England, having recovered from his wounds sustained near Gueudecourt the previous September. During his long convalescence, Ellenberger had toyed with the idea of joining the Royal Flying Corps, but eventually came to the conclusion that 'the infantry is the thing'.[1] His journey back to France had been punctuated by a short stay in London and punctured by an inoculation in Boulogne.

On arrival, he was given command of 'D' Company, Spicer's old company. In a letter home written just after this welcome reunion he remarked that his old friend A.E. Day was now in command of 'A' Company, and that 'The CO, whom I didn't know, seems a very decent fellow.'[2]

On the Monday afternoon there was a cricket match between officers of the battalion and officers of Brigade HQ. The result was a tie. Tactical exercises planned for the following day were cancelled due to rain, but the weather had improved sufficiently for a Battalion Camp Fire Concert that evening. This marked the end of what must have been a very welcome spell out of the line, away from the consistent dangers and irritating discomforts of the trenches. On 30 May, the battalion marched off to bivouacs in Boyelles, arriving at 6.15 p.m., and getting soaked by a sudden thunderstorm on the way.

The following day, the brigade was heading back into the line, the 9th KOYLI relieving the 4th Suffolks in the old German support and front lines of the Hindenburg system west of Fontaine, and north of the Sensée River. This was the stretch of the line that the 3 May attack had failed to capture. Four hundred and seventy men of the 9th KOYLI completed the relief just before midnight with no casualties. Intermittent heavy German shelling of the line between midnight and 3.30 a.m. welcomed the arrival of both the Yorkshiremen and the month of June. Second-Lieutenant Frederick John Nock, aged twenty-four, from Sheffield, who had arrived only ten days earlier, was wounded. He succumbed to his wounds two days later and was buried in Sunken Road Cemetery near Boisleux St Marc.

Stints in the line, punctuated by working parties, reliefs and time in reserve at Boyelle, occupied the next fifteen days.

Writing home on 2 June, Lt Ellenberger, in the Hindenburg Line for the first time, expressed his opinions on the scale of the excavations, and whilst impressed by the feats of engineering, his British 'offensive spirit' is still evident as he doubts its overall efficacy:

Writing in part of the allmächtige Hindenburg Line. The Bosche still seems to think that the depth of a hole is the height of its salvation, for here is the deepest hole I have ever seen; [a tunnel] 50ft deep running right along the length of the Hindenburg Line... He doesn't seem to think that while it may save his casualties from shell fire, it increases the number of prisoners.[3]

Some few days later, on 11 June, Harold Yeo on 64th Brigade Staff also wrote home, part of his letter concerning his recent good news: 'All sorts of people seem to have written to say they are pleased to hear of my getting the Military Cross... not that I've ever done anything in particular except to trot along and do as I was told.'[4]

Coinciding with an unsuccessful attack by 11th Brigade (12th and 13th Northumberland Fusiliers), on 16 June, the 9th KOYLI relieved the 1st East Yorks in the front-line trenches and extended their line southwards across the river to the Croisilles-Fontaines road. The battalion's main task over the next couple of nights was to improve the wire in front of their positions. Second-Lieutenant Cox also led two patrols out to recce enemy positions. Success was limited, but one Other Rank was reported wounded and one killed. The latter was 16378 Pte William Henry Harrison.

The 19 June was a wet day, the trenches becoming very muddy, but the 9th KOYLI were able to leave this problem to the relieving 10th Argyll and Sutherland Highlanders as they moved back to the relative comfort of the Hénin-Croisilles road. A rest period of eight days followed, with the usual refitting and inspections. Thirty-two Other Ranks reported for duty during this period, ten of who were rejoining the battalion. Along with them came 2nd-Lts Moseley (likewise rejoining), P.D. Stanley, L.B. Spicer and G.A. Hyde. On 23 June, the courts martial of Pte Oxley, Adj.-Cpl Davis and Pte Bidwell took place, though the War Diary notes neither their offences nor their punishments.

The battalion was on the move again on 29 June, this time to Moyenneville. The CO and company commanders visited the reserve line west of Croisilles held by the 2nd Royal Welch Fusiliers to arrange details of the relief, which took place the following day, without incident, being completed by 4.45 p.m.

The new month, the first anniversary of the start of the Battle of the Somme, saw the battalion working on the accommodation for the reserve troops. Enemy shelling of the Hénin–St Leger road killed one soldier from 'A' Company. ('Soldiers Died in the Great War' has no casualties listed for the 9th KOYLI on that date.) The enemy shelled the road again the following night, this time without success. On the 4th, 9th KOYLI relieved the 1st East Yorks in the front line, taking up their position as right-hand battalion of the 64th Brigade. Wet weather greeted them and the trenches became heavy.

That night, whilst in charge of one of several wiring parties in no man's land, Lt Walter Ernest Smith[5] was wounded. He died from his wounds the following day whilst being transported from the advanced dressing station to the casualty clearing station. Whilst similarly engaged two nights later, 39649 Pte Tom Norcliffe of 'A' Company was killed outright by a stray shell.

Relieved by the 7th Leicesters on the 8th, the battalion spent the next day resting back in Moyenneville at 'F' Camp, in preparation for the Inter-Company League Football

Competition. Unfortunately no results of the matches have survived, and the story is the same for the officers versus 10th KOYLI cricket match, held on the 12th. A football match against the 1st East Yorks on the 13th sinks into comparable obscurity, though the brigade wiring competition of the 14th is inexplicably better documented: 'D Company 9th KOYLI won easily.'[6]

More stints in the old Hindenburg Line interspersed by working parties followed before another sojourn at 'F' Camp allowed the Inter-Company Football League to continue, though officers only were allowed to enjoy a cricket match against the Brigade Staff. A Divisional concert and a bath rounded off the month.

The 1 August being Minden Day, the battalion wore white roses as they marched up to relieve the 6th Leicesters in Brigade reserve. Working parties were required the following day for the 181st Tunnelling Company, RE and the 126th Field Company, RE along with some for the KOYLI's own Signal Test Station. The only light relief during a week of remarkably similar activities that followed was a German aircraft being 'brought down on fire in a fight with one of ours.'[7]

The 7 August saw the battalion move to new positions east of Bullecourt and relieve the 2nd Queen's Regiment. They were settled in by 9.00 p.m., but were cursing the elements twenty-four hours later as a heavy thunderstorm flooded the trenches.

The 9th KOYLI spent eight days in the line: patrols were regularly sent out and two of them met like-minded enemy expeditions in no man's land. One German party of six men dispersed as soon as they were fired upon; another, out repairing their own wire, fled headlong into their trench when faced with similar action. Second-Lieutenant Davis received a slight shoulder wound on 13 August whilst out trying to locate an enemy sniper (who presumably located him!) and the following evening one unnamed soldier had the misfortune to be wounded accidentally, though not seriously, by a Mills bomb that he dug up whilst filling sandbags.

Relief from the line brought with it the inevitable working parties, though an SOS sent up from the front line very early on the morning of 20 August meant that all companies stood to immediately. They had no idea what to expect, but opened up a machine-gun barrage anyway. The enemy made no approach and with no further alarms from the front line, the state of emergency was allowed to lapse amidst the groans and grumbles of those who had lost valuable rest.

The battalion was relieved by the 1st Royal Munster Fusiliers on 26 August and transported by light railway to Boisleux-au-Mont, where they were very pleased to receive a previously unheralded free issue of beer, prior to marching, once more in heavy rain, to a camp east of the town, where a draft of thirty-seven Other Ranks caught up with them. Another march of eight miles, this time in a north-westerly direction, saw them arrive at Simencourt around 5.30 p.m. Those who had managed to dry out their uniform and kit from the previous day needn't have bothered: the meteorological curse struck again; three and a half hours on the road were accompanied by a long and hefty downpour. Waiting for them at Simencourt was a bedraggled draft of another sixty-seven Other Ranks.

Company training dominated the next nineteen days, but light relief was built into the otherwise exacting timetable. On 9 September, the Inter-Unit Football Competition began, with the 9th KOYLI bowing out somewhat ignominiously in the first round by losing 2-0 to the 1st East Yorks team. The 1st East Yorks were subsequently beaten 3-0 in the semi-final by the 10th KOYLI who in turn were roundly defeated in the final by the 15th DLI by five goals to two. Meanwhile, the officers' relay at the Divisional

Gymkhana held at Wagnonlieu was won by the 9th KOYLI team, and on a more practical footing, the Lewis Gun Competition was won by the Durham Light Infantry.

It soon became obvious that the High Command had plans for the 21st Division: practice attacks began to creep into the training timetable, and on 16 September orders were received transferring the Division to X Corps, 2nd Army. The move was immediate: the battalion entrained that morning at 5.00 a.m. and arrived in Cassel, six miles from the Belgian border, at 11.30 a.m. A five-mile march to the south saw them in billets in a farm near Hondeghem. The pace increased; more company training and more practice attacks took place before the first of several moves eastwards towards the sound of the guns. Bivouacs in a field near Thieushouk were home for five days before the battalion met up with the 10th KOYLI on 28 September at Chippawa Camp near Reninghelst, only six miles west of Ypres. German aeroplanes welcomed the newcomers to Belgium by bombing the neighbourhood the following night.

On the last day of the month, the battalion made another move eastwards, this time into the salient proper. They spent the night at railway dugouts, south-west of Zillebeke Lake, before moving up across a shell-pocked wasteland which had been wrested from the Germans inch by inch all through that late summer. Their destination was Polygon Wood; a few tree-stumps and a low, rectangular, man made mound known as the 'Butte' were all that were left of it. Its capture had cost thousands of casualties, many of whom still lay unrecoverable on the battlefield. The battle was ready to move on: another grand effort was required. The assault on the German lines was to be launched on 4 October and the men of the 9th KOYLI would once more be in the front line.

9

PASSCHENDAELE

If the war was cutting into the heart of the nation, the battle of Passchendaele came near to breaking it.[1]

This was General Sir Douglas Haig's chosen ground. He had long-nurtured plans to regain the high ground to the south and east of the small Belgian town known to his men as 'Wipers', ground which had been lost in the desperately fought and very costly 'First and Second Battles of Ypres', in 1914 and 1915 respectively. The British were clinging on to a salient, Ypres at its hub, overlooked from three sides, and stubbornly refused to surrender what was left of this shell-ravaged town, whose symbolic relevance had come to outweigh its strategic importance. Typical of Haig, these ridges were only stage one of his objectives: the British commander once again had the glint of break-through and overall victory in his eyes.

Any immediate riposte to the 1915 losses was rendered impossible by the requirement of the British forces to co-operate with the French plans for that autumn by attacking at Loos. Nine months later, the Somme became top priority, as did Arras in the spring of 1917. The failure of the Nivelle offensive and the subsequent French mutinies meant that the future prosecution of the war on the western front depended solely on the BEF and Haig was finally able to attack not where politics and diplomacy demanded, but across terrain of his own choosing.

Originally, Haig had been convinced that after the attacks of spring 1917, the German forces in Belgium would have been stripped of their reserves, these having been required further south in order to hold back concerted French assaults. The chances of overrun-ning the remnants of an over-stretched Army would never be better.

The proposal would see the British advancing north-eastwards in two phases: firstly as far as Passchendaele ridge and then onwards from there as far as Roulers and Thourout, the former being a vital railway centre whose capture would almost inevitably force a German tactical withdrawal from the Belgian coast and its hinterlands. The second stage would see the attack turning northwards toward the coast. Simultaneously, an amphibious landing would take place behind the German lines. The liberation of the ports of Zeebrugge and Ostend would hand Haig his great strategic victory. The Royal Navy were more than enthusiastic: the channel ports would be protected, Germany's ability to wage submarine warfare would be severely curtailed, 'and most importantly [it would] remove the nightmare of Germany retaining post-war control of the channel ports in any negotiated settlement.'[2]

Planning had begun in earnest in November 1916 when Sir Herbert Plumer, (commanding the Second Army which had been occupying the Ypres Salient since 1915), was asked to submit plans for an offensive the following spring. Initial proposals suggested a preliminary attack to drive the Germans off the Messines–Wytschaete ridge to the south of Ypres, thus depriving them of high ground from which they would overlook and dominate the right flank of the subsequent main assault. These assaults would be 'phased', the rate of advance being dependent upon the speed at which artillery could be moved up to support the next stage. The idea of a phased attack found little favour with the Commander-in-Chief, who perceived it as too reminiscent of the style of the Somme offensive. Haig realised that previous set battles had lacked momentum, and asked the Second Army commander to review his plans accordingly. Clearly unconvinced by Plumer's ability to come up with the goods, and despite Plumer's intimate knowledge of the ground, Haig asked Sir Henry Rawlinson to submit his own ideas.

Plumer and Rawlinson, as it turned out, by the very nature of their plans and recommendations, did themselves out of a job. The advance, at least as far as Roulers, would be a succession of infantry battles, with pauses between to allow artillery to be brought forward in support – 'Bite and Hold' by any other name.

Haig was by now seeking a commander who could share his vision of producing a decisive breakthrough, someone with a more ambitious philosophy: in short, in the language of the period, a 'thruster'. He decided to appoint Sir Hubert Gough, commander of Fifth Army, a cavalryman, young at just forty-seven years of age, a man with little or no knowledge of the Flanders area. Gough was told on 30 April 1917 that he would command the northern part of the operation, that is to say the main assault, the official order confirming this on 13 May. Plumer would be left with the Messines–Wytschaete ridge operations.

Between the above dates, at the Army Commanders' Conference at Doullens on 7 May, it was decided that the 'main blow will be struck by the British forces operating from the Ypres front, with the eventual object of securing the Belgian coast and connecting with the Dutch frontier... There the operations would be continued in two phases: the attack on Messines–Wytschaete Ridge, about 7 June; and 'Northern Operations' to secure the Belgian coast some weeks later.[3]

The permission to go ahead with preparations for 'Third Ypres' had not come from the War Cabinet until 14 March, and on 16 May, they had told Sir Douglas Haig that the Flanders project could only go ahead if the French contributed to the overall picture by launching supporting offensives. On 2 June, however, Pétain, still struggling to rebuild French morale, informed Haig that French support would not be forthcoming (in the end, two French Divisions were able to go into the attack north of Boesinghe). The whole Flanders assault was plunged into doubt.

Nevertheless, the attack on Messines Ridge was going ahead as planned. Sappers had been tunnelling under the ridge since January 1916, and by the time the assault was ready to begin, almost a million tons of explosive were in place, in the form of twenty-four deep mines, under the German lines atop the ridge. The preliminary artillery bombardment had begun on 21 May, with over 2,000 guns pummelling the German lines and artillery positions for over two weeks.

Zero hour was 3.10 a.m. on 7 June, and, on cue, 933,200 tons of ammonal went up, all within a time-span of nineteen seconds, blowing the top of the ridge and thousands of German soldiers into oblivion. Simultaneously, the guns, standing almost axle to axle, opened up a stupendous final barrage.

Eighty thousand assault troops in the leading Divisions left their assembly trenches and advanced across no man's land. For once, enemy machine gun fire and retaliatory shelling were almost non-existent and the first objectives were taken within the allotted thirty-five minutes. Subsequent resistance stiffened, but the ridge and much of its reverse slope were in British hands by 9.00 a.m. 'The situation... was undoubtedly better than even Plumer had dared hope for. Second Army was firmly established along the whole line of the Messines–Wytschaete Ridge from the River Douve to Mount Sorrel.'[4]

By the end of the day, the battle was as good as over; however, the chance to exploit the weaknesses of an enemy on the back foot was lost. Preparations for the next stage, originally measured in hours, were to drag on for weeks. It was not until 19, 21 and 22

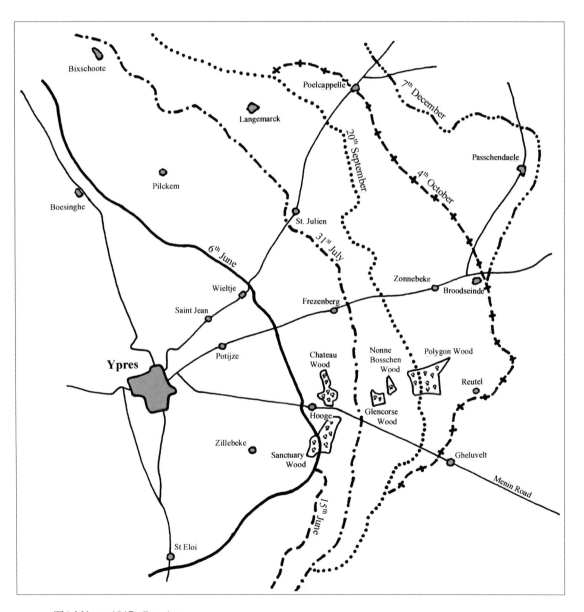

Third Ypres, 1917. Overview.

June that Sir Douglas Haig put his cards on the War Committee's table in person, and it was not until a month later, on 20 July, that a letter from the War Cabinet authorised the Commander-in-Chief to carry out his planned offensive.

Incredibly, the preliminary artillery bombardment had begun four days before this consent was given. This assent contained a caveat. If 'it appeared probable that the results would not be commensurate with the effort made and the losses incurred, the whole question would be re-examined by the War Cabinet with a view to the cessation of the offensive... '[5] They did later assure Haig that his views would be sought before any such decision were taken, but Sir Douglas wrote in reply that the only way to win was to continue attacking, even if the amount of ground gained did not match initial expectations. Zero day was to be 31 July: six weeks of reasonably good campaigning weather had been lost since Messines fell.

The land around Ypres is generally low-lying. The ridges, whose captures were vital to the British operations, were by general standards low and gentle, Gheluvelt Plateau reaching only sixty-four feet at its highest point. Small valleys and woods dotted a landscape crossed by numerous streams, many of them traversing the British line of attack. The land between these streams was kept relatively dry only by a substantial drainage system: artillery bombardment destroyed this system and any rain could quickly turn the salient into a quagmire. It is for such conditions, above all else, that the Passchendaele campaign is remembered.

With the water-table so high, it was impossible for the German defenders to construct the deep dugouts seen on the Somme and at Arras. Instead, a network of concrete emplacements and pill-boxes above ground level became an essential part of enemy defensive strategy (a large number of these still litter the Flanders countryside some eighty years on.)

The preliminary bombardment threw four-and-a-half million shells into the salient, from just over 3,000 guns. At 3.50 a.m. on 31 July, troops from twelve British Divisions advanced on a front of some eleven miles, into mist and rain, which, with impeccable timing, had begun to fall the previous evening.

Substantial progress was made on the first day: XIV Corps in the north captured two German defensive lines at the cost of only 750 fatal casualties. Pilckem Ridge had been taken and the line of the Steenbeek reached, an advance of 3,000 yards. Further south, 39th Division (XVIII Corps) crossed the stream and captured the village of St Julien. To their right, XIX Corps made the greatest initial advance of the day: three defensive lines fell to them as they advanced 4,000 yards – some advanced parties were only the same distance from Passchendaele itself.

Unfortunately, the right-hand Division of the Corps, 15th Division, was taking enemy fire from the right rear. This could only mean one thing: the attack on II Corps front had not gone too well. II Corps was to advance across the Gheluvelt Plateau. Initially, the left flank of the Corps made reasonable advances, Château Wood and Bellewaarde Ridge being overrun. Unfortunately, to their right, Nonne Boschen and Glencorse Woods had not fallen to the 30th Division and troops in strong points there were able to enfilade the more successful British troops, forcing them to fall back to more practical defensive positions. Difficult ground conditions and the thus inevitable loss of the creeping barrage meant that the right-hand portion of the attacking front had stalled by 7.00 a.m. after an advance of no more than 1,000 yards. Later in the day, German counter-attacks enjoyed some measure of success in the centre. St Julien had to be relinquished, but the line of the Steenbeek was the extent of the British withdrawal.

The weather broke well and truly that evening and the rain did not stop for a week. Gough renewed his efforts on the Gheluvelt Plateau, but the terrain became so difficult that the troops' best efforts were mostly in vain.

The battle progressed through the late summer and early autumn in stages. It had been originally envisaged that Roulers would be reached by 7 or 8 August. It was not until the 16th that any substantial attempt could be made to improve on the gains of the first day of the campaign. The Battle of Langemarck, as this phase became known, ran for three days. The ruins of the village after which the battle was named were taken, but on the right 'a heavy price was paid for nought'.[6]

Following further attacks on 22 and 24 August, the Fifth Army had suffered 60,000 casualties and the Gheluvelt Plateau remained in enemy hands. Rain began to fall on the 23rd and by the 28th the salient was once more reduced to a swamp. General Gough informed his Commander-in-Chief that he believed that under the prevailing conditions, the campaign should be abandoned.

Haig, persuaded partly by his Intelligence Chief Charteris' insistence that German morale was deteriorating, and in line with his own attitude as expressed in his aforementioned letter to the War Cabinet, decided that the battle should continue. However, he determined that the effort on the Gheluvelt Plateau should fall to Plumer and his Second Army. Gough's Fifth Army would play a more subsidiary role from now on in the north.

Plumer submitted his plans for the continuation of the battle on 29 August. Basically, it consisted of a series of limited set-piece battles, each requiring an advance of about 1,500 yards. The first of these would be launched on 20 September. The infantry advanced at 5.40 a.m. after a three-week artillery bombardment and had taken most of its objectives by midday. German counter-attacks were repulsed, and the salient drew breath and awaited the next phase of the assault. Up to this point, the British front line had advanced about three-and-a-half miles at a cost of 86,000 casualties: Roulers and Thourout were still between twelve and seventeen miles away.

On 26 September the Battle of Polygon Wood was launched. In the north, XVIII Corps was to establish a defensive flank near Aviatik Farm, while V Corps would take the ruins of the village of Zonnebeke. First Anzac Corps would capture what was left of Polygon Wood as X Corps on the right aimed for the high ground around Tower Hamlets. For once, the artillery barrage which fell on the German positions on the morning of the attack raised a 'dense wall of dust and smoke'[7]. The ground was dry after several days of good weather. Zero hour was 5.50 a.m.

All did not go well. In the north, the mist was so bad, visibility being down to thirty yards, that the attacking troops lost direction and were only able to advance 100 yards. In the south, the ground remained boggy and troops could not keep up with the creeping barrage: Tower Hamlets remained in enemy hands.

The main objective lay in the centre. The Anzacs followed their barrage into Polygon Wood. Resistance from strong points and pill-boxes was unable to check the advance and two platoons reached the Butte. Bombing parties worked their way through the tunnels and galleries: finally, the remaining fifty-eight Germans inside surrendered. Other battalions leapfrogged their compatriots and the final objectives just to the east of the wood were reached before 9.00 a.m. By the end of the day, a victory could be claimed: final objectives had been gained across most of the front, and nine enemy counter-attacks had been successfully repulsed. The cost: 15,375 casualties.[8]

The third stage of Plumer's campaign was brought forward two days to 4 October. Haig's optimism, the perceived state of the enemy and good weather were the decisive

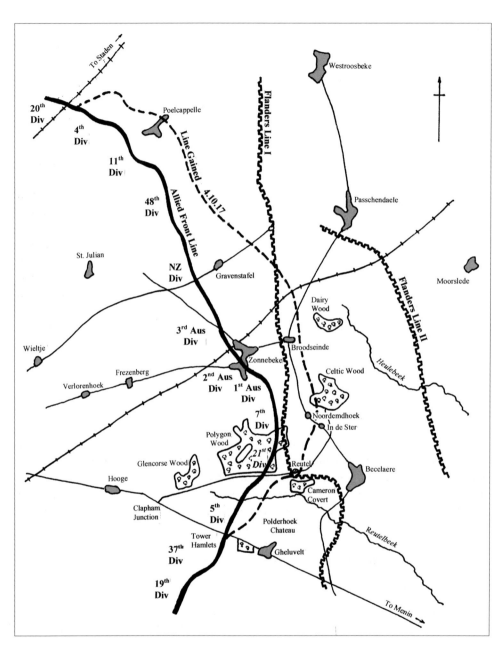

Battle of Broodseinde, 4 October 1917.

factors in this move. Haig had not yet ruled out the final exploitation, including the amphibious landings. This required a further advance of twenty miles.

As he explained to Plumer and Gough on 28 September, this next planned step would complete a definite phase in the operation: subsequent battles would not necessarily be strictly limited in their scope. The two Army commanders were not convinced.

The main assault on 4 October would be by four Divisions of the Anzac Corps in the centre. I Corps, under Birdwood, was to capture the Broodseinde Ridge on a 2,000-yard frontage astride the Moorslede road. II Corps, under Godley's command, was to overrun the Gravenstafel spur on a frontage of 3,000 yards.

On the left, the Fifth Army was destined to attack towards the village of Poelcapelle, using four Divisions (left to right the 20th, 4th, 11th and 48th), their left flank resting on the Ypres–Staden railway. The right flank of the Anzac attack was to be protected by a simultaneous advance of X Corps (Morland), to the eastern edge of the Gheluvelt Plateau, an average distance of some 1,200 yards. On the 1,400-yard frontage, Plumer intended to use both reserve Divisions of X Corps, the 7th and 21st. These were to take and hold the In der Ster and Reutel areas in order to prevent the Germans being able to observe and dominate the flank of the main attack.

Haig made the suggestion that the ground north of the Menin Road not taken in the previous assault should be added to the plan of attack. Fifth Division was accordingly transferred to X Corps for the purpose. The southern defensive flank would be formed by 37th Division of IX Corps. This made a total of twelve Divisions spread over a frontage of 14,000 yards.

Plans for the artillery bombardment were designed to give the enemy no clue as to when the attack would commence. The Menin road assault (20 September), had been preceded by a seven-day bombardment. The Battle of Polygon Wood (26 September), enjoyed a twenty-four-hour overture. Other than normal counter-battery work, however, the Battle of Broodseinde was to have no preliminary bombardment. The barrage would commence at Zero hour.

The troops already in the British front-line trenches had to repulse several small German attacks during the first few days of October before the assault brigades marched up to relieve them on the evening of the third. Fears that the reasonable weather might break were heightened by the presence of a strong south-westerly wind with its accompanying rain showers, which had sprung up around dusk. As the men marched up, most used the duckboard tracks to avoid ground made greasy by the evening precipitation.

The 9th KOYLI had received their orders to move up earlier than most. At 5.00 p.m. on 1 October they were ordered to be at the disposal of 110th Brigade who were holding a line along the track running north–south along the eastern edge of Polygon Wood. This move was in response to German attacks made that morning on the front held by 110th Brigade. The 9th Leicesters in the front line had been forced to concede some ground at first, but managed to regain it when Lt-Col. Bent personally led a counter-attack, which succeeded in recapturing the original positions: he was killed upon reaching this objective, but his actions gained him a posthumous Victoria Cross.

The 9th KOYLI reached Clapham Junction on the Menin Road, about two kilometres to the west of the British front line, by 11.00 p.m., sustaining no casualties on the way. They remained there until 8.00 p.m. on 2 October, sustaining one fatality, 35704 Pte A. Frost, whereupon they began the relief of the 9th Leicesters. This was complete by 11.00 p.m. The battalion held the front-line trench for the next twenty-four hours under continuous heavy shelling. About fifty casualties were reported, many of them

View back to Joist Farm and Polygon Wood from near Reutel Village. (Present day)

designated as shell-shock. Four were, however, fatal: 9307 Cpl Stangroom, 42997 Cpl Thompson, 43990 Pte Bidwell and 43553 Pte Edwin Stocks. Only the last named of these has a known grave (in Hooge Crater Cemetery), the rest being commemorated on the Tyne Cot Memorial.

During the darkness of the early morning of 4 October, the 9th KOYLI troops took up their battle positions in the assembly trenches. They were ready and waiting by 5.00 a.m. As usual, a percentage of the officers and men were kept back in reserve away from the front line to act as either readily available reinforcements or, if the worst should happen, a nucleus around which the battalion could be rebuilt. This time, Lt Ellenberger was among them. On 3 October he wrote home: '... we live in stirring times. But you needn't bother about me as I am at present on the 'nucleus' – i.e. a sort of reserve the same as Spicer on July 1st though the idea is carried to even greater lengths now than it was then.'[9]

In front of the 9th KOYLI troops, directly across their line of advance, was the shallow valley of the Polygonbeek. The ground sloped gently down to this streambed for some 500 yards. The far bank rose more steeply for a further 300 yards. The village of Reutel lay just out of sight over the crest, behind the crossroads that marked the KOYLI's objective (see map).

The nature of the ground over which they were to advance – would it be dry or not? – weighed heavily on the minds of those who would lead the attack. Throughout the summer, rain had appeared with almost malevolent regularity. Just as the British mounted an attack and made some progress, the weather would turn the ground into a morass and movement of any kind became almost impossible. As previously mentioned, however, the days leading up to this attack had been dry. Harold Yeo, in a letter home dated 1 October 1917, wrote: 'Thousands of flies and tons of dust are the chief features of the situation.'[10]

A report from 21st Division on this subject reads: 'The ground presents no formidable natural obstacles. Going should be extremely good on the high ground, and though the low ground is rather wet in places, and the Reutelbeek and Polygonbeek are broken up by shell fire, it ought not to be difficult to make headway.'[11] In an hour's time, the infantry would find out for themselves the true state of affairs.

At 5.20 a.m. the British front line was hit by a German artillery barrage. What the British did not know was that the enemy was planning to attack that same morning. [The original date for the German attack was to have been 3 October, but this had been put back by one day.] The bombardment was particularly heavy on the assembly trenches of the two Anzac corps: I Anzac Corps suffered casualties estimated at 1 in 7 in the forty minutes prior to the assault.

Six o'clock saw the British barrage crash down on the whole depth of the German positions, pre-empting the enemy assault and catching many of the German soldiers in relatively open assembly positions. The British forces left their trenches and went forward in groups or columns as rehearsed.

On the left flank, the XIV Corps were forced to attempt to cross terrain turned into a swamp by the shelling. Bogged down and raked by machine-gun fire, they lost the protection of the creeping barrage and failed to reach and hold their objectives, losing over 1,600 casualties in the process. To their right, the main attack in the Fifth Army area was made by Maxse's XVIII Corps. The 11th and 48th Divisions' main objective was the village of Poelcapelle. With the help of a dozen tanks, they were successful in

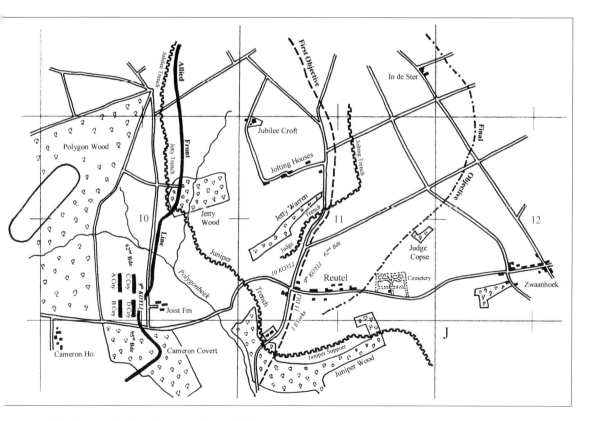

64th Brigade. Attack on Reutel, 4 October 1917.

capturing all but the very northern edge of the village at a cost of just over 2,600 casualties.

In the centre, the II Anzac Corps (3rd Australian and New Zealand Divisions), went forward. Despite suffering severe shelling as their attack began, the New Zealanders succeeded in crossing the Hannebeek swamp and managed to capture strong points behind Gravenstafel, taking over 1,100 prisoners as they did so. The 3rd Australian Division swept over Hill 40 following their 'excellent' barrage, reaching their final objectives by about 9.00 a.m.

On their right, I Anzac Corps (2nd and 1st Australian Divisions) also fared well. Despite their initial casualties, the 1st Division swept over the crest of Broodseinde Ridge and the pill-boxes of the Flanders I defensive line and on to the final objective 400 yards further on. The proposed one-hour halt at 7.15 a.m. before the second stage of the advance was deemed unnecessary and by 8.10 a.m., the struggle was as good as over. The 2nd Division captured the ruins of Zonnebeke and pushed on to take what was left of the hamlet of Broodseinde. The exposed nature of their final positions prompted their commanders to decide to dig in along an old British trench line, last occupied in the winter of 1914-15, about 200 yards short of their final objective. The four Anzac Divisions had paid the price of over 8,000 casualties for their success.

On the extreme right of the British frontage, IX Corps failed to capture Gheluvelt Wood and the Tower Hamlets spur. On the right of X Corps, 5th Division was able to occupy Cameron Covert and Polderhoek Chateau, though the latter had to be given up by nightfall. Seventh Division, on the left of X Corps, managed to keep in touch with the Australians on their left and were able to advance their 20th Brigade as far as the plateau edge between Noordemdhoek and In der Ster Cabaret, some 1,500 yards. The 91st Brigade on its right kept pace and it too ended the day overlooking the Heulebeek depression.

The 9th KOYLI lined up for the attack with 'C' and 'D' Companies in front, left and right respectively, 'A' and 'B' Companies likewise behind them. The 3/4th Queens of 62nd Brigade were on their left, the 2nd DCLI of 95th Brigade, 5th Division on their right. Directly behind them, the 10th KOYLI formed up, ready to pass through and capture the second objective, which included the village of Reutel (see map). 1st East Yorks were in support, and 15th DLI in reserve.

Waiting for the off, two sources of annoyance were evident. Twice they were bombarded by the German artillery, at midnight and at 5.30 a.m., and probably equally galling was the fact that the rations and the rum were late. Enemy shelling of the rear areas from east of Polygon Wood to Clapham Junction meant that the attacking troops were effectively cut off. It was not until 8.00 p.m. that a carrying party under the command of 2nd-Lt H.N. Teaz made it up to the line with water and small arms ammunition.

'We were in position by 5.00 a.m. with our leading waves fifty yards behind the road running north and south in J.10.d. We were in touch with our flank battalions.'[12] Thus wrote Capt. J.H. Frank and Capt. A.E. Day of 9th KOYLI in an account penned six days after the action. The rear-most waves of 'A' and 'B' Companies were some 160 yards behind them. The men of the battalion were to find, as they advanced, that the valley of the Polygonbeek was far from dry:

This sector was broken by the Polygonbeek... and the Reutelbeek, which drain this south-eastern corner of the plateau. Normally a few feet wide and a few inches deep, the bed of these brooks, broken by shell craters, had become belts of oozing mud of uncertain depth; joining near the objective, they

9th KOYLI graves from October 1917.

formed a muddy valley of well over half a mile wide between Reutel village and Polderhoek spur to the south.[13]

The two captains take up the narrative again (the grammar is their own!):

Just before six o'clock all was more or less quiet, at zero the barrage opened with a fearsome noise and we leapt from our shell holes and went forward in snake formation. It was the darkness that precedes the dawn and one could recognise nobody. We are thankful to say that we got away from our own assembly positions before the full force of the German barrage descended – but were immediately subjected to a withering machine-gun fire, men were falling right and left but, who cared?, our one care was to get forward. Joist Farm proved to be our first stumbling block and was a tough nut to crack. Even when our left had reached the swamp lights were being fired at us from this point which was eventually mopped up by two sections of 'D' Coy under Capt. Sykes and one section of 'B' Coy under Sgt Pyott. This place was found to contain one officer, twelve men and four machine guns. As soon as we left our assembly positions we found a party of DCLI crossing our front to the north, it is evident that this battalion completely lost direction.

The swamp proved a veritable death trap we were up to our knees in slush and at the same time subjected to enfilade machine gun fire from the right. A small strongpoint not concreted and immediately on the west bank of the swamp we took by surprise and the garrison surrendered without firing a shot. On the same bank were a considerable number of German bivouacs constructed of 'elephants' and filled with Germans, most of these had been blown in by our bombardment. The remainder containing Germans were bombed by our men and the Germans shot as they ran out. On the east side the ground rose rapidly and contained a number of concreted strongpoints two of which were in our area. These fired at us until we were within 50 yards. The garrisons then surrendered, the majority of them being bombed and shot. The left strongpoint turned out to be battalion HQ and was an elaborate concern. Each contained two machine guns.

Juniper Trench was strongly held but the garrison preferred to retire rather than fight. 2nd-Lt. [L.B.] Spicer by a quick manoeuvre cut off the majority of these who gave themselves up to him. On the right the garrison showed a little more pluck and attempted to counter-attack us. They were immediately squashed by 'D' Coy, after attacking these strongpoints we received little opposition until our objective was reached.[14]

Communications with the rear were proving difficult. It was not until 10.40 a.m. that the first report from 9th KOYLI was received by Division, this being to the effect that the battalion had secured its objective and that 10th KOYLI along with a single company from the 1st East Yorks were advancing on their final objectives at 9.10 a.m.

Frank and Day's report goes on to say that the troops of 64th Brigade were completely mixed up by this point: a considerable number of Northumberland Fusiliers and men from the Queen's were sharing their positions. A strongpoint on the eastern edge of Reutel was also proving to be a considerable nuisance. It was eventually knocked out by a tank. The assistance rendered by tanks during this attack was confirmed by part of the 21st Division's Operations Report:

11.30 a.m. a message received from 64th Brigade that a tank had just returned from Reutel. It had been through the village to the cemetery, and was followed by infantry, but returned after being hit. Another tank had proceeded to engage a strong point North of Reutel.[15]

The captains' narrative takes us further:

It was at this time that we realised that our right flank was absolutely in the air, At the allotted time, the 10th [KOYLI] and NF's attempted to go forward to the eastern extremity of the village,

Name of 9th KOYLI Commanding officer Lieutenant-Colonel Neville Reay Daniell on the Tyne Cot Memorial.

they were not successful and we dug in slightly in advance of our first objective, i.e. 100 yds in front of the road running N and S on the western extremity of the village. We were in touch with the NF's on our left. We were now joined by the remnants of one Coy of the 15th DLI and one Coy of the East Yorks: these were sent out to the right to form a defensive flank... [16]

Reports from the rear positions confirm that German prisoners began to trickle back within half an hour of Zero. At 7.00 a.m., however, the enemy laid down an intense barrage on the rear positions, once more as far back as Clapham Junction. It was impossible to move Battalion HQ forwards, and no communication could be established with the front line. Capts Frank and Day continue:

About noon the enemy commenced to advance up the valley out of the village of Gheluvelt and massed about the road in front of POLDERHOEK CHATEAU about J.16.d.8.10 this continued until about 3 in the afternoon. We should say at least 3 battalions left the village. We sent out a party under 2nd-Lt Spicer with two Lewis Guns and one Vickers to flank the advancing enemy and get enfilade fire to bear on them, later in the day this party disappeared and that evening, we searched the ground both to the right of us and in front of the village for signs of them or their bodies but found nothing. We can only conclude that they were cut off and probably taken prisoners. [17]

Another party of about one platoon strength under 2nd-Lt Burton was also sent out with similar orders. This party eventually returned, but Spicer's group was never seen again. Spicer's death was later confirmed, but he has no known grave, being commemorated on the Tyne Cot Memorial.

'As a result of this counter-attack the Germans got up a machine gun to POLDER-HOEK CHATEAU and this gun persistently fired at us in the rear.'[18] Fearing more counter-attacks, the front-line troops in their precarious positions on the outskirts of Reutel sent up an SOS signal at 9.30 p.m. and the British artillery opened up accordingly. In reply, Polygon Wood and the rear areas were once more heavily bombarded by the enemy's guns. During this bombardment, at about 10.30 p.m., a German shell exploded at the entrance of 9th KOYLI Battalion Headquarters. The signalling corporal was killed outright and both the signalling officer and intelligence officer wounded. The commanding officer, Lt-Col. Daniell DSO, was hit by shrapnel in the stomach and right thigh. The wounds proved mortal. Inexplicably, the twenty-eight-year-old lieutenant-colonel has no known grave and is commemorated on the Tyne Cot Memorial.[19] On the orders of the Brigadier, Lt-Col. Festing, CO 10th KOYLI took command of both battalions.

During the night, the two KOYLI battalions combined to dig one line of defence. The 1st East Yorks continued to the south and faced south-east as there was still a gap of some 700 yards to the next Division. The next morning, Capt. A.E. Day, now in command of the forward troops of both KOYLI battalions, had an estimated 150 rifles at his disposal. (Some of the Yorkshiremen were still mixed up with other units in the locality.) Large numbers of German soldiers were seen in Reutel. Fearing a counter-attack, the KOYLIs opened up with their Lewis guns, dispersing the enemy force. KOYLI snipers were busy for the rest of the day.

On the night of 5/6 October, reserve officers were sent forward by Lt-Col. Festing, and on the evening of the 6th, commencing at 9.00 p.m., 64th Brigade was relieved by troops of the 7th Leicesters. The last unit of the battalion reached the relative safety of Railway Dugouts at about 4.00 a.m. on the morning of the 7th. 'Numbers here amounted to 120 all ranks.'[20] That evening, the remnants of the battalion were in bivouacs in Scottish Wood near the transport lines. Major Harry Greenwood MC took command of the battalion.

The 64th Brigade had suffered heavily in its efforts of the previous days, but '[their] success gave possession of a dominant position overlooking the Reutel valley to the north-east, and so completed the security of the southern flank of the main Broodseinde battlefront.'[21]

The Official History puts 64th Brigade casualties at sixty-one officers and 1,293 Other Ranks.

Appendix I shows that the 9th KOYLI fatal casualties from 3 to 6 October 1917 number 103, eight of them officers.

10

WINTER 1917-1918

The Battle of Third Ypres rumbled on with no further direct involvement for the 21st Division. On 6 November, the patch of ground, 'a pile of bricks with a ruin of a church, a mass of slaughtered masonry and nothing else left on this steel-swept height',[1] where once stood the village of Passchendaele, was finally taken by the 2nd Canadian Division. On 10 November, Third Ypres officially ended. Taking this final stretch of ridge had cost the Canadians over 1,200 casualties.

The entire battle had cost the Second and Fifth Armies 244,897 casualties killed, wounded and missing. The bodies of over 40,000 of these were never found. They have no known graves, but are commemorated on seemingly endless walls of stone at Tyne Cot Cemetery and elsewhere. Of the 103 fatal casualties suffered by the 9th KOYLI between 3 and 6 October 1917, as quoted in the previous chapter, seventy-seven have their names carved on one of the huge white tablets at Tyne Cot.

As the remnants of the 9th KOYLI licked their wounds in Scottish Wood on 7 October 1917, Harold Yeo wrote home: '… met Arthur Frost on the afternoon of the 4th... and he was slightly wounded in the hand. He was quite cheery and I told him the way to Blighty via a motor ambulance... It is beastly weather and keeps pouring with rain. Our region is subsequently all mud.'[2] The following day, Arthur Frost appeared as a statistic in the Battalion War Diary which listed total casualties, killed, wounded and missing since 1 October as twenty officers (though two of these had remained at duty), and 360 Other Ranks.

By this time, Maj. Harry Greenwood MC had taken command of the battalion and had marched his men to the railhead at Ouderdom, five miles south-west of Ypres, where they met up with the nucleus of the battalion which had been kept out of the line before the battle. Reunited, they boarded a train which took them further to the south-west, into France and on as far as Ebblinghem, a small village a few miles east of St Omer, arriving at four o'clock on the morning of 9 October. The next three days were spent resting, refitting and, no doubt, reflecting. Lengthy introspection was not the order of the day, however, and on the 12th, working parties were taken by bus back into the salient to bivouacs at Ridge Wood, near Zillebeke, where they were attached to the X Corps ADS and were put to work laying cables. They were supposed to work from 9.30 a.m. to 5.00 p.m., but enemy artillery fire disrupted this pattern. Heavy shelling on the 14th cost the battalion two fatal casualties, 34450 Pte Thomas Rochford and 23892 Pte Herbert Rollinson, along with an unspecified number of wounded. Little work could be done on the 15th and 16th as the enemy shelling continued. The next day, after parading at 3.00 a.m., the working parties went even further forward to work in Glencorse Wood, just east of Clapham Junction. The cost of this excursion was one more fatality; 39742 Pte William Brown. Private Brown's body was recovered and now lies in Ypres Reservoir Cemetery. A quiet day and the possibility of taking a bath on the 19th were a precursor to a move back into the trenches. Fate decreed that they would relieve the 13th DLI in trenches near Reutel. The 15th DLI were in trenches immediately to the north. The relief was complete by 9.15 p.m., though news of this did not reach HQ until seven o'clock the following morning due to runners losing their way in the dark wilderness. Heavy shelling had accompanied the battalion's arrival back in the front line but only one man was wounded as a result of this. Between 4.00 a.m. and 7.00 a.m. the following day, the Germans shelled the KOYLI positions very heavily. 'C' Company caught the worst of the bombardment and nine men were killed that morning. Two more were to join the list of fatalities before the battalion was relieved the following afternoon. One of the guides leading the battalion to the rear lost his way, and 'A' Company dutifully went with him. It was not until the following morning that the whole battalion had found its way back to Railway Dugouts. The weather continued very wet and the camp was soon ankle deep in mud.

Brigades in the front line were being shuffled: as a result of this, the 64th Brigade was to take over the left brigade front of the Divisional sector. In practical terms this involved the 9th KOYLI moving forward to relieve the 1st Lincs in the front line. The march commenced at 2.20 p.m. on the last day of October. They passed Hooge Crater at about 4.00 p.m. and it was realised that the enemy had spotted the troop movements and had heavily shelled the 15th DLI who were en route ahead of the Yorkshiremen, their gas shells causing a number of casualties. The KOYLIs halted for fifteen minutes, put on their gas masks, and then continued on their way. Several men became casualties after losing their way in the darkness and falling into shell holes. Their gas masks either became dislodged or they removed them in their efforts to clamber back out. The eventual order to remove their masks must have been received with genuine relief when it was given as they approached the Butte in Polygon Wood. A sudden fall of more gas shells at this point however caught some of the men unprotected and further casualties ensued.

With the Battalion HQ at the Butte, the men spent the next four days in the front-line trench system. Heavy shelling on the 1st of the month caused no casualties as the majority of the enemy shells fell either neatly between the front and support lines or to the rear of the latter. On the 4th, however, during an enemy bombardment which had commenced at 5.30 a.m., one shell fell directly onto the support line, killing 2nd-Lts Hawling and Niven, along with 39752 Pte Charles Gellatly and 9344 L/Cpl Leonard Simpson. By 9.00 p.m., the battalion had been relieved by the 10th KOYLI; 'A' and 'C' Companies remained in support, but 'B' and 'D' Companies were back at Railway Dugouts. Two more uneventful days past before further relief saw 'B' and 'D' Companies in new hutments at Café Belge Camp (H29 b 8.3) and 'A' and 'C' Companies in similar luxury at Forrester Camp (I25 a 2.4).

On 10 November, Lt-Col. A.J. McCulloch arrived and took command of the battalion. Two days later, it was reunited at Cornwall Camp, Ouderdom. Route marches and company training occupied the next four days and on 17 November, the 21st Division commenced its transfer to First Army. The move was to be made, in practical geographical terms, by a series of route marches lasting five days.

The 9th KOYLI left Ouderdom at 10.00 a.m. on 17 November, and marched south to Steenwerk, arriving in fine weather just over four hours later. Moving via Neuf

Berquin, two days later the battalion was in billets in Annezin, just west of Béthune. By 20 November, the men were further south still, this time in hutments in Compigny. They had been reviewed on the march by the Divisional Commander just outside Béthune, and McCulloch was, as ever, congratulated on the appearance of the men.

The village of Compigny received the attention of enemy gunners as they sent over high-explosive shells at half-hour intervals. Some casualties were caused within the brigade, but 9th KOYLI remained unscathed. The weather had been kind up to this point, but on the 21st, the slog from Compigny to Lancaster Camp was made under continuous rain. Despite the poor conditions, the War Diary was able to make the proud boast that not one man fell out during the march.

The 21st Division was in reserve to the 31st Division in the line opposite Oppy. A training programme commenced on the 23rd; the following day a draft of 156 Other Ranks and two officers arrived and were immediately inspected by the new CO. A training schedule was worked out for each company as follows:

'A' Company	'B' Company
9.00 a.m. to 1.00 p.m.	9.00 a.m. to 11.00 a.m.
Musketry and Lewis Gun	Close order drill, arms drill,
Instruction and range practice.	Saluting.
Bray Range available from	12.00 noon to 1.30 p.m.
10.30 a.m. to noon.	Musketry and Lewis Gun
	Instruction and range practice.
	Mt. St Eloy range.

'C' Company	'D' Company
9.00 a.m. to 1.00 p.m.	9.00 a.m. to 1.00 p.m.
Wiring and bombing.	Close order drill and PT and BF.
Bombing ground at F7 a 7.0	PT and BF Ground at F15 c 2.8
available from 11.00 a.m. to 1.00 p.m.	available from 11.00 a.m. to 1.00 p.m.

This schedule would rotate in the days following to allow each company to experience all the facilities and activities.

The battalion was able to enjoy a concert on the evening of 28 November, but by this time it had received a warning order that it was to be prepared to move at short notice. The morning after the concert, these orders came into force: the battalion was to be ready to move to an as yet unknown destination on 3 December. The move was in the end brought forward to the 1st of the month, a draft of fifteen signallers arriving just in time to accompany the battalion to Savy, where it would board a train bound for Tincourt, two miles east of Péronne, arriving there shortly after noon. The following day, the men moved a few miles north-east into an RFC Camp at Longavesnes.

On 3 December, the battalion was back in the front line, having relieved the 1st East Yorks in trenches to the east of Epéhy. On 8 December, Lt Ellenberger wrote home describing the battalion's new surroundings: 'There is a distinct resemblance to open warfare. The ground in front of me is full of dead cavalry horses and the Bosches are the best part of a mile away'.[3] He resisted the temptation to paint a completely optimistic picture, however, adding that the weather was bitterly cold and frosty, and remarking that he had not seen his kit nor been able to take his clothes off for over a week.

The 9th KOYLI were in the front line near Vaucelette Farm by 5.00 p.m. on 21 December. The 15th DLI were to the south, the 1st East Yorks to the north. They were to occupy these positions over the Christmas period. The weather was still very cold, but it was fine, and the enemy was quiet.

Ellenberger found time to write home again on the 18th, stating: 'We are pretty comfortable, and this is a 'cushy' section.'[4] 'Cushy' or not, reminders that they were at war were ever present. On the evening of the 23rd, Lt Chalk took out a patrol made up of nine members of 'A' Company and attacked an enemy post garrisoned by around 30 Germans. They had the element of surprise on their side and managed to bomb the enemy dugouts, killing at least three. Enemy reinforcements were quick to arrive, however, and the KOYLI patrol withdrew in the face of by now vastly superior numbers, being forced, reluctantly, to abandon a captured machine gun. The KOYLI force suffered no casualties. German artillery was busy early the next morning and 9th KOYLI suffered one fatal casualty that Christmas Eve: 13811 Pte William Longworth. He is buried in Heudicourt Communal Cemetery Extension.

Christmas Day saw a slight thaw set in, and the Germans shelled Vaucelette Farm during the morning. The War Diary noted that 'no attempts at fraternisation by the enemy were observed. He still remains hostile.'[5] Frost set in on Boxing Day as the battalion was relieved by the 3/4th Queen's. By the evening they were in Middlesex Camp at Heudicourt. The following day, the men were able to enjoy a belated Christmas dinner, thanks to the profits from the Regimental Canteen and a donation of £100 from A. Wynne, treasurer of the KOYLI War Fund being made available to finance the event. Ellenberger was absent, however. He had felt ill on Boxing Day, and a visit to the doctor had revealed a temperature of 102°, resulting in a stay in the casualty Clearing Station hospital. He wrote home on the 28th: 'Rotten luck as yesterday (27th) the battalion was having its Xmas dinner, two big fat pigs for the men and turkeys for the officers... the old story – a touch of Trench fever.'[6]

Festivities were soured, however, by events late that evening. At around 11.00 p.m., a German artillery shell fell in the camp, severely wounding 'C' Company's Quartermaster Sergeant. 15445 CQMS John Pollard DCM died of his wounds three days later.

The year ended quietly. The Battalion Concert Party entertained the men on New Year's Eve, and McCulloch went off on a commanding officers' course at the 5th Army School, leaving Maj. H. Greenwood in charge.

The New Year dawned with the 9th KOYLI still in Middlesex Camp: the adjutant was able to enter 'Nothing to report' in the War Diary for the first two days of 1918. The rest of the month was likewise relatively uneventful. The men had to put up with blizzards, subsequent thaws and the inevitable digging and repairing of trenches that naturally ensued from such meteorological vagaries. By 16 January, the War Diary was describing the trenches as 'practically untenable due to the thaw.'[7] The following day saw the men doing their best to maintain and repair them. The Diary adds: 'Enemy v. quiet and apparently in as much trouble over the trenches as we are, as he allowed our men to expose themselves without shooting at them.'[8]

The KOYLIs were out of the trenches by the 20th and at Haut Allaines were able to rest and refit, bathe and practise their musketry skills on a thirty-yard miniature range. On the 25th, they were moved to huts in Gurlu Wood, where for the next week they were employed, 300 at a time, in digging a defensive line which would be given the code 'Green Line'. This gainful employment continued into February.

On 6 February, the 9th KOYLI War Diary notes that a draft of twelve officers and 250 Other Ranks were transferred from 10th KOYLI on their disbandment. The background to this apparent drastic turn of events is as follows: following the 1917 battles at Arras, Ypres and Cambrai, the BEF was quite simply short of men. In response to Haig's demands for appropriate reinforcements to bring his units up to strength, Lloyd George and his War Cabinet proposed a scheme which would indeed bring units up to strength, but would not entail providing any extra men. The British Division had traditionally consisted of twelve battalions. As from January/February 1918, this number would be reduced to nine, requiring each brigade within a Division to lose one battalion. Throughout the BEF, this required the disbanding of 141 battalions and the subsequent redistribution of the men thus freed up. Consequently, the 10th KOYLI drew the short straw and ceased to exist. The 64th Brigade was now made up of 9th KOYLI, 1st East Yorks and 15th DLI only. The problem was, however, that three battalions were expected to do exactly the same job as had previously been done by four.

February's round of reliefs, working parties, patrols, along with the novelty of some tunnelling, had little of note to punctuate a relatively routine time in and out of the trenches. By the 17th, half the battalion was bathing while the remainder were at Divine Service, the men having been relieved by the 2nd Battalion Royal Irish Regiment. The battalion was not to enter a trench for the rest of the month. Drill of varying kinds was practised, musketry skills were honed on the firing range and on the 27th the 15th DLI won the Brigade Football Competition by beating the 9th KOYLI 4-0 in the final.

On the same day, the CO and the company commanders reconnoitred the section of the line held by the 2nd Munster Fusiliers with the intention of taking over on 1 March. The next day, 28 February, the battalion entrained at Aizecourt-le-Haut, north of Péronne, and was soon at Ambush Camp in Saulcourt, thus being able to take up 'Battle Positions' in Guyencourt, behind Epéhy, with the 64th Brigade in Divisional Reserve. On 2 March, they were issued with orders detailing the course of action to be taken in the way of counter-attack should the forward areas need either reinforcement or something altogether more drastic.

Despite the obvious rise in the levels of tension along the front as the BEF held its breath in anticipation of a massive German assault, the positions held by the 64th Brigade were far enough to the rear to allow for some vestiges of 'normality' to persist. A football match on 4 March against the 1st East Yorks saw the 9th KOYLI lose once more, this time 3-1. Two companies per day were working on defensive positions, while the other two took part in training exercises. On the 12th, the battalion was able to start work on its own two-acre agricultural plot at the transport line camp, but on the 15th, the War Diary notes that captured German prisoners had revealed that a large German offensive was imminent. Numerous raiding parties were organised and sent out to try and capture anyone who could put an exact date on the apparently inevitable attack. A prisoner caught by 62nd Brigade said that the assault was due about 20 March.

On the 19th, the battalion was allocated positions in the 'Brown Line' in case events necessitated them actually occupying it, and at 5.00 a.m. the CO instigated a practice alarm. The speed of turn out was not up to the mark and company commanders held a conference on the subject.

On the 20th, the CO was working on plans for a two-company-strength raid, this to be supported by a strong artillery barrage, along with covering trench-mortar and machine-gun fire. Events were to pre-empt this adventure. At 4.30 a.m. on the morning of 21 March, the commencement of a 'slight' enemy bombardment of small-calibre guns was noticed. Intensity increased until by 5.00 a.m. 5.9's were dropping freely around the 64th Brigade positions.

The 9th KOYLI had had no one 'killed in action' since Christmas Eve. The gods of war were about to redress the balance.

11

KAISERSCHLACHT[*]

On 3 December 1917, Sir Douglas Haig spoke to a gathering of his Army commanders. With the situation both in Italy and Russia in mind, he was forced to conclude that this,

... combined with the paucity of reinforcements which we are likely to receive, will in all probability necessitate our adopting a defensive attitude for the next few months. We must be prepared to meet a strong and sustained hostile offensive. It is therefore of first importance that Army commanders should give their immediate and personal attention to the organisation of the zones for defensive purposes and to the rest and training of their troops.[1]

Why was Haig forced to make 'defence' the BEF's priority for the start of 1918? Since becoming Commander-in-Chief, his overriding philosophy had been one of attack: he had instigated offensives on the Somme, at Arras, Ypres and Cambrai; the BEF had not fought a sizeable defensive action since the middle of 1915. Let us examine the factors contained in his address to his commanders.

Fighting on the Italian Front had not gone well for the Allies during 1917. Offensives fought in May and August had met with little success and mounting casualty figures, and on 24 October, an Austro-German force attacked the Italian Second Army at Caporetto. In ten days, the Italians were driven back eighty miles on a ninety-mile front. The attack petered out with the onset of winter and the Italian Army was able to halt on the River Piave, but only with the help of eleven Allied Divisions rushed to their aid. Five of these Divisions were British, Divisions Haig could ill afford to 'give away', as he saw it. For the foreseeable future, all that could be realistically hoped for was that with continued Allied support, the exhausted and demoralised Italian Army would be able to avoid any repetition of Caporetto. But at least the Italian Front still stood; weakened and propped up by Anglo-French forces it may have been, but it was still there. The situation on the Eastern Front was infinitely worse.

The new Bolshevik Government there wasted no time in pursuing an armistice. Firing on the Eastern Front had ceased by the end of November 1917: the armistice itself was signed on 15 December and a week later peace talks opened in the town of Brest-Litovsk. Ludendorff and Hindenburg were determined to exact severe retribution on the new Russian government and its people. The proposed peace terms involved annexation of

---

[*]*Kaiserschlacht* is the name given by the German Army to its offensive of late March 1918. It translates literally into English as 'Emperor's Battle'.

land and partition of Russia itself. The Bolshevik delegates refused to accept the harsh terms offered and would not sign. Negotiations broke down and on 18 February 1918 the German Armies once more went onto the attack. The Russian Army had, by now, all but ceased to exist in practical terms and the Germans were able to advance 150 miles in five days, meeting only negligible opposition. The towns of Kiev and Odessa were swallowed up, the Ukraine was occupied along with Estonia, and the German troops were within 120 miles of Petrograd. Russia surrendered. The treaty was signed on 3 March 1918.

Even leaving a million troops in the east, Ludendorff was now able to switch his attention to the Western Front. The cessation of hostilities in Russia meant that he could transfer vast numbers of men. At the end of November 1917, Germany had 150 Divisions on the Western Front. By the end of February 1918 this had risen to 180, and by 21 March there were 192.

Ludendorff and Haig saw eye to eye on at least one important point. They both believed that the war would be finally won and lost not in Italy, not in the Balkans, not in Palestine, not in Russia, nor as the result of any other 'side-show', but on the Western Front.

Both of these commanders also knew that time was running out and Ludendorff in particular understood that Germany had one more throw of the dice before the arrival of sufficient American troops tipped the manpower balance irrevocably in the Allies' favour. America had been 'at war' for almost a year, but by the spring of 1918 they were not yet ready to play a major role.

It was in November 1917 that Ludendorff had met with his Chiefs of Staff to discuss the prospects for 1918. A major assault, for the reasons mentioned above, was the only option on the table. Where the offensive should take place was a matter for debate.

One proposal was for an attack in Flanders. An obvious advantage was the proximity to the front of the Channel ports vital to the BEF's continued participation in the war. The need to wait until at least April for the terrain to dry out sufficiently was enough to render the option unacceptable.

Another crack at Verdun was a possibility, but Ludendorff concluded that the British would be unlikely to rush to the aid of their French counterparts and in his view it was vital that the attack target the BEF. His own preference was for an attack, codename 'Michael', in the St Quentin area, this being near the junction of the British and French Armies.

After a tour of the entire Western Front, Ludendorff finally decided on this plan, which would break through the front between the Scarpe and the Oise rivers and would take his troops across the old Somme battlefields in the direction of Amiens. 'Mars', at Arras, would follow a few days later. Preparation of other attacks was to continue. If 'Michael' failed, Ludendorff would look elsewhere. If it succeeded, the German Army would follow up its breakthrough by turning northward and rolling up the British line.

Let us now view the situation from the other side of no man's land. Haig, in his December address, had raised the question of reinforcements and more than hinted that his requests in this area might not be met. As far as Haig was concerned, the obvious main theatre of the war was the Western Front. It was there that the war was going to be won, there that the German Army must be defeated. Lloyd George did not share this view. As 1918 approached, the Prime Minister was strongly opposed to the possibility of Haig mounting further offensives in France or Flanders, which could only end, as he saw it, in the senseless slaughter of more British soldiers. John Terraine takes the view that this feeling was not restricted to the Prime Minister: '... by January 1918 some members of the British Government had become well-nigh hysterical about the casualties of a manpower war. This was not entirely surprising: British casualties by the end of 1917 totalled over two million, a figure far beyond all previous experience or imagining.'[2]

For many reasons, none of which lie within the scope of this work, Lloyd George could not simply dismiss Haig. Stuck with him, 'the only way to stop Haig throwing away lives by the tens of thousands in hopeless offensives was to delay his reinforcements.'[3]

Without them, Haig would not be able to build up the reserves required to launch an offensive. He would have no option but to stand on the defensive. Even so, he estimated that he would need 615,000 men to bring even his current Divisions up to strength, the average Division being 2,000 men short at that time. The Cabinet Committee set up to examine this very question concluded that the Navy, the RFC, shipbuilding, munitions and food production were the priorities. The Army on the Western Front would have to make do with 100,000 Category 'A' men (i.e. deemed fit for active front line duties), along with a similar number in lower medical categories. This was barely enough to keep up with the normal daily casualties, or 'wastage' and sickness.

It is not as if the reserves did not exist: almost 200,000 men had been allocated to the Armies in the Near and Middle East and Balkans, and in total, a staggering 38,225 officers 607,403 men, all Category 'A', were in the United Kingdom, in uniform, trained and ready to be used.

The theory has recently been put forward that Lloyd George had another reason for keeping trained soldiers in the country: following the Bolshevik revolutions in Russia, it was feared that similar insurrection might occur in Britain. Many of these troops were concentrated in and around the major industrial regions, and therefore able to deter or quickly put down any serious manifestation of social unrest.

A recommendation by the Supreme War Council, set up by the Allied nations on 7 November 1917, placed Haig and the BEF in an even more difficult situation. The Commander-in-Chief had already reluctantly agreed to extend the British front southwards, taking over twenty-eight miles of front-line trenches from the French. A further twelve miles were deemed necessary, and Gough's newly created Fifth Army now had its right wing extended to the town of Barisis, five miles south of the River Oise. The entire frontage of the 'Michael' offensive would now be faced by British troops.

Haig's reaction was understandable: he remarked that 'the whole position would be laughable but for the seriousness of it.'[4] The War Council also recommended the creation of a Reserve Force which could be held back and then used to bolster any part of the front which found itself in peril. The idea was fine, but where were the troops to come from? Haig, having to cope with an extended front and a lack of reinforcements, refused to give up any men for its formation. Pétain, for differing reasons, took the same stance. The two commanders were to rely on mutual agreements for support, should it become necessary: troops from an unopposed sector would move to support any area encountering real difficulties, regardless of national considerations and Army boundaries. That was the theory, anyway.

The British line, as it stood in March 1918, extended from Ypres in the north to the River Oise in the south. In the north, Second Army manned a frontage of twenty-three miles with twelve Divisions around Ypres. First Army, with fourteen Divisions on a thirty-three-mile frontage extended almost as far south as Arras. From there, the next twenty-eight miles belonged to the fourteen Divisions of Third Army, including, on its right, the Flesquières Salient, a remnant of the gains made during the Battle of Cambrai. The Fifth Army extended southwards from there for forty-two miles, but only had twelve Divisions with which to cover them. As can be seen, the Fifth Army was at a distinct disadvantage if Divisions per mile of frontage are taken into consideration: each Division was responsible for three-and-a-half miles. The equivalent figure for Second Army was just less than two miles.

This was, to some extent, a sensible strategy on Haig's part. He had to keep his left wing strong: with less than fifty miles between the front and the Channel ports he would have little room for manoeuvre should the German Offensive fall here. Nor could he envisage the possibility of losing this lifeline to Britain. Any failure here would leave the rest of his forces in an untenable position, cut off as they would be from their main lines of supply. If the Germans were to break through in the centre, near Arras, the BEF would be effectively cut in half. On the right wing, however, Fifth Army would be able to give ground if necessary, and by doing so surrender nothing of real strategic importance to the German Army. The town of Amiens, it is true, was vital, but this was over forty miles from the front line. 'Elastic defence' was a possibility here.

The stretch of line taken over from the French on the Fifth Army front was in poor condition and needed a great deal of work if was to be able to stand up to a concerted German attack. The number of Pioneers and Sappers available for this work was nowhere near sufficient, and so the infantry out of the line, which by rights should have been resting and training, were needed to dig trenches, wire defensive positions and fulfil their tertiary role as pack mules. 'This wore them out and reduced their effectiveness still further.'[5] Add to this the number of men trailing along the roads in the rear areas on the move to find their new battalions following the disbandment of their own in the Divisional reduction from twelve battalions to nine and we have even more manpower not being utilised to the full.

Just how was the British Army, imbued with 'offensive spirit', and basically unused to defence on the grand scale, going to cope with this rapidly imposed new philosophy? Holding the front line trenches at all costs, though heroic and 'simple', was looked upon as naïve. A more flexible approach was deemed necessary. The theory runs as follows: the front line system would be called the Forward Zone, code-named the Blue Line. This would be no more than an outpost line, from where pockets of infantry would inflict as many casualties as possible on an advancing enemy before giving ground. The main defensive area, or Battle Zone (Red Line), would be carefully sited some 2,000 to 3,000 yards behind the front line and would be of similar width itself. It was here that an attack would be held up and turned back. Behind it, the Brown Line or Corps Line would be from where reserve troops were moved forward into the Battle Zone as required. Green and Yellow lines even further back were also planned. These were 'to be constructed as opportunity offered'.[6] In reality, the situation was far from ideal. Martin Middlebrook puts it succinctly:

... the entire front of the Fifth Army... never did achieve the status of a fully defended front. The British had come too late, the front was too long, there were not enough men. The front line was reasonably well protected by barbed wire but not by a continuous trench. The Battle Zone was not complete, especially in the extreme south, and the Corps Line in the rear was almost non-existent... scattered outposts ...watched the front, hoping to cover the empty ground between the posts with machine-gun fire. Scattered along the front line area, usually just behind the true front line but well in advance of the Battle Zone, were a series of 'redoubts' or 'keeps'. These were all-round defensive positions sited on natural features dominating the surrounding ground. Like the smaller posts further forward, they covered the gaps to the neighbouring redoubts with machine-gun fire, but the redoubts were too distant from each other to give much mutual support.[7]

As mentioned, the trenches further to the rear were either scratched out to a minimum depth in the grass awaiting completion or simply marked out by lines of tape. On occasion they were no more than lines on a map, with no actual physical manifestation whatsoever. Terraine describes them as 'pious hopes rather than military realities.'[8]

Generals Byng and Gough, commanding the Third and Fifth Armies respectively, going somewhat against the overall strategy dictated by their new defensive systems, placed the majority of their troops in the Forward and Battle zones. This would seem, however, to make sense: they saw little profit in keeping too many reserves in the rear as they would have had few, or indeed no trenches or strongpoints to man. Not that the British commanders had a surfeit of reserves anyway: Haig, on his entire front of more than 120 miles, had the grand total of eight Divisions in reserve.

The 21st Division formed part of VII Corps under Lt-Gen. Sir W.N. Congreve. This Corps was positioned on the extreme left wing of the Fifth Army front. Its 15,000-yard frontage was divided almost equally between its three Divisions; the 16th (South Irish) on the right, the 21st in the centre and the 9th (Scottish) on the left, abutting the Flesquières Salient to the north of Gouzeaucourt (see map). Each Division had one brigade and its Pioneer battalion in reserve. The 16th Division had five battalions in the Forward Zone, the 21st and 9th each having four similarly positioned. This left only five for the entire Corps Battle Zone.

This strong manning of the Forward Zone was judged necessary on account of the short field of view on the high ground, on which the front line had settled down after the Battle of Cambrai, and the ease with which the enemy could mass in the defile, through which the Schelde canal ran close at hand, free from ground observation.[9]

The 21st Division front contained two natural defensive positions: Chapel Hill and the village of Epéhy. Between the two sat Vaucelette Farm, garrisoned, but not so advantageously placed as the other two. These three positions were technically in the Battle Zone, but Vaucelette Farm, for example, was only about 500 yards behind a very scant Forward Zone.

Chapel Hill was held by the 1st Lincolns of 62nd Brigade; Vaucelette Farm was the responsibility of 12/13th Northumberland Fusiliers, also of 62nd Brigade. In and around Epéhy were the 6th, 7th and 8th Leicesters, that is, the 110th Brigade in its entirety. 64th Brigade stood in reserve.

The magnitude of the German March offensive was unprecedented. At 4.40 a.m. on 21 March, the launch of a single white rocket into the air over St Quentin signalled the commencement of the artillery bombardment. Over 6,000 guns, supported by almost 3,500 trench mortars, poured 1,160,000 shells onto the positions of Fifth, Third (and as a feint, First) Armies.

The bombardment was timed to last five hours, and designed, by its sheer weight and ferocity, to stun the defenders, destroy communications and silence the artillery. The first two hours were concentrated mainly on drenching the gun positions in the Battle Zone with gas: then, in the remaining three hours, a mixture of high explosive and gas swept to and fro over the Forward and Battle zones, focusing primarily on the infantry in the front positions. The situation in the Forward and Battle zones, after the conclusion of the bombardment, was one of almost total chaos.[10]

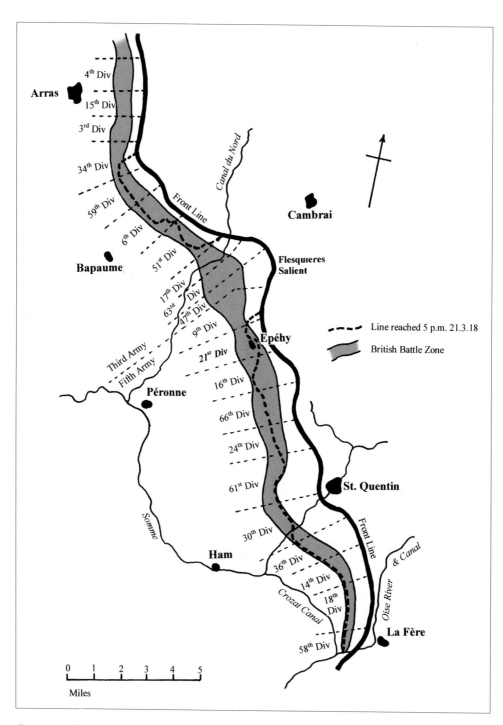

Operation Michael 21 March 1918.

As the soldiers of sixty-six German Divisions, led by specially trained 'storm troopers' left their assembly trenches, they advanced, across most of the front, through thick fog, this made worse by the lingering smoke from the artillery barrage. British outposts, strongpoints and keeps, which depended upon good visibility for their system of mutual support to work, were now blind. Many defenders did not see their attackers until they were upon them, or in some cases until they were infiltrated from the rear, the Germans having originally bypassed their positions.

The 64th Brigade was not directly involved in the fighting on the first day of the battle. Ahead of them, the 110th and 62nd Brigades did their best to halt the tide of field-grey. The 1st Lincolns fought desperately to hang on to Chapel Hill, and were supported by units from their sister battalion the 2nd Lincolns and by the South African Scottish who came down from the Division on their left.

Vaucelette Farm, held by the 12/13th Northumberland Fusiliers, held out during the morning, but after mortars were brought up to pound the area, the Germans were able to take the position from the rear at around noon. The attackers now had the chance to advance along this valley between Chapel Hill and Epéhy. However, the fog lifted earlier here than on other parts of the front, and the now visible German columns were halted by intense fire from the flanking strongpoints, now able to work as they had originally been intended.

The 6th, 7th and 8th Leicesters at Epéhy fared well that day. The Divisional Commander, Campbell, had ordered the front trenches to be evacuated an hour before dawn, and as a result, initial casualties among the Leicester battalions from the bombardment had not been too heavy. Epéhy was not encircled and stood firm.

To the right of Epéhy, the Irish units had not done so well: the Forward Zone had to all intents and purposes disappeared and the Germans were able to penetrate into the Battle Zone. The Fifth Army front had begun to crumble. Isolated units held out, but German first-wave troops were ordered to press on and leave such cases of stubborn resistance to their back up Divisions. Speed of infiltration was the key.

The British Army of this time, as has already been mentioned, was new to the tactics of 'elastic defence'. The 'Tommy' fought best in a line, with his flanks secure and the enemy to his front. Withdrawals of flanking units were cause for great concern for those who were proving able to stand their ground. The temptation was for these also to withdraw to 'conform' with their neighbours. It is a confusing story of such stands, withdrawals and fighting retreats which characterises the next few days of the offensive.

The story of the 9th KOYLI is not untypical. At 11.55 a.m. on 21 March, over two hours after the initial onslaught had begun, the battalion was ordered to take up its allocated positions in the Brown Line. Twenty-five minutes later it was there, in and around the village of Guyencourt. By 1.00 p.m., modifications to those orders saw the battalion move to the high ground to the south of the village. As far as possible, the men were in trenches and away from buildings in order to give some sense of security from the German bombardment. This 'was now steady, though hardly intense, enemy's shells bursting every half minute. Our artillery appeared to be replying with a shell every three minutes.'[11]

By 5.00 p.m., the battalion was back in its original Brown Line positions. During the afternoon, 2nd-Lt Harrison, commanding 'C' Company, and CSM Grimshaw were wounded by an eight-inch shell and evacuated. Fatal casualties that day numbered seven.

The next day also dawned foggy. The bombardment of the 64th Brigade positions continued, but at first with 'much less intensity'.[12] As noon approached, the artillery fire

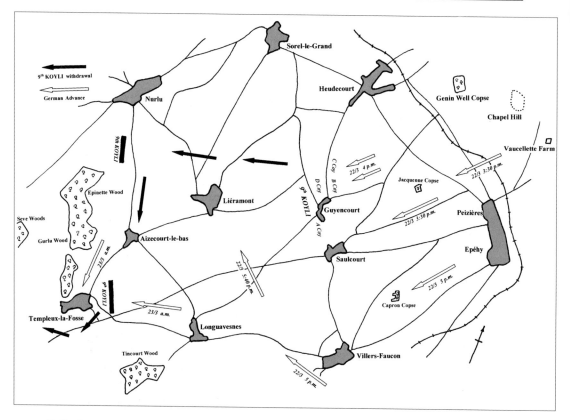

Epéhy Sector, 21 March 1918.

increased, with a heavy barrage of eight-inch shells falling particularly on the unfortunate 'C' Company who suffered thirty-eight casualties, killed or wounded. Communication between units during battle was an accepted problem, but nevertheless reports of German progress were reaching the battalion. It appeared that by midday the enemy had got into Vaucelette Farm, as far as Genin Well Copse and into parts of Epéhy and Peizières. Two front line brigades of 21st Division were being attacked, so it was reported at the time, by four German Divisions.

From about 2.00 p.m., the KOYLI positions were the object of enemy low-level aircraft reconnaissance flights. The pilots expended a great deal of ammunition in strafing the Battalion's positions while they were about it. The results of their efforts were, however, limited to the wounding of 2nd-Lt Hargreaves and two Other Ranks of 'D' Company.

An hour and a half later, the 9th KOYLI got their first view of German ground troops as they were spotted advancing from Peizières along the road to Saulcourt and across country towards Jacquenne Copse directly in front of the battalion's elevated positions. Small arms fire from 'A', 'B' and 'C' Companies held them up, and during the firing, a German officer was seen to fall from his horse. A Lewis Gun team from 'C' Company was able, in addition, to knock out a German limber team. The CO had also sent a Vickers machine-gun team to the south of the battalion positions to give them a better field of fire. He also reported the enemy advance to the artillery battery to the battalion's right rear and they were able to add their not insignificant efforts to stopping the German

9th KOYLI graves from March/April 1918.

advance. Numerous parties of Germans were determined to get forward onto the higher ground, but were stopped each time. The Battalion War Diary estimates that 250 Germans were killed.

Any stability was short-lived. Soon after 5.00 p.m., the situation on the battalion's right appeared to be turning to the Germans' advantage. 64th Brigade HQ had already given the CO information that the Germans were in the village of Villers-Faucon and had supplied co-ordinates of a position to which the battalion was to withdraw should the possibility of being outflanked and cut off from that side occur. Two German battalions had advanced towards Capron Copse Ridge, but had been held up by fire from Saulcourt and from the guns behind it, but 'the rattle of musketry and machine guns seemed to become much more intense from the direction of Villers-Faucon, and it was suspected that the enemy had to some extent broken through on our right.'[13] Observers were dispatched to find out what they could: they were able to report that the enemy was advancing across the ridges to the southwest of Villers-Faucon, and that the possibility of being cut off was very real. Companies were to be ready either to counter-attack or to move to their rear at very short notice. By now, machine-gun fire onto the KOYLI positions from those troops advancing on the right was becoming quite intense. Runners and reconnoitring officers moved across country at their peril. Despite telephone wires being cut by artillery fire eight or nine times that afternoon, the Signallers repeatedly managed to effect repairs on every occasion demanded of them. It was just as well, because at about 5.40 p.m., the 1st East Yorks were seen to be withdrawing from their positions in the Brown Line at Saulcourt and were involved in a running fight through the town. A telephone message to 'A' Company on the 9th KOYLI right meant that the orders to retire reached them just in time to avoid the whole company being surrounded. The rapidity of the German advance meant that one platoon, under Captain V.R. Chalk, was in fact cut off. Their subsequent fate was observed by luckier members of the battalion:

These gave a good account of themselves, and killed more than their own number of Germans. Some Germans indicated, by motions of holding up their hands, that our men should surrender. The men did not take the hint, but shot the enemy down. Capt. Chalk, 'A' Company, shot a German officer with his pistol at five yards.[14]

It is not recorded whether any members of the platoon were able to effect their escape. One must presume that most, if not all, either became casualties or were captured. Captain Chalk survived the action. With the situation becoming more and more desperate by the minute, the CO sent 2nd-Lt Gregg running to 'B' and 'C' Companies to relay instructions to withdraw (presumably the telephone lines had once again been cut). The Germans managed to 'get into' the right flank of 'B' Company and Capt. Teaz's batman was wounded. Wire entanglements held the Germans back and a determined rearguard action managed to account for most of the front line of enemy troops. The organised withdrawal was now possible. Forced to cross the valley behind them under intense enemy artillery fire, they inevitably suffered casualties. 'C' Company, the last to retire under the cool and skilful command of 2nd-Lt Greenshields, were almost cut off as the Germans advanced on Liéramont from the south-east. It was only their 'wonderfully *unenterprising*'[15] assault on the village that allowed the last KOYLI troops to make it back to their new positions between Epinette Wood and Nurlu village. It was almost 8.00 p.m. by the time the battalion got there: reports from the four companies seemed to indicate that five officers and seventy men had been killed or wounded during the withdrawal, and that about 200 were still unaccounted for. Atop this ridge, the appointed rendezvous point, stood sixteen officers and 160 Other Ranks. They were not to stay there long. At 8.15 p.m., the battalion moved to new positions in the Green Line some two miles to the south-west. Halting at Aizecourt-le-bas to fill their water bottles, the battalion was in position in front of the small town of Templeux-la-Fosse, facing slightly north of east, overlooking Longavesnes, by 10.30 p.m. Patrols were sent out to establish, if they could, the whereabouts of the nearest enemy units. They found them about 1,000 yards in front of their main position.

The day's action had cost the battalion seventy-two fatalities, three of them officers: Lt Arthur Hetherington and 2nd-Lts Stanley Makin and Clifford Moon. Their names, along with fifty-six of their comrades, appear on the Pozières Memorial, no trace of their bodies having ever been found.

There was to be little rest for the survivors of the battalion. Daybreak on 23 March found their positions once more swathed in a thick mist, and at 6.30 a.m., under the cover it offered, the Germans launched a frontal attack. Like old-fashioned skirmishers of a previous century, the main enemy force was preceded by a thin line of machine gunners. For once, the German artillery let its soldiers down badly. The accompanying barrage was both weak and inaccurate, with almost all the shells falling harmlessly behind the KOYLI positions. This allowed the defenders to concentrate small arms fire on the attackers with impunity. Some German troops managed to get within thirty yards of the KOYLI but the attack 'was repulsed with slaughter'.[16]

They tried again an hour later, this time moving with more care along the ditches and amongst the mud heaps of the Longavesnes–Péronne road. The KOYLIs were selective with their fire, waiting until obvious targets presented themselves. Once more the Germans lost heavily and were forced to withdraw under cover of their own very intense machine-gun fire. Once this second attack had been successfully repulsed, Maj. Harry Greenwood MC and 38787 Pte H. Wright, accompanied by a Lance-Corporal from the 1st East Yorks, rushed out to the point where the afore-mentioned road reached the KOYLI wire to recover two abandoned German machine guns. These would prove useful, as some of the battalion's Lewis Guns had been lost during the previous evening's withdrawal. The Major came upon a heap of German dead as he reached the road, and suddenly from amongst them appeared a German officer and two soldiers, their hands in the air. They were less inclined to go through with their surrender once they realised that Greenwood was unarmed, but the arrival of the other two with rifles settled the issue. The prisoners and the machine guns were brought back to the British lines. The former were from the 221st Machine Gun Company, and were taken back to Division by the 9th KOYLI adjutant who had been wounded and needed to be evacuated. 'The action of Major Greenwood MC and the two O.R. was worthy of the highest praise, and did much to cheer up the spirits of the troops, who were anxious to witness deeds of retaliation.'[17]

Hard on the heels of this success, at 9.00 p.m., came orders to retire some two miles to trenches in front of Aizecourt-le-Haut. The War Diary describes these orders as a 'terrible blow', as the battalion, having successfully seen off two German attacks, was hoping to stay put. What was more, the line of retirement would mean the KOYLIs crossing open ground in full view of the enemy. As predicted, all 'hell [was] let loose'[18] as the withdrawal began.

The reason for the order soon became evident. The Gloucesters on the brigade's left had already been forced to withdraw and German troops were in Templeux-la-Fosse, half

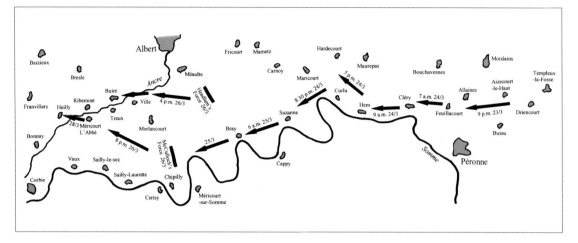

KOYLI withdrawal, 23-26 March 1918.

a mile directly *behind* the KOYLI positions. This discovery led to a forced detour to the south of the village. 2nd-Lt James, in command of 'D' Company, in order to facilitate the manoeuvre, defended the northern flank of the retreating KOYLIs with a screen of Lewis Guns. The move was far from smooth, however. As feared, losses were heavy. Only half a dozen were killed, including Captain Teaz MC,[19] but six officers and about 100 Other Ranks of the 180 remaining members of the battalion were wounded. The detour had also caused isolated units to lose direction and the remnants of the battalion did not recognise their new positions when they reached them and found themselves in the village of Feuillacourt, north-west of Péronne.

What was left of the 15th DLI had halted as required in front of Aizecourt-le-Haut, but the 1st East Yorks were in the same boat as the KOYLIs. The German advance was following close on their heels, but paused as if for breath on the ridge south of Sève Woods, still just to the east of Aizecourt-le-Haut. By 1.15 p.m., their compatriots had made further ground to the north and had taken the town of Moislans. The fear of once again being outflanked precipitated a further withdrawal and the 15th DLI rejoined their comrades in Feuillacourt.

Soon after 4.00 p.m., the enemy also captured Mont St Quentin and as a result the 21st Division were forced to continue their withdrawal, this time across the Canal du Nord to a line east of Cléry, extending northwards for 2,000 yards along a spur. The battalion was once more on the banks of the River Somme, but had no idea where their Battalion HQ was to be found.

Some semblance of order was restored to this 'fluid' situation early on the morning of 24 March when yet another withdrawal was ordered, allowing the KOYLIs to conform with the rearward movement of the rest of the Division. The 9th KOYLI found itself strung out atop a ridge. At about 7.00 a.m., they were entertained by low-flying German aircraft who in turns reconnoitred their position and then fired at them. By 9.00 a.m., the Lincolns and East Yorks on their left, along with the rest of 62nd and 110th Brigades had been forced back to the high ground south east of Maurepas, and the KOYLIs once more followed suit, taking up positions at Hem Wood. Soon after arriving there, they were treated to the encouraging spectacle of a counter-attack by troops of 39th Division throwing the Germans back a little way.

At 12.50 p.m., a German attack was seen building across the battalion front. It and two further attempts to move forward by the enemy were halted by small arms fire from the KOYLIs, but at 2.30 p.m., the Germans brought a number of 5.9's into position, each, it could be observed, pulled by a team of eight horses. The developing attack had grown in scale: troops, preceded by machine gunners, stretched as far as the eye could see. The KOYLIs held on as best they could until about 4.00 p.m. The main thrust of the attack was to the north of the battalion, and an hour later the Division made a short retirement to a line from Curlu to Hardecourt. It was then ordered to move back to Suzanne, three miles to the south-east, on the northern banks of the Somme.

The 9th KOYLI arrived there at about 8.30 p.m. that evening, rejoining their HQ staff. Accommodation for the night stretched to the relative comfort of barns in the town itself. Firing could still be heard from the direction of Maurepas during the night, but the author suspects that it did not unduly disturb the slumbers of the battalion's exhausted survivors for long.

By the time the men awoke the following morning, 25 March, VII Corps had been transferred to Third Army. It is doubtful that any of the men even knew, and less likely that they would have cared much anyway. The change of management did nothing to alter the direction of movement, however, as at 6.00 a.m. they received orders to move the few miles to the town of Bray. It was deemed far enough back this time to allow the establishing of bivouacs, followed by a rest and a substantial meal. After this dinner they were visited first by the Brigade Commander and then by no less a person than Maj.-Gen. Campbell, Commander of 21st Division. Congratulations and encouragement were swiftly followed by inevitable reorganisation: even allowing for a number of stragglers to have found their way back to the fold, it is unlikely that the battalion was at much more than company strength, and as such it could only really be of any effective use once combined with remnants of other equally depleted units. Firstly, a composite company of 120 was formed under the command of Capt. Shaw. These were then sent to join a composite battalion under Maj. Coles, which then moved off northwards to the vicinity of Carnoy to take up a defensive line. As soon as they had left the camp, the further depleted remnants of the battalion were moved into billets in Bray, but were only there two hours before they were moved back to join the transport lines north of Chipilly. There they bivouacked for the night, but the extreme cold, combined with the lack of coats or blankets, rendered sleep almost impossible.

The following morning, two other composite units were formed and despatched to their appropriate places on the battlefield. A staff officer arrived at the camp with instructions for Lt-Col. McCulloch to form and command a force made up of all the nucleus parties of battalions throughout the Division. Two hundred and twelve men of 9th KOYLI under Lt Greenshields joined this force and took up their positions extending northwards from Chipilly as far as the Bray–Corbie road. The total strength of this new unit was 1,200 men and two Vickers machine guns.

Brig.-Gen. Headlam, in the meantime, had organised what was left into a third composite force comprising 650 men from 62nd Brigade, 400 from 64th Brigade and 450 from the 110th, along with a machine gun company of eight guns. These joined the remnants of 35th Division along the Bray–Albert road.

What little there was left of the 9th KOYLI, transport, the band, etc., moved back, not to put it too unkindly, 'out of the way', to Baizieux, well to the north of the main Amiens–Albert road.

VII Corps orders for the rest of the day were to become a little confused. Originally, orders were given to the effect that the forces presently between Albert and the River Somme would withdraw gradually during the course of the day, pivoting on the former, crossing the River Ancre and taking up positions along its northern banks, its right wing resting on the village of Ribemont. Just before 3.00 p.m., a message was received at VII Corps HQ, stating that the retirement had begun as planned. A message from Third Army HQ arrived at almost the same time insisting that no 'voluntary' retirement from the Bray–Albert line was to take place. The present line was to be maintained.

It was too late. Conforming with the rest of 35th Division, McCulloch's force began a steady retirement at about 5.30 p.m. The message to stay put arrived fifteen minutes later, and McCulloch and his staff were able to hold back only the last 500 of his men and these took up positions south of Marlencourt to await developments. Still there at 7.15 p.m., it now faced advancing German troops. They kept up rifle fire for half an hour or so, delaying the inevitable. Once the danger of encirclement from the north became evident, they quickly withdrew in the gathering darkness to their designated crossing point at Méricourt l'Abbé, under fire for most of the way. Casualties were mercifully slight; one officer wounded along with six Other Ranks. The only fatality was 'Sawdust', a riding horse of the 9th KOYLI, 'an old battalion pet, whose loss was much deplored'.[20]

They had arrived at Méricourt l'Abbé at half past nine, and were met at the level crossing by Headlam and were given instructions not to cross the river, but to take up positions between the present location and Sailly, coming under the command of Brig.-Gen. Cummings.

Headlam's force, on the Bray–Albert road, watched the 104th Brigade on their left begin its retirement shortly before 3.00 p.m. Headlam had not intended to commence his movement before dark, and sent a message to that effect to 104th Brigade HQ. The latter continued their rearward movement regardless, however, and were soon joined by the 105th. The left wing of Headlam's force – anxious not to be left behind – began to slip away too, but were stopped before the trickle became a flood. The Commander was eventually forced to bow to the inevitable and sent a telegram to 21st Division HQ explaining the situation:

I was finally forced to leave my line at 4.00 p.m. as the left and centre brigades were then in full retreat. The Bosches were bringing up guns very quickly and there were considerable numbers following on. It is quite possible that some of the extra foot weary men will get cut off but I hope not. The men will be very weary and really not fit to put up a show in defence of the river if Bosches push on hard. Necessity is food and hot drink. Can I have 1,500 rations put at Sucrerie (27.b) and also some cookers brought there for all battalions. Please give me orders re an entrenching Bn and the Reinforcing Bn who were put under my orders. They are no use, in my opinion, and were the cause of several 'stampedes'. They might be a more useful reserve after a day's rest. They also want rations – no. about 800 each. I am trying to get these Bns assembled just east of Buire.[21]

The story of the rest of the month can be quickly told. On the 27th, troops of 3rd Australian Division took up positions in advance of McCulloch's force, which was ordered, on the following day, to move to Heilly on the north bank of the Ancre and once more to come under the orders of Brig. Headlam. Once there, they went into billets. Orders received on the 30th to take up positions on the Amiens outer defence lines were cancelled just in time to prevent them setting out, but not before McCulloch himself had reconnoitred the location.

A march to Fréchencourt, just across the Amiens–Albert road was completed by 1.00 a.m. on the 31st, from where they moved to Allonville, just to the north-east of Amiens, where the disparate units of the 9th KOYLI were finally reunited.

On 1 April, they marched into Amiens and entrained for Hopoutre at 2.00 p.m. By the early hours of the next morning, the battalion was back in Belgium. Captain Harold Yeo, having been in England between 2 and 26 March had missed most of the excitement, but saw enough to provoke a passing comment on the new style of fighting in his next letter home: 'Open warfare is all very well, but it is much too continuous'.[22]

12

KEMMEL

Early in the morning of 2 April 1918, the 9th KOYLI disembarked from the train that had brought them from Amiens to Hopoutre and climbed into lorries, which deposited them two-and-a-half hours later at Kemmel Shelters Camp, a few miles south-west of Ypres. They were joined that day by a badly needed draft of 264 men.

At 10.15 a.m. the following day, the Divisional Commander, Maj.-Gen. Campbell, visited the battalion. The men assembled to hear him congratulate them on their conduct during the recent fighting. No doubt he gave similar messages to all the other battalions in the Division: whether such orations had a hollow ring to them for the 'older' soldiers can only be speculated. The majority of the men were probably just happy that respite had come.

Respite, such as it was, was to be short-lived. By 3.00 p.m. the same day, after first visiting the 2nd Australian Brigade HQ, company commanders were reconnoitring a sector of the line held by the 8th Australian Battalion prior to relieving them. They each spent the night with the company they were about to relieve, and accordingly, on 4 April, the 9th KOYLI moved forward into the trenches between Green Wood and Hollebeke. 'A' and 'C' Companies were in the front line, with 'B' Company in support and 'D' Company in reserve. 'A' and 'B' Companies of the 15th DLI were also put under Lt-Col. McCulloch's command, effectively putting him in charge of all troops in the brigade sector. His Battalion HQ was situated in Onraet Wood, just to the north of the village of Wytschaete.

The entry in the War Diary for 5 April was short and simple, but could not have suited the men better: 'Quiet day, nothing to report.'[1] Captain Ellenberger put his thoughts about the new location down on paper at about the same time:

The comparative safety of the front line, except in an actual attack contrasted strikingly with the increasing harassment of the areas behind. In reserve, by Dickebusch Lake, we spent nights and days moving up shell-beaten paths to dig fresh targets in ground merely to pass over which was fearsome, and on which the gunners stayed for weeks. Our rest was nightly disturbed by German aeroplanes – we had scarcely known them on the Somme: to watch their silvered wings shining like angels' toys in the crossed searchlight beams was entrancing enough; but tents afforded no sense of security either from enemy bombs or from our own avenging missiles. Up in the line, on the other hand, it was often strangely quiet; the enemy's guns found better targets behind us, and when his shells dropped short, the 'lengthen range' signal flared up from a German forward post: maybe we should have mopped up that isolated 'pill-box', but as it was it served us well.[2]

A similarly inactive time at Staff HQ allowed Harold Yeo to put his thoughts on recent events into a letter to his father:

It is a wonderfully interesting stage of the war, isn't it? With overwhelming forces at his disposal, the Hun has failed to break through. The only reason he has got so far is that he used such a weight of numbers as has never been seen before: even then it needed all the assistance the dense fog gave him on the first day to enable him to succeed at all. On our Division's front he hadn't won any of the line, except a small bit in the centre, at the end of the first day's show, and it was only owing to his coming right in on the right that they had to leave their positions. Despite the fog his casualties were very heavy indeed from all accounts, in the scrap for the first positions. After that for about four days they had a running fight, steadily withdrawing in the face of a most persistent follow-up by the Hun, necessitated by the general withdrawal to keep an intact line. That part of the show wasn't very costly and seems to have been very interesting.[3]

On the day that Yeo penned these lines, Ludendorff 'called a halt to Operation Michael, admitting that the attempt at a breakthrough had failed'.[4]

Although the Germans had made great advances, it was mainly against the Fifth Army in the south under Gough, who in February had been given permission by his superiors to fall back if heavily attacked. He had done exactly this, and although his lines of defence had been severely bent, they had not irreparably broken. Ludendorff had not followed through with his plan to 'roll up' the British Army from the south: the German advances were significant, but *in the wrong direction*. True, they had captured Bapaume, Albert, Bray, Péronne, Montdidier in the south along with Noyon and Soissons, but in the final analysis, this territory was of negligible strategic value. The French and British Armies had not been split, the latter had not broken and no effective breakthrough and follow-up had been forthcoming. A final attempt to capture the important railway town of Amiens failed on 5 April.

The German infantry were tired. They had been marching and fighting for over two weeks. Their supply lines were overstretched and heavy artillery was finding it difficult to keep up. German morale also took a severe blow when troops found how well supplied British soldiers had been. Foodstuffs aplenty, along with good quality clothing and boots found in trenches, dugouts and stores were too great a temptation. Instead of pressing on, German soldiers were stopping to loot. Some officers were forced to report that their now drunken and gorged troops were in no fit state to fight.

In what now seems a desperate attempt to re-ignite this stalled offensive, 'Mars', the planned attack on Arras, had been put into operation on 28 March. It failed to make any significant ground and was called off the very same day. All this came too late to save General Gough. The day before the 'Mars' offensive, CIGS had instructed Haig to remove Gough from command of Fifth Army. Haig was very reluctant to comply, but Lloyd George insisted: the deed was done on 4 April. This Army was to be renamed 'Fourth Army' and given to General Sir Henry Rawlinson.

'Michael' was over. It had taken over 90,000 prisoners and 1,000 guns, and had overrun more territory than all the Allied advances of the past three years. But it had not won the war.'[5] Casualties had been heavy, the majority being suffered by the British Army, a total of 178,000 (including 70,000 prisoners). The French had lost 77,000. German casualties more or less matched those of the Allies.

'Michael' may well have been over and at a cost of over 30,000 casualties per day, but Ludendorff was not ready to admit defeat. On his map of the Western Front, his eyes had wandered northwards: even before 'Michael' had finally petered out, orders were given (on 3 April) to instigate 'Georgette', a modification of earlier plans 'George I' and 'George II'. This offensive became known to the British as the Battle of the Lys. The attack was launched between the La Bassée canal, just south of Festubert, and Frelinghem, three miles north east of Armentières, on 9 April 1918. Once again the attacking troops, going in at 8.45 a.m., had a thick fog to cover them.

The preliminary blow was delivered by eight Divisions, four of those directed against the Portuguese Corps between Neuve Chapelle and Laventie. By 10.00 a.m., a precipitate Portuguese retreat had become a rout. The 55th Division, on the Portuguese right, managed to hold their ground, but the 40th on the left was forced to withdraw. The result was a German advance of nearly three miles on a ten-mile-wide front, the forward troops reaching the River Lys at Estaires.

The second phase of 'Georgette' went in again under cover of fog on the following morning, further north still, this time between Armentières and the Ypres–Comines canal in the direction of Hazebrouk. Ploegsteert and Messines had been taken by noon, although the latter was recaptured later in the day. Armentières was outflanked and had to be abandoned.

The situation was becoming desperate for the Allies: Haig's request to Foch for assistance had been fruitless, and other than two cavalry Divisions moved northwards from the Somme, he had no reserves upon which to call. If Hazebrouk fell, along with its important railway junction, vital lines of communication would be cut and the Channel ports threatened. Haig's worst nightmare was in danger of becoming a reality. As the German assaults were renewed on 11 April, Haig issued his now famous 'Special Order of the Day'. This uncharacteristic exhortation concluded:

There is no other course open to us but to fight it out. Every position must be held to the last man: there must be no retirement. With our backs to the wall and believing in the justice of our cause each one of us must fight on to the end. The safety of our homes and the Freedom of mankind alike depend upon the conduct of each one of us at this critical moment.[6]

German successes that day were limited to an enlargement in the original re-entrant, though in the north, IX Corps had been forced to surrender Messines Ridge. By 15 April, Bailleul had fallen and the line to the north of it had been 'adjusted'. Troops to the east of Ypres also shortened their lines, falling back some 3-4,000 yards in the centre, although an outpost line was left in the original advanced positions, giving troops time, it was hoped, to prepare their new defensive line properly.

The 9th KOYLI's quiet day on 5 April was followed by two more, and relief came just as Wytschaete received a few enemy shells. More new troops arrived on the 9th, a draft of 137 managing to rendezvous with their new battalion at Birr Camp, Locre, two miles south-east of Ypres. News of the Lys offensive reached the battalion on 10 April and the men moved into positions in the Polderhoek sector ready to repel the anticipated attack. No attack ensued, and the next few days saw the battalion move to and fro in the sector, presumably in response to the ever-changing situation to the south. Harold Yeo summed up the position nicely in a letter to his mother, dated 13 April 1918: 'One can't analyse the situation at all, chiefly because one doesn't know much about it.'[7]

German attacks were still making gains and on 16 April, the town of Wytschaete fell. The response to this was that at 7.00 p.m. on the 17th, the 9th KOYLI received orders to attack the town the following morning. The KOYLIs were to make the assault alone, but fortunately, and in true Army style, the order for the attack was cancelled within an hour of its receipt at Battalion HQ. A conference the next day concluded that an attack would indeed go ahead, but in conjunction with at least four other battalions, and in any case not before 20 April. Forthcoming events would lead to a further postponement.

On 19 April, the battalion was ordered to relieve the 1st East Yorks and the 15th DLI in Onraet Wood. The relief was described in the War Diary as 'intricate': there were many gaps in the line and no communication trenches. Despite this, the relief was successfully completed at 3.00 a.m. on the 20th when two platoons of 'C' Company took over North House trench from the 2nd South Africans.

These new positions were very close to the town of Wytschaete, which was of course by now in German hands. British artillery, in attempting to shell enemy positions there, managed to drop a number of rounds onto 'B' Company's trenches at around 2.00 p.m. Tragically, the response to an SOS flare sent up at 9 o'clock that evening led to shells once more falling short: our own eighteen-pounders killed four and wounded four of our own men. Although messages sent back were partly effective, one gun continued to shell 'B' Company's positions during the early hours of the 21st, inflicting further casualties. 'Friendly fire' resulted in the deaths of ten soldiers of 9th KOYLI, including 2nd-Lt Stanley Cundall. A similar number were wounded. The War Diarist for once gave vent to his feelings on the matter when recording the day's events: 'The strongest protest was made against this discreditable performance and it is to be hoped that the officer of the artillery concerned will be tried at Court Martial for this carelessness.'[8]

One of the 'Other Ranks' killed by shellfire during this period was 24554 Pte S. Waldron. It is unclear whether friend or foe fired the shell that killed him, but this would have been of little importance to his mother in Bulwell, Nottingham, as she read the War Office telegram. She wrote to one of Sid's friends, asking for any details to fill in the gaps left by the necessarily brief official communication. The friend, Willie Simpson, posted the reply on 10 May:

Dear Mrs Waldron,
Just a few lines answering your most welcome letter which I received today. I was very pleased to hear from you, and I know how you will feel about Sid. I can hardly realize it yet because we were chums. I cannot tell you much more about him because I was only up the line at the time and had to come down again with the CO. He was in a dugout at the time, and a shell hit it, but none of the shell hit him, it must have been a beam or something that hit him or shock because he was not marked anywhere, it is hard luck. I was only telling him a week or two ago we would have a good time when we got home, I should like to get home to tell you but I don't think their [sic] is much luck this time. I am getting a lot better, but gas is an awful thing. I don't want any more of that, I only got a slight wound besides I will give you a call if I get to Blighty. I expect I shall be in hospital a little while yet. I must conclude now. Hoping you are getting over your great loss, which I know will be very hard.
*   I Remain Your Sincere Friend, Willie Simpson.*
*   P.S. Write back and let me know if you get this.*[9]

Sid Waldron's final resting place remains unknown, and his name, along with those of four of his comrades who also died on that day, appears on the Tyne Cot Memorial.

Shaken by their ordeal, 'B' Company were taken out of the line and replaced by 'D' Company. The whole battalion was relieved by the 1st East Yorks on 23 April: 9th

KOYLI was to be rested for two days in preparation for its imminent attack on Wytschaete. The attack was now scheduled for the morning of 26 April. In preparation, the battalion CO went out with his opposite number from the 9th Black Watch to recce the ground. This turned out to be a fruitless exercise: on 25 April, the Germans launched an offensive between Bailleul and Ypres, the main initial objective being the capture of Mount Kemmel.

The *Official History* describes this stretch of the Allied line as an 'international front': the right was held by the 34th, 154th and 28th French Divisions, the left being held by the British, comprising XXII Corps (Lt-Gen. Sir A. Godley), with 9th and 21st Divisions (with the 39th Division Composite Brigade under the latter), and II Corps (Lt-Gen. Sir C. Jacob), with 6th, 41st and 36th Divisions. Occupying the actual front-line trenches were six French regiments, each of three battalions, on a 9,000-yard front, and five 'very weak' British brigades, likewise of three battalions each, on a 7,000-yard front. The defences were organised in three lines: the front line, the Vierstraat Line and the Scherpenberg/Cheapside Line. (The Voormezeele Line ran between the Vierstraat and Cheapside Lines in the northern part of the British-held sector) (see map).

On the evening of 24 April, prisoners taken by the French 28th Division had asserted that a gas attack would be made at 3.00 a.m. the following day. A warning was circulated to troops, but the 28th Division still attempted to push its line forward that night by some 500 yards near Lindenhoek. Success was only partial and the inevitable disorganisation that resulted was not fully remedied by the time the German attack commenced.

In the British sector, XXII Corps was not entirely ready either. Between Lagache Farm and Dome House it had been decided that the front line should be the main line of resistance, not the Vierstraat Line. With this in mind, the curve in the line forming the salient around Onraet Wood was to be straightened by digging a new line across its base from Petit Bois to The Mound. This undertaking had not been completed.

At 2.30 a.m. on 25 April, the first stage of the German bombardment began, drenching the rear areas with gas and high-explosive shells. At 5.00 a.m., after a pause of thirty minutes, the barrage resumed, this time targeting mainly the front-line trenches. The bombardment proved particularly effective against Allied artillery positions: by 8.30 a.m., hardly one gun per battery was still in action in the French sector. The British artillery, having spread out their guns more than their French counterparts, suffered slightly less. Even so, the gunners were forced to keep their gas masks on until 11.00 a.m. and '[the artillery] incurred heavier losses per battery than on any other day in the war'.[10]

The assault on the French line commenced at 6.30 a.m. and involved three-and-a-half German Divisions: 22nd Reserve, 4th Bavarian, the Alpine Corps and part of the 56th Division. The French front positions were very quickly overrun and by 7.10 a.m., the Leib Regiment of the Alpine Corps, advancing with the aid of supporting fire from low-flying aircraft, had reached the summit of Mount Kemmel. So rapid had been their advance that many French support troops were still in their dugouts: within thirty minutes of the Germans' arrival, the position had been consolidated and 800 prisoners taken. However, uncertainty amongst those in the rear areas as to who held the summit meant that it was spared any retaliatory artillery fire until late in the afternoon.

As the Alpine Corps established themselves on the high ground, the 450th Regiment of 56th Division captured the town of Kemmel, taking 1,600 prisoners in the process. One company of the 19th Lancashire Fusiliers and members of the 456th Field Company RE who were attached to French forces in the area tried to counter-attack, but were nearly annihilated by machine-gun fire both from ground positions and from the air.

German forces pressed on down the northern slopes of Mount Kemmel, crossed the Klein Kemmelbeek and halted around 11.00 a.m. behind a defensive artillery barrage in the valley of the Kemmelbeek itself.

On the French right, the 154th and 34th Divisions had fared little better than their compatriots in the 28th. The front positions were also quickly overrun and the 4th Bavarian and 22nd Reserves had formed a defensive flank facing Locre. The German plan was to pause at this juncture and wait for artillery to be brought up before pressing on to their final objectives. Such plans rarely run to schedule, and this one being no exception, by 6.00 p.m., the German troops were still waiting.

The French had managed to bring up two battalions of the 99th Regiment from reserve. These men, hopelessly spread out over nearly three miles from Locre to La Clytte, were all that the French could offer in the way of a line of resistance. The German timetable this time favoured the French. The publication *Les Armées Françaises dans la Grande Guerre* (Tome VI, Volume I) states on page 502, quoted in translation in the British *Official History* that 'After 11 a.m. the pressure on the French virtually ceased.'

It was lucky that the Germans were unaware of the true state of the defensive line which faced them. The gap in this line between La Clytte and the British units was eventually filled by British troops late that afternoon. Meanwhile, General de Mitry was making plans to counter-attack and re-take Mount Kemmel, with the help of British troops.

The British front line, manned by the 27th, 146th, 64th, 26th and 39th composite brigades, was attacked by the right wing of the German 56th Division and by the 19th Reserve, 13th Reserve and 7th Divisions. The right of the line, as it abutted the French positions, was held by three companies of the 12th Royal Scots (27th Brigade). A gap of 600 yards to the Onraet Wood salient was covered only by four Lewis gun detachments of the 4th Tank Brigade. In the salient were the 1/5th West Yorks (146th Brigade). In the vicinity of Dome House were the 1st East Yorks (64th Brigade) and the 1/6th West Yorks (146th Brigade). Two companies of the 7th Seaforth Highlanders were in close support behind the left flank. Beyond here, in the outpost line, were two companies of the 5th Cameronian Highlanders and No.2 Battalion of the 39th Composite Brigade. Each brigadier held one battalion in the Vierstraat Line, with other units further back in Cheapside or beyond.

As soon as the enemy could be seen advancing out of the fog (by this time they would have almost reached the British wire), they were met by concentrated machine-gun and rifle fire, nullifying all German attempts at a quick breakthrough. By seven o'clock, however, with the French in full retreat to their right rear, the 12th Royal Scots were already outflanked. Even the King's Own Scottish Borderers behind them were in danger of encirclement. These two battalions therefore fought their way back to the Vierstraat Line, only to find it partly in German possession, forcing them to continue their withdrawal to the Cheapside positions. The cost was appalling: they arrived there three officers and forty men strong (these numbers doubled after nightfall as stragglers were able to come in, but the losses remain staggering). As they arrived, they found the 9th KOYLI holding the flank on Hill 44.

Further up the line, the 1/5th West Yorks managed to hold out for two-and-a-half hours, but on their left, flamethrowers and trench mortars had helped the Germans break through the lines held by the 1st East Yorks and 1/6th West Yorks. Fighting in the rear of these units became very confused as the two battalions fell back fighting rearguard actions as they went. The 1st East Yorks put up very stubborn resistance in Onraet Wood. Both units lost very heavily, being reduced to twenty-nine and forty-six men respectively

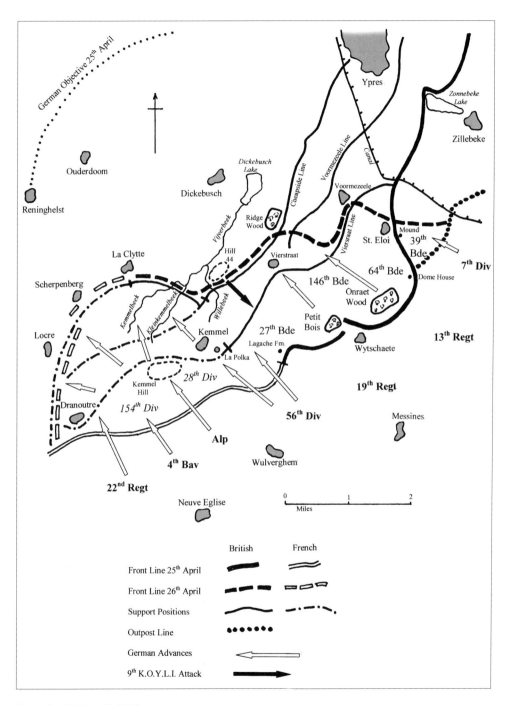

Kemmel, 25-26 April 1918.

as they reached the Cheapside Line. Now isolated in the front trenches, the 1/5th West Yorks fell back to the Vierstraat Line, reaching it at 11.00 a.m., where they joined the 1/7th West Yorks (146th Brigade reserve) and the 9th Scottish Rifles (attached 26th Brigade). Here they attempted to form a defensive flank. A similar manoeuvre was forced upon the 26th Brigade units on the extreme left of the British positions. They had held out against the initial German assaults, but were required to take up south-facing positions as the 64th Brigade units on their right retired.

Soon after midday, the Germans took the village of Vierstraat, but then paused. To the west of this location, German attacks came up against McCulloch's 9th KOYLI and were brought to a standstill.

At 2.45 a.m. that morning, just prior to the commencement of the German artillery bombardment, Brig.-Gen. Headlam had ordered the 9th KOYLI, who were in camp behind the Cheapside Line, to stand by and send out a patrol to assess the situation. A warning message had also gone back to the 15th DLI in Dickebusch. At 5.15 a.m., the KOYLI positions were peppered with gas shells and they expected a German attack at any moment. The attack did not materialise and by 6.15 a.m. the gas had been dispersed by the breeze and breakfast was ordered! By 6.30 a.m., however, more gas shells had arrived and the men were forced to move to higher ground, to Hill 44, many of them suffering from the effects of both gas and a ruined breakfast.

Soon after, French soldiers could be seen retreating on the battalion's right, and German machine-gun bullets were beginning to find the KOYLI positions. The French troops were streaming back from Kemmel in seemingly demoralised fashion. KOYLI officers who tried to get useful intelligence from them could barely get a coherent sentence: many replied to the enquiries with the single word, 'gaz'. The arrival of a French orderly at 64th Brigade HQ at 8.30 a.m. confirmed the earlier sightings and affirmed that the French front line had collapsed. Headlam immediately sent an order to the effect that the 9th KOYLI were to hold the Cheapside Line at Hill 44. By the time the message arrived, the battalion was already immersed in the task. Stubborn resistance and accurate small arms fire brought the German advance to a halt.

'This unexpected resistance took the Germans by surprise; they were thrown into considerable disorder and suffered many casualties.'[11] Thus ran the *Official History's* account: the Battalion War Diary makes the same point, but in a far less objective manner: '[The battalion] got into position and dealt out death with such success that the German attack came to a standstill and nothing could be seen except for a few furtive skirmishers and some more stout-hearted machine gunners who kept up a desultory fire on our front.'[12]

The situation was helped by the fact that 'we had one field gun with us and a couple of sporting artillery officers. They swung the gun round and fired direct at some Bosches advancing 1,200 yards away in our right rear: at the same time we opened up on him and he fled.'[13]

The situation was still fluid, however. The Germans began to work their way around the KOYLI right flank towards La Clytte, and with both flanks well and truly 'in the air', McCulloch decided to counter-attack. Events fortunately pre-empted this perceived necessity; friendly troops were observed coming up on both right and left flanks. Ten Lewis Gun teams from the 13th Tank Battalion had turned up by 12.30, and a company of the 8th Black Watch came on the scene a couple of hours later. The Lewis Guns were commented upon by the War Diarist as 'a most welcome addition'. Finally, 240 men from the 15th DLI arrived and were put under McCulloch's command.

For the rest of the day the 9th KOYLI and its attached units continued to hold off the Germans, despite shelling, 'checking any attempts of the enemy to advance against or past them.'[14] Brig.-Gen. McCulloch's personal diary fills in a few more details:

As soon as the Germans got it too hot from rifle fire in the open they rushed back into the shelter of some huts and stables which lay between Hill 44 and the main Vierstraat-Kemmel road. As soon as they got there our guns [artillery] opened up on them and drove them out of the stables again. The consequence was, severe loss was inflicted on the Germans and they were completely disorganised.[15]

At about 10.00 p.m., the Germans had obviously decided to call it a day, as they were seen to be digging in just to the west of Kemmel village, opposite the KOYLI positions.

The KOYLI stand that day cost them twenty-four fatalities. At some point during the action, Lt-Col. McCulloch was hit in the face by sniper fire but was able to carry on. The overall British position at nightfall ran as follows: from the junction with the French just south-east of La Clytte to join the Cheapside Line at Hill 44, onwards along Cheapside for two miles as far as Ridge Wood, then across to the Vierstraat Line 2,000 yards north-east of the village, thence along that line to Voormezeele before finally running forward to the outpost line north-west of St Eloi.

General Plumer had wanted to organise a counter-attack for 5.00 p.m. that same evening, but the French could not be ready in time; the 39th Division, moving up, would not reach the start line in time to add their weight to the proceedings. Zero hour was postponed to 3.00 a.m. on the 26th. The French 39th and British 25th Divisions would bear the brunt. During the night the weather turned very wet, with heavy rain after midnight. As the rain eventually ceased in the small hours, fog descended. The two Divisions advanced as ordered at three o'clock and, despite the muddy ground and the flooded Kemmelbeek, made it into the village of Kemmel.

The Brigade-Major had personally brought orders to the 9th KOYLI at 1.00 a.m. for the battalion to attack at 4.25 a.m., the aim being to advance in a south-easterly direction, the objective being the re-taking of part of the Vierstraat Line. They were promised a creeping barrage advancing at the rate of 100 yards every four minutes, finally coming to rest on a line 250 yards beyond the Vierstraat-La Polka trench line. Once the KOYLIs moved off, their positions were to be taken by the 15th DLI.

The battalion formed up as required for the attack: 'A', 'C' and 'B' Companies in the front line, left to right, with 'D' Company behind them in close support. They were to go forward in two waves of two lines each. Each company would have two platoons in the front line and the remaining two forty yards in the rear. 'D' Company was to be 150 yards behind the front wave.

The promised artillery barrage failed to materialise: a few eighteen-pounders firing at a rate of one round per minute was all that was forthcoming. Nevertheless, the men advanced at the appropriate time. As the assault got under way, it became clear that the 9th KOYLI were on their own. The right front company ('B') became aware that the Black Watch battalion on their right had not left their trenches. A similar situation was noticed regarding the West Yorks on the left. Both flank companies of the KOYLIs suffered heavily from machine-gun fire once the Germans realised that only one battalion was on the move. On the right, 2nd-Lt Marsden, in charge of 'B' Company, went to talk to the Black Watch who informed him that they had received no orders for the attack and refused to budge. On the left, the West Yorks complained that their attack had been stalled by machine-gun fire almost as it had begun.

As Marsden's company formed a defensive flank on the right, 2nd-Lt Dove, commanding 'D' Company, saw from his rearward position that 'A' Company in front of him and to his left was in serious trouble. He steered his company across and moved through them to form a stronger defensive flank, but suffered heavy casualties in the process from close-range machine-gun and rifle fire.

The centre company, under Capt. Ellenberger, had by this time managed to get forward some 1,200 yards. They too suffered heavy casualties from small arms fire, but even an SOS flare sent up from the German trenches failed to bring down very much in the way of shelling. At 6.30 a.m. a report was received back from 'C' Company, who, well aware of their exposed position, had decided to withdraw to a line approximately 400 yards ahead of their jumping-off point. This was effected without too many casualties under cover of the still lingering mist. In fact, the battalion had managed to capture about seventy prisoners. Between 4.30 and 5.15 a.m., only twenty-three of them had passed Battalion HQ. The War Diary comments that 'summary action' had been taken by the escorts with the remainder.

By noon, all companies had withdrawn to come into line with the centre company. German artillery opened up a bombardment along the whole front, but the 9th KOYLI were lucky this time: most shells burst about 300 yards in the rear. This barrage lasted until 3.00 p.m.

The Diarist estimated that the effective fighting strength of the battalion was by this time only 100 rifles. McCulloch's wound was becoming painful and this, combined with the effects of gas from the previous morning, led to him being relieved by Maj. Greenwood, who took over command of what was left of the battalion.

Trials and tribulations were not over for the day, however. The whole front line was being reorganised, requiring the 9th KOYLI to move down to the right, allowing two companies of the 15th DLI to occupy their vacated trenches. This prompted a further enemy artillery bombardment to open at 4.00 p.m. This time it was the turn of Battalion HQ to suffer a number of casualties and the personnel was forced to move into the cellar of a nearby farm for safety.

At 5.00 p.m., orders were received that the 64th Brigade was to be relieved by the 148th Brigade. 9th KOYLI and 15th DLI surrendered their trenches without a fight to the 1/4th KOYLI, completing the manoeuvre by 2.00 a.m. on 28 April. The battalion moved back to Redhorseshoe Camp near Reninghelst and the literary bent of the Diarist was allowed to come to the fore: 'The first grey of dawn was in the sky as the last HQ'ers moved into camp.'[16]

He went on to mention that casualties sustained during their short spell in the front line ran to 262 Other Ranks. Appendix I shows that 102 of these were fatal. They had also lost one officer killed: 2nd-Lt Paul Nicholson had died during the abortive attack on 26 April. His body was never recovered and his name joins those of so many of his comrades on the Tyne Cot Memorial.

At 2.00 p.m. that day it is recorded that five officers and 155 Other Ranks rejoined the battalion from the nucleus party left behind out of harm's way. Companies were now approximately seventy strong. A German bombardment that evening and an SOS flare saw the 9th KOYLI moved up to a position of readiness along the Ouderdom road. In position by 9.45 p.m., they were ordered back to camp fifteen minutes later as the bombardment subsided.

This pantomime was repeated at four o'clock the next morning to coincide with another German bombardment. At 6.30 a.m. shells were falling amongst the 9th KOYLI

Private Leonard Calvert, killed 27 April 1918.

and three soldiers paid for this state of readiness with their lives, although no infantry attack had developed.

One of the three men killed was Pte L. Calvert. Just under a month later, the *Dewsbury Reporter* ran the full story:

Batley Carr Tuner Killed
Information of an unofficial character, but which unfortunately bears the impression of being only too true reached Mr and Mrs George Henry Calvert of Warwick Road, Batley Carr on Sunday concerning their son, Pte Leonard Calvert, KOYLI, and it has cast a gloom over the household. They had heard nothing from Pte Calvert for some time and in consequence they had begun to feel very anxious about him. The communication containing the sad news of his death was addressed to Miss Laycock, of Eastfield Road, Northorpe – to whom Pte Calvert was engaged – by Pte G. Metcalfe of the Transport Section, KOYLI. Pte Metcalfe said: 'I am sorry to have to inform you of the death of Pte Leonard Calvert. He was left out of the line to stay with the transport where he had the misfortune to be killed. I saw him killed and he suffered no pain, because death was instantaneous. I assisted to bury him. I took possession of his pocket wallet from which I got your address and also a letter which you had sent him. I will get his personal belongings and send them to his home as soon as I can.' Private Calvert was born at Howden Clough and would have been twenty-seven if he had lived until August 3rd. His parents lived in Leeds for a time and later returned to Ravensthorpe where they lived for seven years. They have now been at Batley Carr the same length of time. Prior to becoming head tuner for Messrs J. Fenton & Sons Leeds Mill (formerly Messrs Ibbotson & Co), Mr G.H. Calvert was head tuner at Messrs Joseph Newsome & Sons Mill, Batley

Carr. Pte Calvert was a tuner for Messrs G.H. Hurst & Co at Bright's Mill, Batley. He had a painful experience when he first arrived in France. After being in the trenches for four days he was brought out suffering very acutely from rheumatism and trench feet which necessitated his return to England, where he spent twelve months. On Easter Monday last he returned to France. On Wednesday official news reached Batley Carr to the effect that Pte Calvert was killed in action on April 29th. His brother, Pte John Calvert is also in the Army.[17]

Ten o'clock brought with it orders to return to camp once more, and two hours later a move to Lederzeele was proposed. The arrangement was that the battalion would be transported by rail, but the scheduled train was cancelled and the men marched as far as Steenvoorde, just over the border into France, where they were able to bivouac in field for the night. The following day, the 30th, the battalion continued its march westwards, presumably abandoning all hope of rail transportation, finally arriving at their original destination, Lederzeele, a few miles north of St Omer, at 4.30 p.m. Here, they expected to find billets, but Fortune grimaced once more: the area was full of French, American and British troops. All available buildings were fully occupied and the battalion was faced instead with a final march of just over a mile to fields north of St Omer where they were able to bivouac. Thirty bivouac sheets arrived shortly after they did and were fixed up by those fortunate enough to get them.

After a cold night in the open, the men were able to wash in nearby ponds. The 1 May dawned bright and the temperature rose with the sun. A further twenty-five tents and a marquee arrived, the latter due to Maj. Greenwood beating the CO of 15th DLI on the toss of a coin. Company strength was up to eighty-five, and the whole battalion was under canvas.

The following day was quiet and reasonably uneventful. The men received new shirts and underwear and the brigade received a visit from the Corps Commander, Lt-Gen. Sir A.J. Godley KCB KCMG. No comment in the Diary is made as to which of the two were more gratefully received, but the latter complimented the battalion commanders on the 'Magnificent fighting spirit they had shewn under his command'. Godley took pains to impress on the battalion commanders that he was sincere in his remarks and said that he had 'never commanded better troops'. This message, along with the contents of a letter in similar vein from Brig.-Gen. Campbell was conveyed to the troops.

On arrival at this camp, the battalion had received notification that McCulloch and Greenwood had both been awarded the DSO and that 2nd-Lts. J.A. Greenshields and V.R. Gregg were to get the Military Cross.

The 3 May, along with the arrival of a new doctor, Capt. G. de H. Dawson, a Mons veteran who had recently returned from Italy, saw the presentation of Military Medals by Major Greenwood to the following men:

17733 Sgt C. Weldon	37286 Pte C.D. Nixon
34912 A/Cpl A.J. Harrison	30318 L/Cpl H. Davill
24380 Sgt T. Armstrong	38787 Pte H. Wright
39756 Pte J. Dixon	39652 L/Cpl Tindall (Bar to MM)
37076 Pte T.A. Heseltine	16501 Cpl G. Morgan
34063 Pte S. Fox	37665 Pte J.D. Thompson
39852 Sgt A. Potter	23657 Cpl O. Simmonds.

The same day, the battalion received orders to proceed the few miles to St Omer the following morning. Once there, the entire battalion boarded a train and set off south-wards. They were on the train for the whole of 5 May, which allowed Capt. Ellenberger the time to put down his thoughts on the recent attack in a letter home:

Rather sudden and a bit of a rush, but we did it and got on pretty well, only the people on either flank who were supposed to come with us never left their trenches, so we killed some Bosches, took some prisoners, and had to come back again. A complete muddle on the part of the Staff from beginning to end. All they can do is send us complimentary chits – they don't come up and see the situation themselves: they rest content to call the situation 'obscure'; it's safer for them that way. Well there's not much more about it that I can put in here. Except, as I told you, that I've been put in for a bar to my MC – rather amusing, but very silly: just a reward for not being killed!![18]

Ellenberger was not the only one putting his thoughts on paper. Lt-Col. McCulloch wrote a letter of complaint to 64th Brigade HQ regarding the same attack. He bemoaned the failure of both neighbouring battalions to advance, adding that the Black Watch had mistakenly opened fire on the 9th KOYLI men, believing them to be German. He was most disparaging about the artillery support:

In addition to that I wish to complain about the artillery barrage which was put down, which was of the most futile description, in fact, unless one had been told, one would not have known it was intended for a barrage at all. I cannot see how more than four guns could have been firing over my front, and it had absolutely no effect on the German machine gunners, who remained at their posts and worked their guns with their accustomed skill.[19]

Any reply from 64th Brigade HQ was not preserved.

13

CHEMIN DES DAMES

South of Ypres, the German forces had made one last effort to bring about a decisive result: an attack between Meteren and Zillebeke against the Franco-British positions, at 5.00 a.m. on 29 April, had won some ground, but only temporarily. A counter-attack soon restored the situation. A simultaneous German assault against Belgian forces near Langemarck, to the north of Ypres, had also failed. These were to be the Germans' final efforts here. Hazebrouk was still in Allied hands, as were the heights of Cassel and Mont des Cats. Ypres survived, and the threat to the Channel ports was, for the time being at least, over.

The Allies were to get something of a breather. Foch saw the opportunity to create a sizeable General Reserve force, this to be positioned behind the Franco-British front in the north, where both he and Haig feared a renewal of the German offensive. In order to be able to add fresh French Divisions to this reserve, Foch and Haig had agreed to a system of *roulement*: the French units would be withdrawn from a quiet sector of the line and their place taken by tired British Divisions. Four of the five Divisions chosen were placed under the command of the staff of IX Corps (Lt-Gen. Sir A.H. Gordon), and sent to the French Sixth Army on the Aisne River, west of Reims. The four were the 8th, 21st, 25th and 50th Divisions. All had suffered heavy losses in the previous two months and none was yet back up to full strength.

[They] had been only partly filled up to establishment, mainly with drafts of imperfectly trained young recruits. Casualties among the more experienced officers and NCO's had been exceptionally heavy, so that a period of rest for organisation and training was most necessary to render the Divisions again fit to take part in active operations.[1]

Some anxiety was expressed by the British General Staff as to the suitability of the sector chosen for this rest and recuperation, but they were assured by the French that the region was 'suitable and quiet'.[2]

The 21st Division was certainly in need of a break from the rigours it had endured through March and April 1918. Casualty figures for the periods were calculated to total 8,392.

It was under these circumstances that the 9th KOYLI found themselves travelling southwards on 4 and 5 May. A one-hour halt on the morning of the fifth at Pointoise near Paris for breakfast allowed the men to stretch their legs. The War Diary expresses the men's delight at being amongst new surroundings, in a green and fertile countryside untouched by the war. They reached their penultimate destination, Bouleuse, at eleven o'clock that evening, and marched on the seven miles from there to Romigny, about thirteen miles south-west of Reims. On arriving, at about 2.30 a.m. the following day, they were billeted in a 'splendid'[3] French camp, where all officers and Other Ranks had a proper bed each. When they awoke on 6 May, they bathed, received some new clothing and were paid.

The Champagne region in which they now found themselves must have been a stark contrast to the areas of war-ravaged France and Belgium they had thus far encountered. Sidney Rogerson, author of *The Final Ebb*, is quoted by John Terraine:

To battered, battle-weary troops, whose only knowledge of France was based upon their experience of the Northern front, the Champagne country in the full glory of spring was a revelation. Gone the depressing monotony of Flanders, drab and weeping, with its muds, its mists, its pollards and its pavé; gone the battle-wrecked landscapes of Picardy and the Somme, with their shattered villages and blasted woods. Here all was peace. The countryside basked in the blazing sunshine. Trim villages nestled in quiet hollows beside lazy streams, and tired eyes were refreshed by the sight of rolling hills, clad with great woods golden with laburnum blossom; by the soft greenery of lush meadowland, shrubby vineyards and fields of growing corn.[4]

Harold Yeo, writing home soon after his arrival in this sector, puts it more briefly, yet his phonetic spelling conveys all that he and the men must have felt about their new surroundings: 'We have at last... settled down in a bee-autiful spot.'[5]

After a quiet and restful day on 7 May, a training program commenced the next morning: musketry was the first item on the agenda, to be enjoyed by all, including the Lewis gunners. A route march followed in the afternoon, and thus the pattern was set for the next three days. Instructions given by a visiting French officer and some of his NCOs on the intricacies of the French-style grenade were to enlighten the troops on the 9th, and on the 10th the battalion's officers were treated to a talk by Brig.-Gen. Maxwell Scott on 'Relations with the French Army'.

As training continued on 11 May, the Battalion CO and his company commanders recced the trench line between Berry-au-Bac and Bruant (to the north and slightly west of the town of Reims). This twelve-hour jaunt was described by a returning participant as a 'tiring day, but very interesting'.[6]

Orders were received that evening for a move northwards, and accordingly, at 9.15 a.m. on 12 May, the battalion marched off. It was a depressing day, weather-wise; the rain was falling in torrents and a cold wind as an accompaniment did nothing to lighten the men's spirits as they covered the fourteen miles to Prouilly. They crossed the River Vesle at a point about ten miles west of Reims and arrived at their destination at half past two in the afternoon, thoroughly wet through. Only two men had dropped out during the march, and these were able to hitch a ride with the Transport Section, which luckily had followed the same route as the marching column. Their luck was indeed in, as Division had refused to allow a motor ambulance to bring up the rear for any such instance.

Waiting to welcome the men to Prouilly was an order to relieve the 5th Battalion of the 299th French Infantry Regiment in their trenches on the night of 13/14 May. This necessitated a 3.00 a.m. departure from Prouilly the day after they had arrived there, so after reaching camp at Champignonnières at 5.00 a.m., the battalion was able to rest until nine that evening. It was important to execute the relief under the cover of darkness, as the high ground over which both battalions would have to move was under direct observation by the enemy. The task was completed without mishap between 10.00 p.m. and 1.30 a.m. This put the 9th KOYLI into the support line. The tone of the War Diary returned to a level of cheerfulness, prompted by an upturn in the weather conditions and the pleasant surroundings. It described the area as calm and peaceful, 'far removed from the stress and turmoil of the fighting in the north... weather took a turn for the better; promises to be hot.'[7]

In the letter from Harold Yeo quoted earlier, he goes on to describe the almost idyllic scene from the point of view of Staff HQ, idyllic in the sense that neither side seemed at that point in time keen to inflict any damage on their adversaries:

... a few miles away we can see where the Hun Brigade headquarters sit on a similar hill. Every morning at eleven o'clock the Hun shoots five shells at our hill and we shoot five at his – but of course care is taken to shoot where nobody lives, and at a nice convenient time too when everyone is usually out.[8]

The 18 May was another quiet and uneventful day, allowing the men to get to know their way around the trench system. It seems to be a tradition that a battalion taking over trenches from an alien unit never find their new surroundings quite up to scratch. This occasion was to be no exception. Although the trenches themselves were described by the War Diary as clean, sanitation and hygiene apparently left a great deal to be desired. The day turned out very hot and sunny, and the men were able to observe the half dozen or so enemy aircraft that flew over their sector from time to time. The following day, the weather was still hot, and the enemy planes were still active. Meanwhile, the Divisional Commander paid a hurried visit to the battalion and complimented the men both on their appearance and on their trench discipline. Company commanders also accompanied the CO on a recce of the front-line trenches, this being the inevitable precursor to a move by the battalion in that general direction. A few days' grace remained, however, and during the interim Lt-Col. McCulloch was able to rejoin his battalion from leave.

The expected relief was ordered for 21 May; the 9th KOYLI was to take over the 15th DLI positions in the front line. Prior to the move, however, that day saw the arrival of good news. XXII Corps Routine Order No.1684 announced the award of more Military Medals to men of the battalion. The recipients were: 37655 Cpl C. Martin, 18968 Pte T. Slater, 21003 Pte W.H. Lancashire, 18969 Pte J. Vickers, 34683 Pte J. Scales and 34968 Pte W. Laidler.

Between 9.15 p.m. and 1.00 a.m., the 9th KOYLI and the 15th DLI successfully exchanged positions. Thirty minutes later, the CO and his Adjutant commenced a tour of these new front-line positions, returning to Battalion HQ by 8.00 a.m. The actual front line was held during daylight hours only by small sentry groups (along with observers and snipers,) which withdrew at night to a 'line of resistance' some 4-500 yards to the rear. The most advanced of these positions were actually north of the Aisne–Marne canal. The battalion was to adopt the French defensive scheme while being part of their Sixth Army, whereby in response to a raid, all wire gates in the trenches were to be closed and a stand made on the line of resistance. In response to a large-scale attack, the battalion was to withdraw over the canal, blowing up the bridges as they went, and take up a line in the bastions to the south-west of the waterway.

Two more days of calm ensued. At 1.00 a.m. on the 25th, however, the Leicesters on the left launched a raid on the German lines. They did not penetrate far, finding the front line trenches full of wire and more or less impassable. The German artillery did not respond to the British preparatory barrage; a few machine guns opened up, but other than that the Germans took no notice.

On the right of the 9th KOYLI at this time was a French Zouave Regiment (91st Brigade, 3rd Zouave Regiment), a unit made up of colonial troops. Their CO and machine-gun officer came to lunch at 9th KOYLI Battalion HQ on 26 May.

Later that day, a reorganisation of the brigade front took place: right and left sub-sectors were created, the 1st East Yorks on the right and the 9th KOYLI on the left. Companies were concentrated in and around so-called 'bastions': 'C' Company was in 'Chasseur' and 'Wattignies', 'A' Company in 'Jemmapes', 'B' company in 'Ouvrage de la Meule (one platoon), Redoute des Mousequetaires (one platoon), and Redoute des Grenadiers (two platoons). These three companies were all to the south of the canal. It fell to 'D' Company to man the advanced positions to the north of it. The 1st East Yorks were deployed in similar fashion, with only the one company in the forward positions.

At 9.30 p.m. that same day, 2nd-Lt Marsden of 'C' Company (on the battalion right), sent a message to HQ saying that he had been warned by the French that there were signs of an impending attack apparent in the German lines. These had been observed for two or three days, but there is no indication that any such information had been imparted to HQ Staff by the Zouave CO during lunch. Apparently, new ammunition and supply dumps were being built; new trenches had been dug and wire had been cleared. Large numbers of troops were also reported to be on the roads in the German rear positions. Coinciding with this communication came another reporting unusual telephone activity from the other side of no man's land: the Germans were speaking in clear, uncoded language about barrages, trenches and troop dispositions.

A prisoner captured by the French that day had told them that a barrage was to commence at 1.00 a.m. the next morning, the 27th, and that Zero hour for the attack was set for one hour later.

Although the reorganisation and reliefs were still in progress, all 9th KOYLI units had received their first warning of impending events by 11.00 p.m. The idyll, such as it was, was clearly over.

The Germans had been preparing for this attack for some time, initial orders for an assault in this sector having gone out as early as 17 April. One week later, Maj.-Gen. von Unruh, Chief of Staff of 4th Reserve Corps, was instructed to undertake a reconnaissance of the Allied positions and address the feasibility of the proposed offensive. His report was favourable, and preparations went ahead. On the evening of 26 May, thirty German Divisions and 1,150 artillery batteries stood ready. Fifteen of these Divisions were completely fresh, and none of the others had taken part in the Lys Offensive: 'all had enjoyed at least seven weeks' rest'[9] since their exertions in March.

Facing the attack frontage were, left to right, the French 61st, 21st and 22nd Divisions, covering nearly twenty miles between Leuilly and Craonnelle. Then came the British 50th, 8th and 21st Divisions (with 25th Division in reserve), stretching eastwards and then south eastwards for a further fourteen miles, where the right flank of 64th Brigade abutted the French 45th Division near Loivre.

The principles on which a defensive battle was to be fought had been laid down by Foch on 19 April. Unlike on the Franco-British sector in the north, where every yard of ground was to be tenaciously contested, elsewhere 'it was possible, without serious incon-venience, to abandon a certain amount of ground in the face of a violent enemy onslaught.'[10]

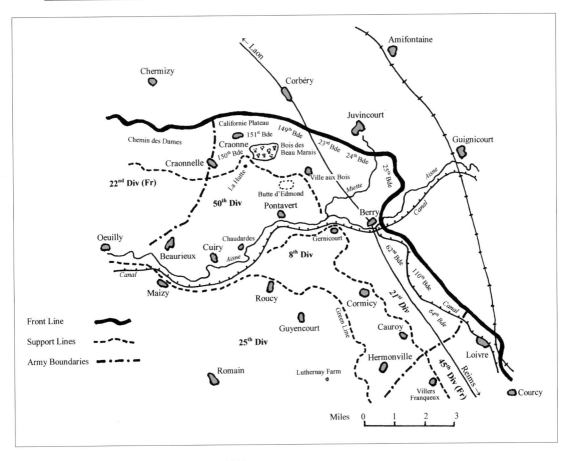

Chemin des Dames: British Sector, May 1918.

Accordingly, the Front Zone (or 'First Position' as it was known to the French), should be lightly held; the enemy should be properly engaged and stopped in the Battle Zone or 'Second Position'. General Duchêne, commanding the French Sixth Army, was, however, of the opinion that in a sector so close to Paris, no ground should be voluntarily surrendered to the enemy, and accordingly placed the majority of his troops in forward positions with orders to defend the narrow Chemin des Dames ridge, won at such great cost during the Nivelle offensive the previous year, at all costs. Foch, faced with this situation, had to either remove Duchêne from command, or give way to his subordinate. He chose the latter course. The French Sixth Army thus lined up with twenty-six battalions in the First Position, five in the Second, and a further seven behind them. The situation on the British front was similar: the line of resistance of the Battle Zone was to run from the Californie Plateau on the ridge itself, through the Bois des Buttes (just south west of Ville aux Bois), and thence across the Gernicourt Plateau and through the villages of Cormicy, Cauroy and Villers Franqueux. Nevertheless, most units were placed in advance of this line, and when Lt-Gen. Gordon expressed his concern, he was met by General Duchêne's curt reply: *'J'ai dit'* (I have spoken).

At 1.00 a.m. on 27 May 1918, as predicted by the German prisoner, some 4,000 guns opened a tremendous barrage. 'Every battery position, village, farm and railway station, every bridge and road junction'[11] as far back as the River Vesle, that is to a depth of about twelve miles, was targeted with high explosive and gas. The First Positions, crowded with French and British defenders, were in places simply obliterated.

Practically all Allied battalion and brigade HQ's too had come under fire and communications had been seriously disrupted. 'So thorough had been the preliminary destruction that all resistance was crushed and the [German] infantry had only to advance to take possession of the front positions.'[12]

At 3.40 a.m., (and not at 2.00 a.m. as predicted by the prisoner), twenty minutes before it began to get light, the barrage lifted and moved on. This was the signal for the German infantry to leave their positions and advance through the mist and smoke towards what was left of the Allied front line.

The Allies were outnumbered by seventeen Divisions to six (the Germans held six more in reserve, the Allies four). The German forces were not distributed evenly along the front, however: the French 21st and 22nd Divisions bore the brunt, facing three and five German Divisions respectively along the main Chemin des Dames ridge.

The French 61st and 21st Divisions on the extreme left wing of the attack were unable to hold their front positions and by 11.00 a.m. the villages of Charonne and Vailly on the northern bank of the River Aisne, and some four-and-a-half miles behind the original front line, were in enemy hands.

The 22nd Division fared little better: the enemy were in full possession of their sector of the Chemin des Dames ridge by 5.30 a.m. They were approaching the Aisne by 9.00 a.m. and the bridge over the river at Oeuilly was in German hands by 10.00 a.m. Two more bridges at Bourg and Pont Arcy were lost before midday: the Germans were swarming across the river between Oeuilly and Maizy, although Villers en Prayères, a mile or so to the south of Oeuilly and just across the river, held out for another half hour.

Moving eastwards, the next sector of the line was the responsibility of the British 50th Division. Their left sector, including the Californie Plateau, the eastern extremity of the Chemin des Dames ridge, was manned by troops of the 150th Brigade. Only small, isolated parties of these units managed to escape the initial onslaught: the plateau was completely overrun by six o'clock. 'By 8.00 a.m., therefore, the 150th Brigade, except the usual detachments left in billets for administrative duties, had ceased to exist.'[13]

To their right was the 151st Brigade: they had the 6th and 8th DLI and a pioneer company of the 7th DLI in the front positions. They were attacked from both left and front: they managed to hold up the enemy on the edge of the Bois de Beau Marais for three-quarters of an hour, but each position was successively outflanked and surrounded, resulting in the almost complete destruction of these DLI units. At Cuiry, on the north bank of the Aisne, the remnants of the brigade held out until eleven, but were soon after taken from the west and rear.

Riddell's Brigade, the 149th, only had one battalion in the exposed front position: the 4th Northumberland Fusiliers. The brigade plan was to hold the enemy on a line along the Reims–Corbéry road. Four German tanks helped their infantry to break through this line, and the survivors of the 4th, along with their sister battalion, the 6th Northumberland Fusiliers, held out as best they could near Ville au Bois. The tanks turned the flank and the trenches were lost. Some redoubts in the Battle Zone fought on, but the defenders were by now surrounded and their fate inevitable.

The 8th Division had nine under-strength and battle-weary battalions facing twenty-one fresh, full-strength German battalions. Of the 23rd Brigade, on the left, only three companies of the 2nd West Yorks were in the front lines, and their resistance was inevitably brief. The enemy advance to the Battle Zone was rapid, and the three companies of the 2nd Middlesex holding a line of redoubts in front of it were quickly overwhelmed. There remained 'D' Company of the 2nd Middlesex and the 2nd Devonshires in the Bois des Buttes, a wood covering a conical hill south west of Ville au Bois. They were engaged by the enemy by 5.15 a.m., and were able to hold out for nearly three hours; by 8.00 a.m., the Devonshire battalion had all but ceased to exist and their CO, Lt-Col. Anderson-Morshead, decided to try and fight a rearguard action back to the River Aisne. Only about fifty men were lucky enough to make it across the river, and many of those were wounded. For its gallant stand against overwhelming odds at the Bois des Buttes, the battalion was later awarded the Croix de Guerre.

The 24th Brigade front battalion, the 2nd Northants, was quickly forced to withdraw to the Battle Zone where the 1st Worcesters were in position. They held out until about 5.00 a.m. when their flank was turned by a German advance down the Miette Valley and their positions overrun. By 6.00 a.m., both battalions had effectively been destroyed.

The 25th Brigade sat in what was in effect a mini-salient: they were attacked from both the north and the south-east, and were forced back. Brigade HQ, north of Berry au Bac, was surrounded almost before the Staff were aware of the situation, and they had to fight their way back to the village of Gernicourt, but Brig.-Gen. Husey was badly wounded and captured. He succumbed to his wounds three days later.

Gernicourt, south of the Aisne, overlooked the river from its elevated position. It was garrisoned by the 22nd DLI and the French II/23rd Territorial Regt, who between them could muster twenty-four machine guns. They were reinforced early in the morning by the other two companies of the 2nd East Lancs and by members of the 2nd and 490th Field Companies RE. On their left, in the woods, were the 1st Sherwood Foresters, who, at 7.00 a.m., were able to watch all but one bridge over the canal in this sector blown up. The troops were able to concentrate such intense fire on the one remaining bridge that the Germans were held up here for several hours. The Gernicourt position had, however, been outflanked on both sides by 1.00 p.m., and with their situation becoming rapidly and obviously untenable, survivors retired to the Green Line. 'Less than ten companies had held up twelve enemy battalions for over six hours.'[14]

The British 21st Division held a frontage of nearly five miles on the flat ground to the south of the Aisne. It had all three brigades in the line and each brigade had two battalions in the Forward Zone and one in reserve. Between the two zones was the Aisne–Marne canal as it ran south-east towards Reims. This was about twenty yards wide, not quite full of water but still unfordable, with swampy ground on both sides. The front of the battle zone consisted of a chain of redoubts running in front of the Berry au Bac–Reims road on the Division right and behind that road on the left. This was considered to be the main line of resistance.

The Division was attacked initially by only one German Division and part of another. Later, other German units from the broken 8th Division front joined in the fray from the north. All eleven companies positioned north-east of the canal were to suffer the same fate: in the darkness, the front positions were quickly overrun, and although several bridges remained intact, very few men succeeded in getting back over the waterway. These companies were: two from the 12/13th Northumberland Fusiliers and three of the 2nd Lincs in 62nd Brigade, two each of the 7th and 8th Leicesters in 110th Brigade and one each of 9th KOYLI and 1st East Yorks in 64th Brigade.

On the 62nd Brigade front, Divisional left, the remnants of the forward battalions had been driven from the redoubts on the main road and were falling back to the Cauroy–Cormicy–Gernicourt line. The 1st Lincs, moving up from reserve, had advanced to positions north of Cormicy and, managing to repulse three assaults on their trenches, they were still holding out at 2.00 a.m., although the Germans advancing through the Bois de Gernicourt in the 8th Division front were threatening their left flank.

The 7th and 8th Leicesters in the front-line positions of 110th Brigade were swept away, though resistance in the Battle Zone was sterner. Two successive frontal assaults were turned back by rifle and Lewis gun fire, but the enemy changed tactics and after bombing their way up the communication trenches and employing concentrated trench-mortar fire on the British positions, they were able to surround and take all the strong-points by 1.00 a.m. The 6th Leicesters were sent up between Cauroy and Cormicy from their positions in the rear along with a company-strength unit formed from the nucleus parties of 7th and 8th Leicesters. The road between the two villages became the front line.

The 64th Brigade were lined up in their reorganised positions: 9th KOYLI in the front line on the left of the brigade sector, the 1st East Yorks on the right, and the 15th DLI in reserve at Chalons le Vergeur, close to Divisional HQ.

The barrage, when it commenced at 1.00 a.m., consisted of large amounts of gas, the rest being high explosive. 'The gas used was of several kinds, but there appeared to be a large proportion of "Yellow Cross".'[15] The 15th DLI was immediately ordered forward into its assembly positions in the sunken roads running south west of Cauroy. By 1.30 a.m., the 21st Division War Diary reports that 'All communication with battalions was cut.'[16] All messages would have to be carried by hand, or, where necessary, by pigeon.

'D' Company, 9th KOYLI, in their exposed positions east of the canal, sent out patrols during the bombardment which were able to report that by 2.15 a.m., no attempt had been made by the enemy to cross no man's land and cut our wire (the company may have been expecting the predicted 2.00 a.m. assault). The men sat, waited and watched as best they could in the darkness and the smoke for signs of a German advance. They were forced to wear their box-respirators the whole time: the War Diarist bemoans their predicament: '… our men were sore about the face, fatigued and without breakfast to commence a long day's battle.' He added ruefully that the Germans 'probably had breakfast in comfort.'[17] In Brigade HQ, the staff were also suffering the effects of the gas attack and 'sucked [their] gas helmets and cursed the Hun.'[18]

The Germans finally appeared through the mist and smoke in front of 'D' Company's positions at about 3.00 a.m. Rifle fire, grenades and, more importantly, intense Lewis gun fire from the KOYLI trenches held up the Germans as they struggled initially to get through the British wire. The attack developed into a grenade fight, and although 'D' Company held out for over an hour, their posts were eventually surrounded. Almost all were either killed, wounded or captured. Only a handful of men (the Diary actually puts the figure at five or six), were able to escape from their grave predicament, along with two officers who had been captured but had managed somehow to escape. Lt Robert Kenneth James, in command of 'D' Company, was killed.

Instructions to blow up the bridges over the canal had been given, but at least one remained intact at this point, and the Germans were able to cross the waterway without too much difficulty.

By 4.30 a.m. the Redoute des Chasseurs, and the three platoons of 'C' Company defending it, were under attack. Here too the initial assault was repulsed, but the enemy was happy to pause and pour rifle fire and grenades into the KOYLI positions from the east, north and west. It was only a matter of time before the inevitable happened: at 8.45 a.m., Brigade HQ received a message carried by pigeon, stating that the Germans had crossed the canal and that Chasseurs had been taken.

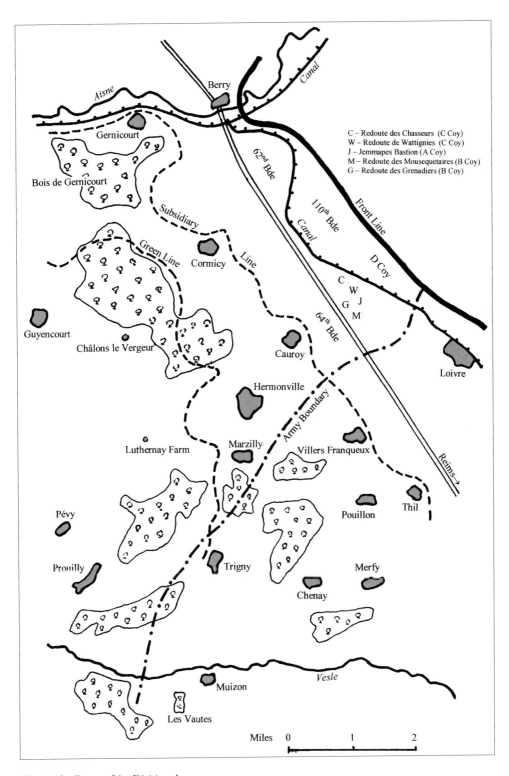

C – Redoute des Chasseurs (C Coy)
W – Redoute de Wattignies (C Coy)
J – Jemmapes Bastion (A Coy)
M – Redoute des Mousequetaires (B Coy)
G – Redoute des Grenadiers (B Coy)

Chemin des Dames: 21st Division Area.

Captain Ellenberger, commanding 'C' Company, was wounded and captured here. He was able to recall his experiences some days later in a letter home from captivity:

My Company, 'C' Coy, was relieved in the front line, or outpost line as it really was, only that evening [26 May] by 'D' Coy and I did not get back to Chasseurs Redoubt (my new post west of the canal) until about 10.30 p.m. I had three platoons and my headquarters together in Chasseurs and the remaining platoon in Wattignies – though it was really absurd to talk of having platoons, as the total strength of the company was only about eighty men. About midnight came a message to the effect that prisoners stated the bombardment would commence at 1.00 a.m., and the attack at 2.00 a.m. We did not really, even then, believe that an attack was actually coming on such a quiet sector. I went down with Shaw, my Second in Command, to see the French 'listening set' operators, who had their instrument in Chasseurs, to ask if they had any information. We took a tin of Gold Flake cigarettes with us to promote the 'entente' feeling – how I wish I had that tin here now!

The Frenchmen were quite certain nothing serious was taking place: but even while they were saying it was only to be a 'coup de main', the bombardment started. Shaw and I went at once to see how things were.[19]

The two were making their way to Wattignies Redoubt when a gas shell exploded nearby. Ellenberger seems to have suffered from the effects; Shaw managed to get him back to his dug out in Chasseurs. Ellenberger carries on the narrative, initially with uncertainty, but his recollections become more detailed and assured as the events of the morning progress:

… the rest of the night seemed like a dream. I remember going on with Shaw in a sort of nightmare. I think he was trying to get me back to the dugout. We passed my servant, Miller – I think he said he was gassed. I saw him no more, but hope he got away. In the dugout I remember Shaw told me Sgt. Tilbrook was badly and probably fatally hit, but he was taken down alive.

Shaw gave Sgt. Watson Tilbrook's respirator as Watson had lost his in hospital two days before. My next recollection is of finding myself with Shaw standing in the trench two or three hours later in the early morning. The Germans suddenly appeared and seemed to be all around us in no time. No 'SOS' went up from the front line.

We fired at figures advancing through the mist: one Lewis Gun, I remember, was completely driven from its position by a machine gun firing from somewhere close at hand. We were bombed from both sides, and found the French bombs, which were all we had, absolutely ineffective and outclassed.

The trenches, too, made the confusion worse as the French make their trenches very deep with insurmountable sides – you cannot see out of them and it is very hard to get up anywhere to have a look. It was soon all over, and we found ourselves prisoners. Shaw, I lost, he was wounded I believe, but I hear he was brought back safely by the Germans. [Evidence seems to point to the fact that Shaw was one of the officers who managed subsequently to escape, along with 2nd-Lt Holmes; these brought the first news of the attack to Battalion HQ at about 5.00 a.m.] *I was wounded in both legs… but could hobble along… after crossing the canal we met Taylor, another of my officers, untouched. We were passed back through our old trenches and taken over no man's land and along the old German line to a dressing station at Mont Spin. We were decently treated all the way. One German gave me a stick to help myself on with, but another, less polite, took it from between my knees while we were sitting outside a dressing station.*[20]

Ellenberger's family must have been very surprised and relieved to receive this letter, as an Official Telegram had by this time reached them, informing them that he had been killed in action. This communication was backed up by one from Lt-Col. McCulloch, written on 6 June:

Your son's company was holding the post close to the Aisne-Marne canal about five miles SE of Berry-au-Bac. On Mon. morning 27th May the Germans attacked. Your son and his men offered most gallant resistance. Eventually your son's company was surrounded and he died in a hand to hand encounter with the enemy.
McCulloch
Lt-Col. CO 9th KOYLI [21]

The Lieutenant-Colonel even wrote another letter some days later, giving a more detailed version of events: '... killed instantaneously at close quarters whilst making a counter-attack on Germans who had entered his trench. This is the account I got from Lt J. Shaw who was with him.'[22]

Lt Shaw was obviously mistaken: Ellenberger spent the rest of the conflict as a prisoner of war. It was while he was in captivity that the Bar to his Military Cross was confirmed.

The under-strength platoon of 'C' Company in Wattignies Redoubt was also in a precarious position: surrounded by the advancing German troops, they managed to hold out for three hours before they were finally overwhelmed. At 7.30 a.m., the full weight of the enemy attack fell on 'A' Company in the Jemmapes Bastion. Lieutenant Greenshields had by this time been seriously wounded by a shell and evacuated. Two counter-attacks by the men of 'A' Company held up the German advance. The enemy stood back and bombarded the position for two hours. A second assault then proved successful: the position finally fell at about 9.30 a.m. 2nd-Lt Hurley and thirty-eight men

Soissons Memorial.

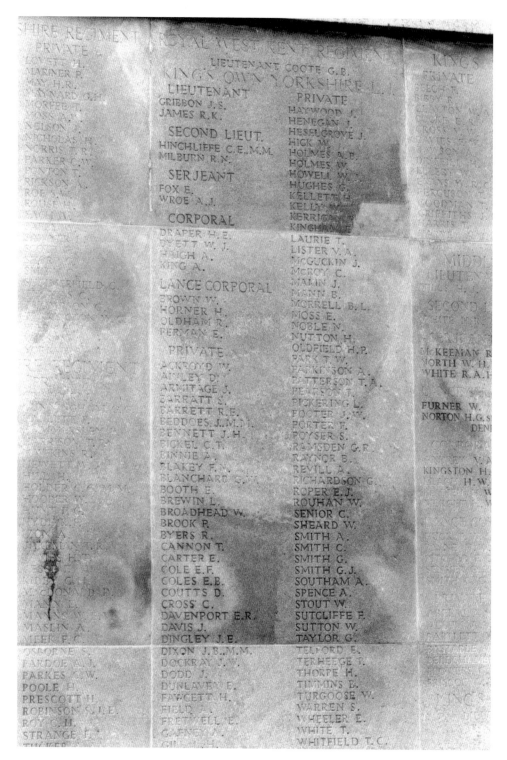

KOYLI tablet at Soissons Memorial.

managed to escape to the south-east where they joined the troops of the 1st East Yorks. At this point, the War Diarist backs up Capt. Ellenberger's opinion of the French hand grenade:

It was found during grenade conflicts that the French grenade with the tin cover inflicted few injuries on the enemy. Good up to a point for intimidation purposes, but of little use compared to the Mills grenade when it came to killing and mutilating Germans. Our men were not as proficient in grenade fighting as men of the battalion a year ago as it had been relegated to a secondary position in training of the last six months. Still, 'A' and 'B' Coys' hand-grenade fights ('B' Coy under 2nd-Lt Scott) were carried out in a courageous and determined manner against superior forces.[23]

2nd-Lt Scott and his 'B' Company men, in the Mousequetaires and Grenadiers redoubts, were in a similar position to those in Jemmapes. It was reported that both redoubts were holding out, though with the enemy all around them, at 10.30 a.m.

9th KOYLI HQ had, by this time, reported to Brigade HQ that the enemy were working their way round their left flank, moving up Antoine Trench and were across the main road which ran behind the bastions in this sector of the line. The 15th DLI also reported that the 1st East Yorks on the right were being forced back, but this withdrawal was actually by order of their commanding officer.

No more information ever came back from Mousequetaires and Grenadiers redoubts, and by 2.00 p.m., these and Jemmapes would seem to have been finally overwhelmed, as sounds of grenades and rifle fire had ceased from that direction.

Thirty Other Ranks, Battalion HQ and six men of the 1st East Yorks, under the command of Lt Holmes, took up a position to the south of that presently held by the 15th DLI. The CO moved this small force, which was in effect the only properly formed body of troops left of the battalion, to a shallow trench in front of a farm about a mile north-east of the village of Hermonville, thus about half a mile south of Cauroy, in order to get a better field of fire. They were joined here later by sixteen men of 15th DLI under Capt. Clarke who prolonged the line southwards and gained touch with the Zouaves on the right.

The Germans' final effort of the day here was a grenade attack up one of the communication trenches on the 15th DLI positions near Cauroy. They came within thirty to forty yards of the KOYLI trench during the night, but made no attempt to attack. The Yorkshiremen sat and awaited developments.

Along the rest of the front, things had continued to go badly. By the time darkness fell, the German troops in the centre, on the French 21st and 22nd Divisions' front, had even managed to cross the River Vesle. The French 13th Division, sent up from reserve positions, were trying to hold a line between Romain and Bazoches and were clinging on to the town of Fismes in their centre on the south bank of the Vesle.

In the course of a summer day the enemy had crossed two, and in places three, rivers; he had driven a salient twenty-five miles wide at the base and extending nearly twelve miles into the Allied line; he had destroyed four of the Divisions originally in the line, and nearly destroyed two more (the British 21st and French 61st), besides two others (British 25th and French 157th) sent up from the reserve.[24]

During the night, the 21st Division had received orders to withdraw to a line in touch with the French on the right, to the north of Hermonville (64th Brigade), thence south-westwards through Luthernay Farm (110th Brigade), with 62nd Brigade on the left to the south of Pévy. The 9th KOYLI did not receive any such orders, and dawn found them still in position south of Cauroy, completely alone and exposed. The Germans began to advance through Cauroy at 5.30 a.m., but were temporarily held up by this small detachment of thirty or so men. Probably more surprised than anything else to find British troops here, the Germans halted and poured rifle and machine-gun fire into the KOYLI trench. Lt-Col. McCulloch was hit in the side by a bullet at about 6.00 a.m. and was forced to go off to hospital, leaving Lt Walby in command.

The German attack reached as far as the trench-block the men had constructed during the night, and it was at about this time that the KOYLIs became aware of their precarious position: an NCO sent out to find out the situation from the 15th DLI came back with the news that they had gone. Awareness coincided with a realisation that their present position was potentially disastrous, and the decision was made to form a defensive flank along Champagne Trench to a position about 400 yards north of Hermonville. This was only a temporary measure, however; the Division had been outflanked on the left, the Germans being seen on top of the Vesle ridge by 8.00 a.m. Orders had accordingly gone out for another withdrawal, this time to positions farther to the south-east, along the heights between Trigny and Prouilly. This time, it was the 64th Brigade who did not receive the orders: by midday, the 62nd and 110th Brigades (and 7th Brigade to their left) were in their new positions and the 64th was still out on a limb. It was 2.00 p.m. before the last stragglers of the 1st East Yorks, by now reduced to about forty men, joined their compatriots on the Trigny Heights. The 9th KOYLI contingent had by this time moved southward through Marzilly to Trigny. To their left, as they made the move, they could hear quite clearly the sounds of machine-gun fire from the villages of Prouilly and Pévy. The men were joined in the new line by a Lewis Gun team from the nucleus party. The Brigadier, who had had one horse shot from under him that morning, went around the new positions and found them thus:

The line was held by a somewhat mixed party of troops. On the right, there was a French battalion, then came mixtures of the 64th Brigade with a fair percentage of officers, and then a French battalion. The French commander had a liaison officer of the 62nd Brigade with him, and the 62nd Brigade were on his left. The situation on the left of that was somewhat obscure, as the enemy were known to be in Prouilly and Jonchery. The line was situated just on the forward slope and was about 2' 6" deep and had good wire, but thick woods in front of most of it obscured the view.[25]

The 9th KOYLI War Diary describes the rest of the day as uneventful: the main German thrust was once again in the centre; Soissons was lost, the Vesle was crossed everywhere from there as far as Jonchery on the right. The most advanced German troops had reached Branges, Mareuil and Cohan. By German admission, their follow-up attacks in front of the British positions had been less than energetic:

The infantry of the 7th Reserve Division was greatly lacking in attack ardour on this day [and] stopped in the face of weak resistance… went forward very slowly with hour-long pauses, without there being a question of any real fighting… The 86th Division went forward even more slowly than the 7th Reserve and, going no further than Thil-Trigny, lost all touch with the Allies.[26]

At 3.00 a.m. the following day, 29 May, an officer going on his rounds discovered that the troops to both the left and right of the 64th Brigade's 'mixed' force had disappeared.

German troops were coming through the wire in front of the trench by this time, though only in twos and threes: possibly they did not expect to find the position manned. A quick reconnaissance by the Adjutant revealed that the Trigny defensive system had indeed been evacuated, and an even quicker decision to withdraw followed. To where, exactly, was impossible to know: they just had to move southward until they came across units they recognised. The party crossed the bridge over the River Vesle at Muizon. Here, they found the rest of the troops who had received their orders shortly after midnight, and they joined the line along the southern edge of the river; the bridge was now destroyed and the 9th KOYLI party, with the addition of another Lewis Gun team from the nucleus, was attached to what was left of the 1st East Yorks and held in reserve in a wood about half a mile south-west of Muizon, near Les Vautes.

Though not under direct attack here, the War Diary still describes their new positions as 'an unhealthy spot, and owing to the number of HQ's of various units that were in it, and the number of Mounted Orderlies which came up to it every minute, was made more unhealthy by gas, 5.9's and 4.2's.'[27]

Several French battalions soon moved up into the area and the 64th Brigade was moved back to a position in the hills between Rosnay and Germigny, a mile or so further to the rear. At 1.00 a.m. on 30 May, after the arrival of more French troops in the sector, the brigade received orders to move back to Marfaux to join the Transport Section. On arrival, at about 7.00 a.m., the remnants of 9th KOYLI numbered thirty-four, this including some stragglers who had somehow managed to rejoin their comrades. It was found that two other officers with about forty-five men and the band had already joined the Transport; the total strength of the battalion therefore amounted to 217. Those who had been involved in the fighting and were still there to tell the tale enjoyed their first real rest since the offensive had begun. After a morning resting at Marfaux, another march to the south saw them arrive at Forêt d'Epernay, having crossed the River Marne at Damery at 7.30 p.m. They bivouacked for the night in a large clearing about one-and-a-half miles south of Vauciennes. Here, a few more stragglers caught up, and a small draft of nine men increased total numbers to 236.

The last day of May 1918 saw the battalion on the move once again: a four-hour march concluded with their arrival at Chaltrait just after 1.00 p.m. The rest of the day was spent washing and generally cleaning up. 'The men were very hot, tired and dusty.'[28]

The last word of this episode goes to Harold Yeo:

Since we got up on the morning of the 26th, in the ordinary way I hadn't got any sleep until that night of the 30th (i.e. five days and four nights) except on three occasions when I got about two hours' sleep each time, at the very most. That's the worst part of these shows, the lack of sleep. It seems not to affect some people as much as others; for instance, the General doesn't sleep the whole time and yet never seems to yawn even.

Since then we've been trekking about the place and are now in quite a good village and have got pretty decent billets. Thus ends the third battle we've had since the Bosches started their pushes: so far as we are concerned, it is ended, at any rate, pro tem.[29]

14

ONTO THE OFFENSIVE
AUGUST AND SEPTEMBER 1918

The Chemin des Dames German offensive continued in the 9th KOYLI's absence: by 3 June 1918, the German Army had reached the banks of the River Marne, just as they had done some four years earlier. The fall of the town of Château Thierry, less than sixty miles from Paris, was, effectively, to prove the limit of the enemy advance. The Germans had, in spectacular fashion, created a salient some forty miles wide at its base and extending to a depth of thirty miles. Its defence had cost the Allies dear: the British had suffered almost 29,000 casualties, the French over three times that number. As with 'Michael' and 'Georgette' before, however, the German advance had run out of steam. The depth of the new salient made it difficult to supply and defend, the wings being vulnerable to counter-attack. Even von Unruh, who had originally scouted the ground and pronounced it favourable for the offensive, was forced to admit that the 'brilliant offensive had petered out.'[1]

Ludendorff realised that he would have to try and somehow widen the salient. The Eighteenth Army, under General von Hutier, would attack between Montdidier and Noyon, to the west of the Chemin des Dames ridge, in an attempt to reach Compiègne. The Battle of the Matz saw the Germans advance six miles on 9 June. The following day, however, the pace slowed dramatically, and on the 11th, the French, under General Mangin, who had been brought in to replace the disgraced Duchêne, launched a counter-attack using 144 tanks and aircraft support. The battle ended, in effect, on 13 June. Other small, local actions were fought, but Mangin, prior to the counter-attack, had exhorted his men by assuring them that this defensive battle was over, promising them a renewal of Allied offensives, that the tide had begun to turn. Just how much faith he had in his own pronouncements can only be surmised, but he was to be proved right.

On 1 June 1918, the 9th KOYLI spent much of the day compiling lists of deficiencies and making out casualty rolls. One set of orders received saw three officers and 107 Other Ranks parade for duty and be driven off in motor buses to become part of a composite battalion made up from men from all the units in the 64th Brigade.

On the 3rd, the 9th KOYLI ranks were depleted further when a party of 'first reinforcements' for the 21st Independent Brigade, consisting of thirty-six Other Ranks, one officer from the 1st East Yorks and a Mounted Officers' Patrol led by 2nd-Lt E.S. Parke, were spirited away once more on motor buses. The rest of the battalion moved off to Congy, a 'very pleasant village',[2] and were very pleased to be billeted in houses. Second-Lieutenant Overman, who had joined the battalion the previous day from the 2nd Dragoon Guards (Queen's Bays), took over as Transport Officer in 2nd-Lt Parkes' absence.

Reinforcements and the return of more stragglers saw the battalion strength rise to five officers and 211 Other Ranks (three officers and 143 men were with the composite battalion). Along with these came news of gallantry awards: Lt-Col. McCulloch received a bar to his DSO, 2nd-Lt Dore and Adj.-Capt. Ellenberger added bars to their MC's and Lt H.C. Walby got the Military Cross.

On 5 June, with the Brigadier having gone to England, Maj. Greenwood took command of the Brigade. 2nd-Lt P.L. Farrar also rejoined the battalion, along with eleven Other Ranks who had all been sent on a signalling course just a few days prior to the recent battle.

A move to Les Essart followed a few days later and on 14 June the battalion was ordered to entrain at Fère Champenoise at 5.00 p.m. They moved off eventually at 9.00 p.m., and reached Pont Remy, on the River Somme, at 6.45 a.m. the following day. They marched to Bainest on the main Rouen road, five kilometres south west of Abbeville, and went into some very good billets, Battalion HQ being in a nearby château. Their stay was to be short lived: a very slow and dusty journey by motor bus on 18 June saw them arrive at Beauchamp le Vieux on the River Bresle at 2.45 p.m. The War Diary describes the accommodation as excellent and goes on to say that the mayor and the townspeople were 'most obliging and kind'.[3]

On 19 June, Lt-Col. McCulloch returned to the command of the battalion and the following officers joined: 2nd-Lts W. Teasdale, A.O. Wilson, H.L. Matthew, W.H. Dales, W.S. Grafton, P. Green, J.H. Surtees, J.W. Wilson, S.I. Russell, C. Ashworth, W. Williams, T. Hutchinson, S. Hilditch, H. Prior, E.C. Rust and G.B Bradley. Two days later, 2nd-Lts T. Hindle and G. Harrop also joined the battalion, the former having been wounded in the Champagne Battle.

On 22 June the brigade moved to a new training area around Gamaches on the River Bresle, with 9th KOYLI billeted at Bouttencourt, a few miles upstream of Blangy. Here, more reinforcements arrived on the scene, including four company sergeant majors. The battalion went into billets the next day in the two nearby villages of Rieux and Le Carnet and as company and platoon training got underway on the 24th, the 9th KOYLI received the order for the reduction of the battalion to cadre status. This would entail a drastic reduction in numbers, leaving only a handful of officers and fewer than 200 men. In effect, the 9th KOYLI would cease to exist as an effective fighting infantry force.

On 26 June 1918, the commanding officer 64th Brigade, Brig.-Gen. Headlam, inspected the 9th KOYLI for the last time, and gave what amounted to a farewell speech.

With what appears to be less than perfect timing, A/RSM O. Maltby DCM was taken onto the strength of the officers of the battalion, his commission having been granted that same day.

In the first of the moves to break up the battalion, the Transport Section was ordered to move to the Cucq Camp near Montreuil on 28 June. At 11.30 p.m. on the 27th, however, the message came down from brigade that the reduction of 9th KOYLI had been 'reconsidered'. The battalion was to live on. Company and platoon training resumed as if nothing had happened, and on 29 June, the following men were awarded the Military Medal: 16705 L/Cpl J.T. Poole, 37073 Pte H. Green, 18736 Pte R. Bullock and 35631 Pte J. Jones.

Following Church Parade on 30 June, the warning came that the Division was about to move the very next day. Reveille was at 2.00 a.m. on 1 July, breakfast followed at 3.00 a.m., and by 4.00 a.m. the battalion was on the road to Blangy. There, they waited at the railway station until 11.30 a.m.; their train pulled out fifteen minutes later and headed north-east, passing through Amiens on its way. The average speed of the journey could not have been very high, as it took seven hours to reach their destination at Puchevillers, some thirty miles away. Once there, they marched into camp, a former POW camp, on the Puchevillers–Touttencourt road. The usual routine of cleaning, reorganising and training quickly ensued, and on 4 July, the Brigade Inter-Company Football Tournament began. Sadly for the 9th KOYLI, only 'C' Company survived the first round.

Another round of medal awards meant that the following men were rewarded: Bar to DCM for the newly appointed 2nd-Lt Maltby; DCM to 37492 Pte W.H. Barber; MSM to 43784 L/Cpl W.H. Richardson; MM to 9364 A/Sgt H.J. Routledge, 37654 Pte C.E. Maude, 200412 A/Cpl G.H. Horsfield, 37711 L/Cpl T. Wilbor, 24222 Pte E. Cooke, 36266 Pte H.E. Ogley and 36298 Pte W. Wainwright.

On 8 July, as 9th KOYLI officers reconnoitred the village of Engelbelmer (just north of Albert), a draft of 170 Other Ranks arrived from the West Yorkshire Regt. Tactical exercises, bombing instruction, musketry, inspections and route marches filled the following four days, during which several officers arrived and were taken on the strength of the battalion. These included Lt E.A. Martin, Lt F. Slater (Lewis Gun officer), 2nd-Lt S. Taylor and 2nd-Lt F.A. Powell-Ackroyd. It was also the turn of the officers to receive medals: Bar to MC to Capt. L.D. Spicer, Brig.-Maj. 64th Brigade; MC to Lt H.C. Walby, Lt T. Hindle, Capt. W.K. Pethed and T/Capt. G.H. Dawson, RAMC.

On 12 July, the battalion was to parade early, from 7.30 to 9.00 a.m., in order to leave the rest of the day clear for brigade sports. Neither the parade nor the sports survived the bad weather: unfortunately for the men, the afternoon route march was able to go ahead. The sports took place on the following afternoon, and the battalion was very successful, with four first places, seven seconds and three thirds. Buoyed by their success, 9th KOYLI looked forward with optimism to the Rifle Meeting to be held on the 15th: the team performed well, but not as successfully as had been hoped.

The battalion continued both its training and its build up toward full strength: over one hundred Other Ranks arrived during the next week, along with Lt W.F. Renshaw, 2nd-Lt A.B. Russell and Maj. W.F. Walsh. The 9th KOYLI was once again ready to resume duties in the line. On 25 June, they left camp at 9.00 a.m., halted for dinner at Acheux Wood at 12.30 p.m. and then moved forward to relieve Hood Battalion, 63rd Royal Naval Division, in the reserve positions east of Mailly Maillet. The relief was completed without incident by 5.30 p.m. Major Greenwood was in command, McCulloch being away commanding the Divisional School for company commanders at Acheux, and Maj. Walsh, newly arrived, was second in command. Battalion HQ was on the Mailly Maillet–Vitermont road.

The two days which followed were very wet, and the British artillery continually bombarded the enemy rear areas. On the 27th, Brig.-Gen. Headlam paid farewell visits to his battalions in the line on the occasion of his appointment as Inspector of Training. The next day, McCulloch was given command of 64th Brigade and Major Walsh took his place at the Divisional School.

The 9th KOYLI came under fire for the first time in nearly two months on 29 July when an enemy gas shell bombardment fell on Mailly Maillet and the immediate area. One shell fell on a bivouac causing five casualties, fortunately none of them fatal. A similar bombardment fell on 9th KOYLI positions the following day: 'A' Company on the Mailly Maillet–Vitermont road suffered casualties. Once more shells fell on bivouacs at the commencement of the bombardment and several men were affected by the gas before they had had a chance to put on their masks. Such was the severity of the attack, it was deemed appropriate for the company to move out of the gassed area to their battle positions astride the Engelbelmer–Auchonvillers road.

Following a brief respite on 30 July, when no gas attacks were forthcoming, and the War Diary was able to report a quiet night, the 9th KOYLI then relieved the 15th DLI in the front line on 1 August, taking up positions as right-front battalion on the Brigade sub-section. 'B' Company had three platoons in Beaumont Trench, with another extending southward astride the Auchonvillers-Hamel road, 'A', 'C' and 'D' Companies held positions slightly further back. The relief was completed shortly after midnight, and it was noted that the trenches were in a poor state, particularly the communication trenches. Patrolling began at once, and a small force under 2nd-Lt C.A. Woodley spotted an enemy patrol of about twelve men, but this group scattered and withdrew before proper contact could be made. Further patrols the following day made no contact at all, and although the British guns kept up an almost constant bombardment, the enemy artillery produced little in the way of reply.

On 3 August it was reported that the enemy were withdrawing in the sector facing Albert, and V Corps suspected a similar movement in the Mailly Maillet sector. The like-lihood of this being true was strengthened by information received from prisoners taken from positions on the right of the battalion, but when patrols were subsequently sent out to investigate they found the trenches opposite them still strongly held. Patrols sent out by the 1st East Yorks found exactly the same, though to the south of the 64th Brigade positions it was reported that the enemy had retired to their reserve trenches, just west of the railway line which ran south–north at that point along the Ancre River valley, curving gently toward the east as it followed the waterway past Beaucourt and Grandcourt before swerving northwards once more at Miraumont. The War Diary had one more exciting episode to report that day: an enemy aircraft was brought down in no man's land imme-diately in front of 'B' Company trenches.

A day of heavy rain showers followed, and daylight patrols established that the enemy had remained exactly where they were. The 5 August was wetter still; 'A' Company relieved 'B' Company in the front line and a night patrol drew fire from several enemy machine guns, but without fatality. Two more days of patrolling made no contact with the enemy, but at least the weather was steadily improving. A fine day on the 8th heralded a raid by the brigade to the north of the KOYLI positions: enemy retaliation cost the 9th KOYLI three fatal casualties, the first since they had left the Champagne region. Privates Clement Bamford, Percy Stewart Sandford and George Swift are buried together in Mailly Wood Cemetery. Early on the morning of the 9th, an enemy barrage opened up on the 64th Brigade front line. 9th KOYLI Battalion HQ put up an SOS, but no enemy attack materialised and all was quiet once more by 4.00 a.m. That evening, the battalion was relieved, and the entire brigade front was moved 500 yards to the north.

On 13 August, a message was received from Brigade that the enemy had retired from the village of Serre, just to the north, and as before patrols had to be sent out to check the situation on the 64th Brigade frontage. At 5.00 p.m., orders for two platoons to go forward toward Beaucourt were received. They reached Beaumont Hamel early the following morning and as they moved further eastwards the advanced platoon met some opposition, revealing that the Germans were holding 'Luminous Avenue' along the Beaucourt road. Consequently, the battalion had to spend the following night in the southern sections of 'Lubber Avenue' ('B', 'C' and 'D' Companies) and 'Lux Alley' ('A' Company), prior to continuing the advance the next morning.

At 8.00 a.m. on 15 August, it became clear that the enemy were not going to withdraw without a fight as had mainly happened the previous year when the Germans moved back to the Hindenburg Line. An artillery bombardment fell on the KOYLI positions, causing casualties in all companies. The attempted advance was also being held up by fire from machine-gun posts, and one in particular was proving very troublesome: it was success-fully rushed by 'A' Company with the help of Stokes mortar fire. The whole line was by now pushed forward to 'Artillery Lane', a trench line running north from the town of Beaucourt. 'B' and 'D' Companies occupied this line, with 'A' Company in 'Luminous Avenue'. The advance got no further that day: machine-gun and artillery fire to the east of 'Artillery Lane' was very heavy and checked any efforts in that direction. The action had cost the 9th KOYLI eleven fatal casualties, including 2nd-Lt William Salter Grafton, who had joined the battalion only eight weeks before.

The KOYLIs were relieved by the 15th DLI in the early hours of the next morning and took up reserve positions once more near Mailly Maillet. The procedure cost the KOYLIs more lives: three men were killed; 62687 L/Cpl Charles Cooper is buried in Serre Road No.1 Cemetery. The two others, 46988 Pte John Cunningham and 34089 Pte Samuel Sykes have no known graves and are commemorated on the Vis-en-Artois Memorial.

More heavy shelling at dawn on the 22nd prompted a move into the Luminous Trench area once again, to be precise into the valley running south-east from Beaumont Hamel. Orders for a further move arrived: the 9th KOYLI was to relieve the 12/13th Northumberland Fusiliers on the south side of the River Ancre. However, before the orders could be put into effect, the perceived chance of an enemy counter-attack disrupting the relief saw the move abandoned. On the 23rd, orders were once more received for a move to the south side of the river: this time, however, the trenches to be occupied by the KOYLIs were the jumping-off positions for an attack scheduled for the early hours of the 24th. As dusk approached, the men crossed the Ancre just south of Beaucourt and took up their positions in Logging Lane Trench (see map), guided by battalion scouts. 'Between nine and ten the quiet concentration commenced, and sinuously they threaded their way through the marshes and over the foot bridges, and as coolly as on parade formed up on the south side of the River Ancre.'[4]

The ground over which the attack was to be made sloped down from right to left into the valley of the Ancre. The terrain could be best described as gently 'rolling'. Four shallow valleys ran more or less directly across the line of advance. 'Battery Valley' was the nearest, some 800 yards, on average, from the jumping-off lines. A similar distance further on lay the next 'valley'. This was in effect no more than a sunken road, the last half-mile or so of the Thiepval–Grandcourt road. The also slightly sunken Grandcourt–Courcelette road formed the next obvious transverse feature a few hundred yards further on still. The fourth valley, arguably the only one to merit the name, was known to the Allies as Boom Ravine, approximately a mile-and-a-half from the start line. The objective was the high ground, Hill 135, to the south of Miraumont, a total advance required of just over 4,000 yards.

August 1918 was a good month for the Allies. The German offensives of the spring had all ground to a halt: the early summer saw little of major consequence on the western front. The Allies were gathering themselves after the recent setbacks, the Americans were arriving in larger numbers and the Germans would soon be forced onto the back foot, never to regain any forward momentum.

On 8 August, the Allies launched a massive and decisive attack eastwards from the city of Amiens. One hundred thousand troops of Fourth Army went into the assault at 4.20 a.m., backed by 2,000 guns, and managed to push the enemy back as much as eight miles in places. The Germans were forced back to the line of the original Amiens outer defence line and lost an estimated 27,000 men. Eighteen thousand of those were taken prisoner and 400 guns were also captured. This first day of the 'Battle of Amiens' was, in the words of Ludendorff, a 'black day' for the German Army.

The battle continued for a further two days, but ran out of steam on the 11th, as German resistance stiffened on the Fourth Army front. Haig was looking to keep the pressure on and on the same day ordered General Byng, Third Army, to prepare for an attack in the direction of Bapaume.

On 15 August, German withdrawals from outpost lines south of Bucquoy had allowed British troops to enter Serre and Beaumont Hamel. This type of 'cautious' pursuit of the enemy was not to Haig's liking and he ordered an attack across what was in effect the southern edge of the 1917 Arras battlefield and the northern edge of the 1916 Somme conflict area.

By 21 August, Third Army had twelve Divisions, plus one in reserve, and was faced by eight German Divisions, with two in reserve. The main offensive roles fell to the VI and IV Corps: V Corps, much of whose front was west of the Ancre River, was to play a subsidiary role. The Ancre itself was barely recognisable as such: it was still a waterway, but burst banks resulted in expanses of marsh. Previous bombardments had left tangles of trees littering the area and the Germans, just for good measure, had wired much of it.

By 6.00 a.m., both VI and IV Corps had taken their first objectives. On the VI Corps front, the Guards and 3rd Divisions leapfrogged and reached the Amiens–Arras railway, (except for the half mile on the extreme right) by 11.30 a.m. IV Corps had a harder time: they managed a three-mile advance on a three-mile front, but did not reach the railway. The V Corps made some progress north of the Ancre, taking Beaucourt by 6.30 a.m., and gaining touch with the right wing of the 42nd Division of IV Corps.

Further south, the 38th Division pushed patrols out across the river but met with serious resistance. Byng ordered V Corps to halt until Fourth Army on their right had managed to take the town of Albert. This prize was expected to fall into Allied hands the following day. Accordingly, Third Army paused on 22 August, while Fourth Army launched a substantial attack. The 18th Division on their left secured Albert as predicted that morning in the face of less than determined opposition.

General Byng issued his orders for the furtherance of the advances which were to be designated the nomenclature of 'Battle of Albert' at 5.35 p.m. on 23 August. The Third Army was to continue its advance eastwards early the following day. On the V Corps front, the Ancre valley, as mentioned previously, represented a substantial obstacle: the floods and swamps between the village of Aveluy (just over a mile north of Albert) and a point some 700 yards north of Authuille persuaded Lt-Gen. C.D. Shute (officer commanding V Corps):

to make convergent attacks from south and north of this flooded area, which would join up on the line La Boisselle-Ovillers-Grandcourt. This plan had also the advantage of avoiding a direct attack on the strong Thiepval position which lay just to the north of the sector protected by the flooded area.[5]

Zero hour for the attack would be 1.00 a.m. The southern wing, comprising the right flank of 38th Division and the left and centre of 18th Division to their right, would attack north-eastwards. The northern wing, made up of the remainder of 38th Division, one brigade (50th) of 17th Division and the 21st Division, would advance in a south-easterly

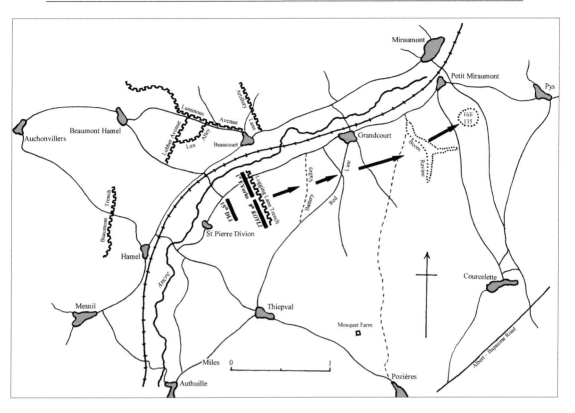

64th Brigade Attack, 24 August 1918.

direction. The two forces would converge about half a mile north–north-east of Ovillers. Thus, Thiepval and the high ground beyond it would be outflanked on both sides, enabling its capture without the need for direct and inevitably costly assault.

The long ridge which extends east-south-east from Thiepval towards Morval has a northerly spur which overlooks the village of Miraumont as it sits snugly on the north bank of the Ancre. The village was still firmly held by German forces, and it was deemed vital that the high ground to the south-east of it, the spur, be taken as soon as possible to 'cut off' the village and prevent the garrison from destroying the bridges over the Ancre and withdrawing.'[6] The 21st Division was thus ordered not to wait for Zero hour, but to take this high ground as soon as possible.

'It appeared that information which the Army had received showed that the Bosche were likely to retire and wanted hustling.'[7] Thus wrote Brig.-Gen. McCulloch in his personal diary.

At around 5.30 p.m., the Brigadier, now in command of 64th Brigade, was summoned by telephone to 21st Divisional HQ at Mailly Maillet. Here, he was informed that his brigade had been selected for the task, and plans were hastily discussed and finalised. His diary continues:

… it was decided that an early attack was to take place, and that I was to advance without troops on my right or left. I did not care much for the idea but I quite realised that others knew the situation in rear of the German outposts better than I did. I took care to impress battalion commanders that the situation demanded boldness.[8]

Before leaving the headquarters, McCulloch issued the orders which moved the men of the brigade to the south of the River Ancre. Support for the brigade flanks would, it was planned, arrive later: the 110th Brigade on the right and the 42nd Division on the left would follow on only at the original Zero hour of one o'clock. The 64th would leave their assembly positions at 11.30 p.m., and the expectation was that they would await the arrival of their comrades at the final objective, the high ground between the two roads which run southwards from Miraumont to Courcelette, known to the Allies as Hill 135.

The 9th KOYLI and 1st East Yorks (each minus one company) were to lead. One company of the 15th DLI and the other two detached companies formed the reserve, under the command of Maj. Constantine of 9th KOYLI. Each battalion had two companies in the front line, with their third in close support behind. Each individual company was in a square formation, with a platoon at each corner of the square, twenty yards between them in either direction. Companies were separated by a similar distance. The supporting companies were 100 yards to the rear. Divisional HQ gave orders that the men were to be as lightly equipped as possible, each man carrying two grenades. They were also insistent that no more than twenty officers per battalion were to join the action. It was made clear to these officers that any Germans encountered directly in the line of the advance were to be rushed at once: conversely, no heed was to be paid to any who fired from the flanks. Any machine guns which menaced said flanks were to be rushed and captured by a party placed on each battalion's exposed flank for that express purpose. The War Diary of 21st Division sums up the overall philosophy of the action: 'These attacks will be pushed with the greatest boldness and risks will be taken which, at other times, would be unjustifiable.'[9]

At 11.15 p.m., a rather weak preparatory artillery barrage commenced, and the men advanced through the outpost positions held by the 12/13th Northumberland Fusiliers into the pitch black over ground 'pitted with craters, gulleys and small ravines. The advance was in the face of the enemy, but no signs of his presence were obvious at first.'[10]

The 9th KOYLI, under the command of Lt-Col. Harry Greenwood, encountered some strongly held machine-gun posts, but these were quickly dealt with and Battery Valley was reached with a final rush, urged on by Brig.-Gen. McCulloch, who gave the word for the charge as he realised that they were nearing this first objective: 'Charge! Charge! The shout was quickly taken up by everyone, and the battalions vied with each other in the vigour of their shouting, and their rush into Battery Valley.'[11] On descending into the valley (the War Diary of 64th Brigade puts the time at around midnight), their own artillery deposited five shells onto the front-line brigade troops causing about thirty casualties. Once there, the KOYLI troops cleared several dugouts and strongpoints, capturing one machine gun and a 4.2 gun in the process. The battalion formed up once more for the next stage. This next advance was made under heavy machine gun fire towards the 'Red Line', the Thiepval–Grandcourt road. Before they got there, although the British barrage should have lifted and moved on by that time, some more shells from the heavy batteries fell short, causing several casualties. Friendly fire had once more come back to haunt the men of the 9th KOYLI, including this time Lt-Col. Greenwood, who was blown violently from his feet against a post, injuring him internally. In spite of this, he was able to continue and lead his men towards the final objective.

The brigade was able to report that the Red Line had been taken by 12.30 a.m. Greenwood found it difficult to hold his men back at this point, as they were 'eager to proceed.'[12] Some of the men in the brigade were not so keen, however. In his personal diary, McCulloch relates an incident regarding an unidentified platoon:

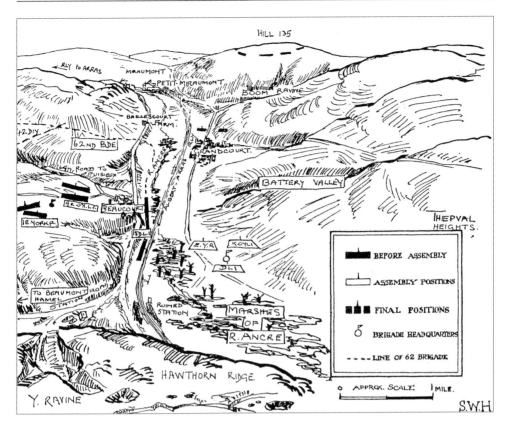

Sketch to illustrate the Night Attack of 23/24 August 1918 of 64th Brigade.

... one platoon only, when leaders had been killed or wounded, came back. They were brought to me and reported that they had lost touch and were trying to find the rest of their company. They were somewhat shame-faced when I cursed them for heading away from the enemy and went forward again willingly and rejoined. I do not think that these men were panic-stricken. They simply had faced a blow – had their directing hand removed and were in a sort of invertebrate state with no will to guide them. I mention this because it is in this that the danger of night fighting lies. Directly these men met me and found someone who meant business they responded willingly and went on with their task.[13]

Reorganisation was necessary: the right flank was still obviously in the air, and the 15th DLI were brought up to form a defensive flank, though they did not arrive until 2.15 a.m. On the left, the support and reserve companies of the 1st East Yorks had been sent to mop up the village of Grandcourt. They overran it quickly, capturing four field guns, twenty machine guns and over 100 prisoners.

The 9th KOYLIs dug in about 400 yards ahead of the Red Line; the establishment and securing of this position was complete by 1.30 a.m., but prompted by 'the isolated position of the brigade, the absence of the 15th DLI... and the number of Germans around, Brig.-Gen. McCulloch decided to postpone further advance until 3.15 a.m.'[14]

At the appointed hour, the advance resumed. With the 15th DLI now in position on the right, Boom Ravine was reached 'with exceptional dash and courage.'[15] A number of Germans were killed or captured and the rest fled, discarding their equipment as they went. The men pressed on, encountering heavy machine-gun fire from the flanks, and from machine-gun nests and outpost positions directly ahead, but the final objective, Hill 135, was reached by 4.30 a.m. The men now had about fifteen minutes of darkness left in which to reorganise before they became targets for the nearby German defenders. The 9th KOYLI were now occupying a line of shell holes: the 15th DLI arrived some three-quarters of an hour later and formed a short defensive flank on the right. On the other flank, the 1st East Yorks had not managed to reach the line gained by the KOYLIs, and settled into positions from where they would try to guard the left flank, albeit a thousand yards or more to the rear.

By this time it was daylight. McCulloch was doing his best to make a tour of his battalions' positions, but was unable to complete his task. Just as he located the 15th DLI he was hit in the thigh by a bullet from a German machine gun. His diary completes the story: 'As I was bleeding a lot and unable to walk I considered that if I stayed, I would be more of a hindrance than a help.'[16] He was carried back by some German soldiers that he had captured. Command of the brigade passed to Lt-Col. C.E.R. Holroyd-Smyth of the Durhams. His message, to the effect that the high ground in square 'R 11 b' had been taken, reached 21st Divisional HQ at 8.45 a.m. It went on to report that the enemy were working their way around either flank and that reinforcements were urgently needed. Communication on the Great War battlefield remained a real problem: signallers tried to set up a lamp station on the hill, but German riflemen managed to smash the lamps.

The position became more critical, and a more traditional communication method came into its own: a pigeon message timed at 7.28 a.m., (received 9.20 a.m.), reported that their positions had by then been completely surrounded. The enemy were back in Battery Valley, cutting off all communications with the rear. Casualties were becoming heavy: the enemy had counter-attacked both flanks but had been repulsed. They also held very strong positions a 'few yards' in front of the KOYLI line and 'subjected us to very deadly sniping, machine gun fire and bombing.'[17] From their adjacent positions, the Germans called upon the KOYLIs to surrender: it is doubtful that the reply given was polite; suffice it to say that it was definitely in the negative.

Headlam, on receipt of these messages back at Divisional HQ, ordered 110th Brigade to advance and support the right flank of the 64th. Captain Spicer, Brigade-Major of 64th Brigade, had managed to break out of the Hill 135 positions at about 10.30 a.m. and rode back to 21st Division HQ in Mailly Maillet to present his report personally. The 64th Brigade positions roughly encircled the hill, units were mixed up – the enemy was back in Boom Ravine. In short, they were cut off and running out of time. The report was confirmed by aerial reconnaissance flights and these planes dropped messages onto the hill promising that help was on its way.

By noon, the sun had dissipated the mists from the river valley and the day had turned out hot. At about this time, British troops could be observed to the north advancing on Miraumont. Enemy fire suddenly ceased: influenced by the sight to the north and no doubt by the general Allied advance now underway elsewhere, the Germans (16th Reserve Division) retired. Lieutenant Howard of 1st East Yorks had been separated from his battalion earlier in the day, and found himself amongst members of the 15th DLI on Hill 135. As the situation developed around midday, he stood up from his shell hole and saw Lt-Col. Greenwood of the KOYLIs walking about. Others began to do the same: soon the collection and evacuation of wounded was being organised. The War Diary of 9th KOYLI also reports that 130 enemy dead were found in front of their positions.

By 2.30 p.m., the 110th Brigade had gained touch with the 64th Brigade 'outpost' and a few remaining enemy troops were being mopped up in Boom Ravine. Late in the afternoon, the 62nd Brigade pushed through the 64th's positions and advanced south of Pys, joining up with the 42nd Division to the north. The 17th and 38th Divisions had advanced to the south and made good their objectives. Thiepval Ridge had fallen as planned. The V Corps had also captured La Boisselle, Ovillers, Pozières and of course Grandcourt.

At 7.00 p.m., the 64th Brigade was withdrawn into Divisional Reserve positions. The 9th KOYLI spent a chilly night in Boom Ravine. Lt Howard's article in *The Snapper* sums up the day as follows:

The 64th Brigade had some cause for self-congratulation, having fought its own bridgehead positions, crossed the Ancre, and on a pitch dark night advanced from 2.5-3 miles to their allotted objective over craters and shell hole country and holding that objective in face of determined outflanking enemy until relieved some fifteen hours afterwards.[18]

McCulloch, by now safe and well to the rear, was still concerned for his men's welfare: 'From hospital in Le Treport I wired to know how the fight ended and to ask that the ground between St Pierre Divion and Miraumont be searched for my wounded.'[19]

The cost to the 9th KOYLI could be said to be have been relatively light: fatal casualties for 23-24 August numbered twenty-three. One officer was amongst that number; 2nd-Lt Frederick Gillard is commemorated on the Vis-en-Artois Memorial.

Four days later, the battalion received a 'Special Order' from 21st Division congratulating them on their achievements on 24 August:

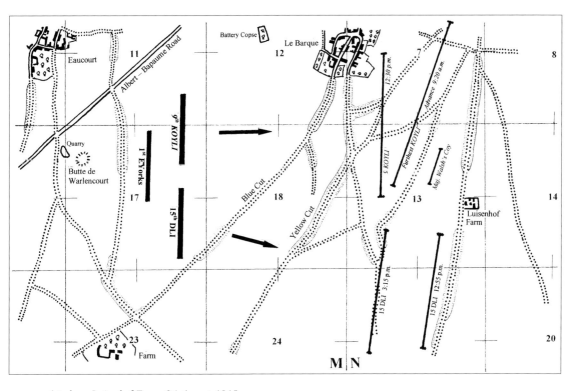

Attack on Luisenhof Farm, 26 August 1918.

The magnificent work done by the Division during the recent fighting equals, if it does not surpass, any previous performance done by it in the past. The manner in which the 64th Brigade occupied and, although completely surrounded, held the high ground south of Miraumont will certainly rank as one of the finest deeds performed by any brigade in this war. That such deeds were possible, after the serious casualties which the Division has suffered during the past few months, clearly shows the fine spirit and determination which all ranks possess.[20]

Harold Yeo, writing home immediately after the receipt of this 'encouraging' message, expressed his feelings more succinctly: 'We had the devil of a battle last week and secured great results, far better shows these modern battles than the old-fashioned ones.'[21] By the time these thoughts were being put on paper, the 9th KOYLI had been in action again. On 25 August they had spent the day reorganising, receiving orders at 5.00 p.m. to move forward into trenches in a quarry north-west of the village of Le Sars. Other brigades of the Division had not been idle, being involved in further advances during that day: Le Sars itself had fallen, along with the Butte de Warlencourt, Contalmaison, Bazentin-le-Petit, Martinpuich and Courcelette.

Orders for 26 August involved the First, Third and Fourth Armies: the general advance in the face of the retreating German Army was to continue, but they were preparing to halt and hold the old Hindenburg Line, and this was to prove a difficult obstacle once more. The overall picture does not need to be detailed here: it will suffice to say that V Corps were to continue their advance eastwards. Narrowing the field of vision even further, 21st Division was to advance towards and occupy the road running north–south between Ligny-Thilloy and Factory Corner (just north of Flers). The road was sunken for most of its length: except at its highest point, halfway between the two villages, where the terrain was dominated by the German-held strongpoint of Luisenhof Farm.

On the left flank of 21st Division, 38th Division would clear the Bazentin Woods and advance on Longueval and High Wood. On their right, 17th Division would have Flers as its objective. An early start was envisaged, but some brigades did not receive their orders until one or two o'clock in the morning, and this, combined with a severe thunderstorm that night, meant that the assaults would have to commence in daylight. The German machine gunners would have visible targets from the outset.

Just before dawn on the 26th, 62nd Brigade were withdrawn to the valley behind Le Sars, and the 64th Brigade assembled for the attack, HQ being established in a dugout in a quarry behind the Butte de Warlencourt. This ancient Gaulish mound, just to the east of the Albert–Bapaume road, is about 100 feet high, and at this time still had many white crosses on its summit, a memory of the 1916 attacks.

The battalions formed up on a front of approximately 1,000 yards, the 15th DLI on the right, the 9th KOYLI on the left, the frontage equally split. The 1st East Yorks were about 300 yards behind in support positions. The two front battalions were now in the dead ground just to the west of 'Blue Cut' (see map), approximately 1,500 yards from their objective.

The advance began at 5.00 a.m., with little artillery support, over open ground. Both flanking Divisions were held up, and the 64th Brigade found itself taking machine-gun fire not only from the front but from both flanks. 'Advancing over Blue Cut the increasing hail of machine-gun bullets from the enemy broke up the advance, and it soon became a shell hole scramble.'[22] The 9th KOYLI pressed on and crossed Yellow Cut, harassed by machine-gun fire from low-flying German aircraft, but by 10.00 a.m. the advance had faltered and the Yorkshiremen found cover in shell holes as best they could. Reconnaissance patrols were sent out along trenches on the flanks and various German machine-gun posts were located. The right-hand company under Maj. Walsh managed to get even further forward, to within 300 yards of the objective, but were soon forced to withdraw.

The 15th DLI on the right of the brigade frontage had managed to get within 150 yards of the sunken road, but by mid-afternoon, they and the KOYLIs were holding on to positions some 7-800 yards short of the objective. At about 4.00 p.m., a German counter-attack was repulsed by Lewis gun and rifle fire. It was obvious to all that the attack had failed: the men on the front line could now only hope that discretion would prevail.

As far as HQ were concerned, the position was extremely hazy: no runners had managed to get back over the open ground. Observers on the Butte had reported that the fighting seemed to have died down, with only occasional machine-gun fire to be heard. It was decided that a withdrawal was necessary, but also that it could not be executed before nightfall.

The three battalions were able to move back once darkness had begun to fall: 9th KOYLI withdrew to positions in Yellow Cut, a line they were to hold for the night, with the 15th DLI on their right, the 1st East Yorks having been withdrawn to shelters in a sunken road to the south of the Butte de Warlencourt. Eighteen men from 9th KOYLI had been killed in action during the day, and as Lt Howard put it: 'the only tangible result of our day's operations was to prove that the German resistance was thickening, and that it was getting increasingly necessary to have artillery preparation and assistance for further advances of any distance or importance.'[23]

The KOYLIs spent the next day holding the same ground, and were rewarded by an enemy artillery bombardment of some twenty minutes' duration at around 6.00 p.m. Several casualties were inflicted, but none of them proved fatal. At 8.30 p.m., the battalion was relieved by the Northumberland Fusiliers, the entire brigade moving back into Divisional Reserve.

Further enemy retirements on the 28th saw the battalion moved forward into trenches near Blue Cut at about three in the afternoon. The CO, Lt-Col. Greenwood, wounded and sick, went back to the dressing station, leaving Maj. Walsh in charge. The next two days were taken up by refitting and reorganising and by the collection of large quantities of salvage from the forward areas.

On the first day of September, a further Allied advance meant that the 9th KOYLI was able to move forward and occupy trenches east of Luisenhof Farm without a fight, relieving two companies of the 15th DLI and the 1st East Yorks. The following day, the East Yorks made an attack on Lubda Copse, near the village of Villers-au-Flos, with the 9th KOYLI in reserve: the KOYLI's role that day consisted of supplying carrying parties for the attacking units, but it still suffered one fatal casualty, a namesake of the still absent Commanding Officer; 43139 Pte Harry Greenwood is buried in Vaulx Hill Cemetery.

Over the next three days, while the battalion, in Divisional Reserve once more, was bathing, refitting, training and practising musketry, eleven new officers and 237 Other Ranks arrived to replace the recent losses. A move forward to the Sailly Saillisel area on the 5th was followed on the 6th by the news of a further German retirement from their positions along the Canal du Nord at Etricourt. Orders were received to cross the canal at a new bridge being built by the Royal Engineers at Etricourt, but a reconnaissance

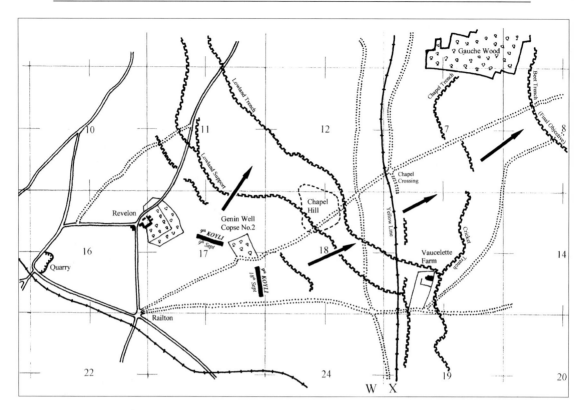

Attacks made on 9 and 18 September 1918.

revealed that the bridge was only suitable for foot traffic. The Transport Section was forced to move down the canal and cross at Manancourt. Once across the waterway, HQ could be established in a cottage in the village of Equancourt. The next morning, the enemy was reported to be holding positions on Lowland Ridge and Chapel Hill, some miles to the east, and, that afternoon, orders came through to the effect that the 9th KOYLI would attack on 9 September, their objectives being Lowland Support and Lowland Trench. Accordingly, the battalion moved off from Equancourt at midnight. They marched via Fins and Heudecourt to the jumping off point on a track to the west of Genin Well Copse No.2 (see map). 'B' and 'D' Companies were in the front line, 'C' Company was in support, and 'A' was in reserve in trenches east of Revelon Farm. Battalion HQ was in a quarry approximately 1,000 yards further back.

At 4.00 a.m., the troops went forward with artillery support. 'Some gas shelling, which affected the eyes, made it difficult to keep direction in the darkness; but in the early stages, this darkness prevented the enemy's machine gun fire from being very effective, and good progress was achieved.'[24] Lowland Support Trench was quickly occupied, and the battalion paused to reorganise before pressing on to its second objective. In this attack, however, considerable resistance was met in the form of heavy machine-gun fire, trench mortars and bombs. Despite this, and after some vicious hand-to-hand fighting, the trench was reached, taken and held. Unfortunately, neither flank was supported, and, in the face of enemy counter-attacks, it was eventually deemed necessary to withdraw to positions back in Lowland Support. The trench was consolidated and outposts were pushed out into the communication trenches in the direction of the recently abandoned line. Also during the morning, Battalion HQ in the quarry had been shelled, and the Transport Section, also located there, lost eight horses killed and suffered considerable damage to their vehicles. Headquarters was quite understandably moved back half a mile into a sunken road.

At 5.00 p.m., Lowland Trench was assaulted once more. As before, the objective was reached, but the Germans had outflanked the KOYLIs on their left and inflicted heavy casualties. With both flanks once more exposed, the battalion was frustratingly soon back in Lowland Support. More German counter-attacks were feared, so a company of the 1st East Yorks was put at the disposal of the CO just in case. No such attacks materialised and in the early hours of 10 September, the 1st East Yorks leapfrogged the KOYLI positions to mount the 64th Brigade's third attempt at capturing Lowland Trench. It was not to be third time lucky: the attack failed, the East Yorks suffering heavily in the process.

That night, after a day sheltering in Lowland Support under trench mortar fire and artillery shelling, the 9th KOYLI was relieved by the 1st Wiltshires and moved back to the safety of Equancourt, where they were billeted in buildings and huts in the village, with HQ initially in the church. The attacks had cost the battalion twenty-three men killed in action, including three officers. 2nd-Lt Henry Cooil was attached to the 9th KOYLI, 2nd-Lt John Overman was on the HQ staff, and 2nd-Lt Percy Green had joined the battalion less than three months earlier. All three were buried close together in Gouzeaucourt New British Cemetery.

The next day, the battalion paraded in the morning and commenced a training programme. The officers had organised a revolver shooting competition amongst themselves; unfortunately, the Adjutant, when writing the War Diary entry for that day, failed to note the results. Enemy shelling of the village that night meant that the men had to spend an uncomfortable night sheltering in trenches nearby. A move to relieve the 6th Leicesters on the night of 14/15 September was ordered and then cancelled. Instead, on the 14th, the battalion received a warning that it was to take part in an attack near Vaucelette Farm, to the south-east of the Lowland Ridge trench systems they had so recently assaulted. The officers were called together and briefed on the matter.

On the 16th and 17th, the men rehearsed the attack on ground between Equancourt and the Canal du Nord. At 9.00 p.m. on the second day, the battalion paraded and marched off in single file via Railton Crossroads to their jumping off point just to the south of Genin Well Copse No.2.

The V Corps had three objectives that day: the first included Chapel Hill and was only about 500 yards from the front line. The second included Vaucelette Farm and Chapel Crossing on the north–south railway line. A pause of fifteen minutes was envisaged here, after which the third objective would be approached. This was a mile further on, running from Limerick Point, past the western outskirts of Villers-Guislan, up to Gauche Wood and thence westwards along its northern edge.

On the 21st Divisional front, the hurricane artillery barrage opened up at 5.20 a.m. on 18 September. The first troops away were from 62nd Brigade. The 1st and 2nd Lincolns, along with the 12/13th Northumberland Fusiliers, were successful in capturing the first of the objectives: the retaking of Vaucelette Farm was particularly sweet; they had held the position bravely and successfully on 21 March as the massive German Spring offensive had got under way.

At 5.30 a.m., the 9th KOYLI moved forward, with 'B', 'C' and 'D' Companies in the front line and 'A' in support, and passed through 62nd Brigade to the Yellow Line, on the aforementioned railway line (see map). There, the battalion paused and reorganised, a forty-five minute halt having been scheduled into the artillery barrage at that point. At 9.47 a.m., the KOYLIs dashed forward as far as Beet Trench, the final objective, and, after a sharp fight, the enemy were cleared and the trench occupied. The positions were consolidated and the companies were disposed as follows: 'D' Company on the left, 'B' in the centre and 'C' on the right. 'A' Company was in close support, Battalion HQ being at 'X7.d.95'. The War Diary describes the situation on the battalion's left as 'somewhat obscure'. Considerable rifle and machine-gun fire was enfilading the KOYLI positions from the eastern end of Gauche Wood. An enemy counter-attack from that area at half-past twelve drove the troops to the left of the battalion's positions back several hundred yards: finding the battalion's left flank in the air, a platoon from 'A' Company was rushed forward under Maj. Walsh to fill the gap. The arrival of this force seemed to rally the other retreating troops and the original line was eventually regained. Major Walsh was unfortunately wounded during this desperate action, and it fell to Capt. A.F. Ennals to take command of the battalion. Two more platoons from 'A' Company were despatched to reinforce the extreme left, and with additional troops from 62nd Brigade and the 15th DLI soon arriving on the scene, the situation was stabilised and the night passed with little incident.

From their positions in Beet Trench, the men of 9th KOYLI were able to observe an extended artillery bombardment of the enemy lines during the next day. Both sides exchanged shells during the evening, but no infantry action developed and the KOYLIs were relieved during the night by the 6th Queens, marching back into Equancourt. This episode had cost the battalion a further twenty-three fatal casualties, fifteen of which have no known grave and are commemorated on the Vis-en-Artois Memorial.

The 20 September was spent in positions west of Equancourt resting and cleaning up. The Battalion was earmarked for Divisional Reserve, and accordingly, at 8.00 a.m. on the 21st, they paraded and marched to Les Boeufs, where Maj. H.W.H. Taylor joined from the 7th Leicesters and assumed command. Church parades on the morning of the 22nd were followed by more cleaning and refitting. All companies were able to bathe on the Monday before they were once more on the move. A march to Etricourt at 2.00 p.m. on the 24th was a precursor to the receipt of orders for yet another attack, this time on Gonnelieu.

Before moving off into reserve trenches on the evening of 25 September, a special afternoon performance by the Divisional Concert Party the 'Soarers' was enjoyed by the brigade. The battalion remained in reserve in Quivering Trench for the next two days, receiving Lewis gun and grenade training. On the 28th, orders were received to move at very short notice to Gonnelieu itself, the attack on the village having been rendered superfluous by an enemy withdrawal. Training continued on the 29th, but not without interruption: attack orders were again received, only for them to be subsequently cancelled. As the month drew to a close, the battalion moved into new positions in Heather and Lowland trenches to the north west of Chapel Hill.

The events of August and September 1918 had set the pattern for the rest of the conflict. It was clear that the Germans were in serious trouble and that the tide of movement toward the east was inexorable. What was also set was the pattern of Allied losses: the stunning series of victories had been gained only at substantial cost. Indeed, if the 9th KOYLI casualties can be taken as typical, the August and September fatality totals of sixty and sixty-eight are surpassed only by the huge set-piece battles of earlier in the war; in fact, the 'victorious' actions of 1918 were to account for over eighteen per cent of the battalion's total for the entire war (the first day of the Somme, in comparison, accounts for just under thirteen-and-a-half per cent).

The 29 September had witnessed a massive and successful Allied attack on the Hindenburg Line some way to the south of the KOYLI positions, along the Fourth Army front. The III and IX Corps had advanced up to 6,000 yards on a 10,000-yard frontage, the Hindenburg Main System and its support system having been broken and over 5,300 prisoners and over ninety guns captured. At a conference that same day at the Hotel Britannique in Spa, Belgium, Hindenburg and Ludendorff met with the Kaiser and advised him to seek armistice terms. The request was subsequently made by the German Government to President Wilson on 4 October. It was to take a further thirty-eight days of fighting for the request to become reality, and the 9th KOYLI would have their part to play.

15

A BLUE SUIT
AND A BOWLER HAT

As October 1918 dawned, the 9th KOYLI Commanding Officer and his company commanders were engaged in a complete recce of their section of the front line. Gone were the days when a battalion was able to prepare to advance over ground that had become familiar to it over weeks and even months of careful observation from entrenched positions. Almost every move made at this stage of the war was over territory unfamiliar to the field commanders whose responsibility it was to make sense of, and subsequently put into action, the attack plans drawn up by brigade, corps and Army staff officers.

While their commanding officers were gainfully employed in this manner, the men were salvaging everything in the immediate area behind their forward positions, making one central dump of any items deemed 'useful'. The War Diary also notes on this day that the number of men parading sick was remarkably low. Indeed, only one man presented himself to the medical officer that day.

It would seem that one particular item found and collected during the salvage operation (which continued into the next day's activities) in great number was the German hand grenade. So plentiful were they, it was deemed necessary that part of the training schedule for this and the next day would be instruction and practice in their use. On 4 October every man in the battalion was able to take a bath and was given a change of clothing: this, as ever, was 'much appreciated by the men.'[1] The same day, Maj. W.C. Ratcliffe joined the battalion and assumed his position as second-in-command.

The next day, the 9th KOYLI received orders to move up to the Banteux area, this town being situated on the west bank of the St QuentinCanal, a mile or so to the north of Honnecourt. The three battalions of 64th Brigade duly marched off, the 1st East Yorks in front, 15th DLI next and the 9th KOYLI in the rear, the required gap of 500 yards between battalions being strictly maintained. The men did not stop at Banteux, but crossed the canal and immediately took up positions in trenches, the Germans having abandoned the canal, the Hindenburg Line and the Hindenburg Support Line. The latter was duly occupied by 3.00 p.m., an unopposed advance from the canal of 2,000 yards.

On 6 October, the battalion moved forward at 5.00 a.m. to support the 15th DLI and the 1st East Yorks in what can best be described as 'aggressive manoeuvring' in an attempt to push as far forward as possible toward the Beaurevoir Line prior to assaulting it. The final objective for the day was the village of Walincourt, but it soon became clear that such a move was unrealistic, considering the given policy that no frontal attacks were to be made if strong opposition was met: the enemy was to be 'manoeuvred out of position'.[2] As it was, the 15th DLI occupied Montcouvez Farm and pushed out patrols some distance further and dug in. The 1st East Yorks tried to take Bonne Enfance Farm a mile or so to the north. They managed a brief hold of the position, but by midday heavy casualties forced them to withdraw to the Vauroy Line.

The positions were set: 21st Division was flanked by 37th Division to the north, 38th Division to the south, and the next major assault was timed for 8 October. The orders given on 4 October by General Byng had originally been for the Third Army to attack on the 7th, but this was amended the following day to the 8th. The Third and Fourth Armies were to advance together, but close co-operation between the two would be difficult. The Fourth Army, to the south, had advanced further east than the Third, having already taken the Beaurevoir Line along its frontage. V Corps, on Third Army's right wing, were still facing this major obstacle. In an attempt to enable all units to stay abreast of each other, the attack would have three start times. Shute's V Corps would launch a preliminary assault on the Beaurevoir Line at 1.00 a.m. The rest of Third Army would move at 4.30 a.m. and Fourth Army (along with parts of the French 1st Army), would join in at 5.10 a.m.

The 9th KOYLI and 15th DLI formed up in the assembly positions at half past midnight, along the road running south-east from Montcouvez Farm. Half an hour later, dead on time, the artillery barrage opened up and the troops advanced as close to it as they dared, the KOYLIs on the left, the DLI to their right. The Beaurevoir Line was 'carried with a rush by assaulting troops who then pushed on.'[3] By 2.30 a.m., all their objectives had been taken, including part of the Green Line running northwards from Angle Château, and at very little cost. The château, once taken, was lost to a German counter-attack, regained at 6.00 a.m., abandoned to allow the removal of enemy mines, and then finally and definitively occupied. The German counter-barrage had overshot the advancing British lines, causing little damage. (Some shells did land near 9th KOYLI Battalion HQ.)

At this point, the 9th KOYLI ceased their active part in this episode. The 15th DLI consolidated and held the line taken, and the 9th KOYLI withdrew to join the 1st East Yorks in the Beaurevoir Line. At 6.00 p.m., 62nd and 110th Brigades attacked the village of Walincourt, and at the same time the 9th KOYLI moved up to garrison the trenches in Walincourt Wood vacated by the attacking troops. The 1st East Yorks, under 62nd Brigade orders, eventually captured and held Hill 18 to the north of Walincourt that night, though the original attack orders had given the task to the KOYLIs. The village itself, however, remained in enemy hands.

By dusk, V Corps had taken the Beaurevoir Line along the whole of the Corps front, along with the villages of Villers Outreaux and Malincourt. Angle, Walincourt and Hurtebise Woods were also captured, thus making the average advance some 5,000 yards, 873 prisoners being collected along the way. The 64th Brigade share of the haul of prisoners came to five officers and about 100 Other Ranks.

It would appear that the brigade's only officer killed during that period was 2nd-Lt Charles Woodley of 9th KOYLI, lost during the attack on 8 October. He is buried in Prospect Hill Cemetery between Le Catelet and Beaurevoir. The battalion lost six men that day: two of the other five have no known grave and are commemorated on the Vis en Artois memorial. The remaining three are all in separate cemeteries in the area (see Appendix I).

By the evening of 8 October, the German High Command concluded that the town of Cambrai was no longer tenable and that night issued orders for a general retreat to the Hermann Position I, a distance of almost ten miles, to the River Selle, on which nestled the town near which the 2nd KOYLI had held up von Kluck's advance in August 1914, Le Cateau.

The 9 October saw the 9th KOYLI resting, having concentrated in the area of Walincourt Wood. The medical officer, Captain Guy de H. Dawson, was able to treat some of the civilians who had remained in the area during the fighting. The following day, the battalion was moved into billets in Walincourt village itself, these being described by the War Diary as 'evidently satisfactory'. At 5.00 p.m., the battalion band gave a concert from the village bandstand, a treat much appreciated by both soldiers and locals alike.

A draft of ninety Other Ranks and ten officers joined the battalion that day, the officers being: 2nd-Lts J. Hayes, J.H. Williamson, L. Lawton, S. Taylor, W.B. Smith, J.T. Kidd, A. Hunter, W.L. Percival, J. Robinson and A.C. Grant. At this late stage of the conflict, it is particularly ominous to note that three of these officers would not survive the war.

After reorganising, re-equipping and bathing, the battalion was paraded in the afternoon of 12 October and Brig.-Gen. Edwards passed on the congratulations of the Divisional Commander for their recent successes. The first part of the message contained the usual slightly over-the-top congratulatory phrases, but the last few lines reveal much:

I would ask all ranks to note the ruthless havoc wrought by the enemy on the person and property of defenceless women and old men. You are fighting a vicious beast and you must treat him as such. The enemy is rapidly reaching the end of his tether and it is up to you to see that his final defeat is as complete as possible. What you suffered in the early days of the war, the enemy is suffering now with, moreover, the prospect of an overwhelming defeat staring him in the face.

Good luck,
Signed: David G.M. Campbell
Major-General Commanding 21st Division.

A training programme devised by Maj. Tyler commenced two days later. Sessions ran from 8.00 a.m. to 12.00 noon and 2.00 p.m. to 3.30 p.m. That evening, 'C' Company 9th KOYLI played football against 'D' Company 15th DLI. An embarrassed entry in the War Diary does not reveal the score, but admits that the 15th DLI won 'rather easily'.

On 15 October, Lt-Col. Greenwood made a welcome return from sick leave. A battalion tactical exercise planned for the following day was postponed for twenty-four hours due to inclement weather. The exercise actually took place two days later, with 9th KOYLI and 15th DLI in the front line of a practice attack. The 1st East Yorks were, as the Diary put it, in 'imaginary' support. The East Yorks obviously had more pressing matters to attend to! That same day, three more officers were taken on the strength of the battalion: Lt J.P. Webster, Lt J.P. Carrington and 2nd-Lt G.W. Garbutt.

Parades, training, and a demonstration platoon attack on a 'strongpoint' took up the next two days before the battalion moved up to new billets in the village of Montigny, just to the south of Caudry, the move being completed by 8.30 p.m. Divine services were held the following morning in the town theatre, and the rest of the day was set aside for exactly that: rest.

The battalion paraded in full fighting order the next day, the 21st, and was addressed by the newly returned CO. He complimented the men on the way they had maintained the good traditions of the regiment, and almost predictably, with 22 October, orders arrived for the 9th KOYLI which would enable them to add to their growing list of Battle Honours. The battalion duly moved off to the north-east, reaching Inchy by 11.00 a.m. where the brigade halted for tea. By 5.00 p.m., the men were in their assembly positions for the planned attack, along a railway embankment just to the east of Neuvilly, the 1st East Yorks on their left. There they remained until 11.30 p.m. At this point, both battalions moved to their jumping-off positions on high ground near the small village of Amerval. Zero hour was 2.00 a.m., 23 October.

In the two weeks since the 9th KOYLI had been out of the front-line trenches, the Allied advance had continued. The Second Army in Flanders made a four-mile advance on 14 October, renewed their attacks the following day and once more forced the enemy back: the German Fourth Army pulled back initially to the Lys, then to the Hermann Positions.

On 17 October, the Fourth Army broke into the Hermann Positions, attacking across the River Selle. Le Cateau had fallen by dusk. The attacks continued for the next two days, and a total advance of 9,000 yards on a seven-mile front was achieved: the right wing of the offensive saw the Germans pushed back as far as the Sambre-Oise Canal. By 20 October, with their left flank approaching the Forêt de Mormal, the Fourth Army advance ground to a halt: the Third Army was to pick up the baton.

Facing Byng's troops, to the east of the River Selle, were six Divisions of the German Seventeenth Army. Orders had gone out on the 17th for an attack to drive these enemy troops off the ridge they presently held. Surprise was to be the thing: no preliminary bombardment was fixed. Byng decided to make it a night attack, and Zero hour was set for 2.00 a.m. on the 20th: a full moon was to light their way.

All four corps advanced under a heavy artillery barrage: the VI and XVII Corps were able to reach their objectives during the morning, but V and IV Corps had met considerable resistance. The 21st Division was not involved, but ahead of their positions the 17th Division managed to take Neuvilly.

The high ground to the east of the River Selle was taken, but operations were then halted in order to allow artillery to be brought up.

The second phase of the Battle of the Selle was to involve the Fourth, Third and First Armies. Originally scheduled for 21 October, it had been postponed twice because of the delay in getting ammunitions trains up in the Third Army area. 'Its purpose was to swing the left forward so that the Armies should stand opposite or beyond the Hermann Position II'.[4] This ran from Oisy in the south, through Ors, on northwards between Bousies and Robersart (Fourth Army), onward to Poix du Nord, Ghissignies and Ruesnes (Third Army), and finally north-westwards into the First Army area through Querenaing to the Schelde canal at Trith. The *Official History* describes the German trenches along this line as poor, but the delay in continuing the attacks had given the enemy time to wire the positions and the hedges. An outpost zone had also been constructed, with strongpoints dug into the fields and orchards.

The First Army, on the left of the attack frontage, had little ground to make on 23 October: their advances were made with the minimum of drama and do not really merit detailed examination here. By the end of the 24th, their Divisions stood almost on the banks of the Schelde.

The role of the Fourth Army was to form a defensive flank for the main part of the assault undertaken by the Third Army. The IX Corps on the extreme right was to advance two miles to the Sambre Canal, and XIII Corps, on their left, had before them a five-mile advance to Landrecies–Englefontaine road. The troops moved off at 1.20 a.m., with ground mist limiting visibility. Slow progress at first meant that the creeping barrage was soon lost, but resistance was patchy and almost all the objectives were taken, despite many of the twenty-three tanks employed ditching or falling victim to mechanical failure.

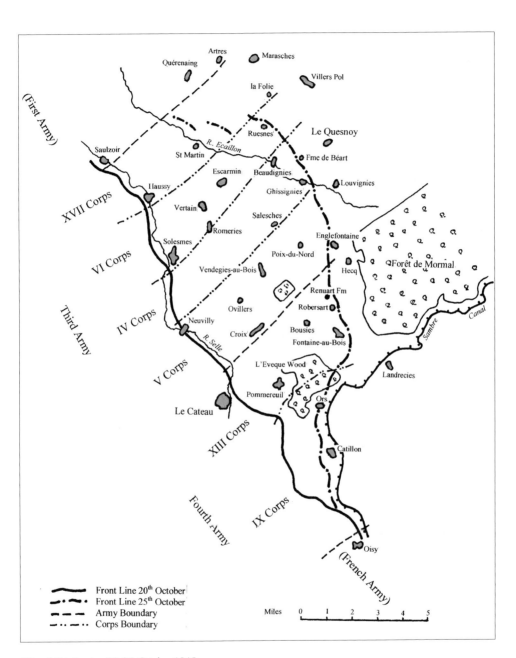

III and IV Armies, 20-25 October 1918.

The Third Army positions ran approximately north–south. The advance was to be made mainly in a north-easterly direction, however: this meant that the right wing of the Army, V Corps, had much further to go than the rest. The left wing of XVII Corps, on the extreme north of the Third Army front, by comparison, had actually reached its objectives on 20 October, and therefore stood its ground and formed the pivot around which the rest of the Army would wheel to the left. The right wing of XVII Corps had under a mile to make, but V Corps had a succession of five objectives spread over 9,500 yards. 'The ground in front presented no special difficulties: it consisted of a series of long, low ridges with the valleys of small streams between them descending to the Schelde; it was closely cultivated, and dotted with small villages, nearly all in the valleys, surrounded as usual by orchards.'[5]

The difficulties with the supply of artillery shells meant that ammunition for the supporting barrage was quite limited: in an effort to compensate, each brigade was to have at least two mobile six-inch mortars to be used against strongpoints and machine-gun posts. A number of tanks were also allocated: six to V Corps, four to IV Corps and twelve each (held in reserve), to VI and XVII Corps.

The 2.00 a.m. Zero hour was forty minutes later than that of Fourth Army. (The right of Third Army was approximately 1,000 yards ahead of Fourth Army's left wing.) The artillery barrage was to advance at a rate of 100 yards every four minutes as far as the Green Dotted Line (see map): the barrage would not extend beyond there. The rate of advance of the troops was also strictly timetabled: the Red Dotted Line was to be reached at 3.40 a.m.: forty minutes later the men would move off from there and arrive at the Red Line at 6.00 a.m. The rest of the schedule was as follows:

Leave Red Line:	0800
Arrive Green Dotted Line:	0840
Leave Green Dotted Line:	0920
Arrive Green Line:	1050
Leave Green Line:	1250
Arrive Brown Line:	1520

64th Brigade started on the right of the Divisional frontage, 110th Brigade on the left, and 62nd in reserve. The 62nd was to leapfrog the others and lead the advance from the Green Dotted Line onwards. Needless to say, once the advance started, the timetable very quickly and inevitably became a work of fiction. Even before Zero hour, at about 12.15 a.m., the enemy opened a heavy counter preparation barrage on the positions of the 7th Leicesters, 110th Brigade, this lasting for about an hour.

At 2.00 a.m. the men rose from their jumping-off positions, 9th KOYLI on the right of the brigade frontage, 1st East Yorks on the left. They moved through the 15th DLI, who were holding positions in front of them and made for the first objective. By 4.30 a.m. the line had been taken and a message to 64th Brigade HQ timed at 7.30 a.m. reported that the 1st East Yorks and 9th KOYLI were about 300 yards east of the village of Ovillers and that enemy shells were falling amongst the troops. Progress had not been smooth: approaching Ovillers, the battalion was held up by fire from a machine-gun post bypassed by units of 33rd Division on the right. Lt-Col. Greenwood rushed this post single-handed, killing the crew of four. He, along with two battalion runners, was forced to repeat this act of gallantry very soon afterwards as the outskirts of Ovillers were reached. The crew suffered the same fate as their comrades. The village was left behind

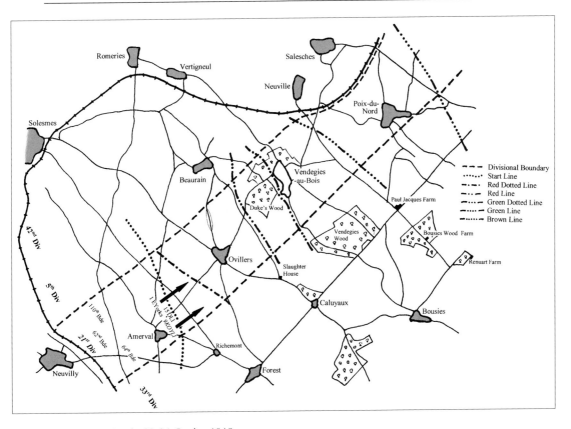

21st Division Attack, 23-24 October 1918.

them and the Red Line was reached, though by 7.50 a.m., German soldiers were still in Ovillers and the 1st Wiltshires were dug in before them to the south-west of the village. Meanwhile, the 7th Leicesters had outflanked the village to the north, reaching the sunken road (see map). They were apparently in some disarray, coming under machine-gun fire from the village of Beaurain to the north.

The 9th KOYLI was the first unit to reach the second objective, but Lt-Col. Greenwood found his men, about 250 of them, isolated, both flanks in the air. The Germans counter-attacked from the right flank and made it to within forty yards of the KOYLI positions before they were halted.

The few Germans left in Ovillers did not hold up the general advance for long: at 8.00 a.m., RAF observers high above the battlefield reported British troops advancing through the village and tanks advancing to the south-east.

By 7.45 a.m., the 19th Brigade on the right and 110th Brigade on the left were level with the KOYLI positions: the Brigade-Major, returning from the front-line positions, was able to report that the Green Dotted Line, their final objective, was reached by 8.05 a.m., the 9th KOYLI having arrived there before their own barrage; buoyed by their success in holding off the German counter-attack, and led by the enthusiastic Greenwood they had taken 150 prisoners, eight machine guns and a field gun in the process.

At this point, the 15th DLI took over the Green Dotted Line and the 9th KOYLI and 1st East Yorks were able to form a defensive flank facing south-east. Even so, machine-gun fire was still coming from Duke's Wood, by now behind the forward troops.

The 62nd Brigade, which had started the day's advance in reserve, now came up and leapfrogged the 15th DLI positions at about 11.00 a.m. and attacked the fourth objective, the Green Line, half way between Vendegies au Bois and Poix du Nord.

By midday, the advancing troops were still a thousand yards short of their objective, though Vendegies au Bois and Duke's Wood had been completely cleared of enemy soldiers by then. The attack continued, and by 1.00 p.m. the distance to the Green Line had been more than halved, and enemy artillery was shelling the British troops from Vendegies Wood in the 33rd Division area to the south. The Germans, worn down by the frontal attacks, and being pushed back on the flanks, retired to the Green Line and by 3.45 p.m. the 62nd Brigade were able to report that position captured.

Of the three tanks that had been allocated to the Division, two had reached the second objective and had helped in the mopping up of machine-gun nests in and around Ovillers. The third had lost direction in the dark and ended up operating in the 33rd Division area.

No more advances were made that day: 'Attempts to advance further, however, were frustrated by machine gun fire from the Poix du Nord ridge and the 21st Division had to be content with the capture of the fourth objective.'[6] Nevertheless, V Corps had managed to push forward about three-and-a-half miles.

On the 21st Division's right, the 33rd Division had reached the same objective line by nightfall: the town of Forest had fallen, along with 200 prisoners. The Red Line was reached by 7.00 a.m., the only real resistance coming from the slaughter house between Ovillers and Caluyaux. The bound to the Green Line followed. There, they were held up until dark, pinned down by fire from Paul Jacques Farm. The farm was eventually taken that day, but by then the darkness meant that any further plans for further movement were postponed until the next day.

On the IV Corps front, to the north, the final objective was successfully reached when Neuville and Salesches fell.

At 9th KOYLI Battalion HQ, which was, by the evening, in Vendegies au Bois, orders were received at 9.15 p.m. for the continuation of the attack on Poix du Nord the following morning. Up to this point, the battle had cost the Battalion twenty-eight fatal casualties.

On 24 October, the First, Third and Fourth Armies were to continue their joint operations in order, where necessary, to reach the final objectives set for the 23rd, and, in other places, to improve upon the previous day's gains.

On the Fourth Army front, on the right of the frontage to be assaulted, IX Corps (extreme right), did not have far to go and were able to set their Zero hour at 9.30 a.m., allowing their men a proper rest overnight. When they advanced, patrols made it as far as the western outskirts of the village of Catillon, and they discovered that the Germans had more or less evacuated the west side of the Sambre Canal, leaving only a few snipers and machine gun crews. L'Eveque Wood, the major geographical feature facing them, was cleared, all but in its extreme eastern corner.

Zero hour for XIII Corps was 4.00 a.m. They had left themselves rather more to do: the fourth and fifth objectives from the previous day remained untouched, and to reach them, the Hermann II positions still had to be crossed. Despite heavy machine-gun fire from these positions, the 25th Division had secured its fourth objective by 10.00 a.m. The advance was renewed at 2.00 p.m., and four hours later the final line was taken. The 18th Division, on the 25th's left, indeed on the Army's left wing, encountered heavy resistance and made only slow progress. The village of Robersart, behind the Hermann positions, was stubbornly defended, but the church in the centre was finally captured at 6.00 p.m. An attempt to reach the fourth objective, some 2-300 yards further on, went in at eleven that night, but failed. A further attempt at dawn on the 25th met with the same fate.

Fifty-fourth Brigade (18th Division), actually bordering Third Army, reached Renuart Farm, adjacent to the village of Robersart, at 5.00 p.m., in touch with troops on both of its flanks. (An officer, a sergeant and a Lewis gun section of the 6th Northants managed to put six enemy machine guns out of action north of Renuart Farm, and captured their crews in the process. The officer, Lt F.W. Hedges, was awarded the Victoria Cross.)

The Third Army plan was to push forward to a ridge of high ground running from Englefontaine (a village near the western edge of the Forêt de Mormal), north of Ghissignies, Ruesnes and Quérenaing). To the north of the KOYLI positions, IV Corps had made a five-mile advance for the cost of just 400 casualties, Ghissignies and Beart Farm having fallen.

Further north still, VI Corps were able to keep touch with those units on their right and captured the village of Ruesnes. XVII Corps had not matched this rate of progress, however, faltering at La Folie, and VI Corps had to form a defensive flank on their left to avoid leaving a gap which might entice German counter-attacks.

V Corps front, in the centre of the whole advance, was the domain of 33rd and 21st Divisions. 33rd Division, on the right, had orders to keep touch with the Fourth Army, sending forward 98th and 19th Brigades. The 98th Brigade made it as far as the Poix du Nord–Hecq road, but were there held up by machine-gun and other small arms fire enfilading them from the right, as Fourth Army units had not kept pace. The 19th Brigade, free from such nuisances, were able to reach the road running northward through the western outskirts of Englefontaine. At midday, 100th Brigade came up and leapfrogged the 19th, but were unable to penetrate into Englefontaine itself. They had to be content with taking over and holding the line gained that day by 33rd Division.

The 21st Division sent forward 64th and 62nd Brigades. They were presented with two objectives, neither of which coincided with the fifth, the Brown Line, of the previous day: the first was the Englefontaine–Salesches road, the second the road running north from Englefontaine to Ghissignies.

A regular barrage was to be available as far as the first objective, delivered by four brigades of field artillery and heavy machine guns. Only one of these artillery brigades would be able to help the advancing troops towards the second. No fire at all was to be directed on the village of Poix du Nord as it was still full of French civilians (2,600 were subsequently found to be there).

Divisional Order No.249 placed the 64th Brigade on the right, 62nd on the left, and 110th in support. The barrage began as planned at 4.00 a.m. and the men moved forward. Troops of 62nd Brigade made good time and were reported on the line of the first objective by 6.00 p.m. On the 64th Brigade front the 15th DLI and 9th KOYLI were held up on the wire of the Hermann II position on the ridge in front of Poix du Nord. For two hours, extremely intense machine-gun fire pinned the men down. Lt-Col. Greenwood, recceing the position himself, spotted that a stretch of the ridge in front of the KOYLI positions was held by just one German machine gun. He rushed the emplacement single-handed, and despite fire from this post being directed at him, he got to within twenty yards of the position and was able to kill the crew. 'A' Company was then ordered to advance into this newly created gap: the breakthrough was rapidly followed up, the flank of the machine-gun posts on the ridge turned, and Poix du Nord subsequently taken with little resistance encountered. The KOYLIs came up against another

Lieutenant Webster and Private Inch, killed 24 October 1918.

line of machine-gun posts to the north of the town, but these crews did not prove to be as stubborn as their compatriots and the line of the first objective was gained by 8.00 a.m. The 1st East Yorks came up on the right at about 10.00 a.m., and the 15th DLI were in position on the left by midday. Before this support arrived, the 9th KOYLI, somewhat isolated, had fought off a German counter-attack. Once more, Lt-Col. Greenwood proved inspirational: he walked up and down in full view of the enemy, in front of the advance posts, encouraging his men.

Momentum had been lost to some extent, and it was decided that the attempt on the second objective would not be launched until 4.00 p.m. The DLI and East Yorks, left and right respectively, would lead this time. The 9th KOYLI would be in support and were required to form a defensive flank facing south-east.

The attack went forward as planned, and the road running south-east from Grand Gay Farm to the crossroads north of Englefontaine was successfully taken by 6.00 p.m. The 9th KOYLI, in forming the defensive flank, came under severe fire from the right. Greenwood and his men dealt with several machine-gun posts outside the brigade boundary and later handed these over to troops of 33rd Brigade. By darkness, positions had been established at the previously mentioned crossroads. The remainder of the night was spent digging in.

Patrols sent out on the morning of 25 October encountered heavy machine-gun fire and further attempts to advance were abandoned. The position on the brigade front remained unchanged for the rest of the day, and 64th Brigade was relieved by 51st

*Grave of 2nd-Lt A. Hunter, the last 9th KOYLI
officer killed in the Great War. Doulers
Communal Cemetery.*

Brigade. The men moved back into billets in Vendegies au Bois for the night. Further
relief on the following day saw them back in Inchy by the afternoon. Kit deficiencies
were made up, billets were organised and on the 27th the men were able to bathe.
Voluntary church services were followed by a concert in one of the town squares by the
battalion band.

The battalion could once more pause and count its losses: a further nineteen fatal casualties were suffered on the 24th, including Lt John Philip Webster, who had joined the
KOYLIs only seven days before. Second-Lieutenants Walter Lowe Percival and William
Byron Smith died of wounds on the 24th and 25th respectively, their stays with the
battalion likewise fourteen and fifteen days. Casualties for the 9th KOYLI for this month
were 265 killed, wounded or missing.

If it is assumed that a battalion went into action with the habitual 750 men, or there-
abouts, it can be seen that more than one in three men of the 9th KOYLI became casualties. Appendix I gives final fatal casualties for October 1918 as four officers and
fifty-seven Other Ranks, not including the seven men recorded as dying whilst in
captivity in Germany.

In a reversal of the previous relief, the 64th Brigade relieved 51st Brigade in Vendegies
au Bois on 29 October. A new draft of about 100 Other Ranks joined, and they were
inspected by the CO and 'told of the traditions of the battalion.'[7] Although warned to be
ready to move at twenty minutes' notice and take up positions in the Green Line, the
battalion remained in Vendegies au Bois for the remaining two days of the month, under-

going Lewis gun training and enduring PT Drill. On that last day of October, a note of congratulation was received from the Commander-in-Chief in recognition of the recent actions. He expressed his confidence that 'any further test which the future might bring would be met with the same unflinching resolution.'[8]

From his perspective at Staff HQ, Capt. Harold Yeo wrote home to his mother on 30 October, giving his by now familiar slant on recent events: 'We got all we set out for and did in a decent tally of Huns. It was far more interesting than the old murderous shoves as far as I was concerned.'[9]

One final aspect of the story of this action remains untold: for his gallant actions on 23 and 24 October 1918, Lt-Col. Greenwood, commanding 9th KOYLI, was awarded the Victoria Cross. The full citation reads as follows:

For great gallantry, devotion to duty, and fine leadership of his battalion during the fighting of 23rd/24th October 1918. Whilst advancing eastwards towards Ovillers on the early morning of the 23rd, the advance of the battalion was checked by an enemy machine-gun post which had not been mopped up by the unit on its right and which was causing heavy casualties. Lt-Col. Greenwood single-handed rushed this machine-gun post, which was firing at point blank range, and killed the crew of four. At the entrance of the village of Ovillers, another machine-gun post was encountered, which again held up the advance. Again, Lt-Col. Greenwood rushed this post with two of his battalion runners, killing the occupants. On reaching the objective west of Dukes Wood, touch had been lost with both flank units. Lt-Col. Greenwood found himself with 250 men, almost surrounded by the enemy machine-gun posts which were held in great strength. The enemy, seeing this force almost isolated, counter-attacked on the right flank and succeeded in getting within forty yards before the attack was broken up. Led by Lt-Col. Greenwood the men swept forward cheering and took the last objective, actually in front of our own barrage, taking 150 prisoners, eight machine guns and one field gun in doing so. At the commencement of the attack on the Green Line, south of Poix du Nord on 24th October, the advance of the brigade was held up by withering fire from wired-in machine gun posts on the ridge. Lt-Col. Greenwood, by a personal reconnaissance, discovered a part of the ridge that was held by one enemy machine gun only. This post he rushed single-handed, killing the occupants who were firing at him at a range of about twenty yards. He then threw a company into this gap. The whole flank of the machine-gun posts was turned and the advance proceeded through Poix du Nord, the battalion led by Lt-Col. Greenwood sweeping aside a further line of machine-gun posts that was encountered north of the town, reaching its objective with both flanks in the air. Heavy machine gun and field gun fire was then opened against the battalion from the front and right flank. Heavy casualties caused the line to waver and it was only due to Lt-Col. Greenwood walking up and down in front of the advanced posts (under heavy machine gun fire in full view of the enemy) encouraging his men that the line was held and an enemy counter-attack beaten off. During the further advance on Grand Gay Farm Road on the afternoon of the 24 October, Lt-Col. Greenwood was given the right flank of the brigade to advance on and protect. Despite the fact that no troops advanced on his right flank, thereby allowing very heavy enfilade machine-gun fire to be concentrated on the right flank of the brigade, he led his battalion forward, cleared up all the machine-gun posts, took an objective well to the right of the objective that had been allocated to the brigade, subsequently handing this over to the Division on his right and made the right flank of his own Division absolutely secure. During the two days of fighting Lt-Col. Greenwood, by the magnificent example he set his officers and men, showing utter contempt for danger, contributed greatly towards the success of the operations during the advance. He was twice blown up by a shell dropping near him and was hit several times by the fragments, on one occasion being badly stunned. His conduct and example during the fighting was beyond all praise.

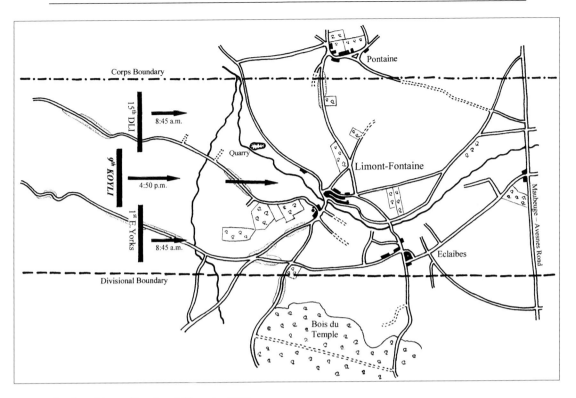

Attack on Limont-Fontaine, 7 November 1918.

Greenwood's own thoughts on the episode do not come to light until early in 1919 when he wrote a letter to Ellenberger who had by that time been released from captivity and was back home in England:

My Dear Ellenberger,
Many thanks for your letter which turned up last evening and for the nice things you say therein about myself. I'm afraid I don't deserve them all, however, as I did really nothing save drive on, kill a few Huns and cheer our own fellows on a bit when they flagged. It was topping fighting really and I would not have missed it for anything. Lots of Bosche to kill and plenty of time to kill them in, in fact one could almost always choose one's bird. Our fellows were splendid and with any kind of leadership would have gone anywhere. It is a great shame of course that you were not there to get a little of your own back.[10]

The first days of November 1918 for the 9th KOYLI consisted of training, including more Lewis gun work, and various movements and reliefs. Training sessions were not limited to familiarisation and practice with the Lewis gun: captured weapons were to be turned upon their previous owners. Second-Lieutenant M.W. Williams, in Command of 'D' Company, wrote to his counterpart in 'B' Company on 1st November: 'To CO 'B' Coy, May I have the loan of your (Light) Boche machine gun for an hour this morning 10.00 a.m. Please, M. Williams, OC 'D' Coy 1.11.18'[11]

By the early hours of 4 November, the battalion was in support positions near Futoy, ready to follow in the wake of advances planned for that day. V Corps, as part of the general attack, faced a fight through various hamlets west of the Forêt de Mormal, followed by an assault through the forest itself. The attack was prosecuted by the 17th and 38th Divisions, Zero hour being 6.15 a.m. The most serious resistance was encountered before they actually reached the edge of the forest. Once into the woodland, the task, unexpectedly, became easier.

By nightfall, troops had advanced well into the forest, and when the advance was renewed the following morning, it became more of a careful pursuit of an Army in retreat. The west bank of the Sambre was reached and bridges were built during the night, enabling troops to cross as it became light. Third and Fourth Armies had made excellent progress along the whole of the attack frontage. The 'Battle of the Sambre' had seen the two Allied Armies take about 10,000 prisoners, and move their line forward an average of three miles. By 4.00 p.m. on 5 November, the 9th KOYLI, uninvolved in the actual fighting (though still sustaining one fatal casualty that day, 51874 Charles Thornton being killed in action), were moving into the village of La Grande Carrière, on the *eastern* edge of the Forêt de Mormal, where they were to spend the night.

The 21st Division was to continue its advance on 7 November: 110th Brigade was required to push on to the Avesnes–Maubeuge road. The 64th Brigade was to be ready to pass through their compatriots and take over the advance should the assault falter.

At 4.30 a.m., the 64th duly left La Grande Carrière and followed the front-line assault troops. By this time, resistance from the retreating German forces was limited to rearguard actions fought in certain fortified villages. Some of these garrisons proved very stubborn and the Third Army units fought some severe actions that day. One of these villages was directly in the path of the 21st Division advance: the German garrison at Limont-Fontaine (just to the west of the Avesnes–Maubeuge road) was in no mood to surrender the ground that they held.

At 8.45 a.m. 64th Brigade passed through the by now halted 110th, 15th DLI and 1st East Yorks (left and right respectively), in front, 9th KOYLI in support. Morale was high, a heavy mist hung over the battlefield, and the men were confident of a swift victory. Intense German artillery and machine-gun fire held up the advance, however, and the village remained, for the time being, in enemy hands. Recce patrols were sent out to try and locate exactly the artillery batteries and machine-gun posts during the day, and with this newly gathered intelligence another attack was arranged. The 9th KOYLI was to lead the attack, supported by the 1st East Yorks. The only existing account of the action is to be found in the War Diary of the 9th KOYLI, and this is short on detail: the attack went in at 4.50 p.m., supported by covering machine-gun and artillery fire. The enemy made a determined stand, but after fierce fighting in the approaches to the village and in the streets themselves, the KOYLIs emerged victorious. By 9.30 p.m. Limont-Fontaine and its smaller neighbour Eclaibes, 'thoroughly cleared of the enemy, were both added to the growing list of Allied gains.'[12]

Although the men could not have known it at the time, the 9th KOYLI had fought its last action of the war: the cost that day was sixteen lives; a further half dozen or so were to succumb to their wounds in the days following. Second-Lieutenant Archibald Hunter was killed in action during the liberation of Limont-Fontaine, the last officer of the battalion to die in the service of his country. He had been with the battalion only twenty-seven days.

As midnight approached on the 7/8 November, the men of 64th Brigade were holding their newly established line to the east of Limont-Fontaine, just short of the main Avesnes–Maubeuge road. The 17th Division passed through these positions rendering them redundant as the general advance moved on. The 9th KOYLI were therefore able to move back some two-and-a-half miles, arriving in Bachant at 6.30 a.m. Tea, ever welcome, was issued, and, starting at 8.00 a.m., a march of a similar distance took them to Berlaimont on the west bank of the Sambre. The rest of the 8th and the whole of 9 November were spent resting, and the men were able to clean up both themselves and their equipment. The 10th saw the resumption of training, and on Monday 11 November 9th KOYLI were once more marching eastwards. They arrived at Limont-Fontaine at midday, and found comfortable quarters in the area north of the river, 'glad to be billeted in a village which is of peculiar interest to them by right of capture.'[13]

During their march, the Great War had come to an end, the order having been given for hostilities to cease at 11.00 a.m. 'En route, news of the signing of the Armistice arrived, and while inward satisfaction was undoubtedly felt, no outward demonstration was made.'[14]

The War Diary does not record the extent to which the news was celebrated that night, once it had had time to sink in and the constraints of march discipline had been removed. Harold Yeo provides the only clue in a letter home written that evening:

Everyone smiling and sounds of cheers ringing out in all the villages. What a strange feeling! These great events never are quite so great when they actually come about. I think one's senses have been rather numbed by all the shocks they have received during the last four and a half years... and now to go to bed to dream of a blue suit and a bowler hat.[15]

16

PEACE AND AFTERMATH

The 30 October 1918 was an eventful day: Ludendorff had resigned five days earlier, and it was on this date that his successor, General Wilhelm Gröner, the fifty-one-year-old son of a non-commissioned officer, arrived at Supreme Command HQ in Spa. The same day, though several hours later, the Kaiser himself turned up: the demands for his abdication were mounting at home. To round off the day, Turkey signed an armistice with the Allied powers.

In the meantime, the Prime Ministers of Great Britain, France and Italy, and President Wilson's representative, Colonel House, were in Paris discussing the terms for an armistice. On 5 November, Wilson was able to send a note to Berlin advising the German Government that Foch was authorised to meet German representatives and advise them of the terms of the armistice on offer.

The chosen German representatives were in Spa by the morning of Thursday 7 November, and on their way westwards by noon. They crossed the front lines at about 9.00 p.m. that day and were met by French representatives at La Capelle. They spent the night in a château on the Aisne and the following morning, the 8th, they were taken by train to a siding in the Forest of Compiègne. At 9.00 a.m., they were shown into a Wagon Lits saloon coach: Foch, General Weygand, Admiral Sir Rosslyn Wemyss (First Sea Lord), with Admiral Hope and Captain Marriott of the Royal Navy made their entrance shortly afterwards.

The terms of the armistice were read; Erzberger asked for an immediate cessation of hostilities while the terms were considered by the German Government and Supreme Command. Foch replied that although he too was eager for the fighting to end, this could not happen until the armistice carried German signatures. A courier was despatched to Spa with the full text of the Allied demands at 1.00 p.m.

The situation in Germany was by now critical. A General Strike in Berlin was followed by the setting up of revolutionary councils in various cities: troops sent to re-establish order had in some places joined the rebels. The Chancellor tried to persuade the Kaiser that the only way to prevent civil war was for the latter to announce that he would abdicate, but Wilhelm remained obdurate, refusing to comply with the demand. On 9 November, Hindenburg and Gröner were forced to inform the Kaiser that the Army would no longer stand behind him. The declaration of a Socialist Republic from the steps of the Reichstag building in Berlin and the resignation of the Chancellor left Hindenburg with no choice but to tell his monarch: 'I cannot accept the responsibility of seeing the Emperor hauled to Berlin by insurgent troops and delivered over as a prisoner to the Revolutionary Government. I must advise Your Majesty to abdicate and to proceed to Holland.'[1]

On 10 November, at 5.00 a.m., the Kaiser left Spa and reached the Dutch border two hours later. On the evening of the same day, the German Armistice Commission, anxious for news and instructions, received two messages: the first was to the effect that Germany accepted the terms offered. The second authorised Erzberger to sign the armistice. Final negotiations recommenced at 2.15 a.m. on Monday 11 November. The German delegation signed the document at 5.10 a.m., and Foch declared the meeting closed. A telegram was immediately sent out:

1. *Hostilities will cease on the entire front on November 11th at 11.00 a.m., French time.*
2. *Allied troops are not to pass until further orders beyond the line reached on that day at that hour. Exact report must be made as to this line.*
3. *All communication with the enemy is forbidden until receipt of instructions by Army Commanders.*

The message was relayed to the headquarters of the five British Armies, and all were in possession of it by 7.30 a.m. All that remained to be done was to ensure that the order was communicated to the front-line units. Communications being what they were, however, the message often took some time to reach its destination and operations continued in places up to the last moment. Indeed, the last officially recorded British fatality was timed at 10.58 a.m.

Corporal Harry Davill M.M., died of wounds 14 November 1918.

On 12 November 1918, the War Diary of the 9th KOYLI declared that 'No parades were engaged in, it being considered that for this day at least, training was subservient to rest.'[2]

Training reappeared on the daily schedule the very next day, this leading up to a Brigade Ceremonial Parade held on the 16th. Church Parade on Sunday 17 was followed in the afternoon by various sporting activities, football and running included, under the official title of 'recreational training'.

On 18 November, a Memorial Service was held in the village church at Limont-Fontaine in memory of those who had fallen in its liberation. A 'magnificent wreath'[3] was made by the villagers and presented to the battalion. The local curé, the Abbé J. Hégo, gave a stirring speech. In it he praised the British Army for its valiant efforts since 1914. He spoke in emotive terms of the battle that had resulted in the liberation of his village:

But our hearts, those of the inhabitants of Limont-Fontaine, share a commonly and acutely felt pain when we reflect upon the cost paid by the English Army for the retaking of our tiny village. A Division (an elite Division, of that we are sure), had thrown forward its best battalions: the fight was hot and deadly; it was necessary to flush out one by one the machine-gun nests that the enemy, taking every advantage offered by the location, had concealed behind every hedge or placed astride each fold in the terrain: the assailant, as he rose from cover, found himself immediately the target of their bullets. Artillery batteries had been forced to take up their positions under intense bombardment themselves, galloping forward under a hail of shells: successive pockets of resistance were taken at bayonet point. Blood flowed... many brave men fell... officers, as well as their men, were offered up as sacrificial tributes to Death, and it seems that he chose those amongst you of whom you were most proud.

So, it is to recognise the qualities of all the brave men that the English Army has lost in the course of this war: it is to celebrate the memory of the officers, NCO's and men who have fallen in our homeland: it is to beseech the Almighty to have mercy upon their souls: it is for these reasons that the young people of this commune wanted this ceremony. In the name of all my parishioners, I thank you, General, you the officers, for being able to enhance it by your presence, and for allowing your men to take part.[4]

He went on to apologise for the conditions in which the ceremony had to be held: the Germans had burned his church in 1914 and shelled it in 1918. '*Quelle triste église pour vous recevoir, Messieurs.*'[5]

For the following four days, the battalion fell into a routine of drill and salvage in the morning, sports in the afternoon. Another Brigade Ceremonial Parade was held on the 23rd, and such was the improvement since the last one that the Brigadier-General felt he had to write a congratulatory letter, complimenting the entire brigade on their appearance and discipline.

Two days later, a scheme was put into place which would both occupy the men and perhaps prove useful to them in the long term. The Battalion Educational Scheme was launched. Nearly 300 men enrolled for courses on a variety of subjects: Elementary English, grammar and composition, Advanced English, Mathematics, Languages, Technical subjects including the theory of engines, Electricity and Magnetism. The teaching staff had been culled from the officers and men of the battalion.

The end of the month saw the 9th KOYLI succeed on the sporting field: Brig.-Gen. Edwards had provided a silver cup for a football competition, and on the afternoon of

The Church at Limont-Fontaine. (present day)

28 November, the final was played between 'A' Company 1st East Yorks and 'B' Company 9th KOYLI After extra time, the KOYLI team emerged triumphant by a score of two goals to one, watched by almost the entire battalion.

The Brigade Cross Country Competition came next: the 9th KOYLI were the first team to get twenty-five runners home, thereby winning the team competition, and also scooped first and second positions in the individual contest.

December 1918 saw the commencement of the long and inevitably slow process of demobilisation. To begin with, as the War Diary details, it was men with specific trades and skills particularly needed back in Britain who were the first to be released. On the 2 and 6 December, groups of miners (122 of them on the second of these dates) left for the examination centre at Cambrai prior to being sent home. On the day that the first of these two groups departed, the rest of the battalion was treated to a lecture by the Demobilisation Officer on the Government Plan for the Extension of Military Service. Clearly, the men, each eager to return home to their families and loved ones would have to try to remain patient. The extent of the popularity of the officer in question is not recorded in the War Diary. Neither are the men's thoughts on the content of his speech.

On the 12th of the month, the battalion was on the move once more, and over the next three days a series of marches took them through Berlaimont and Vendegies to Inchy, where they briefly occupied billets they had last seen in October. The following day, the 15th, they boarded motor buses at 7.30 a.m. for an eight-hour, seventy-mile road journey westwards to the village of Seux, about five miles west of Amiens. 'Great interest was attached to this run as the way led over some of the most historic battle-fields of France, fields sacred to the memory of all those who saw them again that day. In this part of the line, the immortal 21st Division has from time to time won undying fame.'[6]

'C' and 'D' Companies were billeted in Seux itself, with 'A' and 'B' Companies in the neighbouring village of Briquemesnil. Battalion HQ was established in Château Seux.

Three days after their arrival, 18 December was described by the War Diary as a 'red-letter day in the history of the battalion'. News of Lt-Col. Greenwood's Victoria Cross reached the 9th KOYLI. The Colonel was, as it happens, away at the time, commanding the 64th Brigade in Brig.-Gen. Edwards' absence. A telegram was immediately sent to him, conveying the congratulations of all the officers and men of the battalion:

Every officer and man was intensely proud to learn that the bravery of their leader had met with such signal reward. Only to the few does this distinction come. The cross is awarded for valour and it was felt that the dignity of the decoration had been maintained. If the distinction was great, so was the rejoicing. Honour had been bestowed on the commanding officer, thus honour had come to the Bn and the Bn felt a thrill of reflected glory. In battle Col. Greenwood is ever in front with his men. For him, to be in [the] rear in action is to be out *of it. That useful work may be done from the rear he does not deny, but coupled with this belief he holds other views. For him there is only one position, that is in the van. He does not urge, he leads.*[7]

The Brigade Ceremonial Parade held on Christmas Eve was another proud moment, with Lt-Col. Greenwood VC in command. Christmas Day, the first peacetime celebration of the holiday for five years, was also a special occasion. The officers had done their best to ensure that plentiful supplies of appropriate food and drink were available: in some companies, the officers waited upon the men, a 'touch of camaraderie and much appreciated'.[8]

In the morning, the sergeants had played the officers at football, losing 1-2, and in the evening the Battalion Concert Party gave of their best to a hut full to overflowing. In honour of Greenwood's Victoria Cross, Boxing Day was declared a battalion holiday.

The year drew to a close with the usual round of educational classes, training and salvage work. At Seux, Nissen Huts were being erected to house the men. Seux, it would seem, was to be improved by this construction scheme: in Greenwood's letter to Ellenberger written in January 1919, the CO gives his candid opinion of the location after telling his newly released comrade of the changed make-up of his old battalion:

There is hardly anybody you know here now, Hendricks is back with us, also Gregg who was with 'C' when you commanded it. There are no other Officers that you would know. We are in the doldrums just now, being billeted in a poverty-stricken area just west of Amiens. The billets are bad and the people inhospitable.[9]

The routine continued into the New Year: on 3 January, the men were given the opportunity to watch a rugby match. The game was apparently growing in popularity amongst the men of the battalion, largely due to the efforts of Capt. W. Robb MC, captain of the team. A large number of men turned out to watch a fast and exciting game played on a very heavy pitch. The officers of 64th Brigade lined up against those of 62nd Brigade, only to go down 0-3.

Demobilisation was still proving to be a slow process: on 6 January, in a talk given to the 1st East Yorks and the 9th KOYLI in the hangars at Bovelles aerodrome, General Sir David Campbell, after praising the 'magnificent' work of both battalions, deemed it necessary to explain the considerable delay before General Demobilisation took place,

Limont-Fontaine was the last village to be captured by this Bde.

L.D.F.

EN MÉMOIRE

DES

OFFICIERS, SOUS-OFFICIERS ET SOLDATS ANGLAIS,

TOMBÉS À LIMONT-FONTAINE,

LES

6, 7 and 8 NOVEMBRE, 1918.

Sous-officiers et Soldats Anglais.   5

Hélas! sans parler des blessures qui énorgnérent à peine et par miracle quelques-uns d'entre vous—combien, combien de vos compagnons ont payé de leur vie la gloire qui rayonne dans les plis de vos drapeaux!

On frémit quand on songe a ce million de vies anglaises, débordantes de jeunesse et d'espoirs, sacrifiées pendant plus de trois ans d'une monotone et indécise guerre de tranchées . . . ou pendant ces batailles acharnées de la Somme et des Flandres qui arrachèrent a l'ennemi quelques précieux lambeaux d'un territoire où il semblait s'être enracine.

On frémit quand on songe aux assauts perpétuels de la victorieuse offensive déclenchée il y a quatre mois.

Mais notre cœur, a nous, habitants de Limont-Fontaine, se serre avec une particulière douleur, quand nous réfléchissons à ce que coûta a l'armée anglaise la reprise de notre tout petit village. . . . Une division (division d'élite, nous le savons), avait lancé en avant ses meilleurs bataillons; la lutte fut chaude et meurtrière; il fallut nettoyer un a un les nids de mitrailleuses que l'ennemi, profitant des avantages que lui offrait l'endroit, avait dissimulées derrière chaque haie ou à cheval sur chaque pli de terrain; l'assaillant qui se découvrait devenait immédiatement le point de mire des balles; il fallut poster les batteries sous un intense bombardement, galoper sous la pluie des obus; ce fut aussi l'enlèvement a la baïonnette des points successifs de résistance. . . . Le sang coula. . . . Plus d'un brave tomba. . . . Les officiers payèrent comme leurs hommes leur tribut à la mort; et parmi eux il semble qu'elle ait choisi ceux dont vous étiez les plus fiers.

Eh bien! c'est pour reconnaitre le mérite de tous les braves que l'armée anglaise perdit au cours de cette guerre; c'est pour célébrer la mémoire des officiers, des sous-officiers et des soldats tombés chez nous; c'est pour implorer en faveur de leurs âmes la miséricorde du Tout-Puissant; que les jeunes gens de notre commune ont voulu cette cérémonie. Au nom de tous mes paroissiens, je vous remercie, Monsieur le Général et Messieurs les Officiers, d'avoir bien voulu la rehausser de votre présence, et d'y avoir fait participer vos soldats.

Certes, nous devons nous excuser de la pauvreté, de la misère de l'appareil exterieur au milieu duquel nous vous recevons. Pour la seconde fois au cours de cette guerre, notre église vient d'être la victime de ceux qui prétendaient combattre dans la société de Dieu: Gott mit uns! En 1914, ils l'ont incendiée, en 1918, ils l'ont bombardée, les Barbares! Quelle triste eglise pour vous recevoir, Messieurs!

Nous aurions voulu aussi de somptueuses tentures, un parterre de fleurs et de couronnes symboliques.

Front cover and extract from the Order of Service for the ceremony held at Limont-Fontaine church on 18 November 1918.

64th INFANTRY BRIGADE

Order of Ceremonial
at the
Unveiling of the Brigade Memorial
in
Cojeul British Cemetery,
on
Henin Hill, France,
by
Brigadier A. J. McCulloch,
D.S.O., D.C.M.

Saturday, July 4th, 1931,
at 5 o'clock p.m.

This Memorial is erected by the Survivors of the 64th Infantry Brigade to the glorious memory of the Officers, N.C.O.'s and Men who laid down their lives in the Great War, 1914-1918.

The unveiling of the 64th Brigade Memorial at Cojeul British Cemetery.

and asked the men to show patience. In the first three months of the year, 351 Other Ranks and eleven officers were demobilised.

On 14 January, the battalion was once more at the aerodrome at Bovelles, this time in the presence of the Bishop of Leicester, who performed the ceremony of consecration of the battalion colours.

Routine thereafter took on a predictable pattern. Becoming equally routine seemed to be the success enjoyed by the 9th KOYLI in various sporting competitions: on 15 January, the battalion Tug of War team won the Brigade Competition, to be followed five days later by equal success in the Divisional Boxing Competition: another silver cup for the trophy cabinet.

Honours of a different kind were bestowed on 24 January. The following WOs and NCOs received the Military Service Medal: 15152 RQMS Wool, H.E.; 16131 CQMS Smith, J.W.; 17664 CQMS Wynn, R.W.; 18999 Sergt. Dee, J.H. Just over a month later, on 25 February, the Military Medal was awarded to: 17384 CQMS Wynn, H.E. and 34850 Cpl Barron, J.

The Battalion War Diary chronicles the months of January, February and March 1919. Route-marches, church parades, salvage working parties, sporting distractions, educational classes: all these continued, disturbed only by a couple of heavy falls of snow.

At the end of March, the War Diary ends. With it ends the history of the 9th Battalion KOYLI, its duty to the nation completed. The list of Battle Honours reflects the magnitude of the part played in the struggle:

Loos
Somme
Arras
Third Ypres
March Offensive
Kemmel
Chemin des Dames
Albert
Scarpe
Epehy
Cambrai
Selle
Sambre

The deeds of the 9th (Service) Battalion King's Own Yorkshire Light Infantry have now passed from the realm of first-hand human memory, but to borrow words found on the memorial stone in the Commonwealth War Graves Commission cemeteries which record the names of the 1338 men of the battalion who gave their lives for their country:

Their Name Liveth For Evermore

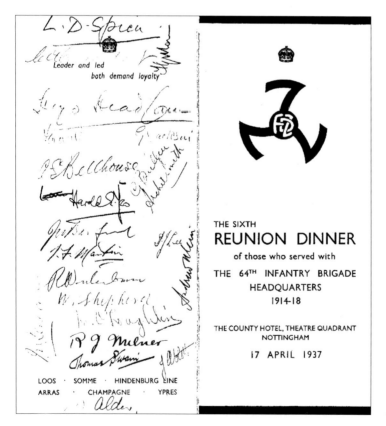

Menu Card from the 64th Infantry Brigade HQ Reunion Dinner, April 1937.

NOTES

NB: The PRO record for the War Diary of 9th Bn KOYLI is WO95 2162.

Introduction

1 *History of the First World War*, B.H. Liddell Hart, p.16.
2 *The Times Diary and Index of the War* 1914-18, p.3.
3 *Official History 1914*, Vol. I, p.29.

Chapter 1

1 *Kitchener's Army*, Simkins, p.64
2 *A Short History of the King's Own Light Infantry 1755-1965*, Huxley, p.1.
3 Ibid., p.2.
4 Ibid., p.2.
5 *Official History 1949* Vol. I, p.176.
6 *Dewsbury Reporter*, 22.08.14.
7 Ibid.
8 Ibid., 05.09.14
9 *Kitchener's Army*, Simkins, p.69.
10 Ibid., pp. 199-200.
11 Ibid., p. 128.
12-17 Unpublished handwritten memoirs of an unidentified officer of the Battalion. Papers held by the KOYLI Association.

Chapter 2

1 The First World War Letters of Colonel H.E.Yeo, MBE MC 1915-1919, Imperial War Museum.
2 *Letters from France*, Spicer, p.2
3 Letters of H.E.Yeo, IWM.
4 *Letters from France*, Spicer, p.2.
5 Letters of H.E.Yeo, IWM.
6 War Diary of 21st Div.
7 Ibid.
8 *Official History 1915*, Vol II, p.278.
9 Ibid., p. 114.
10 Ibid., p.118.
11 Ibid., p.129.
12 Ibid., p.284.

13 *Official History 1915*, Vol II. p.265.
14 Ibid., p.267.
15 War Diary of 21st Division, WO95 2128 PRO.
16 *Official History 1915*, Vol II, p.306.
17 Ibid., p.312.
18 Ibid., p.315.
19 Ibid., p.317.
20 Ibid., pp.328-329, Footnote.
21 Letters of H.E.Yeo, IWM.
22 War Diary of 21st Division.
23 Ibid.
24 Ibid.
25 *Official History 1915*, Vol II, pp. 343 and 345.

Chapter 3

1 The author's father used a similar device in a letter sent to his wife in 1941 whilst serving with the 1/4th KOYLI in Iceland. The first letters of the first seven words spelt out the location.
2 Letters of H.E. Yeo, 17.10.15, IWM.
3 Ibid., 7.11.15.
4 *Daily Mail*.
5 Letters of H.E. Yeo, 27.11.15, IWM
6 War Diary of 9th Bn KOYLI.
7 Letters of H.E.Yeo, 17.11.15, IWM.
8 Ibid., 18.11.15.
9 The First World War Papers of Brigadier G.F. Ellenberger MC. Letter dated 22.12.15, IWM.
10 *Letters from France*, Spicer, letter dated 22.11.15.
11 Letters of G.F. Ellenberger, 27.12.15, IWM.
12 Letters of H.E. Yeo, 2.1.16, IWM.
13 War Diary of 9th Bn KOYLI.
14 Letters of G.F. Ellenberger, 27.01.16, IWM.
15 War Diary of 9th Bn KOYLI.
16 Letters of G.F. Ellenberger, 10.2.16, IWM.
17 Ibid., 16.2.16.
18 *Letters from France*, Spicer, p.16.
19 Letters of G.F. Ellenberger, 21.2.16, IWM.
20 Ibid., 28.2.16.

21 Ibid., 14.3.163.
22 *Letters from France*, Spicer, p.41.
23 Letters of G.F. Ellenberger, 27.3.16, IWM.

Chapter 4

1 *Official History 1916*, Vol I, p.44.
2 Ibid., p.44.
3 Ibid., p.266.
4 *Command on the Western Front*, Prior and Wilson, p.147.
5 *The First Day of the Somme*, Middlebrook, p.77.
6 *Somme*, Macdonald, pp.10-11.
7 Ibid., p.11.
8 Letters of G.F. Ellenberger, IWM.
9 Ibid.
10 Ibid.
11 Letters of G.F. Ellenberger, 20.4.16, IWM.
12 *Letters from France*, Spicer, pp.45-46.
13 Ibid., p.47.
14 Ibid., pp.50-51.
15 Letters of G.F. Ellenberger, 7.6.16, IWM.
16 The 'Pals' brigades of 31st Division adopted this method and were slaughtered.
17 Order No.36, War Diary, 9th Bn KOYLI
18 Ibid.
19 Ibid.
20 War Diary of 21st Division, WO95 2029 PRO.
21 *Bugle* Vol.24, No.6., Article by B.L. Gordon, p.28.
22 The toast was not forgotten; it appeared subsequently in the Memoriam column of *The Times* each year until well into the 1960s. Both Lynch and Haswell were killed on 1 July. They lie close together in Norfolk Cemetery, Becourt, Somme.
23 Letters of G.F. Ellenberger, 25.6.16, IWM.
24 *Bugle* Vol.24, No.6. Article by B.L. Gordon, p.28.
25 Ibid., p.30.
26 Ibid., p.30.
27 Ibid., p.30.
28 Ibid., p.30.
29 Letters of G.F. Ellenberger, 7.7.16, IWM.
30 Ibid.
31 *Bugle* Vol.24, No.6. Article by B.L. Gordon, p.31.
32 *Bugle* Vol.24. No.7 Article by L.D. Spicer, p.10.
33 Ibid., p.11.
34 Ibid., p.11.
35 War Diary of 9th Bn KOYLI.
36 Papers of G.F. Ellenberger, IWM. Fragment from *When the Barrage Lifts*, B. Liddell Hart, 1920.
37 War Diary of 9th Bn KOYLI.

Chapter 5

1 Letters of G.F. Ellenberger, 27.7.16, IWM.
2 Letters of G.F. Ellenberger, IWM.
3 Ibid.
4 Letters of H.E. Yeo, 13.7.16, IWM.
5 War Diary of 9th Bn KOYLI.

6 Letters of H.E. Yeo, 20.7.16, IWM.
7 *Memoirs*, Liddell Hart, p.25.
8 Letters of H.E. Yeo, IWM.
9 *Memoirs*, Liddell Hart, pp.25-26.
10 War Diary of 21st Division, WO95 2031 PRO.
11 Ibid.
12 War Diary of 9th Bn KOYLI.
13 *The Tanks at Flers*, Pidgeon, p.180.
14 Letters of G.F. Ellenberger, 23.9.16. IWM.
15 Ibid.
16 Papers of G.F. Ellenberger, IWM.
17 Ibid.
18 War Diary of 9th Bn KOYLI.
19 *Letters from France*, Spicer. p.74.

Chapter 6

1 Letters of G.F. Ellenberger, 4.10.16, IWM.
2 War Diary of 9th Bn KOYLI.
3 Papers of G.F. Ellenberger, IWM.
4 Ibid.
5 Letters of H.E. Yeo, 4.3.17, IWM.
6 Letters of H.E. Yeo, IWM.
7 Ibid.
8 Captain 'Stanford' is quite clearly named thus in the Battalion War Diary. The publication *Officers Died in the Great War* record him as Capt. Clement Richard Folliot Sandford MC, of the 5th Battalion KOYLI. He is buried in Cambrin Military Cemetery, Plot G. 55. All other KOYLI burials in that cemetery are 9th and 10th Battalion, and one can only assume that he was attached to the 9th KOYLI at the time of his death.

Chapter 7

1 *History of the First World War*, Liddell Hart, p.332.
2 *The Great War Generals*, Neillands, p.322.
3 *Official History 1917*, Vol.I, p.62
4 *Official History 1917*. Vol.I, p.185.
5 Ibid. p.183.
6 Ibid. p.201.
7 *Cheerful Sacrifice*, Nicholls, p.117.
8 *Official History 1917*, Vol. I, p.207.
9 War Diary of 21st Division, WO95 2159. PRO.
10 *Official History 1917*, Vol. I, p.205.
11 War Diary of 64th Brigade, WO95 2159.
12 War Diary of WO329 2524.
13 Ibid.
14 War Diary, 64th Brigade, WO95 2159.
15 *Official History 1917*, Vol. I, p.247.
16 *Huddersfield Examiner*, 27.4.17.

Chapter 8

1 Papers of G.F. Ellenberger, IWM.
2 Letters of G.F. Ellenberger, 28.5.17, IWM.

3 Ibid., 2.6.17.

4 Letters of H.E. Yeo, IWM.

5 Lt W.E. Smith is mentioned quite specifically in the War Diary of the 9th KOYLI (WO95 2162 PRO). The publication *Soldiers Died in the Great War* and the equivalent CD ROM give him the rank of Acting Captain and place him in the 8th KOYLI. This battalion was already in the Ypres area at the time of Lt Smith's death, so the author has no hesitation in including him in the 9th's Roll of Honour.

6 War Diary of 9th Bn KOYLI.

7 Ibid., entry for 04.8.17.

Chapter 9

1 *The Great War Generals*, Neillands, p.381.

2 *Passchendaele in Perspective*, Ed. P. Liddle, p.12. (Ch.1 by John Bourne).

3 *Official History 1917*, Vol. II, pp.24-25. (The original 48-72 hour interval was evidently forgotten by this time).

4 *Pillars of Fire*, Passingham, p.126

5 *Official History 1917*, Vol. II, p.105.

6 *History of the First World War*, Liddell Hart, p.332.

7 *Official History 1917*, Vol. II, p.284.

8 Ibid., p.293.

9 Letters of G.F. Ellenberger, 3.10.17, IWM.

10 Letters of H.E. Yeo, 1.10.17, IWM.

11 War Diary of 21st Division, WO95 2132 PRO.

12 WO329 2524 PRO.

13 *Official History 1917* Vol. II, p.313.

14 WO329 2524 PRO.

15 War Diary of 21st Division, WO95 2132 PRO.

16 WO329 2524 PRO.

17 Ibid.

18 Ibid.

19 Lt-Col. Neville Reay Daniell's name appears on the panel of the memorial dedicated to his original regiment, the Duke of Cornwall's Light Infantry.

20 War Diary of 9th Bn KOYLI.

21 *Official History 1917*, Vol. II, p.313.

Chapter 10

1 *The Great War Generals*, Neillands, p.405.

2 Letters of H.E. Yeo, 7.10.17, IWM.

3 Letters of G.F. Ellenberger, 8.12.17, IWM.

4 Ibid., 18.12.17.

5 War Diary of 9th Bn KOYLI.

6 Letters of G.F. Ellenberger, 28.12.17, IWM.

7 War Diary of 9th Bn KOYLI.

8 Ibid.

Chapter 11

1 *Official History 1918*, Vol. I, p.37.

2 *To Win a War*, Terraine, p.43.

3 *The Great War Generals*, Neillands, p.445.

4 *To Win a War*, Terraine, p.47.

5 *The Great War Generals*, Neillands, p.455.

6 *The Unexpected Victory*, Johnson, p.24.

7 *The Kaiser's Battle*, Middlebrook, p.80.

8 *To Win a War*, Terraine, p.60.

9 *Official History 1918*, Vol. I, p.130.

10 *The Unexpected Victory*, Johnson, p.27.

11 War Diary of 9th Bn KOYLI.

12 Ibid.

13 Ibid.

14 Ibid.

15 Ibid.

16 Ibid.

17 Ibid.

18 Ibid.

19 The War Diary also lists Makin and Moon as killed during this withdrawal. CWGC records indicate 22 March as the date of death. The discrepancy cannot be resolved at the time of writing.

20 War Diary of 9th Bn KOYLI.

21 War Diary of 21st Division, WO95, 2133 PRO.

22 Letters of H.E. Yeo, 5.4.18, IWM.

Chapter 12

1 War Diary of 9th Bn KOYLI.

2 Papers of G.F. Ellenberger, IWM.

3 Letters of H.E. Yeo, 5.4.18, IWM.

4 *The Great War Generals*, Neillands, p.472.

5 *The Western Front*, Holmes, p.201.

6 *Official History 1918*, Vol. II. Appendix 10. p.512.

7 Letters of H.E. Yeo, 13.4.18, IWM.

8 War Diary of 9th Bn KOYLI.

9 Liddle Collection, Item 55.

10 *Official History 1918*, Vol. II, p.413.

11 Ibid., p.422.

12 War Diary of 9th Bn KOYLI.

13 Letters of G.F. Ellenberger, 2.5.18, IW.

14 *Official History 1918*, Vol. II, p.423.

15 War Diary of 64th Brigade, WO95 2160.

16 War Diary of 9th Bn KOYLI.

17 *Dewsbury Reporter*, 25.5.18.

18 Letters of G.F. Ellenberger, 2.5.18, IWM.

19 War Diary of 9th Bn KOYLI.

Chapter 13

1 *Official History 1918*, Vol. II, p.31.

2 Ibid., p. 31.

3 War Diary of 9th Bn KOYLI.

4 *To Win a War*, Terraine, p.70.

5 Letters of H.E. Yeo, 18.5.18, IWM.

6 War Diary of 9th Bn KOYLI.

7 Ibid.

8 Letters of H.E. Yeo, 18.5.18, IWM.

9 *Official History 1918* Vol. II, p.29.

10 Ibid., p.39.

11 Ibid., p.47.
12 Ibid., p.49
13 Ibid., p.53.
14 Ibid., p.55.
15 Ibid., p.61.
16 War Diary of 21st Division, WO95 2133 PRO.
17 War Diary of 9th Bn KOYLI.
18 Letters of H.E. Yeo, 5.6.18, IWM.
19 Letters of G.F. Ellenberger, 4.6.18, IWM.
20 Ibid.
21 Ibid., 6.6.18.
22 Ibid., 22.6.18.
23 War Diary of 9th Bn KOYLI.
24 *Official History 1918*, Vol. II, p.84.
25 War Diary of 21st Division, WO95 2133 PRO.
26 *Official History 1918*, Vol. II, p.119.
27 War Diary of 9th Bn KOYLI.
28 Ibid.
29 Letters of H.E. Yeo, 5.6.18, IWM.

Chapter 14

1 *To Win a War*, Terraine, p.73.
2 War Diary of 9th Bn KOYLI.
3 Ibid.
4 *The Snapper.* Story of the 1st Battalion [East Yorks] in
   the War, Part VII., Lt Howard, KOYLI Association
5 *Official History 1918*, Vol. IV, p.243.
6 Ibid., p.243.
7 War Diary of 64th Brigade, WO95 2160 PRO.
8 Ibid.
9 War Diary of 21st Division, WO95 2134 PRO.
10 *The Snapper*, p.59
11 Ibid., p.59.
12 War Diary of 9th Bn KOYLI.
13 War Diary of 64th Brigade, WO95 2160.
14 *Official History 1918*, Vol. IV, p.245.
15 Ibid.
16 War Diary of 64th Brigade., WO95 2160 PRO.
17 War Diary of 9th Bn KOYLI.
18 *The Snapper*, p.61,
19 War Diary of 64th Brigade., WO95 2160.

20 War Diary of 15th DLI, WO95 2161 PRO.
21 Letters of H.E. Yeo, 29.10.18 and 30.10.18, IWM.
22 *The Snapper*, p.61.
23 Ibid., p.63.
24 *Official History 1918,* Vol. IV, p.454.

Chapter 15

1 War Diary of 9th Bn KOYLI.
2 Ibid.
3 Ibid.
4 *Official History 1918*, Vol. V, p.321.
5 Ibid, p.361.
6 Ibid, p.364.
7 War Diary of 9th Bn KOYLI.
8 Ibid.
9 Letters of H.E. Yeo, 30.10.18, IWM.
10 Papers of G.F. Ellenberger, IWM. Letter from
   H. Greenwood, 5.1.19.
11 Notebook of M.L. Williams, held by KOYLI
   Association.
12 War Diary of 9th Bn KOYLI.
13 Ibid.
14 Ibid.
15 Letters of H.E. Yeo, 11.11.18, IWM.

Chapter 16

1 *To Win a War*, Terraine, p.252.
2 War Diary of 9th Bn KOYLI.
3 Ibid.
4 Extract from a copy of the Programme of the
   Ceremony held by the KOYLI Association,
   Pontefract. Translated from the French by the
   author.
5 Ibid.
6 War Diary of 9th Bn KOYLI.
7 Ibid.
8 Ibid.
9 Papers of G.F. Ellenberger, IWM. Letter from H.
   Greenwood, 5.1.19.

APPENDIX I

ROLL OF HONOUR

Fatalities are recorded chronologically.

Within a single day, officers are recorded first, alphabetically, followed by Other Ranks.

Key:

d. Home	died at home in the United Kingdom	d.	died, usually of illness
dow	died of wounds	kia	killed in action

1915

5.1.15	BROOK James Pte 15847 d. Home	Normanton Upper Cem. P.3.7
14.1.15	ELLIS Charles William Pte 17626 d. Home	Sleaford Cem. X. 'U' 125
15.1.15	WORSNOP William Cliff Pte 13633 d. Home	Leeds Holbeck Cem. 'C' 13028
4.3.15	BODDY James Pte 13446 d. Home	Maidenhead Cem. A.H.61
26.9.15	HILLS Albert Edward Pte 17261 kia	Loos Memorial
27.9.15★	ADAMS George Oswald Pte 17050 kia	Loos Memorial
27.9.15	ANTCLIFFE William Pte 13713 kia	Loos Memorial
27.9.15	BOREHAM William Pte 14111 kia	Loos Memorial
27.9.15	BROADHEAD Willie Pte 17078 kia	Loos Memorial
27.9.15	BURROWS Frederick Pte 14904 kia	Loos Memorial
27.9.15	CAMPBELL George Herbert L/Cpl 13664 kia	Loos Memorial
27.9.15	CLARK Albert Pte 16055 kia	Loos Memorial
27.9.15	CLARKE Peter Pte 19023 kia	Loos Memorial
27.9.15	EARL Richard Thomas L/Cpl 19369 kia	Loos Memorial
27.9.15	EDWARDS Rhys Joseph A/Cpl 16615 kia	Loos Memorial
27.9.15	GARDINER Alfred Pte 16955 kia	Loos Memorial
27.9.15	GILL Frederick William Pte 15600 kia	Loos Memorial
27.9.15	GOSNEY John Pte 13623 kia	Loos Memorial
27.9.15	HAIGH Joseph Pte 12866 dow	Loos Memorial
27.9.15	HEYWOOD William Pte 16814 kia	Loos Memorial
27.9.15	HOLLINGWORTH John Pte 21182 kia	Loos Memorial
27.9.15	HOLMES William Bramwell Pte 3/2504 kia	Loos Memorial
27.9.15	IRWIN Horace Pte 15983 kia	Loos Memorial
27.9.15	JACKSON John William Pte 13361 kia	Loos Memorial
27.9.15	JOWITT Lionel Thomas Pte 17546 kia	Loos Memorial
27.9.15	LAZENBY Thomas A/Sgt 3/2388	Loos Memorial
27.9.15	LIDSTER Edgar Pte 21224 kia	Loos Memorial
27.9.15	MARTINDALE Harry Pte 211711 kia	Loos Memorial
27.9.15	MAYOR Frederick Ernest Pte 14894 kia	Loos Memorial

★The Commonwealth War Graves Commission gives the date of death of forty-two members of the battalion who were lost at Loos as 27 September 1915. It is likely that most of those casualties were from the previous day, the 26th.

27.9.15	MORRIS John Pte 18941 kia	Loos Memorial
27.9.15	MOSLEY John Pte 19376 kia	Loos Memorial
27.9.15	PLATTS George Pte 14274 kia	Loos Memorial
27.9.15	RHODES Walter Pte 14729 kia	Loos Memorial
27.9.15	RICHARDSON John Pte 14857 kia	Loos Memorial
27.9.15	ROSE John Henry Pte 16745 kia	Loos Memorial
27.9.15	SAVILLE Richard Pte 3/2116 kia	Loos Memorial
27.9.15	SMITH Richard A/Cpl 17417 kia	Loos Memorial
27.9.15	SMITH Fred L/Cpl 16550 kia	Loos Memorial
27.9.15	SMITH George John Pte 15887 kia	Loos Memorial
27.9.15	SMITH Percy Cpl 14517 kia	Loos Memorial
27.9.15	STANSFIELD Thomas Henry Pte 17780 kia	Loos Memorial
27.9.15	TAYLOR Cyrus L/Cpl 15539 kia	Loos Memorial
27.9.15	TAYLOR Edward Pte 21176 kia	Loos Memorial
27.9.15	TAYLOR William Pte 19045 kia	Loos Memorial
27.9.15	THORPE George Pte 3/2866 kia	Loos Memorial
27.9.15	WOOD George Pte 17540 kia	Lillers Communal Cem. IV B 30
27.9.15	WROE George Pte 16452 kia	Loos Memorial
29.9.15	RATCLIFFE William Edward Sgt 17387 dow	Etaples Military Cem. IV G 8A
30.9.15	FOWLER Jack Pte 16067 d.	Le Treport Military Cem. I K 8
1.10.15	NORTH Milton Pte 16148 dow	La Pugnoy Military Cem. I D 43
8.10.15	BEDFORD William Pte 19383 dow	Longuenesse Souvenir Cem. II A 53
9.10.15	CHARLESWORTH George Pte 18403 dow Home	Knottingley Cem. 2077
15.10.15	SHAW Horace Pte 19046 kia	Ploegsteert Wood Military Cem. III G
31.10.15	TIPLING Martin Pte 17487 dow	Ackworth All Saints Churchyard
19.11.15	FLINT Fred Pte 19627 dow	Bailleul Communal Cem. Ext. I C 11
20.11.15	VARLEY Walter H. Pte 3/2700 kia	Houplines Communal Cem. II B 29
24.11.15	GILBERTHORPE Clayton Pte 22209 dow	Cité Bonjean Military Cem. IX D 44
27.11.15	CROWCROFT James Edward Pte 16494 kia	Houplines Communal Cem. II B 25
27.11.15	FARR William A/Sgt 12340 kia	Cité Bonjean Military Cem. IX D 49
27.11.15	PAUL Walter Pte 13580 kia	Houplines Communal Cem. II B 26
2.12.15	STOCKS Earnest Pte 17740 dow	Bailleul Communal Cem. Ext. I E 32
5.12.15	HEATON John William Pte 17412 d.	Houplines Communal Cem. III B 30
6.12.15	HEWITT Alfred Pte 17367 d.	Cité Bonjean Military Cem. IX D 88
10.12.15	KENNINGTON Arthur A/Cpl 16365 dow	Bailleul Communal Cem. Ext. I D 122
12.12.15	HOULDEN Harold Pte 11511 dow	Bailleul Communal Cem. Ext. I D 124
17.12.15	MARWOOD Albert Pte 3/1584 kia	Houplines Communal Cem. III B 5
20.12.15	JOHNSON Harold Pte 10752 dow	Bailleul Communal Cem. Ext. I D 142
28.12.15	BUCK William Pte 3/2325 dow	Cité Bonjean Military Cem. IX D 63

1916

2.1.16	STEPHENSON John Joseph Pte 17032 dow	Bailleul Communal Cem. Ext. II C 23
11.1.16	BIRCH Thomas Pte 13457 kia	Cité Bonjean Military Cem. IX D 92
11.1.16	DODDS George Pte 15537 kia	Cité Bonjean Military Cem. IX D 91
16.1.16	BEVAN Thomas L/Cpl 18292 kia	Cité Bonjean Military Cem. IX E 92
17.1.16	NEWLOVE Charles L/Cpl 12936 kia	Cité Bonjean Military Cem. IX E 90
20.1.16	MELLOR Wilfrid Pte 14449 dow	Bailleul Communal Cem. Ext. II C 71
25.1.16	WRIGHT Herbert W.C. Pte 16371 kia	Cité Bonjean Military Cem. IX E 72
26.1.16	ANDERSON William Pte 13805 kia	Cité Bonjean Military Cem. IX E 55
26.1.16	BRUNSDEN John Pte 16043 kia	Cité Bonjean Military Cem. IX E 54
26.1.16	DAYKIN William Pte 14271 dow	Bailleul Communal Cem. Ext. II C 87
26.1.16	GUEST Stanley Pte 21219 kia	Cité Bonjean Military Cem. IX E 57
26.1.16	NORTON Charles Gilbert Pte 15913 kia	Cité Bonjean Military Cem. IX E 58
26.1.16	ROSSELL William Pte 14665 kia	Cité Bonjean Military Cem. IX E 56
26.1.16	SAUNDERS Henry Harold Pte 23357 kia	Cité Bonjean Military Cem. IX E 59
28.1.16	DAWSON Charles L/Cpl 13394 kia	Cité Bonjean Military Cem. IX E 28
28.1.16	HAMBLIN William Oliver Pte 15540 kia	Cité Bonjean Military Cem. IX E 29
28.1.16	HOWDEN Thomas L/Cpl 16726 kia	Cité Bonjean Military Cem. IX E 36
28.1.16	HURP James Pte 15921 kia	Cité Bonjean Military Cem. IX E 38
28.1.16	ROBERTS Thomas Henry Cpl 15208 kia	Cité Bonjean Military Cem. IX E 37

29.1.16	BURDETT Sam Pte 12944 dow	Bailleul Communal Cem. Ext. II C 100
2.2.16	BROADHEAD Pemberton Pte 16852 kia	Cité Bonjean Military Cem. IX E 18
2.2.16	HAYNES Arthur Pte 19032 kia	Cité Bonjean Military Cem. IX E 19
2.2.16	LIVERSIDGE Robert Pte 20141 dow	Bailleul Communal Cem. Ext. II C 107
12.2.16	BRIGNELL Edgar Douglas L/Cpl 16454 kia	Cité Bonjean Military Cem. IX F 97
12.2.16	BROWN Robert L/Cpl 3/2400 kia	Cité Bonjean Military Cem. IX F 98
12.2.16	DAVIDSON Fred Pte 14026 kia	Cité Bonjean Military Cem. IX F 100
12.2.16	EVANS Thomas James Pte 17950 kia	Cité Bonjean Military Cem. IX E 5
12.2.16	LEWIS George Cpl 14368 kia	Cité Bonjean Military Cem. IX F 95
12.2.16	WILKINSON William Pte 17271 kia	Cité Bonjean Military Cem. IX F 94
14.2.16	HALL Edward E. Pte 3/1965 dow	Bailleul Communal Cem. Ext. II C 130
17.2.16	BULLOCK John Pte 12/805 kia	Cité Bonjean Military Cem. IX F 80
17.2.16	STOKELL Charles William L/Cpl 14323 kia	Cité Bonjean Military Cem. IX F 77
22.2.16	WHITHAM Joseph William Pte 19836 dow	Bailleul Communal Cem. Ext. II C 167
25.2.16	HEALEY James Pte 10935 kia	Cité Bonjean Military Cem. IX F 54
26.2.16	MURRAY Felix L/Cpl 13286 dow	Bailleul Communal Cem. Ext. II C 178
27.2.16	GUNN George Pte 3/2156 dow	Bailleul Communal Cem. Ext. II C 181
29.2.16	BELTON Earnest Priestley Pte 13693 kia	Cité Bonjean Military Cem. IX F 50
1.3.16	McNIFF Joseph Pte 19797 kia	Cité Bonjean Military Cem. IX F 51
4.3.16	BOOTH Frederick Pte 3/3589 kia	Cité Bonjean Military Cem. IX F 39
4.3.16	RHODES Horace Pte 3/358 kia	Cité Bonjean Military Cem. IX F 40
4.3.16	ROBINSON Peter Pte 9531 kia	Cité Bonjean Military Cem. IX F 42
4.3.16	SANDERSON Vernon Pte 14447 kia	Cité Bonjean Military Cem. IX F 41
4.3.16	SIDDALL Leonard Pte 24364 kia	Cité Bonjean Military Cem. IX F 43
18.3.16	GOODISON Bertie Pte 3/1306 dow	Bailleul Communal Cem. Ext. II B 3
23.3.16	HALLAM Leonard O. Pte 17266 d.	Outtersteene Communal Cem. Ext. IV E 14
10.4.16	KING James Cedric Pte 19846 dow	Ville-sur-Ancre Communal Cem. C 7
10.4.16	SCOTT John William Pte 12862 kia	Dartmoor Cem. I E 12
11.4.16	COLLINGS James Pte 21220 kia	Dartmoor Cem. I E 14 (also Thiepval Mem.)
11.4.16	KERTON David Williamson L/Cpl 9226 dow	Dartmoor Cem. I E 15
11.4.16	McKENNA Patrick Pte 11003 kia	Dartmoor Cem. I E 13
11.4.16	MERCHANT Arthur Pte 18964 kia	Dartmoor Cem. I E 16
11.4.16	RODGERS James Henry Pte 13642 dow	Corbie Communal Cem. I F 34
13.4.16	McHARD Andrew Morrison Pte 21399 dow	Corbie Communal Cem. I F 32
14.4.16	HARRISON George Haigh Pte 24036 dow	Corbie Communal Cem. I F 30
30.4.16	DAVIES John Henry A/Cpl 16493 dow	Boisguillaume Communal Cem. I F 10
2.6.16	KAYE Harold Pte 18998 kia	Dartmoor Cem. I B 29
3.6.16	BRADSELL Charles Cashmore Pte 18994 kia	Dartmoor Cem. I B 30
3.6.16	JENNINGS Herbert Pte 24923 dow	La Neuville Communal Cem. A 52
4.6.16	SIMMONDS Arthur Pte 14867 kia	Dartmoor Cem. I C 35
4.6.16	SPILMAN Joe Pte 3/1929 kia	Dartmoor Cem. I C 36
4.6.16	WILLIAMSON George Pte 20181 kia	Dartmoor Cem. I C 34
5.6.16	EWART William Pte 3/1529 dow	La Neuville Communal Cem. A 54
6.6.16	DAGLEY Arthur Luke Pte 19388 dow	La Neuville Communal Cem. A 7
8.6.16	LOWE Rowland Cpl 12813 kia	Dartmoor Cem. I B 32
10.6.16	FEELEY William Pte 16272 kia	Dartmoor Cem. I D 37
10.6.16	ROUSE Harry Pte 7351 kia	Dartmoor Cem. I D 38
16.6.16	BOLTON Harry Pte 16864 kia	Norfolk Cem. I C 65
16.6.16	FARR Albert Pte 16770 dow	Corbie Communal Cem. Ext. I A 7
16.6.16	MITCHELL William James Pte 3/2001 dow Home	Norwich Cem. 25.198
30.6.16	MORGAN James Pte 14833 kia	White House Cem. I J 11
1.7.16	ALEXANDER N.L. 2nd-Lt kia	Gordon Dump Cem. II M 10
1.7.16	CAMBIE Edward Maurice Baldwin Lt kia	Thiepval Memorial
1.7.16	ELLIS Clifford Walker 2nd-Lt kia	Gordon Dump Cem. V N 4
1.7.16	FEATHERSTONE George Herbert 2nd-Lt kia	Thiepval Memorial
1.7.16	GOLDING Frank Alfred 2nd-Lt kia	Gordon Dump II N 4
1.7.16	GRIFFIN George Edward Capt. kia	Thiepval Memorial
1.7.16	HASWELL Gordon Capt. kia	Norfolk Cem. I B 92
1.7.16	HEAD Leslie Dymoke Capt. kia	Gordon Dump Cem. X A 6
1.7.16	HOWLETT Charles Wilfred 2nd-Lt kia	Norfolk Cem. I B 88

1.7.16	LYNCH Colmer William Donald DSO Lt-Col. kia	Norfolk Cem. I B 87
1.7.16	MACONACHIE Arthur Delano 2nd-Lt kia	Gordon Dump Cem. Sp. Mem. B10
1.7.16	OLDERSHAW John Joseph Fritz 2nd-Lt kia	Thiepval Memorial
1.7.16	TELFER H.A. Lt (Trench Mortar Bn) kia	Gordon Dump Cem. II N 9
1.7.16	VASSIE Charles Edward 2nd-Lt kia	Gordon Dump Cem. II M 7
1.7.16	WALKER William Capt. kia	Norfolk Cem. I B 91
1.7.16	ALMOND Arthur L/Cpl 16017 kia	Thiepval Memorial
1.7.16	ARMITAGE George Pte 14762 kia	Gordon Dump Cem. VIII I 10
1.7.16	ATKINSON Freeman Clement L/Cpl 11033 kia	Thiepval Memorial
1.7.16	BAILEY Price Robert Pte 16074 kia	Thiepval Memorial
1.7.16	BAMLING Robert Cpl 16396 kia	Gordon Dump Cem. IV R 6
1.7.16	BARKER Frank Pte 19736 kia	Thiepval Memorial
1.7.16	BARKER Thomas James Pte 20384 kia	Thiepval Memorial
1.7.16	BARNES Isaac Pte 16809 kia	Thiepval Memorial
1.7.16	BARRACLOUGH Leonard Pte 14469 kia	Thiepval Memorial
1.7.16	BARTLE Arthur L/Cpl 16945 kia	Thiepval Memorial
1.7.16	BELL Robert Hannah Pte 22981 kia	Gordon Dump Cem. III R 5
1.7.16	BINGLEY John Earle Pte 3/1465 kia	Gordon Dump Cem. IV R 5
1.7.16	BOOTH Herbert L/Cpl 16960 kia	Gordon Dump Cem. VII B 5
1.7.16	BRADSHAW Robert Henry Pte 14898 kia	Thiepval Memorial
1.7.16	BROOKS C.L. Pte 3/1743 kia	Gordon Dump Cem. II Q 10
1.7.16	BRYAN George A. Pte 22033 kia	Thiepval Memorial
1.7.16	CADE Richard Pte 16807 kia	Gordon Dump Cem. VIII H 5
1.7.16	CAIN Martin Pte 9945 kia	Gordon Dump Cem. VII B 7
1.7.16	CAMPBELL Robert Pte 22131 kia	Gordon Dump Cem. VII A 8
1.7.16	CARR Charles Pte 16020 kia	Thiepval Memorial
1.7.16	CHRISTIAN Arthur Pte 24375 kia	Gordon Dump Cem. II Q 9
1.7.16	CLAPHAM Leonard Powell L/Cpl 3/3536 kia	Thiepval Memorial
1.7.16	CLEAVER Albert Pte 13156 kia	Thiepval Memorial
1.7.16	COMER James Pte 15203 kia	Thiepval Memorial
1.7.16	COOKE Wilfred Pte 25959 dow	Méricourt l'Abbé Comm. Cem. Ext. II A 5
1.7.16	COOPER John Willie L/Cpl 16708 kia	Thiepval Memorial
1.7.16	COOPER Lawrence Pte 19878 kia	Thiepval Memorial
1.7.16	COOPER Samuel L/Cpl 19877 kia	Thiepval Memorial
1.7.16	CRAWFORD Thomas Gray Pte 16105 kia	Thiepval Memorial
1.7.16	DIXON James Edgar L/Cpl 10962 kia	Thiepval Memorial
1.7.16	DOCHARTY Daniel Pte 17787 kia	Gordon Dump Cem. X E 4
1.7.16	DRAKETT James Pte 20172 kia	Thiepval Memorial
1.7.16	DRURY George Pte 19909 kia	Thiepval Memorial
1.7.16	ELLIS Edward Sgt 20059 kia	Thiepval Memorial
1.7.16	ENGLAND William Pte 17161 kia	Thiepval Memorial
1.7.16	FLOWITT George Pte 17517 kia	Thiepval Memorial
1.7.16	FOSTER John William L/Cpl 13954 kia	Thiepval Memorial
1.7.16	FOX Albert Cpl 3/1576 kia	Thiepval Memorial
1.7.16	FOX Henry L/Cpl 14712 kia	Thiepval Memorial
1.7.16	GARLAND Albert Pte 24382 kia	Thiepval Memorial
1.7.16	GAUNT John William Pte 24960 kia	Gordon Dump Cem. IV Q 2
1.7.16	GEE Joseph Cpl 13898 kia	Thiepval Memorial
1.7.16	GIBBONS Walter Sgt 17232 kia	Norfolk Cem. I B 78
1.7.16	GODLINGTON Ernest Pte 21196 kia	Gordon Dump Cem. VIII A 7
1.7.16	GOLDTHORPE Fred Pte 9/17134 kia	Thiepval Memorial
1.7.16	GOULDING John Pte 22200 kia	Gordon Dump Cem. IV R 7
1.7.16	GRIFFITHS David Pte 13255 kia	Gordon Dump Cem. IX A 6
1.7.16	HALL Joseph Pte 3/3656 kia	Gordon Dump Cem. IX C 6
1.7.16	HALL Tom Pte 12823 kia	Thiepval Memorial
1.7.16	HANCOCK Henry L/Cpl 13974 kia	Thiepval Memorial
1.7.16	HARRIS Albert Cpl 16003 kia	Thiepval Memorial
1.7.16	HARSLEY Chas William L/Cpl 17279 kia	Thiepval Memorial
1.7.16	HASLEGRAVE Harry Pte 17315 kia	Thiepval Memorial
1.7.16	HAWKINS Charles Edward L/Cpl 14577 kia	Thiepval Memorial

1.7.16	HEPWORTH John A/Cpl 17272 kia	Thiepval Memorial
1.7.16	HILL Alfred Pte 19110 kia	Gordon Dump Cem. VII J 3
1.7.16	HIMSWORTH Albert Pte 13599 kia	Thiepval Memorial
1.7.16	HINCH James North Pte 20292 kia	Thiepval Memorial
1.7.16	HIND Ernest Pte 13968 kia	Gordon Dump Cem. IX S 7
1.7.16	HINDLE James William Pte 13753 kia	Thiepval Memorial
1.7.16	HIRST Thomas Pte 26530 kia	Thiepval Memorial
1.7.16	HOLLAND Edgar Pte 19779 kia	Gordon Dump Cem. IV P 5
1.7.16	HOLLAND Ernest Frederick A/Sgt 14164 kia	Thiepval Memorial
1.7.16	HOLMES Fred Pte 16698 kia	Thiepval Memorial
1.7.16	HOLTON John Pte 24926 kia	Thiepval Memorial
1.7.16	HOPKINS Michael Pte 3/866 kia	Gordon Dump Cem. V K 4
1.7.16	HORNE Arthur Pte 21998 kia	Gordon Dump Cem. IX A 3
1.7.16	HOUGHLAND Percy Colin Pte 14900 kia	Gordon Dump Cem. IV Q 10
1.7.16	HOWDEN Percival Pte 24985 kia	Thiepval Memorial
1.7.16	HUGHES Griffith Thomas Pte 14586 kia	Thiepval Memorial
1.7.16	JACQUES Cyril Pte 19952 kia	Thiepval Memorial
1.7.16	JERRISON George Pte 9938 kia	Thiepval Memorial
1.7.16	JOHNSON Bernard Pte 14287 kia	Thiepval Memorial
1.7.16	JOHNSON George Pte 18859 kia	Gordon Dump Cem. IV R 9
1.7.16	JOHNSON George Henry L/Cpl 13880 kia	Thiepval Memorial
1.7.16	JOHNSON Robert William L/Cpl 24377 kia	Thiepval Memorial
1.7.16	JONES Job Pte 22034 kia	Thiepval Memorial
1.7.16	JUDE John Robert Pte 21215 kia	Thiepval Memorial
1.7.16	KEAN David Patrick Pte 14675 kia	Gordon Dump Cem. Sp Mem. C3
1.7.16	KIPLING George Pte 14317 kia	Thiepval Memorial
1.7.16	KNIGHT Bertie Pte 17478 kia	Thiepval Memorial
1.7.16	KYNASTON Thomas Pte 16424 kia	Thiepval Memorial
1.7.16	LAW Melvin A/Sgt 19467 kia	Thiepval Memorial
1.7.16	LAWTON John Pte 16251 kia	Gordon Dump Cem. V N 7
1.7.16	LEACH Robert Chaplin Pte 14151 kia	Gordon Dump Cem. VII B 6
1.7.16	LEATHER George Pte 3/1527 kia	Thiepval Memorial
1.7.16	LITTLEWOOD Harold Sgt 17442 kia	Gordon Dump Cem. II Q 8
1.7.16	LLOYD Thomas L/Cpl 14582 kia	Thiepval Memorial
1.7.16	McLOUGHLIN John Pte 3/1431 kia	Gordon Dump Cem. Sp Mem. B14
1.7.16	MARSH Joseph Pte 6479 kia	Gordon Dump Cem. X D 2
1.7.16	MARSHALL Ernest Pte 13998 kia	Gordon Dump Cem. III R 8
1.7.16	MERRILL William Pte 20083 kia	Thiepval Memorial
1.7.16	MIDDLETON Elven Pte 19043 kia	Gordon Dump Cem. III R 7
1.7.16	MITCHELL Arthur Pte 3/3672 kia	Norfolk Cem. I C 83
1.7.16	MOORE Henry Thomas Pte 15151 kia	Thiepval Memorial
1.7.16	MOORE Thomas Pte 3/2658 kia	Gordon Dump Cem. IX A 7
1.7.16	MORRILL Harold Pte 15629 kia	Thiepval Memorial
1.7.16	MOUNTAIN Wilfred L/Cpl 15114 kia	Gordon Dump Cem. VIII D 8
1.7.16	MULVEY Andrew Pte 3/1874 kia	Thiepval Memorial
1.7.16	OUTRAM John Barton Pte 19955 kia	Thiepval Memorial
1.7.16	PELL Norman Pte 15858 kia	Thiepval Memorial
1.7.16	PENNINGTON Samuel Pte 20767 kia	Thiepval Memorial
1.7.16	PERKIN George Pte 19806 kia	Thiepval Memorial
1.7.16	PEVERLEY Robert Sidney Pte 25009 kia	Thiepval Memorial
	(Also recorded on the Thiepval Memorial under the pseudonym of Henry Wakely)	
1.7.16	PORTER Ernest Pte 20110 kia	Gordon Dump Cem. IV R 8
1.7.16	POULTER Frederick Pte 13354 kia	Thiepval Memorial
1.7.16	POWELL Thomas Pte 3/569 kia	Gordon Dump Cem. IV Q 9
1.7.16	PRICE Enoch Pte 21238 kia	Thiepval Memorial
1.7.16	PRIDMORE William Henry Pte 21218 kia	Thiepval Memorial
1.7.16	RAMSDEN Stanley L/Cpl 19087 kia	Gordon Dump Cem. V N 9
1.7.16	RENSHAW Norman Pte 25220 kia	Thiepval Memorial
1.7.16	RILEY George K. Pte 14884 kia	Gordon Dump Cem. III R 9
1.7.16	ROBINSON Samuel James Pte 25345 kia	Thiepval Memorial

1.7.16	ROBINSON Walter Pte 13587 kia	Thiepval Memorial
1.7.16	SANDIFORTH Ernest Pte 13730 kia	Thiepval Memorial
1.7.16	SEASTON Alfred L/Cpl 21189 kia	Thiepval Memorial
1.7.16	SEDDON William Pte 21231 kia	Thiepval Memorial
1.7.16	SELLARS Charles Pte 12633 kia	Thiepval Memorial
1.7.16	SHACKLETON Frederick Pte 22549 kia	Thiepval Memorial
1.7.16	SHAW Abraham Pte 12587 kia	Gordon Dump Cem. VIII H 9
1.7.16	SHAW Albert Pte 19370 kia	Thiepval Memorial
1.7.16	SHAW George L/Cpl 8647 kia	Gordon Dump Cem. VIII E 2
1.7.16	SHEPPARD John Pte 21936 kia	Thiepval Memorial
1.7.16	SIMPSON George Leonard Pte 19816 kia	Gordon Dump Cem. IV R 4
1.7.16	SISSON Walter Gether Pte 16343 kia	Gordon Dump Cem. VII B 8
1.7.16	SLAVEN John Pte 15345 kia	Gordon Dump Cem. III R 4
1.7.16	SMALLEY Robert L/Cpl 19656 kia	Thiepval Memorial
1.7.16	SMITH George Pte 15838 kia	Gordon Dump Cem. VIII E 1
1.7.16	SMITH Oswald Pte 21967 kia	Thiepval Memorial
1.7.16	SPIVEY Tom Pte 12709 kia	Thiepval Memorial
1.7.16	STANTON George Pte 21972 kia	Thiepval Memorial
1.7.16	STILL Herbert Pte 17542 kia	Thiepval Memorial
1.7.16	SWALLOW Arthur Sgt 17427 kia	Thiepval Memorial
1.7.16	SWEET James William L/Cpl 9/17006 kia	Thiepval Memorial
1.7.16	SYKES John Sgt MM 18329 kia	Thiepval Memorial
1.7.16	TAYLOR Harry Pte 16818 kia	Thiepval Memorial
1.7.16	TAYLOR John Pte 25481 kia	Gordon Dump Cem. V K 3
1.7.16	TAYLOR Richard Pte 14888 kia	Thiepval Memorial
1.7.16	TERRY Frank Pte 16081 kia	Thiepval Memorial
1.7.16	THOMPSON John William L/Cpl 16006 kia	Thiepval Memorial
1.7.16	TILLOTSON James Willie Pte 13996 kia	Thiepval Memorial
1.7.16	TINDALL Charles Pte 21191 kia	Thiepval Memorial
1.7.16	TINDALL William Padley Pte 3/3293 kia	Thiepval Memorial
1.7.16	UTTLEY Fred Pte 16184 kia	Gordon Dump Cem. IV R 10
1.7.16	WALES Walter Claxton Pte 18944 kia	Thiepval Memorial
1.7.16	WALKER Joseph Pte 13030 kia	Thiepval Memorial
1.7.16	WALL Walter Pte 13502 kia	Thiepval Memorial
1.7.16	WALLIS Arthur Pte 3/1944 kia	Thiepval Memorial
1.7.16	WARD Benjamin Pte 17439 kia	Thiepval Memorial
1.7.16	WASEY George Henry Pte 22184 kia	Gordon Dump Cem. VII A 7
1.7.16	WATERFIELD George Henry L/Cpl 16093 kia	Thiepval Memorial
1.7.16	WEBSTER Joseph Pte 25319 kia	Thiepval Memorial
1.7.16	WESTRAN William Pte 3/2348 kia	Thiepval Memorial
1.7.16	WHITAKER Wilfred Pte 25228 kia	Thiepval Memorial
1.7.16	WHITE Alfred Pte 26414 kia	Gordon Dump Cem. VIII H 5
1.7.16	WHITTINGHAM Ernest Pte 13522 kia	Thiepval Memorial
1.7.16	WHYTE John Pte 23463 kia	Thiepval Memorial
1.7.16	WILD Claude Pte 3/1468 kia	Gordon Dump Cem. IX A 2
1.7.16	WILLIAMS Arthur Edward Pte 12112 kia	Thiepval Memorial
1.7.16	WILSON William Farrah Pte 14822 kia	Thiepval Memorial
1.7.16	WINWOOD Harry CSM 16446 kia	Thiepval Memorial
1.7.16	WRAGG Harry Pte 20422 kia	Thiepval Memorial
1.7.16	WRATHALL Ernest Pte 16525 kia	Thiepval Memorial
2.7.16	MARSH Walter Pte 14683 dow	Corbie Communal Cem. Ext. I B 12
3.7.16	BROADHEAD William Pte 14805 dow	Heilly Station Cem. I B 31
3.7.16	COOPER William Richard L/Cpl 21223 dow	St. Sever Cem. A 21 52
3.7.16	GREATBACH Arthur Pte 25396 dow	Daours Communal Cem. II A 23
3.7.16	HURDUS Broughton Pte 19609 dow	Méricourt l'Abbé Comm. Cem. Ext. II A 2
3.7.16	UTTLEY Herbert Pte 15484 dow	Thiepval Memorial
4.7.16	FRETWELL George Pte 19883 dow	St Sever Cem. A 22 38
4.7.16	MOON Walter L/Sgt 14152 dow	Heilly Station Cem. I D 25
4.7.16	MORRIS Joseph Pte 19646 dow (Real name: Joseph RILEY)	Corbie Communal Cem. Ext. I B 28

5.7.16	HUNTLEY William Gilbert Pte 19998 dow	St. Sever Cem. A 22 41
6.7.16	BETTS Cecil Kenneth Pte 17526	Corbie Communal Cem. Ext. I B 42
6.7.16	WILDE Isaac Pte 15846 dow	Heilly Station Cem. I F 33
7.7.16	EBBAGE Harry Pte 24006 dow	St. Sever Cem. A 24 3
8.7.16	CHAPMAN Frank Pte 13689 dow	Boulogne Eastern Cem. VIII C 113
8.7.16	PRESTON George Richard Pte 3/2526 dow	St Sever Cem. A 24 23
9.7.16	HOWARTH Alfred Pte 13669 dow	Méricourt l'Abbé Comm. Cem. Ext. II A 5
10.7.16	WILLIAMS Douglas 2nd-Lt (attd 9th) dow	St Sever Cem. A 3 4
11.7.16	GARNER Francis Arthur Pte 26572 dow	St Sever Cem. A 28 14
13.7.16	NOTT Edward Ross MC 2nd-Lt dow	Abbeville Communal Cem. V G 1
14.7.16	BECKETT William Pte 12558 kia	Thiepval Memorial
14.7.16	GARFITT Arthur Pte 13986 kia	Thiepval Memorial
14.7.16	SCOTT Sam Pte 27250 kia	Thiepval Memorial
15.7.16	HICKLIN William L/Cpl 14680 dow	St Sever Cem. A 26 14
15.7.16	WRIGHT Joseph Pte 10631 d. Home	Royston New Churchyard III 226
17.7.16	JACKSON John Richard Pte 9/17146 d.	Dantzig Alley British Cem. IV G 4
18.7.16	CLEGG William Pte 14855 dow	Méaulte Military Cem. E 38
22.7.16	HAIGH David Pte 3/839 d. Home	Batley Cem. M 56
25.7.16	RAMSDEN Ralph Cecil L/Cpl 3/1609 d. Home	Adwick-le-Street (St. Lawrence) Cem.
29.7.16	COX Joseph Pte 20388 dow Home	Owston (All Saints) Cem. West of Church
5.8.16	RHODES Thomas Pte 15583 kia	Faubourg d'Amiens Cem. I F 5
6.8.16	RADFORD Ernest Sgt 12568 dow	Faubourg d'Amiens Cem. I F 9
13.8.16	BROADHURST James Watson Pte 14892 kia	Arras Memorial
14.8.16	HODGSON Wilfred Pte 17253 dow	Abbeville Communal Cem. VI D 12
20.8.16	SHARP Frederick Pte 19895 kia	Faubourg d'Amiens Cem. I F 31
27.8.16	LUNN Samuel Pte 21599 d.	Avesnes-le-Comte Comm. Cem. Ext. I B 16
3.9.16	RICHMOND William Pte 24053 kia	Dantzig Alley British Cem. VIII R 10
16.9.16	ASQUITH Ernest 2nd-Lt kia	Thiepval Memorial
16.9.16	BLAKEY George 2nd-Lt kia	Thiepval Memorial
16.9.16	FORRYAN Donald 2nd-Lt kia	Thiepval Memorial
16.9.16	GROSS Herbert George 2nd-Lt kia	Thiepval Memorial
16.9.16	JACKSON Arthur Selby 2nd-Lt kia	Thiepval Memorial
16.9.16	KEAY Wilfred Farrar T/Lt & Adj. kia	Thiepval Memorial
16.9.16	LEASON Thomas Herbert 2nd-Lt dow	Dartmoor Cem. II A 73
16.9.16	SUTCLIFFE Kenneth Wilson 2nd-Lt kia	Thiepval Memorial
16.9.16	WOOLLETT William Charles Capt. kia	AIF Burial Ground III J 28
16.9.16	ADAMSON Ralph Pte 34841 kia	Thiepval Memorial
16.9.16	ANDERSON Arthur Pte 34840 kia	AIF Burial Ground II J 26
16.9.16	ANDERSON Thomas Pte 34838 kia	Thiepval Memorial
16.9.16	ANDERSON William Pte 34843 kia	Thiepval Memorial
16.9.16	APPLEBY Clarence Charles Pte 34846 kia	Thiepval Memorial
16.9.16	BALDAN Thomas Pte 34858 kia	Thiepval Memorial
16.9.16	BECKETT Arthur Pte 10548 kia	Thiepval Memorial
16.9.16	BOYES Harry Pte 34859 kia	Thiepval Memorial
16.9.16	BRAMHAM Harold Pte 18919 kia	Thiepval Memorial
16.9.16	BRAMLEY Thomas Pte 13826 kia	Thiepval Memorial
16.9.16	BRAY William Pte 34862 kia	Thiepval Memorial
16.9.16	BUCKLEY Walter Pte 18052 kia	Thiepval Memorial
16.9.16	BURTON Robert James Pte 18975 kia	Thiepval Memorial
16.9.16	CALLERY Francis Joseph Pte 13376 kia	Thiepval Memorial
16.9.16	CARR Joseph Pte 15239 kia	Thiepval Memorial
16.9.16	CARSON George Arthur Pte 28067 kia	Thiepval Memorial
16.9.16	CATHERALL George L/Cpl 8/13023 kia	Thiepval Memorial
16.9.16	CHAMBERLAIN Ernest Pte 34933 kia	Thiepval Memorial
16.9.16	CHAMBERS George Pte 34867 kia	Thiepval Memorial
16.9.16	CLARKE Alfred William Pte 34934 kia	Thiepval Memorial
16.9.16	COOK Sidney Pte 26898 kia	Thiepval Memorial
16.9.16	COOPE Harold Pte 37678 kia	Thiepval Memorial
16.9.16	CORNISH Robert William Pte 37641 kia	Thiepval Memorial
16.9.16	COTTERILL Charles Henry Pte 37689 kia	Thiepval Memorial

16.9.16	CUNDILL Charles Pte 34871 kia	Thiepval Memorial
16.9.16	DALTON Charles Pte 34875 kia	Thiepval Memorial
16.9.16	DAVIES Cyrus Sgt 11162 kia	Thiepval Memorial
16.9.16	DAVISON William Henry Pte 34877	AIF Burial Ground III E 27
16.9.16	DEARMAN James L/Cpl 3/1504 kia	Thiepval Memorial
16.9.16	DEGG John Edwin Pte 37708 kia	Thiepval Memorial
16.9.16	DELANEY Peter Pte 34881 kia	Thiepval Memorial
16.9.16	DOBSON Arthur Pte 37722 kia	Thiepval Memorial
16.9.16	DUFFIELD Arthur A/Sgt 21212 kia	Thiepval Memorial
16.9.16	EDWARDS Owen Pte 37713 kia	Bray Military Cem. III A 32
16.9.16	ELDIN John Pte 26360 kia	Thiepval Memorial
16.9.16	ELY George Arthur Pte 37673 kia	Thiepval Memorial
16.9.16	FARNSWORTH William Pte 21137 kia	Thiepval Memorial
16.9.16	FISHER Joseph Henry Pte 34959 kia	Thiepval Memorial
16.9.16	FORMSTONE George Henry Pte 34888 kia	Thiepval Memorial
16.9.16	FOSTER Arthur Pte 34936 kia	Thiepval Memorial
16.9.16	GALLAGHER Thomas Sgt 15861 kia	
16.9.16	GARBUTT John Wilkinson Pte 20062 kia	Thiepval Memorial
16.9.16	GEE William Francis Cpl 15710 kia	Thiepval Memorial
16.9.16	GLASPER James Frederick Pte 34898 kia	Thiepval Memorial
16.9.16	GRAHAM George Pte 34987 kia	Thiepval Memorial
16.9.16	GREEN Albert Pte 18666 kia	Thiepval Memorial
16.9.16	GUY John Wormald Pte 25162 kia	Thiepval Memorial
16.9.16	HARKER Leonard Pte 37647 kia	Thiepval Memorial
16.9.16	HARRINGTON James Douglas Pte 34909 kia	Thiepval Memorial
16.9.16	HARRISON George Reuben L/Cpl 21230 kia	Thiepval Memorial
16.9.16	HART John Robert Pte 34856 kia	Thiepval Memorial
16.9.16	HARWOOD John William Pte 34915 kia	Thiepval Memorial
16.9.16	HAWKSWORTH Garnet Pte 37646 kia	Thiepval Memorial
16.9.16	HEATON John Walter Cpl 15546 kia	Thiepval Memorial
16.9.16	HOGG Thomas Pte 14796 kia	Thiepval Memorial
16.9.16	HOLGATE Charles Tom Pte 12948 kia	Thiepval Memorial
16.9.16	HOLTON Philip John Pte 34902 kia	Thiepval Memorial
16.9.16	HOWARTH James Richard Pte 34904 kia	Thiepval Memorial
16.9.16	HULSE Joseph CSM 16409 kia	Contalmaison Château Cem. II E 14
16.9.16	HUMES Richard Pte 34989 kia	AIF Burial Ground III A 15
16.9.16	INMAN Harold Pte 34922 kia	Thiepval Memorial
16.9.16	JACKSON Benjamin Pte 23992 kia	Thiepval Memorial
16.9.16	JARVIS George Pte 34926 kia	Thiepval Memorial
16.9.16	JOBSON Walter Pte 34923 kia	Thiepval Memorial
16.9.16	JONES Edward Pte 34918 kia	Thiepval Memorial
16.9.16	JOWETT Albert Pte 15937 kia	Thiepval Memorial
16.9.16	LAWLEY Lionel Cpl 16491 kia	AIF Burial Ground III G 15
16.9.16	LAZENBY Arthur Pte 34930 kia	AIF Burial Ground III C 24
16.9.16	LAZENBY Walter Pte 34931 kia	Thiepval Memorial
16.9.16	MATTOCKS Samuel Pte 37723 kia	Thiepval Memorial
16.9.16	MIDDLETON Joseph Pte 37669 kia	Thiepval Memorial
16.9.16	MOSS Nicholas Pte 21841 kia	Thiepval Memorial
16.9.16	OGDEN John William Pte 34958 kia	Thiepval Memorial
16.9.16	PALMER Samuel Pte 37682 kia	Thiepval Memorial
16.9.16	PARRY Thomas Pte 16308 kia	Longueval Road Cem. D 6
16.9.16	PARSONS William A/L/Cpl 34979 kia	Thiepval Memorial
16.9.16	PEEL John Pte 15339 kia	Gordon Dump Cem. X D 3
16.9.16	POWELL Harold Pte 25880 kia	Thiepval Memorial
16.9.16	PRIESTLEY Arthur Sgt 19185 kia	Thiepval Memorial
16.9.16	RENWICK Harry Pte 14716 kia	Thiepval Memorial
16.9.16	RICHARDSON Ernest Pte 9/19002 kia	Thiepval Memorial
16.9.16	ROBINSON Ernest Sherwood Pte 34944 kia	Thiepval Memorial
16.9.16	ROWNTREE James Henry Pte 34945 kia	Thiepval Memorial
16.9.16	SALTER Thomas Cpl 9/17125 kia	Thiepval Memorial

16.9.16	SANDERS Frederick Harry Pte 37724 kia	Thiepval Memorial
16.9.16	SEAGLE John Sgt 20700 kia	Thiepval Memorial
16.9.16	SELLARS Eli Pte 37691 kia	Thiepval Memorial
16.9.16	SENIOR Percy Pte 37600 kia	AIF Burial Ground III 15
16.9.16	SKELTON Albert Edward Sgt 14556 kia	Thiepval Memorial
16.9.16	SMITH Albert Pte 13970 kia	Thiepval Memorial
16.9.16	SMITH Albert Pte 24347 kia	Thiepval Memorial
16.9.16	SMITH Ernest Pte 34870 kia	Thiepval Memorial
16.9.16	SMITH Ronald Nelson Pte 27240 kia	Thiepval Memorial
16.9.16	SMITHSON Frank Pte 3/3584 kia	Thiepval Memorial
16.9.16	STAINCLIFFE James Pte 16461 kia	Thiepval Memorial
16.9.16	STERLAND Arthur Ernest Pte 37664 kia	Ville-sur-Ancre Comm. Cem. Ext. C 17
16.9.16	TANSLEY Henry Pte 22095 kia	Thiepval Memorial
16.9.16	TAYLOR George Pte 11656 kia	Thiepval Memorial
16.9.16	TAYLOR Herbert Pte 9/19006 kia	Thiepval Memorial
16.9.16	TAYLOR William Pte 19567 kia	Thiepval Memorial
16.9.16	TEALE George Pte 12876 kia	Thiepval Memorial
16.9.16	THOMPSON Charles Edward Pte 15522 kia	Thiepval Memorial
16.9.16	VAUX Roy Pte 26930 kia	Thiepval Memorial
16.9.16	WALES Joseph Pte 15231 kia	AIF Burial Ground II J 14
16.9.16	WALLER Fred Pte 26933 kia	Thiepval Memorial
16.9.16	WALSH Fred Pte 9/17011 kia	Thiepval Memorial
16.9.16	WARRILOW Enoch Pte 37719 kia	Thiepval Memorial
16.9.16	WATERTON Joseph Pte 25120 kia	Thiepval Memorial
16.9.16	WEBSTER John Edward Sgt MM 16840 kia	AIF Burial Ground IV G 9
16.9.16	WILSON Henry Percival Pte 10231 kia	Thiepval Memorial
16.9.16	WRIGHT Harry Smith Pte 34834 kia	Thiepval Memorial
16.9.16	WRIGHT Tom L/Cpl 19835 kia	Thiepval Memorial
18.9.16	FORD Leonard Pte 19947	Thiepval Memorial
18.9.16	STAPLETON John Henry Pte 15197 dow	Dartmoor Cem. IIA 81
20.9.16	MARSH William Pte 37656 dow	Heilly Station Cem. IV E 55
21.9.16	DAVIES Evan Pte 34883 dow	Heilly Station Cem. IV E 51
25.9.16	TEMPEST W.N. Major	Thiepval Memorial
26.9.16	CLARK Benjamin Pte 26363 kia	Thiepval Memorial
26.9.16	HALL William Edward Pte 38287 kia	Thiepval Memorial
26.9.16	MANN Douglas Pte 15770 kia	Heilly Station Cem. IV H 60
26.9.16	SHARP Thomas Pte 21943 kia	Thiepval Memorial
26.9.16	SMITH Walter Thorpe Pte 17624 kia	Guards Cem. Sp Mem. 55
26.9.16	STEELE Charles Henry Pte 16004 kia	Guards Cem. Sp Mem. 56
28.9.16	CUTTS William Robert Pte 13378 dow	Heilly Station Cem. IV I 37
28.9.16	JOHNSON George Pte 34919 dow	Heilly Station Cem. IV I 55
1.10.16	HERBERT W.A. 2nd-Lt	Thiepval Memorial
1.10.16	MARTIN E.T. 2nd-Lt	Thiepval Memorial
1.10.16	WATERTON Andrew Pte 26509 kia	Thiepval Memorial
1.10.16	WYATT William Henry Pte 24028 kia	Adanac Cem. III J 19
7.10.16	COCKING Ernest Cpl 9/17180 dow	Goole Cem. A West 'C' 1879
18.10.16	ALMOND Joseph Pte 12/2375 kia	Cambrin Churchyard Ext. S 10
19.10.16	IRELAND Fred Pte 34921 dow	Etaples Military Cem. XII A 11A
27.10.16	HENDLEY Thomas Pte 19030 d.	Denaby Main Church Burial Ground 55
28.10.16	JONES Charles Douglas Lt kia	Cambrin Churchyard Ext. S 15
28.10.16	CROMPTON James Edwin Cpl 34977 kia	Cambrin Churchyard Ext. S 18
28.10.16	HARTLEY Thomas Pte 31037 kia	Cambrin Churchyard Ext. S 19
28.10.16	PAULSON Harry Pte 26931 kia	Cambrin Churchyard Ext. S 17
28.10.16	SKELTON Hubert Pte 14551 kia	Cambrin Churchyard Ext. S 16
28.10.16	STOREY Harry Pte 13546 kia	Cambrin Churchyard Ext. S 20
4.11.16	WADDINGTON Wilfred Pte 15147	Morley Cem. A. Gen 286
6.11.16	SIMPSON Charles Percy Pte 16931 d.	Bailleul Communal Cem. Ext. II A 233
18.11.16	McMORDIE James Wilson 2nd-Lt	Thiepval Memorial
18.11.16	SEED Arthur L/Cpl 16153 kia	Cambrin Churchyard Ext. S 26
25.11.16	EDGE John Pte 19759 dow	Leeds (Hunslet Old) Cem. 'C' 4 11213

29.11.16	BROWN George Pte 34861 dow Home	Edinburgh (Seafield) Cem. B 641
2.12.16	CALVERT Fred Pte 38424 dow Home	Wainfleet All Saints Cem. (Skegness)
14.12.16	SUTHERLAND Norman Munroe Pte 35479 kia	Loos Memorial
18.12.16	LILLIE Frank William Capt. kia	Vermelles British Cem. V F 29
22.12.16	BOYLE Frederick Arthur Pte 34857 kia	Vermelles British Cem. V F 32
27.12.16	JACKSON George Pte 32970 dow	Etaples Military Cem. XX M 1A
27.12.16	REED George Frederick Pte 38252 kia	Vermelles British Cem. V E 26

1917

21.1.17	GABBITAS John Pte 16755 dow	Doncaster Old Cem. S 188
31.1.17	WATSON Ernest Ludlow Pte 39689 d.	Bethune Town Cem. VI B 5
8.2.17	BLACKBURN J.H. Lt d.	Lijssenthoek Military Cem. X A 6
19.2.17	STENTON George Pte 25006 kia	Cambrin Military Cem. G 51
19.2.17	WEBB Joseph 20216 kia	Cambrin Military Cem. G 50
19.2.17	WILLIAMSON Jesse Harrop Pte 27244 kia	Cambrin Military Cem. G 49
21.2.17	HEAP Arthur Pte 43036 kia	Cambrin Military Cem. G 52
22.2.17	STANFORD C.R.F. Capt. kia	Cambrin Military Cem. G 55
23.2.17	BUTTERFIELD Leonard Pte 35719 dow	Bethune Town Cem. VI B 72
24.2.17	STOKES Reginald Alexander 2nd-Lt kia	Cambrin Military Cem. H 5
5.4.17	JENKINSON John Pte 30112 kia	Boyelles Communal Cem. I A 3
7.4.17	HAGSTON Oliver Pte 13329 d.	Bucquoy Road Cem. VI K 5
9.4.17	ACKRILL-JONES Robert Roland 2nd-Lt kia	Cojeul British Cem. D 4
9.4.17	CRICK William Edward 2nd-Lt dow	Bucquoy Road Cem. I A 19
9.4.17	HARVEY Stanley 2nd-Lt kia	Wancourt British Cem. V G 31
9.4.17	SPARK Archibald Graham Capt. MC kia	Cojeul British Cem. D 3
9.4.17	ADAMS Robert Pte 39846 kia	Wancourt British Cem. V G 24
9.4.17	ARMITAGE George Pte 43060 kia	Cojeul British Cem. D 42
9.4.17	BALDWIN Willie Pte 35721 kia	Wancourt British Cem. V G 28
9.4.17	BLOOMFIELD Albert Pte 37680 kia	Arras Memorial
9.4.17	BROOKER Albert Amos Pte 43994 kia	Wancourt British Cem. VII H 12
9.4.17	BROWN Joseph Cpl 42992 kia	Cojeul British Cem. D 13
9.4.17	BULLOCK Arthur Pte MM 14856 kia	Wancourt British Cem. VII H 5
9.4.17	BURKINSHAW Herbert Pte 30847 kia	Cojeul British Cem. D 47
9.4.17	CALVERT William A/Cpl 16996 kia	Cojeul British Cem. A 6
9.4.17	CARTER William Sidney Pte 44002 kia	Wancourt British Cem. VII H 6
9.4.17	CHAPLIN Harry Pte 23999 kia	Cojeul British Cem. A 5
9.4.17	CLEWS John Pte 44004 kia	Cojeul British Cem. D 16
9.4.17	CLOUGH Arthur Sgt 35743 kia	Cojeul British Cem. D 8
9.4.17	COCKING Willie Pte 35724 kia	Cojeul British Cem. D 15
9.4.17	COOK Albert Victor Pte 44005 kia	Cojeul British Cem. D 14
9.4.17	DANN Robert Pte 44014 kia	Wancourt British Cem. V G 23
9.4.17	DEAN George William Pte 35746 kia	Cojeul British Cem. A 2
9.4.17	ELLERINGTON Charles Edwin Sgt 8974 kia	Cojeul British Cem. D 31
9.4.17	ELLUM Herbert Pte 39799 kia	Wancourt British Cem. V G 29
9.4.17	FOX Sidney John Pte 44023 kia	Cojeul British Cem. D 24
9.4.17	FROST Leonard Benjamin Pte 44025 kia	Cojeul British Cem. D 63
9.4.17	GREEN William J.W. Sgt 23612 kia	Wancourt British Cem. V G 22
9.4.17	HALL Noah Albert Pte 34937 kia	Cojeul British Cem. D 11
9.4.17	HARDIMAN Thomas William Pte 34912 kia	Arras Memorial
9.4.17	HASLAM Charles Pte 43538 kia	Cojeul British Cem. A 23
9.4.17	HEADLINGTON Sidney James Sgt 37893 kia	Cojeul British Cem. D 27
9.4.17	HEATH Arthur Edward Pte 43627 kia	Arras Memorial
9.4.17	HILL George Pte 235135 kia	Wancourt British Cem. V G 27
9.4.17	HOBSON David A/Sgt 12870 kia	Wancourt British Cem. V G 30
9.4.17	JAMES Sydney L/Cpl 35274 kia	Cojeul British Cem. D 9
9.4.17	JONES Herbert Thomas Pte 44056 kia	Cojeul British Cem. D 48
9.4.17	KEEP Fred Cpl 23287 kia	Wancourt British Cem. VII H 4
9.4.17	KELLY John Pte 22871 kia	Cojeul British Cem. D 17
9.4.17	LEWIS Arthur Sidney Pte 43629 kia	Cojeul British Cem. D 50
9.4.17	LITTLEHALES Albert Pte 44065 kia	Cojeul British Cem. D 18

9.4.17	LUMB Arthur Pte 39596 kia	Henin Comm. Cem. Ext. III D 3
9.4.17	LUPTON Alfred William Pte 25801 kia	Arras Memorial
9.4.17	McMAHON Phillip L/Cpl 42979 kia	Arras Memorial
9.4.17	McMARNISS Isaac Pte 13208 kia	Cojeul British Cem. Sp Mem. B 11
9.4.17	McNALLY Edgar Francis Pte 39939 kia	Arras Memorial
9.4.17	MARSDEN Frederick Pte 41539 kia	Cojeul British Cem. Sp Mem. A 2
9.4.17	MILLER Richard Pte 43631 kia	Wancourt British Cem. V G 21
9.4.17	MOFFIT Charles Pte 43031 kia	Wancourt British Cem. VII H 8
9.4.17	MORRELL Walter L/Cpl 11416 kia	Cojeul British Cem. Sp Mem. A 1
9.4.17	MORTON Arthur Harry A/Sgt 38268 kia	Arras Memorial
9.4.17	MOSS Harold Pte 11120 kia	Arras Memorial
9.4.17	NEILSON Frederick L/Cpl 14880 kia	Cojeul British Cem. D 7
9.4.17	NETTLETON Charles Ernest Sgt 12/462 kia	Cojeul British Cem. D 64
9.4.17	ORME Samuel Sgt 7761 kia	Wancourt British Cem. V G 25
9.4.17	ROBERTS Frederick Thomas Pte 43636 kia	Arras Memorial
9.4.17	ROBSON George Pte 43054 kia	Arras Memorial
9.4.17	RYAN John Pte 39541 kia	Cojeul British Cem. A 4
9.4.17	SATCHWELL Fred Pte 17115 kia	Arras Memorial
9.4.17	SAWBRIDGE Frank Pte 43568 kia	Cojeul British Cem. D 10
9.4.17	SILVESTER Albert Pte MM 12/506 kia	Cojeul British Cem. A 14
9.4.17	SMITH Thomas L/Cpl 23989 kia	Arras Memorial
9.4.17	SWIFT Thomas Pte 34076 kia	Cojeul British Cem. D 32
9.4.17	TAYLOR Joseph Christopher Pte 42998 kia	Cojeul British Cem. D 46
9.4.17	TORDOFF Squire Pte 39660 kia	Cojeul British Cem. A 42
9.4.17	TURNER George William Pte 42353 kia	Cojeul British Cem. D 41
9.4.17	WAINWRIGHT Charles Pte 235164 kia	Cojeul British Cem. A 1
9.4.17	WALKER Willie Pte 39720 kia	Cojeul British Cem. D 29
9.4.17	WARD Thomas Pte 235165 kia	Cojeul British Cem. A 3
9.4.17	WATERHOUSE Herbert Sgt 5857 kia	Cojeul British Cem. D 12
9.4.17	WEST Vernon Sgt 38591 kia	Cojeul British Cem. D 45
9.4.17	WILLIAMSON Sidney George Pte 42968 kia	Arras Memorial
9.4.17	WOODCOCK George Pte 24180 kia	Arras Memorial
9.4.17	WOOLDRIDGE John Pte 44041 kia	Wancourt British Cem. V G 26
10.4.17	CLANCY Matthew A/Sgt 42976 dow	Warlincourt Halte British Cem. VII A 13
10.4.17	HEAMES Sam Pte 44040 dow	Mont Huon Military Cem. III F 4A
10.4.17	MORCOMBE Eddie L/Cpl 38492 kia	Boyelles Communal Cem. I A 8
11.4.17	HART Frederick Pte 43579 dow	Warlincourt Halte British Cem. VIII E 9
11.4.17	JONES Joseph Edward Pte 43570 dow	Warlincourt Halte British Cem. VIII E 11
14.4.17	HOLLIDAY Thomas William Pte 33044 kia	Croisilles British Cem. IV C 33
16.4.17	LINDSTROM William Axel Pte 43040 dow	St Sever Cem. Ext. O VIII D 9
17.4.17	FRANCE Alonza Pte 28186 kia	Hollybrook Memorial (UK)
20.4.17	COLBECK Ernest Pte 30104 kia	Arras Memorial
23.4.17	HOULDEY Frederick Pte 34940 kia	Arras Memorial
25.4.17	CLARK Ernest Pte 22651 kia	Arras Memorial
25.4.17	HEATH Percy A/Sgt MM 3/698 kia	Cojeul British Cem. B 13
25.4.17	LITTLE Henry George Pte 44064 kia	Cojeul British Cem. A 70
25.4.17	TERRY Keiron Pte 43556 kia	Cojeul British Cem. C 61
25.4.17	WRAY Walter Cpl 28097 kia	Arras Memorial
27.4.17	DENBY Samuel Pte 43034 dow	St Sever Cem. Ext. P.I.C. 9A
28.4.17	CLARK John Pte 43598 kia	Cojeul British Cem. B 5
28.4.17	FISHER David Gordon Pte 40255 died	Arras Memorial
28.4.17	FORD Joseph Pte 39956 kia	Arras Memorial
28.4.17	GRANT William Dorkin Pte 39798 kia	Wancourt British Cem. VII D 10
28.4.17	ERVINE James A/CSM 8033 kia	Arras Memorial
28.4.17	THOMPSON Samuel L/Cpl 43088 kia	Arras Memorial
28.4.17	WHITAKER Arthur Pte 43045 kia	Arras Memorial
28.4.17	WOOLF Joseph Pte 43564 kia	Cojeul British Cem. B 48
30.4.17	GILES Percy Pte 43903 dow	Warlincourt Halte British Cem. X E 13
1.5.17	CONNELLY Laurence Pte 43048 dow	Warlincourt Halte British Cem. X G 6
1.5.17	HEAP Arthur Maurice L/Cpl 35734 dow	Bailleul Road East Cem. II E 39

1.5.17	McHUGH Willie A/Cpl 42989 dow	Bucquoy Road Cem. I D 8
3.5.17	WHITE Nicholas Henry A/Sgt 424971 kia	Henin Communal Cem. Ext. I B 2
5.5.17	WATSON John Andrew Gregory Pte 25266 dow	Warlincourt Halte British Cem. X F 6
9.5.17	PARR Herbert Pte 39830 dow	Warlincourt Halte British Cem. IX H 11
11.5.17	APPLEYARD H. Pte 29966	Boyelles Communal Cem. I D 7
12.5.17	HITCHMAN George Pte 43542 dow	Bucquoy Road Cem. I G 5
12.5.17	JENKINS Arthur Sgt 35742 dow	Bucquoy Road Cem. I G 4
22.5.17	HANCOX Charles Arthur Pte 44035 dow	Warlincourt Halte British Cem. XII A 10
23.5.17	FARROW John Charles Pte 43614 d.	Mont Huon Military Cem. II H 2B
1.6.17	BURNE Leonard Pte 235120 dow	Henin Communal Cem. Ext. II A 14
1.6.17	JONES Charles Heseltine Cpl 42986 kia	Henin Communal Cem. Ext. II A 16
1.6.17	JOWES James Pte 34920 kia	Henin Communal Cem. Ext. II A 15
3.6.17	NOCK Frederick John 2nd-Lt (attd 9th) dow	Sunken Road Cem. I E 3
3.6.17	HARDING Harry Pte 253132 kia	Henin Communal Cem. Ext. II A 18
4.6.17	EVERY Frederick Pte 43987 dow	Achiet-le-Grand Comm. Cem. Ext. I I 31
6.6.17	SUTTON Thomas Edward L/Cpl MM 42987 dow	Achiet-le-Grand Comm. Cem. Ext. I J 8
8.6.17	CHAMBERLAIN Frank Pte 43587 kia	Henin Communal Cem. Ext. II B 1
9.6.17	HALL James Thomson 2nd-Lt dow	Etaples Military Cem. XVII B 21
18.6.17	HARRISON William Henry Pte 16378 kia	Cojeul British Cem. E 13
3.7.17	BLUNT George Pte 43925 dow	Grevillers British Cem. VI E 18
4.7.17	KEIGHTLEY Chas Willaton L/Cpl 17648 kia	Arras Memorial
5.7.17	SMITH W.E. Lt	Grevillers British Cem. VI D 3
7.7.17	NORCLIFFE Tom Pte 39649 kia	St Leger British Cem. F 10
20.7.17	JAFFE Israel Pte 40596 kia	Arras Mem and Cojeul British Cem. E 22
22.7.17	BAKER Francis Henry Pte 39736 kia	Cojeul British Cem. E 21
22.7.17	RODGERS William Pte 30148 dow	Sheffield (Burngreave) Cem. V 5 'C' 57
3.8.17	FRANKLAND Fred Pte 38301 kia	Croisilles British Cem. I A 31
10.8.17	BROADBENT Frank A/Sgt 9930 kia	Croisilles British Cem. I D 18
10.8.17	DAY Harold Pte 202477 kia	Croisilles British Cem. I D 19
10.8.17	HEPWORTH Alfred Pte 235134 dow	St Leger British Cem. F 13
13.8.17	JESSUP Joseph Pte 42993 kia	Croisilles British Cem. I E 26
27.8.17	JEFFERSON Hayton Pte 34336 kia	Ypres Reservoir Cem. IX G 14
2.10.17	FROST Albert Pte 35704 kia	Tyne Cot Memorial
3.10.17	BIDWELL Frank James Pte 43990 kia	Tyne Cot Memorial
3.10.17	REES William Henry Cpl 43759 dow	Lijssenthoek Military Cem. XXIV E 9
3.10.17	STANGROOM Walter David Cpl 9307 kia	Tyne Cot Memorial
3.10.17	STOCKS Edwin Pte 43553 kia	Hooge Crater Cem. XII F 8
3.10.17	THOMPSON John Norman Cpl 42997 kia	Tyne Cot Memorial
4.10.17	DANIELL N.R. Lt-Col. kia	Tyne Cot Memorial
4.10.17	BENNETT Robert Granville 2nd-Lt (attd 9th) kia	Tyne Cot Memorial
4.10.17	DAVIS Norman 2nd-Lt (attd 9th) kia	Tyne Cot Memorial
4.10.17	HARDMAN Archibald T/Lt (A/Capt) kia	Tyne Cot Memorial
4.10.17	HYDE Gilbert Arthur 2nd-Lt (attd 9th) kia	Tyne Cot Memorial
4.10.17	LOGSDON Frank Lionel de Marche 2nd-Lt kia	Tyne Cot Memorial
4.10.17	SPICER Leonard Baker 2nd-Lt (attd 9th) kia	Tyne Cot Memorial
4.10.17	STANLEY Percy Douglas 2nd-Lt (attd 9th) kia	Tyne Cot Memorial
4.10.17	ALDRIDGE William Lawson Pte 10841 kia	Hooge Crater Cem. XIII C 12/15
4.10.17	ATKINSON Ernest Pte 43760 kia	Tyne Cot Memorial
4.10.17	AVIS James George Pte 40032 kia	Tyne Cot Memorial
4.10.17	BARNES Christopher Pte 40874 kia	Tyne Cot Memorial
4.10.17	BARRS Thomas Edward Pte 16050 kia	Hooge Crater Cem. XII J 10
4.10.17	BARTON William Pte 43126 kia	Tyne Cot Memorial
4.10.17	BODELL Ernest Pte 43592 kia	Tyne Cot Memorial
4.10.17	BROOK Arthur Hilton Pte 40902 kia	Tyne Cot Memorial
4.10.17	BRUMWELL Harry Pte 35722 kia	Tyne Cot Memorial
4.10.17	BURTON Lewis Pte 235121 kia	Tyne Cot Memorial
4.10.17	BUTLER Ernest Edgar Sgt 9391 kia	Tyne Cot Memorial
4.10.17	CARTLEDGE Maurice Turner Pte 36172 kia	Tyne Cot Memorial
4.10.17	CHAPMAN Harry Cpl 14752 kia	Tyne Cot Memorial
4.10.17	CLAXTON John Pte 27243 kia	Tyne Cot Memorial

4.10.17	COCKERILL Harry Pte 40505 kia	Tyne Cot Memorial
4.10.17	CUMMING Edward Young Pte 36197 kia	Tyne Cot Cem. LX A 11
4.10.17	DAVEY George L/Cpl 2691 kia	Tyne Cot Memorial
4.10.17	DAWSON Ernest Pte 24920 kia	Tyne Cot Cem. LIX E 23
4.10.17	DEAKIN Percy Pte 202541 kia	Railway Dugouts Burial Ground I M 4
4.10.17	DYSON Harold Whiteley Pte 43017 kia	Tyne Cot Memorial
4.10.17	EVERITT William Edward Pte 19189 kia	Tyne Cot Memorial
4.10.17	FREEDMAN Joseph Pte 235130 kia	Tyne Cot Memorial
4.10.17	FROST Joe Pte 36176 kia	Hooge Crater Cem. XIII G 17
4.10.17	FRY George Henry Pte 44026 kia	Hooge Crater Cem. XIII C 12/15
4.10.17	GASKELL John Lee Pte 39735 kia	Tyne Cot Memorial
4.10.17	GILGAN Michael L/Cpl 43622 kia	Hooge Crater Cem. XII H 6
4.10.17	GILYEAT Robert Pte 240879 kia	Buttes New British Cem. XV B 2
4.10.17	GOLDEN Hedley Walter Pte 44029 kia	Tyne Cot Memorial
4.10.17	GORDON William Pearson L/Cpl 40950 kia	Tyne Cot Memorial
4.10.17	HARNAN Bernard Pte 43030 kia	Tyne Cot Memorial
4.10.17	HEAD Richard Augustus L/Cpl 43626 kia	Tyne Cot Memorial
4.10.17	HELLIWELL George A/Sgt 16815 kia	Hooge Crater Cem.
4.10.17	HILL Frank Pte 43153 kia	Tyne Cot Memorial
4.10.17	HIRST Leonard Pte 39590 kia	Tyne Cot Memorial
4.10.17	HODGETTS William Pte 235137 kia	Tyne Cot Memorial
4.10.17	HODGKINSON James Pte 26204 kia	Tyne Cot Memorial
4.10.17	HOWE John Arthur Pte 34056 kia	Tyne Cot Memorial
4.10.17	HUGHES Harry Pte 43545 kia	Hooge Crater Cem. XI L 17
4.10.17	HYDON Edward Thomas Pte 43578 kia	Tyne Cot Memorial
4.10.17	JARMAN John Harold Pte 44053 kia	Tyne Cot Memorial
4.10.17	JOHNSON Walter Cpl 21175 kia	Tyne Cot Memorial
4.10.17	JONES Lloyd L/Cpl 34952 kia	Tyne Cot Memorial
4.10.17	KERSHAW Harry L/Cpl 42953 kia	Tyne Cot Memorial
4.10.17	LANG Willie Pte 43921 kia	Tyne Cot Cem. LXI B 3
4.10.17	LAMPITT George Henry Pte 44060 kia	Hooge Crater Cem. X J 11
4.10.17	LEPORATI Ernest Pte 41594 kia	Tyne Cot Memorial
4.10.17	LOCK Ivor Cecil Pte 44066 kia	Tyne Cot Memorial
4.10.17	LODGE Robert A/Cpl 31025 kia	Tyne Cot Memorial
4.10.17	McLENNAN Murdo Kenneth Pte 35837 kia	Tyne Cot Memorial
4.10.17	MANSELL Albert W.O. 2nd Class 7195 kia	Tyne Cot Memorial
4.10.17	MATTHEWS Thomas Pte 42036 kia	Tyne Cot Cem. LXI A 2
4.10.17	MAW Frank Pte 16310 kia	Hooge Crater Cem. X K 1
4.10.17	MOORE Charles Henry Pte 39978 kia	Tyne Cot Memorial
4.10.17	NASH William Sgt 38580 kia	Tyne Cot Memorial
4.10.17	NUTTYCOMBE Albert Pte 40653 kia	Oxford Road Cem. IV C 3
4.10.17	OATES Edward Pte 17800 kia	Tyne Cot Memorial
4.10.17	O'CONNOR Francis Herbert Pte 34501 kia	Tyne Cot Memorial
4.10.17	ORMONDROYD Reginald L/Cpl 39599 kia	Tyne Cot Memorial
4.10.17	PEACOCK William Dungworth Cpl 13647 kia	Bedford House Cem. XII AA 4
4.10.17	PENTY Kenneth Cpl MM 16012 kia	Tyne Cot Memorial
4.10.17	PERKINS Edwin Alfred Charles Pte 43858 kia	Duhallow A.D.S. Cem. VIII D 17
4.10.17	PYATT William Frederick Sgt MM 19086 kia	Tyne Cot Memorial
4.10.17	POPE George Thomas Pte 44089 kia	Tyne Cot Memorial
4.10.17	POSKITT John William Pte 235152 kia	Bedford House Cem. XIII AA 6
4.10.17	RHODES James Pte 43821 kia	Tyne Cot Memorial
4.10.17	ROBINSON James Pte 35169 kia	Tyne Cot Memorial
4.10.17	SCOTT Charles Pte 42194 kia	Tyne Cot Memorial
4.10.17	SCULL Timothy Pte 40728 kia	Tyne Cot Memorial
4.10.17	SHAW John Leonard Pte 32666 kia	Tyne Cot Memorial
4.10.17	SILKSTONE Alfred Pte 24799 kia	Tyne Cot Memorial
4.10.17	SLATER Joe Clegg Pte 43020 kia	Tyne Cot Memorial
4.10.17	SMITH Harry Sgt 18943 kia	Tyne Cot Memorial
4.10.17	SOUTHWELL Willie Pte 39611 kia	Bedford House Cem. XIII AA 3
4.10.17	SUTTON Everard Pte 35405 kia	Tyne Cot Memorial

4.10.17	TAYLOR George Pte 39860 kia	Hooge Crater Cem. XII H 5
4.10.17	THICKETT Tom Pte 12/1829 kia	Tyne Cot Memorial
4.10.17	TROW Arnold L/Cpl 31036 kia	Tyne Cot Memorial
4.10.17	VIGRASS Edward Cpl 36166 kia	Tyne Cot Memorial
4.10.17	WAINWRIGHT James Cpl 3/1812 kia	Tyne Cot Memorial
4.10.17	WAKEFIELD Albert Ernest Pte 242766 kia	Tyne Cot Memorial
4.10.17	WALKER Joe Pte 235162 kia	Tyne Cot Memorial
4.10.17	WALTERS Joseph Pte 40392 kia	Tyne Cot Memorial
4.10.17	WALSHAW Edwin Pte 40282 kia	Tyne Cot Memorial
4.10.17	WALTON Wilfred Pte 36189 kia	Hooge Crater Cem. XII J 16
4.10.17	WHITTAKER George Pte 20028 kia	Tyne Cot Memorial
4.10.17	WHITWORTH George Herbert L/Cpl 42959 kia	Tyne Cot Memorial
4.10.17	WOGAN Walter Pte 39703 kia	Tyne Cot Memorial
4.10.17	WOODLAND Thomas Pte 43561 kia	Tyne Cot Cem. XLIX A 8
4.10.17	WRIGHT Arthur Pte 235163 kia	Hooge Crater Cem. X K 2
5.10.17	MASON Ernest T/Lt (A/Capt) dow	Godewaersvelde British Cem. I L 35
5.10.17	BORTHWICK John Edwin Pte 9877 kia	Tyne Cot Memorial
5.10.17	ORD John Robert Pte MM 43012 dow	Godewaersvelde British Cem. I N 8
6.10.17	HANSON Benjamin L/Cpl 39597 dow	Lijssenthoek Military Cem. XX E 16
7.10.17	GREENWOOD Wade Pte 43013 dow	Godewaersvelde British Cem. I F 29
10.10.17	LARRARD Harold Martin Pte 45667 dow	Boulogne Eastern Cem. VIII I 46
11.10.17	HOLLYHEAD Samuel Haydn Pte 26869 dow	Nine Elms British Cem. III C 13
12.10.17	CARTWRIGHT Andrew William Pte 36173 dow	Etaples Military Cem. XXX C 6
12.10.17	OGLESBY Albert Pte 22213 d. Home	Stanley Outwood Cem. (Batley) X 'C' H.25
14.10.17	RHODES Sam Pte 43005 dow	Locre Hospice Cem. III B 29
14.10.17	ROCHFORD Thomas Pte 34450 kia	Tyne Cot Memorial
14.10.17	ROLLINSON Herbert Pte 23892 kia	Tyne Cot Memorial
15.10.17	ROYLES William Henry Pte 41073 dow	Etaples Military Cem. XXX D 4A
17.10.17	BROWN William Pte 39742 kia	Ypres Reservoir Cem. IX A 33
22.10.17	CARTER William Pte 13574 kia	Tyne Cot Memorial
22.10.17	HEY Clement Pte 42999 kia	Tyne Cot Cem. XLIII D 2
22.10.17	JONES Joseph A/Cpl 12/1489 kia	Tyne Cot Memorial
22.10.17	MARTIN Fred Pte 44069 kia	Tyne Cot Memorial
22.10.17	SIMPSON Alfred Pte 35738 kia	Buttes New Military Cem. XXII A 16
22.10.17	SORBY George Henry A/Cpl 15766 kia	Tyne Cot Memorial
22.10.17	VERITY Frederick Pte 40595 kia	Tyne Cot Memorial
22.10.17	WANLESS Bertram Pte 31663 kia	Tyne Cot Memorial
22.10.17	YATES George Walter Pte 43565 kia	Tyne Cot Memorial
23.10.17	BRAMWELL Joshua Lister Pte 43462 kia	Tyne Cot Memorial
23.10.17	WHITEWAY Edward John WO2 8512 kia	Tyne Cot Memorial
4.11.17	HAWLING Thomas Albert 2nd-Lt (attd 9th)	Tyne Cot Memorial
4.11.17	NIVEN Alan Scott 2nd-Lt (attd 9th)	Tyne Cot Memorial
4.11.17	GELLATLY Charles George Pte 39752 kia	Tyne Cot Memorial
4.11.17	SIMPSON Leonard L/Cpl 9344 kia	Tyne Cot Memorial
6.11.17	CLOSE Frank Pte 32347 kia	Tyne Cot Memorial
6.11.17	DEEBLE Albert Pte 235129 kia	Tyne Cot Memorial
6.11.17	HUDSON James William Pte 17785 kia	Tyne Cot Memorial
6.11.17	LAWFORD George Pte 20710 kia	Tyne Cot Memorial
8.11.17	HOBBY Ernest George Pte 44046 dow Home	Stone (All Saints) Churchyard 276
6.12.17	EDWORTHY Walter Pte 44017 dow	Tincourt New British Cem. III E 38
6.12.17	HEMMENS John Arthur Pte 34209 kia	Gouzeaucourt New British Cem. V H 1
6.12.17	HOWE Thomas James Pte 37894 dow	Gouzeaucourt New British Cem. VII H 9
6.12.17	PERKINS Gordon L/Cpl 235782 kia	Gouzeaucourt New British Cem. VII H 10
6.12.17	TUDDENHAM Goliath Pte 35740 dow	Epehy Wood Farm Cem. IV A 2
23.12.17	SOLLITT Thomas Henry Pte 42198 dow	Epehy Wood Farm Cem. V C 13
24.12.17	LONGWORTH William Pte 13811 kia	Heudicourt Comm Cem. Ext. E 13
30.12.17	POLLARD John CQMS DCM 15445 dow	Tincourt New British Cem. IV C 18
30.12.17	RHODES Horace Pte 39946 dow Home	Batley Cem. (UK) A 521

1918

17.1.18	BARTER Sidney Pte 37058 dow	Etretat Churchyard Ext. II A 11
19.3.18	REAKES Edward James L/Cpl 44096 dow	Tincourt New British Cem. Sp Mem. 4
21.3.18	BLACK William Percy L/Cpl 18850 kia	Pozières Memorial
21.3.18	CHAMPION George Cartwright Pte 43727 kia	Pozières Memorial
21.3.18	COGRAVE Alfred Pte 47034 dow	Pozières Memorial
21.3.18	CORNES Cyril Pte 37066 kia	Pozières Memorial
21.3.18	COSSINS Charles William Pte 19483 kia	Pozières Memorial
21.3.18	DUNDERVALE William Cpl 23439 kia	Pozières Memorial
21.3.18	WILCOCK Arnold Pte 37097 kia	Pozières Memorial
22.3.18	HETHERINGTON Arthur Lt kia	Pozières Memorial
22.3.18	MAKIN Stanley 2nd-Lt kia	Pozières Memorial
22.3.18	MOON Clifford Abraham 2nd-Lt (attd 9th)	Pozières Memorial
22.3.18	BAIRSTOW Matthew Pte 43056 dow	Pozières Memorial
22.3.18	BARTON George L/Cpl 35189 kia	Pozières Memorial
22.3.18	BATES Reuben Cpl 235784 kia	Pozières Memorial
22.3.18	BRAY Albert George Pte 36582 kia	Pozières Memorial
22.3.18	BREWER Frederick Pte 34851 kia	Pozières Memorial
22.3.18	BRIGGS Lawrence L/Cpl 42967 kia	Pozières Memorial
22.3.18	BYRNE Fred Pte 15095 kia	Pozières Memorial
22.3.18	CHAMBERLAIN Robert Pte 43467 dow	Pozières Memorial
22.3.18	CLARK Arthur Joseph Pte 37025 d.	Saulcourt Churchyard
22.3.18	COLE Tom Alfred Pte 47523 kia	Pozières Memorial
22.3.18	CULTON William Pte 43108 dow	Pozières Memorial
22.3.18	CURTIS Alfred Ernest Pte 44012 kia	Pozières Memorial
22.3.18	DOWNES Albert Pte 37026 kia	Pozières Memorial
22.3.18	DUGGAN Charles Henry Pte 37070 kia	Pozières Memorial
22.3.18	EMMERSON Arthur Pte 38425 kia	Pozières Memorial
22.3.18	EVANS John William L/Sgt 17853 kia	Pozières Memorial
22.3.18	FAWCETT Ernest Pte 42345 kia	Pozières Memorial
22.3.18	FISHER Leonard Pte MM 21195 kia	Pozières Memorial
22.3.18	FOSTER Frank Cyril Pte 37521 kia	Pozières Memorial
22.3.18	GILSON Ernest L/Sgt 17903 kia	Pozières Memorial
22.3.18	GLOVER Harry Pte 36177 d.	Peronne Comm Ext Ste Radegonde III I 2
22.3.18	HAILS Robert Pte 34980 d.	Pozières Memorial
22.3.18	HART James Joseph Pte 37529 kia	Pozières Memorial
22.3.18	HARTLE William Pte 36618 kia	Pozières Memorial
22.3.18	HARVEY Ashton Ellis A/Sgt MM 38953 kia	Péronne Comm Ext Ste Radegonde III H 14
22.3.18	HAWKSWORTH Charles Pte 40029 kia	Pozières Memorial
22.3.18	HETHERINGTON John William Pte 21300 kia	Pozières Memorial
22.3.18	HIRST John T. Pte 33048 kia	Péronne Comm Ext Ste Radegonde V F 6
22.3.18	HIRST Wilfred Heap Pte 39089 kia	Péronne Comm Ext Ste Radegonde IV F 12
22.3.18	HUDSON Frank William Pte 47511 kia	Pozières Memorial
22.3.18	HUTCHINSON Ernest Sgt 3/1601 kia	Saulcourt Churchyard D 7
22.3.18	JACKSON John William Cpl 235790 kia	Pozières Memorial
22.3.18	JAMIESON William Pte 37189 kia	Péronne Comm Ext Ste Radegonde III H 13
22.3.18	JONES Robert Patrick Pte 32864 kia	Pozières Memorial
22.3.18	KAY William Cpl 23879 d.	Pozières Memorial
22.3.18	KNAPTON Herbert Pte 38705 kia	Pozières Memorial
22.3.18	LEWIS Stanley Pte 36637 kia	Pozières Memorial
22.3.18	McDONALD James Pte 43022 kia	Pozières Memorial
22.3.18	McNAUGHTON Donald L/Cpl 42983 kia	Pozières Memorial
22.3.18	MALONEY James Cpl 43002 kia	Péronne Road Cem., Maricourt I C 16
22.3.18	MELLISH Thomas George Pte 37036 kia	Pozières Memorial
22.3.18	MELLON James Pte 24705 kia	Pozières Memorial
22.3.18	MILSON Charles Pte 43905 kia	Pozières Memorial
22.3.18	MORRELL Frederick William Pte 38720 kia	Pozières Memorial
22.3.18	MORRIS Bernard Pte 39844 kia	Pozières Memorial
22.3.18	NICHOLSON Andrew Pte 43487 dow	Pozières Memorial
22.3.18	OTWAY Edward Pte 38741 kia	Pozières Memorial

22.3.18	PEARCE Thomas Harry Pte 37230 kia	Pozières Memorial
22.3.18	RICKARD William Guy Pte 38759 kia	Pozières Memorial
22.3.18	SAYER Reginald John Pte 37249 kia	Pozières Memorial
22.3.18	SCOTT George Pte MM 18361 d.	Saulcourt Churchyard D 6
22.3.18	SENIOR Frederick Sgt 39058 kia	Pozières Memorial
22.3.18	SENIOR Harold Pte 39723 kia	Pozières Memorial
22.3.18	SETTER Herbert Pte 36606 kia	Pozières Memorial
22.3.18	SHAW James William L/Cpl 42960 kia	Pozières Memorial
22.3.18	SHAW Joseph Leonard L/Sgt 235794 kia	Péronne Comm Ext Ste Radegonde IV F 15
22.3.18	STANDAGE Robert Pte 34487 kia	Pozières Memorial
22.3.18	TATTERSALL William Thomas Pte 37047 d.	Pozières Memorial
22.3.18	THACKRAY Fred L/Sgt MM 31052 kia	Roisel Comm. Cem. Ext. III D 14
22.3.18	THOMAS Joshua Pte 37256 kia	Pozières Memorial
22.3.18	THORPE John William Pte 37056 kia	Péronne Comm Ext Ste Radegonde V F 7
22.3.18	WATTS George William Pte 37268 kia	Pozières Memorial
22.3.18	WHITTAKER John Pte 36647 kia	Pozières Memorial
22.3.18	WHITELEY Arthur Pte 13679 kia	Pozières Memorial
22.3.18	WILKINSON Horace Pte 38794 kia	Pozières Memorial
22.3.18	WILKINSON James Pte 235780 kia	Pozières Memorial
22.3.18	WOODFIELD John B. L. CQMS 14150 kia	Péronne Comm Cem Ext. III L 19
22.3.18	WORMALD William Alfred Cpl 15270 kia	Pozières Memorial
22.3.18	YATES George Pte 37053 kia	Pozières Memorial
23.3.18	TEAZ Homer Nevin T/Lt A/Capt. MC kia	Péronne Comm Ext Ste Radegonde III H 29
23.3.18	AUSTIN Harry Pte 43602 kia	Péronne Comm Ext Ste Radegonde IV F 14
23.3.18	FEAST Percy Frank Cpl 16092 kia	Pozières Memorial
23.3.18	HOLROYD Arthur Ernest Cpl 39059 kia	A.I.F. Burial Ground IX J 9
23.3.18	MAUDE John Pte 37033 kia	Pozières Memorial
23.3.18	SPEIGHT Samuel Thompson Pte 32404 kia	Pozières Memorial
24.3.18	BORMAN John George Pte 47490 dow	Rosières British Cem. 12
24.3.18	CLARKSON Horace Pte 34866 dow	Honnechy British Cem. II C 20
24.3.18	McDONALD Thomas A/Cpl 38962 dow	Honnechy British Cem. II C 22
24.3.18	MORLEY Edward Stanley Pte 42262 dow	Honnechy British Cem. II C 23
24.3.18	TIDESWELL Thomas Pte 37712 kia	Pozières Memorial
24.3.18	TOONE Alan Sanders Pte 36619 kia	Pozières Memorial
25.3.18	BAILEY Harold Pte 36622 dow	Pozières Memorial
25.3.18	BURGAN Fred Pte 37015 kia	Tincourt New British Cem. IX A 14
25.3.18	DAVIS John Edwin Pte 37149 kia	Pozières Memorial
25.3.18	HOLTHAM Arthur Thomas Sgt 43004 dow	Honnechy British Cem. II C 19
25.3.18	STEELE Arthur Pte 24838 dow	Villers-Faucon Comm. Cem. Ext. III C 10
25.3.18	WILKINSON Arthur Pte 41288 kia	Pozières Memorial
26.3.18	HUTSON Harold 2nd-Lt (attd 9th) dow	Villers-Faucon Comm. Cem. Ext. III C 5
27.3.18	BENNETT Joseph Pte 25636 dow	St Hilaire Cem. V B 8
27.3.18	SUMMERS Wallace Randolph Pte 205160 kia	Pozières Memorial
30.3.18	AYRE Claude L/Cpl 43459 dow	Tincourt New British Cem. X F 6
30.3.18	CHARLTON Thomas William Pte 43058 dow	St. Souplet British Cem. III E 15
3.4.18	HOULDER John Walter Pte 39732 kia	Saulcourt Churchyard D 5
4.4.18	EAGLE George Henry Pte 43588 kia	Tyne Cot Memorial
4.4.18	TWIGG Tom Pte 24067 dow	Fins New British Cem. IV F 11
5.4.18	COWLES Edmund Wilfred Pte 36592 dow	Le Cateau Military Cem. I B 9
5.4.18	GREEN Harry Pte 23021 dow	St Sever Cem Ext. P VII B 6A
8.4.18	BOWER John Pte 21354 dow	Abbeville Comm. Cem. Ext. IV A 8
9.4.18	CALLAGHAN John Pte 37500 d.	Tourgeville Military Cem. I C 4
12.4.18	BARLOW John William Pte 37747 kia	Tyne Cot Memorial
12.4.18	CURTIS Frederick Herbert Pte 36593	Villers-Faucon Comm. Cem. Ext. III A 2
13.4.18	DOWGILL Richard L/Cpl 35729 dow Home	Farsley Baptist Burial Ground B526
16.4.18	KNIGHT John Pte 36595 dow	Berlin SW Cem. X A 9
17.4.18	JOHNSON Albert Pte 18287 kia	Klein-Vierstraat British Cem. V C 9
19.4.18	BOOTH Arthur Pte 30824 died	Le Cateau Military Cem. I B 56
20.4.18	CUNDALL Stanley 2nd-Lt kia	Klein-Vierstraat British Cem. V A 8
20.4.18	LUSH Joseph Henry Pte 9096 kia	Tyne Cot Memorial
20.4.18	SMITH Ben Pte 37043 dow	Villers-Faucon Comm. Cem. Ext. III A 13

20.4.18	TOLSON Charles Wilfred Pte 26113 kia	Tyne Cot Memorial
20.4.18	WARD Joseph Pte 34708 kia	Klein-Vierstraat British Cem. IV D 2
21.4.18	BROOKS Henry Pte 39307 kia	Tyne Cot Memorial
21.4.18	COLVER Harold Ernest Pte 39299 kia	Tyne Cot Memorial
21.4.18	HARRISON Charles L/Cpl 34833 kia	Tyne Cot Memorial
21.4.18	HOPPER George Watkinson Pte 38695 kia	Tyne Cot Memorial
21.4.18	JENNINGS William Christopher Pte 44055 kia	Tyne Cot Memorial
21.4.18	WELCH Robert Pte 37100 kia	Tyne Cot Memorial
	BORROWDALE William Christopher Pte 49734 dow	Tyne Cot Memorial
22.4.18	BURGES Frederick George Sgt 39289 kia	Tyne Cot Memorial
22.4.18	PEARSON James William Pte 46420	Tyne Cot Memorial
22.4.18	WALDRON Sidney Pte 24554 kia	Tyne Cot Memorial
22.4.18	WRIGHT Percival William Pte 38785 kia	Tyne Cot Memorial
23.4.18	FRYER John Joseph Pte 35509 kia	Tyne Cot Memorial
23.4.18	HOTSTON Frank John Pte 44049 dow	Mendinghem Military Cem. X B 47
23.4.18	LONGLEY Allen Pte 47484 kia	Tyne Cot Memorial
23.4.18	SHIELDS John Pte 50706 kia	Tyne Cot Memorial
23.4.18	THORPE Percy L/Cpl 27268 dow	Lijssenthoek Military Cem. XXVI GG 9
24.4.18	COOKE Charles Pte 14310 kia	La Clytte Military Cem. V D 23
24.4.18	HORNSBY Samuel Pte 39329 kia	Tyne Cot Memorial
24.4.18	MICKLEWRIGHT William Sgt 51393 kia	Tyne Cot Memorial
25.4.18	BAKER Arthur Pte 23526 kia	Tyne Cot Memorial
25.4.18	BINGLEY John Cpl 30035 kia	La Clytte Military Cem. IV D 23
25.4.18	BOLT Ernest John Pte 16655 kia	Tyne Cot Memorial
25.4.18	CRAMMER Samuel Pte 36640 kia	Tyne Cot Memorial
25.4.18	GARSIDE Joseph Pte 2364 kia	Tyne Cot Memorial
25.4.18	GODFREY Edward George L/Cpl 23408 kia	La Clytte Military Cem. IV D 21
25.4.18	GOWERS Harold Pte 18942 kia	Lijssenthoek Military Cem. XXVII H 12A
25.4.18	HODGSON Robert Pte 43140 dow	Tyne Cot Memorial
25.4.18	HORNER John Pte 235778 kia	Tyne Cot Memorial
25.4.18	IRVING John Pte 39331 kia	Tyne Cot Memorial
25.4.18	KEALL Edwin Cpl 11690 kia	Tyne Cot Memorial
25.4.18	LEONARD George Pte MM 200216 kia	Tyne Cot Memorial
25.4.18	LINDLEY Walter Pte 47841 kia	Tyne Cot Memorial
25.4.18	McLEAN Albert Sgt 37755 kia	Tyne Cot Memorial
25.4.18	MALLOY John Pte 43065 kia	Tyne Cot Memorial
25.4.18	NICHOLSON Geoffrey L/Cpl 23092 dow	Harlebeke New British Cem. II D 16
25.4.18	OLDROYD George Henry Pte 205323 kia	Tyne Cot Memorial
25.4.18	PREST Lancelot Pte 34653 kia	La Clytte Military Cem. VI F 7
25.4.18	ROBINSON William Pte 32047 dow	Crouy British Military Cem. I B 13
25.4.18	TATE John Pte 35623 kia	Tyne Cot Memorial
25.4.18	TERRY Harry Pte 40019 kia	Wytschaete Military Cem. IV B 34
25.4.18	WADSWORTH Charles Briggs Pte 14562 kia	Tyne Cot Memorial
25.4.18	WAIN George Pte 30095 kia	Tyne Cot Memorial
25.4.18	WALES William Anderson Pte 37265 kia	Tyne Cot Memorial
25.4.18	WEBB Albert Pte 41134 kia	Tyne Cot Memorial
25.4.18	WILDBLOOD James Edward L/Cpl 15912 kia	Tyne Cot Memorial
26.4.18	NICHOLSON Paul Cheesum 2nd-Lt kia	Tyne Cot Memorial
26.4.18	ADCOCK Harry Pte 39304 kia	Tyne Cot Memorial
26.4.18	ARMSTRONG George Dan Pte 24818 kia	Tyne Cot Memorial
26.4.18	BARBER Herbert Pte 37021 kia	Tyne Cot Memorial
26.4.18	BASS Charles Frederick Pte 39309 kia	Tyne Cot Memorial
26.4.18	BIRD Ernest Pte 29369 kia	Tyne Cot Memorial
26.4.18	BOLTON Willie Pte MM 15271 kia	Tyne Cot Memorial
26.4.18	BRADBURY Robert Pte 39310 kia	Tyne Cot Memorial
26.4.18	BROOKS Harold Pte 24776 kia	Tyne Cot Memorial
26.4.18	BURKILL Arthur Pte 202351 kia	Tyne Cot Memorial
26.4.18	CARROTT Henry Patterson Pte 39316 kia	Tyne Cot Memorial
26.4.18	CASHMORE Edward Clifford Pte 39314 kia	Tyne Cot Memorial
26.4.18	CHADWICK Albert L/Cpl 50708 kia	Tyne Cot Memorial

26.4.18	CHAPMAN Welburn Pte 33104 kia	Tyne Cot Memorial
26.4.18	CONE Ernest Pte 39318 kia	Tyne Cot Memorial
26.4.18	CROSSLEY William Pte 39319 kia	Tyne Cot Memorial
26.4.18	EASON Arthur Frederick Pte 50697 kia	Tyne Cot Memorial
26.4.18	ECCLES Henry Atkinson Pte 43024 dow	Tyne Cot Memorial
26.4.18	ELLIS Alfred Pte 35120 kia	Tyne Cot Memorial
26.4.18	FINLEY Bernard Edward Pte 13427 kia	Tyne Cot Memorial
26.4.18	FOWLER Walter Pte 13638 kia	Tyne Cot Memorial
26.4.18	GILBERT Arthur Ernest Pte 39308 kia	Tyne Cot Memorial
26.4.18	GILL Albert Pte 20260 kia	Tyne Cot Memorial
26.4.18	GLEDHILL Walter Burdon 36784 kia	Tyne Cot Memorial
26.4.18	GREEN Charles Pte 39327 kia	Tyne Cot Memorial
26.4.18	GREEN Isaac Lawrence Pte 37528 kia	Tyne Cot Memorial
26.4.18	GRINSILL Joseph Cpl 201210 kia	Tyne Cot Memorial
26.4.18	HALL Leonard John Pte 17044 dow	Hoogstaede Belgian Military Cem. 948
26.4.18	HANSON John Henry Pte 37531 kia	Tyne Cot Memorial
26.4.18	HARRATT John Pte 47630 kia	Tyne Cot Memorial
26.4.18	HAYWOOD Harold James Pte 22088	Tyne Cot Memorial
26.4.18	HEPWORTH Arthur Pte 1265 kia	Tyne Cot Memorial
26.4.18	JAMES Harold Pte 235779 dow	Haringhe (Bandeghem) Mil. Cem. III D 8
26.4.18	JAMES Thomas Pte 38703 kia	Tyne Cot Memorial
26.4.18	JOHNSON Josiah Pte 39333 kia	La Clytte Military Cem. VI F 2
26.4.18	JOHNSON Percy Pte 37276 kia	Tyne Cot Memorial
26.4.18	JONES Robert Pte 242431 kia	Tyne Cot Memorial
26.4.18	KENNEY John Frederick Pte 37194 kia	Tyne Cot Memorial
26.4.18	KEVITT William Henry Alphonse Pte 38709 kia	Tyne Cot Memorial
26.4.18	LAWRENCE Conrad Pte 39291 kia	Tyne Cot Memorial
26.4.18	LAYCOCK Seth Pte 42368 kia	Tyne Cot Memorial
26.4.18	LOMES Stephen Alfred Pte 203968 kia	Tyne Cot Memorial
26.4.18	MADDOCK Thomas Pte 8804 kia	Tyne Cot Memorial
26.4.18	McARTHUR Samuel Pte 35035 kia	Tyne Cot Memorial
26.4.18	McLEAN Robert Stevenson Pte 37208 kia	Tyne Cot Memorial
26.4.18	MALONE James Augustine Pte 28078 kia	Tyne Cot Memorial
26.4.18	MANN George Percy Pte 39334 kia	Tyne Cot Memorial
26.4.18	MAY Arnold Pte 12/677 kia	Tyne Cot Memorial
26.4.18	MOAKES Ernest L/Cpl 21332 kia	Wytschaete Military Cem. I B 11
26.4.18	MURRAY Walker Pte MM 27373 kia	Tyne Cot Memorial
26.4.18	ORMONDROYD William Pte 201392	Tyne Cot Memorial
26.4.18	PAYTON Arthur William Pte 44086 kia	La Clytte Military Cem. IV D 27
26.4.18	PORTSMITH William Pte 16997 kia	Tyne Cot Memorial
26.4.18	RICHARDSON Percy L/Cpl 29480 kia	La Clytte Military Cem. IV D 22
26.4.18	ROBINSON Tom Pte 37041 kia	Tyne Cot Memorial
26.4.18	ROBSON John Robert Pte 38757 kia	Tyne Cot Memorial
26.4.18	SAYNOR Frank Cyril Pte 40328 kia	Tyne Cot Memorial
26.4.18	SLEDDON Richard Pte 37088 kia	Tyne Cot Memorial
26.4.18	STIMPSON Denman Pte 26406 kia	Tyne Cot Memorial
26.4.18	TAYLOR George CSM 12/331 kia	Tyne Cot Memorial
26.4.18	TAYLOR Richard Alfred Pte 34309 kia	Tyne Cot Memorial
26.4.18	THOMPSON John Dring Pte MM 37665 kia	La Clytte Military Cem. IV D 18
26.4.18	THORPE George L/Sgt 16413 kia	Tyne Cot Memorial
26.4.18	TOWNSEND Geoffrey L/Cpl 27072 kia	Tyne Cot Memorial
26.4.18	WILLIAMS William Owen Pte 36645 kia	Tyne Cot Memorial
26.4.18	WILLIAMSON Harold Pte 205517 kia	Tyne Cot Memorial
26.4.18	WILLS Albert Pte 38783 kia	Tyne Cot Memorial
26.4.18	WOOLLEY Wilfred Pte 24532 kia	Tyne Cot Memorial
26.4.18	YATES John Pte 37818 kia	Tyne Cot Memorial
27.4.18	BURCHER Albert Edward Pte 43678 dow	Longuenesse Souvenir Cem. V A 74
27.4.18	CHESHER Arthur John Pte 23230 kia	Tyne Cot Memorial
27.4.18	COLLINS James Pte 35172 dow	Esquelbecq Military Cem. I A 23
27.4.18	LEATHER Ernest Pte 12/184 dow	Haringhe (Bandaghem) Mil. Cem. V A 6

27.4.18	MARTIN George Pte 35736 kia	Klein-Vierstraat British Cem. V B 4
27.4.18	MORGAN George Cpl MM 16501 dow	Esquelbecq Military Cem. I A 24
27.4.18	SANDERSON John William Pte 235155 kia	Tyne Cot Memorial
27.4.18	TAYLOR John Pte 202675 dow	Longueness Souvenir Cem. V A 77
28.4.18	CRAWLEY Alfred Pte 34517 dow	Arneke British Cem. II A 9
28.4.18	FIELDING Benjamin Pte 39740 dow	Arneke British Cem. II A 1
28.4.18	RICH Douglas Thomas Pte 14851 dow	Esquelbecq Military Cem. I A 43
29.4.18	CALVERT Leonard Pte 242169 kia	Tyne Cot Memorial
29.4.18	SCHOLEY Tom Pte 17680 kia	Tyne Cot Memorial
29.4.18	SOWERBY George Briggs Pte 43051 kia	Tyne Cot Memorial
30.4.18	HARDY Frank Pte 8999 d.	Rue Petillon Military Cem. II A 6
30.4.18	NEWELL James Pte 24745 dow	Harlebeke New British Cem. XII D 9
2.5.18	BURFITT Walter Percy Pte 43998	Boulogne Eastern Cem. IX B 30
2.5.18	PLANT Charles Henry Pte 25464 dow	Boulogne Eastern Cem. IX B 14
6.5.18	BARNES Arthur Pte 37057 dow	Niederzwehren Cem. (Ger) X A 17
9.5.18	WELLS Herbert Pte 12760 dow	Esquelbecq Military Cem. II C 5
27.5.18	JAMES Robert Kenneth Lt (attd 9th)	Soissons Memorial
27.5.18	ACKROYD William Pte 235115 kia	Jonchery-sur-Vesle British Cem. I E 16
27.5.18	ARMITAGE Joseph Pte 242866 kia	Soissons Memorial
27.5.18	BARRATT Stephen Pte 37133 kia	Soissons Memorial
27.5.18	BOOTH Ernest Pte 15274 kia	Soissons Memorial
27.5.18	BROADHEAD Wallace Pte 37275 kia	Soissons Memorial
27.5.18	COUTTS David Pte 43729 kia	Soissons Memorial
27.5.18	DIXON John Bailey Pte MM 39756 kia	Soissons Memorial
27.5.18	HARLING Harold Zetland Pte 38697 kia	Soissons Memorial
27.5.18	HORNER Henry L/Cpl 28868 kia	Soissons Memorial
27.5.18	MOSS Ernest Pte 38729 kia	Soissons Memorial
27.5.18	NORTON John Pte 27989 kia	Jonchery-sur-Vesle British Cem. I E 18
27.5.18	POYSER Samuel Pte 35352 kia	Soissons Memorial
27.5.18	RICHARDSON George Pte 34662 kia	Soissons Memorial
27.5.18	SPENCE Albert Pte 36325 kia	Soissons Memorial
27.5.18	SUMMERSCALES George Pte 200917 kia	Rethel French National Cem. 1717
27.5.18	TERHEEGE Percy Pte 13769 kia	Soissons Memorial
27.5.18	TIMMINS Bertram Pte 35791 kia	Soissons Memorial
28.5.18	BROWN William L/Cpl 242374 kia	Soissons Memorial
28.5.18	NOBLE Joseph Pte 25054 kia	Romigny Churchyard
28.5.18	WOOLLEY Herbert Pte 263014 dow	J-sur-Vesle, Tramery Mil Cem. Menn 2
29.5.18	WALKER George Pte 205475 kia	Jonchery-sur-Vesle British Cem. I H 11
30.5.18	LIGHTFOOT Herbert Pte 21104 dow	Rethel French National Cem. 1741
31.5.18	HIGGINS Gilbert Arthur Pte 44043 d.	Wimereux Communal Cem. XI G 6
4.6.18	BLISSETT Harold Pte 39306 dow	Vittel Communal Cem.
24.6.18	WHITELEY Reginald William Pte 39822 dow	Courtrai (St Jean) Communal Cem. B 32
26.6.18	SYKES George Pte 39696	Poznan Old Garrison Cem. (P) I A 3
30.6.18	JACKSON John Pte 13572 d.	Pozières Memorial
14.7.18	CAIN James Pte 14968 d.	Niederzwehren Cem. (Ger) V E 5
16.7.18	ABBOTT George Cecil Pte 39303 d.	Niederzwehren Cem. (Ger) VIII D 5
27.7.18	WALLWORTH Stanley Pte 37096 dow	St Imoges Churchyard A 19
8.8.18	BAMFORD Clement Pte 39823 kia	Mailly Wood Cem. II P 10
8.8.18	SANDFORD Percy Stewart Pte 64913 kia	Mailly Wood Cem. II P 11
8.8.18	SWIFT George Pte 62785 kia	Mailly Wood Cem. II P 9
14.8.18	BYERS Robert Pte 49737 dow Germany	Soissons Memorial
15.8.18	GRAFTON William Salter 2nd-Lt kia	Mesnil Communal Cem. II C 3A
15.8.18	BATES Joseph Cpl 21236 kia	Serre Road No. 1 Cem. VI H 27
15.8.18	DIXON Arthur Gawthorpe Pte 62695 kia	Vis-en-Artois Memorial
15.8.18	EDWARDS John Pte MM 203042 kia	Serre Road No. 1 Cem. I H 38
15.8.18	GENT Joseph Pte 64855 kia	Vis-en-Artois Memorial
15.8.18	HODGSON Victor Pte 62721 kia	Vis-en-Artois Memorial
15.8.18	NEUMANN Carl Ernst Sgt 13827 kia	Vis-en-Artois Memorial
15.8.18	PILLER Walter Pte 64904 kia	Vis-en-Artois Memorial
15.8.18	ROOK Fred L/Cpl 235812 kia	Vis-en-Artois Memorial

15.8.18	ROWBOTTOM Albert Pte 64986 kia	Vis-en-Artois Memorial
15.8.18	SHIRT Robert Pte 49714 kia	Vis-en-Artois Memorial
16.8.18	COOPER Charles Alfred J. L/Cpl 62687 kia	Serre Road No. 1 Cem. I H 33
16.8.18	CUNNINGHAM John Pte 46988 kia	Vis-en-Artois Memorial
16.8.18	SYKES Samuel Pte 34089 kia	Vis-en-Artois Memorial
17.8.18	MINNETT George Pte 62754 dow	Bagneux British Cem. IV C 31
23.8.18	GIBBS William Thomas Pte 64940 kia	Serre Road No.1 Cem. I J 10
23.8.18	REDIHOUGH Harry Pte 11232 kia	Regina Trench Cem. VIII G 14
23.8.18	TAYLOR Cecil Pte 235567 kia	Vis-en-Artois Memorial
24.8.18	GILLARD Frederick 2nd-Lt kia	Vis-en-Artois Memorial
24.8.18	BEATTY Reginald MM 240205 dow	Fienvillers British Cem. A 21
24.8.18	BOOTLAND Arthur Pte 64830 kia	Vis-en-Artois Memorial
24.8.18	BUXTON Henry Pte 37752 kia	Regina Trench Cem. VII A 7
24.8.18	CARROLL Francis Pte 62683 kia	Regina Trench Cem. IX L 29
24.8.18	CHESTER Paul Pte 64836 kia	Vis-en-Artois Memorial
24.8.18	CROSS F.M. Pte 47474 kia	Regina Trench Cem. VIII K 6
24.8.18	DIXON Harold Pte 33281 kia	Vis-en-Artois Memorial
24.8.18	DRYDEN Robert Pte 62696 kia	Regina Trench Cem. VII A 8
24.8.18	GIBSON Frederick Pte 30312 dow	Bagneux British Cem. IV E 27
24.8.18	GRAYHURST Henry Pte 30096 kia	Regina Trench Cem. VII A 15
24.8.18	HARRISON Arthur Pte 62718 dow	Ancre British Cem. IV D 23
24.8.18	HODGKINSON Leonard Clauden 9048 kia	Vis-en-Artois Memorial
24.8.18	JENKINSON Edward Pte 64872 kia	Regina Trench Cem. VII B 10
24.8.18	MARSHALL Ernest Pte 64883 kia	Regina Trench Cem. VII B 18
24.8.18	OSBORNE Frederick Pte 30709 kia	Vis-en-Artois Memorial
24.8.18	PARKER Frederick Sykes Pte 200217 kia	Vis-en-Artois Memorial
24.8.18	PIGOTT George Henry Pte 39818 kia	Regina Trench Cem. VII A 13
24.8.18	TAYLOR Frank Pte 62791 kia	Regina Trench Cem. VII B 20
24.8.18	WHITEHEAD Ernest Pte 62808 kia	Regina Trench Cem. VII B 5
25.8.18	CARD John Oliver Pte 19475 dow	Rethel French National Cem. 1710
26.8.18	BAXTER Ernest Cpl 235795 kia	Vis-en-Artois Memorial
26.8.18	BEDDOWS Willie Pte 64826 kia	Vis-en-Artois Memorial
26.8.18	BINNS Harris Pte 64829 dow	Bagneux British Cem. VI D 13
26.8.18	BISHOP Bert L/Cpl 23197 dow	Etaples Military Cem. LXVII G 28
26.8.18	CALVERT Ernest L/Cpl 29747 kia	Warlencourt British Cem. IV F 39
26.8.18	DAVIES Thomas WO2 MM 62626 kia	Warlencourt British Cem. IV F 13
26.8.18	EASTER Herbert A/Cpl 23121 dow	Connaught Cem. VIII G 7
26.8.18	FUSSEY Ernest Pte 47469 kia	AIF Burial Ground XI E 7
26.8.18	GREENWOOD Walter Pte 205581 kia	AIF Burial Ground XI E 4
26.8.18	HALL Arthur Pte 238111 kia	Warlencourt British Cem. IV F 36
26.8.18	HARTSHORN Edward L/Cpl 200487 kia	AIF Burial Ground XI E 5
26.8.18	JOHNSON Arthur Preston Pte 62734 kia	Vis-en-Artois Memorial
26.8.18	JOWETT Thomas Lister Pte 62736 kia	AIF Burial Ground IX J 2
26.8.18	KING Arthur Pte 38708 kia	Vis-en-Artois Memorial
26.8.18	LAYBOURN John Roy Pte 64876 kia	Regina Trench Cem. VII B 19
26.8.18	LAYCOCK Joseph Benjamin Pte 64980 kia	AIF Burial Ground IX J 5
26.8.18	MALTAS Ernest Pte 64882 kia	Warlencourt British Cem. IV D 31
26.8.18	O'HAGAN Michael Pte 34760 kia	Warlencourt British Cem. IV F 15
26.8.18	PARKER Frank Pte 64897 kia	Vis-en-Artois Memorial
26.8.18	ROBINSON Henry Hurst Pte 62774 kia	Vis-en-Artois Memorial
26.8.18	SHAW Arthur James Pte 64915 kia	AIF Burial Ground IX E 6
26.8.18	WALLIS William Pte 24429 dow	Warlencourt British Cem. I C 3
26.8.18	WOODWARD Oscar Cecil Cpl 22206 dow	Bagneux British Cem. VI D 14
29.8.18	KAYE Edward Cpl 30920 dow	Pozières British Cem. II A 15
30.8.18	CARTER Charles Frederick Pte 37134 kia	Brie British Cem. II H 12
1.9.18	TAYLOR Joe Sykes Pte 43063 dow	Bagneux British Cem. V F 4
2.9.18	GREENWOOD Harry Pte 43139 kia	Vaulx Hill Cem. I K 8
2.9.18	McDONOUGH William Henry Pte 64887 dow	Terlincthun British Cem. III A 25
4.9.18	MAWSON David Pte 65074 dow	St Sever Cem. Ext. RII J 20
8.9.18	MORRIS Beriah Pte MM 241070 dow	St Sever Cem. Ext. RII H 9

9.9.18	COOIL Henry Stuart 2nd-Lt (attd 9th) kia	Gouzeaucourt New British Cem. I H 11
9.9.18	GREEN Percy 2nd-Lt kia	Gouzeaucourt New British Cem. I A 10
9.9.18	OVERMAN John Gilbert 2nd-Lt (HQ) kia	Gouzeaucourt New British Cem. I H 8
9.9.18	BARTHOLOMEW Raymond Pte 63868 kia	Vis-en-Artois Memorial
9.9.18	CAVELL Walter Pte 27237 kia	Vis-en-Artois Memorial
9.9.18	CROSLAND Hurst Pte 21974 kia	Vis-en-Artois Memorial
9.9.18	DIXON William 63741 kia	Vis-en-Artois Memorial
9.9.18	DUDDING Francis Clifford Pte 36745 kia	Vis-en-Artois Memorial
9.9.18	FERGUSON Gilford Pte 63710 kia	Gouzeaucourt New British Cem. V B 20
9.9.18	GARRETT Frederick Pte 41294 kia	Vis-en-Artois Memorial
9.9.18	GIBSON Joseph Watson Pte 63712 kia	Vis-en-Artois Memorial
9.9.18	GLENDINNING John Joseph Pte 63745 kia	Vis-en-Artois Memorial
9.9.18	GODDARD Ernest Pte 62714 kia	Vis-en-Artois Memorial
9.9.18	HOLDEN George Willie Pte 22012 dow	St Sever Cem. Ext. RII P 11
9.9.18	HOLGATE Herbert Pte 36163 kia	Gouzeaucourt New British Cem. I H 12
9.9.18	MAXWELL James Pte 63687 kia	Vis-en-Artois Memorial
9.9.18	OLDROYD Arthur Pte 53457 kia	Villers Hill British Cem. Sp Mem. 7
9.9.18	OSBORNE Walter Pte 31759 kia	Vis-en-Artois Memorial
9.9.18	RICHARDS David Brynmans Pte 64959 kia	Vis-en-Artois Memorial
9.9.18	SHORT Walter Frederick Cpl MM 18794 kia	Vis-en-Artois Memorial
9.9.18	TITTENSOR George Coomer Pte 47638 dow	Bagneux British Cem. VI F 32
9.9.18	VERRILL Thomas Vincent Sgt 204626 kia	Vis-en-Artois Memorial
9.9.18	WALTHAM Nathan Pte 53433 kia	Gouzeaucourt New British Cem. VI C 11
9.9.18	WARNER Frederick Pte 40749 kia	Vis-en-Artois Memorial
9.9.18	WHITE James Pte 63857 kia	Vis-en-Artois Memorial
10.9.18	ARMITAGE William Pte 52845 dow	Five Points Cem. B2
10.9.18	NESSWORTHY Ambrose Pte 63720 dow	Varennes Military Cem. III L 6
11.9.18	DRURY Leonard George 2nd-Lt MC dow	Mont Huon Military Cem. VIII E 2
12.9.18	WICKER John Arthur Pte 63848 dow	Varennes Military Cem. III L 9
17.9.18	BROADBENT Samuel Pte 11619 dow	Vis-en-Artois Memorial
18.9.18	HUTCHINSON Tom 2nd-Lt (attd 9th) kia	Villers Hill British Cem. II A 25
18.9.18	ASHLEY Fred Pte 63704 kia	Gouzeaucourt New British Cem. VIII D 9
18.9.18	BORTHWICK Francis Pte 63738 kia	Vis-en-Artois Memorial
18.9.18	CATON John Pte 39315 kia	Vis-en-Artois Memorial
18.9.18	CHAPMAN George Pte 63739 kia	Vis-en-Artois Memorial
18.9.18	CLARKSON Henry Pte 53281 kia	Vis-en-Artois Memorial
18.9.18	CRANE Philip Edmund Pte 36198 kia	Vis-en-Artois Memorial
18.9.18	HEALEY Fred Pte 30125 kia	Vis-en-Artois Memorial
18.9.18	HILL Walter Pte 64869 kia	Villers Hill British Cem. IV C 12
18.9.18	LAWLOR Thomas Pte 64875 kia	Vis-en-Artois Memorial
18.9.18	LEES John Thomas Holmes Pte 37205 kia	Vis-en-Artois Memorial
18.9.18	LIDDELL Thomas Pte 63761 kia	Vis-en-Artois Memorial
18.9.18	MITCHELL Fred Pte 49735 kia	Gouzeaucourt New British Cem. VIII D 5
18.9.18	NEWTON Harry Pte 12/1044 kia	Vis-en-Artois Memorial
18.9.18	STUBBINGS George Pte 64923 kia	Vis-en-Artois Memorial
18.9.18	TIFFANY Thomas Pte 53463 kia	Vis-en-Artois Memorial
18.9.18	TOYNE Sydney Pte 50026 kia	Vis-en-Artois Memorial
18.9.18	WATERS Charles William Pte 27813 kia	Gouzeaucourt New British Cem. VI E 6
18.9.18	WOODCOCK John W. Pte 53430 dow	Vis-en-Artois Memorial
19.9.18	CUMMINS Norman Pte 63671 kia	Vis-en-Artois Memorial
19.9.18	METCALFE George Henry Pte 64939 dow	Grevillers British Cem. XIII D 1
20.9.18	McLARTY Hector L/Cpl 43154 dow	Five Points Cem. B19
22.9.18	BOOTH Frank Pte 31619 d.	Vis-en-Artois Memorial
24.9.18	GILL Edward Pte 64970 dow Home	Leeds Armley Cem. (UK) C 622
26.9.18	WEDGEWOOD Herbert Pte 36614 d.	Montcornet Military Cem. B2
3.10.18	KEEN Sidney Pte 34421 dow	Mont Huon Military Cem. VIII H 7A
5.10.18	HAYES Wilton Pte 37182 dow Germany	Maubert Fontaine German Cem. Mem.
7.10.18	WILSON E. Pte 30957	Cologne Southern Cem. XIV G 2
8.10.18	WOODLEY Charles 2nd-Lt	Prospect Hill Cem. V A 20
8.10.18	BARRETT Lionel Pte 62672 kia	Vis-en-Artois Memorial

8.10.18	MORLEY James Cpl 12/1112 kia	Vis-en-Artois Memorial
8.10.18	PITTS John Pte 45067 kia	Marcoing British Cem. II D 8
8.10.18	PLOWMAN George Pte 47132 dow	Rocquigny-Equancourt Rd Br Cem. IX A 23
8.10.18	SLATER Frederick Stanley Pte 49927 kia	Bois-des-Angles Cem. I A 11
10.10.18	WILBY George Pte 27881 d.	Niederzwehren Cem. (G) I G 4
16.10.18	COOPER William Henry Pte 37065 d.	Berlin South West Cem. XVIII C 6
19.10.18	STEAD Joseph Pte 39693 kia	Terlincthun British Cem. VIII C 15
21.10.18	ROBINSON Robert Whitburn Pte 235347 dow	Berlin South West Cem. V F 6
23.10.18	AKED Arthur Pte 64822 dow	Caudry British Cem.
23.10.18	ANDERSON Frank Pte 37905 kia	Amerval Communal Cem. C 5
23.10.18	BELLIS Thomas William Pte 64827 kia	Romeries Communal Cem. VI B 5
23.10.18	BLAND Albert Pte 62673 kia	Amerval Communal Cem. C 18
23.10.18	BREAR Walter L/Cpl 10544 kia	Amerval Communal Cem. C 3
23.10.18	CHALKLEY John Pte 30080 kia	St Souplet British Cem. I D 38
23.10.18	EDGAR Theodore Pte 63742 kia	Amerval Communal Cem. C 17
23.10.18	FOSTER John Henry Pte 35432 kia	Amerval Communal Cem. C 19
23.10.18	FOSTER Joseph Pte 63743 kia	Vis-en-Artois Memorial
23.10.18	FRITH Dorman Brema Pte 63839 dow	Awoingt British Cem. I B 25
23.10.18	GILBANK James Pte 19282 kia	Vis-en-Artois Memorial
23.10.18	HAITHWAITE Frederick Pte 38699 kia	Amerval Communal Cem. B 34
23.10.18	HARLEY Joseph Pte 238022 kia	Amerval Communal Cem. C 11
23.10.18	HARRISON Arthur Pte 42278 kia	Romeries Communal Cem. Ext. VI E 14
23.10.18	KIMBER Richard Pte 63682 kia	Amerval Communal Cem. B 33
23.10.18	LEE Harry L/Cpl 36423 kia	St Souplet British Cem. I E 15
23.10.18	MARTIN Frederick James Pte 38530 kia	Amerval Communal Cem. C 6
23.10.18	METCALF Ralph Pte 35270 kia	Amerval Communal Cem. C 1
23.10.18	MILBURN Arthur Pte 263012 kia	St Souplet British Cem. I E 12
23.10.18	ROBINSON Leslie Pte 53624 kia	Amerval Communal Cem. C 21
23.10.18	SANDERSON Robert Pte 62787 kia	Poix du Nord Communal Cem. Ext. II B 9
23.10.18	SMITH Joseph Henry Pte 62779 dow	Inchy Communal Cem. B 32
23.10.18	STIMSON Frank Molyneux Pte 203356 kia	Romeries Communal Cem. Ext. VI E 15
23.10.18	THREADGOLD William Hill A/Cpl 21244 kia	Amerval Communal Cem. B 36
23.10.18	WALKER William Pte 53613 kia	Neuvilly Communal Cem. B 29
23.10.18	WALL William Pte 37874 kia	St Souplet British Cem. I E 8
23.10.18	WALLS Edgar Stanley Pte 29481	Romeries Communal Cem. Ext. VI E 12
23.10.18	WALTON John Pte 52635 kia	Vis-en-Artois Memorial
24.10.18	PERCIVAL Walter Lowe 2nd-Lt (attd 9th) dow	Poix du Nord Communal Cem. Ext. II B 17
24.10.18	WEBSTER John Phillip Lt dow	Awoingt British Cem. I B 15
24.10.18	EXLEY Henry Pte 37158 kia	Amerval Communal Cem. B 37
24.10.18	FITZPATRICK Cyril Pte 53626 dow	Awoingt British Cem. II D 24
24.10.18	GREEN Arthur Tom Pte 65226 kia	Vis-en-Artois Memorial
24.10.18	GREENWOOD Harry Pte 62713 kia	Poix du Nord Communal Cem. Ext. II B 8
24.10.18	HODGSON Joseph Pte 63714 kia	Vis-en-Artois Memorial
24.10.18	HUNTER Harold Armstrong Pte 63751 kia	Amerval Communal Cem. C 22
24.10.18	INCH James William Pte 62729 kia	Vendegies-au-Bois British Cem. A 4
24.10.18	MUDDIMAN Reginald Pte 53489 kia	Poix du Nord Communal Cem. Ext. II B 7
24.10.18	NEASHAM Thomas William Pte 63767 kia	Poix du Nord Communal Cem. Ext. II B 11
24.10.18	NEWTON Leonard Pte 64891 kia	Amerval Communal Cem. C 16
24.10.18	PALFREMAN Charles Pte 53616 kia	Romeries Communal Cem. Ext. V A 15
24.10.18	SALES Robert Harold L/Cpl 205695 kia	Amerval Communal Cem. Ext. C 10
24.10.18	SHELDON Luther Henry Pte MM & Bar 33362 kia	St. Souplet British Cem. I E 7
24.10.18	SLINGER John Davis Sgt 62630 dow	Inchy Communal Cem. B 40
24.10.18	SMITH Percy Harry William Pte 40584 kia	Vis-en-Artois Memorial
24.10.18	WETHERS George Osmond Pte 203964 kia	Amerval Communal Cem. C 20
24.10.18	WRIGHT Harold Thomas Pte 64933 kia	Englefontaine British Cem. D 46
25.10.18	SMITH William Byron 2nd-Lt (attd 9th) dow	Awoingt British Cem. I E 11
25.10.18	MOODY Boaz Pte 44075 dow	Awoingt British Cem. I G 9
25.10.18	SWINBURNE Thomas Pte 62784 dow	Awoingt British Cem. I G 23
26.10.18	GARGIN John Pte 63746 dow	St Sever Cem Ext. S.II KK 15
27.10.18	DOBSON Thomas Pte 235371 kia	Vis-en-Artois Memorial
28.10.18	BROWN Frank Pte 37490 d.	Houyet Churchyard A 8

29.10.18	ROOKS Francis Pte 43574 dow	Berlin South West Cem. XIII C 3
30.10.18	FEARNLEY Sam Pte 49741 d. Germany	Niederzwehren Cem. V M 5
1.11.18	NELSON John Pte 53491 d.	Hautmont Communal Cem. IV D 9
1.11.18	SMITH Walter Pte 235160 dow	Givet German Cem Memorial
3.11.18	COATES Frederick Pte 17640 d.	Hamburg Cem. (G) IV E 3
3.11.18	HUTCHINSON Richard Pte 3/1919 d.	Cologne Southern Cem. XII B 27
5.11.18	THORNTON Charles Henry Pte 51874 kia	Fontaine-au-Bois Communal Cem. B 11
7.11.18	HUNTER Archibald 2nd-Lt kia	Dourlers Communal Cem. II C 22
7.11.18	ALLAN Ronald Pte 235470 dow	Ghissignies British Cem. B37
7.11.18	BRODIE Robert Pte 68073 kia	Dourlers Communal Cem. II B 10
7.11.18	BULLOCK Richard Cpl MM 18736 kia	Dourlers Communal Cem. II B 3
7.11.18	BUTTERFIELD Eddie Pte 59000 kia	Dourlers Communal Cem. II B 4
7.11.18	COOK Percy William Pte 65225 kia	Dourlers Communal Cem. II B 5
7.11.18	FOWLER George Pte 59201 kia	Dourlers Communal Cem. II B 9
7.11.18	FURNISS Ernest L/Cpl 53476 dow	Aulnoye Communal Cem. A 10
7.11.18	JACKSON Ernest Cpl MM 3/1629 kia	Dourlers Communal Cem. II B 1
7.11.18	LAING Alexander Kewen Pte 62740 kia	Maubeuge Centre Cem. D 37
7.11.18	MOUNSEY Joseph Pte 63686 kia	Dourlers Communal Cem. II B 12
7.11.18	RIPLEY Squire Pte 15015 kia	Vis-en-Artois Memorial
7.11.18	SHAW Joseph Osborne Pte 53617 kia	Dourlers Communal Cem. II B 8
7.11.18	SUTCLIFFE Herbert A/Cpl 242522 kia	Maubeuge Centre Cem. D 2
7.11.18	WAITE Sidney Pte 62252 kia	Dourlers Communal Cem. II B 7
7.11.18	WHITE Jack Pte 59001 kia	Dourlers Communal Cem. II B 6
8.11.18	BROOKES Enoch Lot Pte 36213 d.	Berlin South West Cem. XIII C 9
8.11.18	DODD Fred L/Cpl 62699 dow	Ghissignies British Cem. B 39
8.11.18	HOWLETT-TURNER Edward Francis Pte 59217 dow	Caudry British Cem. IV D 28
8.11.18	LEARY Arthur Pte 38714 d.	Niederzwehren Cem. (G) IV F 15
8.11.18	MASSEY Oliver Pte 53483 d.	Etaples Military Cem. XLIX D 26
8.11.18	SOAMES George Pte 43712 d. Germany	Hautrage Military Marche Ger. Cem. Mem 1
8.11.18	STACEY Francis Joseph Pte 64938 dow	Caudry British Cem. IV H 37
8.11.18	WILSON George Pte 41327 d.	Ingolstadt Cem. (G) Mem 10
9.11.18	CONNOLLY Thomas Pte 23036 d.	Hautrage Military Cem. IV A 19
9.11.18	GRAY James Joyce A/Cpl 36888 dow	Caudry British Cem. I B 21
11.11.18	MILLINGTON John Pte 34644 dow	Delsaux Farm Cem. III A 12
12.11.18	CURTIS John William L/Cpl 64842 dow	Caudry British Cem. I B 29
12.11.18	HESELTINE Thomas Arnold Pte MM 37076 d.	Niederzwehren Cem. (G) IV D 14
12.11.18	STROTTON George Leonard Pte 44155	Vis-en-Artois Memorial
12.11.18	WOOD Harry Pte 41288 dow Germany	Hautrage Military Cem. IV A 16
14.11.18	DAVILL Henry Cpl MM 30318 dow	Caudry British Cem. I D 24
14.11.18	LEE Louis Alfred Pte 40567 dow Home	Camberwell Cem. (UK)
14.11.18	THOMPSON Henry Stancer Pte 201145 d. Germany	Berlin South West Cem. VIII P 8
15.11.18	HUGHES W.C. Cpl 17169 d.	Berlin South West Cem. XV B 3
16.11.18	ROOKES Ernest Pte 15057	Normanton Upper Cem. (UK) L 9 20
20.11.18	TRAVIS Ernest Pte 28293 d.	Terlincthun British Cem. XI C 19
27.11.18	WALKER Albert Pte 209964 dow	Etaples Military Cem. LI C 17
28.11.18	LILEY Harry Pte 39301 d.	Niederzwehren Cem. (G) VI K 18
2.12.18	HOPE Joseph Thomas Pte 63677 dow Home	Langley Park All Saints Ch'd (SE Corner)
8.12.18	SPINK W. Cpl 19304 d. Home	Leeds Holbeck Cem. (UK) Gen. 1831
10.12.18	WHITHAM Tom Pte 202616 dow Home	Meltham Wesleyan Burial Ground (UK) 294

1919

4.2.19	COOPER W.G. Pte 37497	Dewsbury Cem. (UK) B 'C' 401
15.2.19	ISLE Robert William Pte 64983 d. Home	Goole Cem. (UK) A Centre 'C' 754
28.2.19	GRIFFITHS Harold Pte 21201	Wakefield Cem. (UK) A 'U' 1132
5.7.19	INGLE James A/Cpl 62730 d.	Beaulencourt British Cem. I D 13
25.7.19	HAMILTON John James Pte 43105	Newcastle St John's (UK) 179

1920

19.9.20	TIMSON S. Pte 19843	Kippax (Sts May & Nicholas) Ch'd North

APPENDIX II

FATAL CASUALTY STATISTICS

The statistics used in this section are based not on the total number listed in Appendix 1 of 1,338, but on the figure of 1,324, that being the number killed between September 1915 and the end of November 1918, that is, the period of 'Active Service'.

A: The first table shows the percentage casualties for each year of the conflict. It is 1918, with its three defensive actions and the offensives that followed, which shows the highest.

PERCENTAGE BY YEAR:

YEAR	%	NO. KILLED
1915	4.83	64
1916	33.53	444
1917	21.82	289
1918	39.80	527

(Due to decimal places being rounded up, the total percentages do not add up to 100!)

B: The second table presents the heaviest days. It is surprising to find that *over 49%* of all fatal casualties for the period specified were suffered on only *seven* particular days.

HEAVIEST DAYS:

27 September 1915	42
1 July 1916	178
16 September 1916	121
9 April 1917	72
4 October 1917	97
22 March 1918	72
26 April 1918	69
Total	651

C: The final table shows fatal casualties for each month during the specified period, and is graphically illustrated by the bar chart.

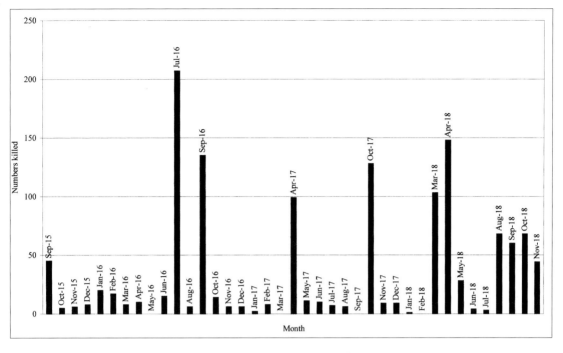

9th (Service) Battalion KOYLI fatal casualties, September 1915-November 1918.

MONTHLY FATAL CASUALTIES:

	1915	1916	1917	1918
January		20	2	1
February		17	8	0
March		8	0	103
April		10	99	148
May		0	11	28
June		15	10	4
July		207	7	3
August		6	6	68
September	45	135	0	60
October	5	14	128	68
November	6	6	9	44
December	8	6	9	

BIBLIOGRAPHY

Bond, *History of the KOYLI Vol. III The Great War*
Brown, M., *The Imperial War Museum Book of the Somme* (Sidgwick & Jackson, 1996)
Edmonds, (Sir) J., *Military Operations France and Belgium 1914* (Vols I & II)
—, *Military Operations France and Belgium 1915* (Vols I & II)
—, *Military Operations France and Belgium 1916* (Vols I & II)
—, *Military Operations France and Belgium 1917* (Vols I & II)
—, *Military Operations France and Belgium 1918* (Vols I, II, III, IV & V) (Imperial War Museum)★
Fletcher, D. (Ed.), *Tanks and Trenches* (Alan Sutton Publishing, 1994)
Gliddon, G., *When the Barrage Lifts* (Alan Sutton Publishing, 1987)
Griffith, P., *Battle Tactics of the Western Front* (Yale University Press, 1994)
Harris, J.P., *Amiens to the Armistice* (Brassey's, 1998)
Haythornewaite, P., *The World War One Sourcebook* (Brockhampton Press, 1992)
Holmes, R., *The Western Front* (BBC Books) 1999
Huxley, C. (Major), *A Short History of the KOYLI 1755-1965* (Wakefield Express Services, 1965)
Johnson, J.H., *1918 The Unexpected Victory* (Arms & Armour Press, 1997)
Liddell Hart, B.H., *History of the First World War* (Penguin, 1972)
Liddell Hart, B.H., *Memoirs* (Cassell, 1965)
Liddle, P. (Ed.), *Passchendaele in Perspective* (Pen & Sword, 1997)
Livesey, A., *The Viking Atlas of World War I* (Viking, 1994)
Macdonald, L., *1914* (Penguin, 1989)
Macdonald, L., *Somme* (MacMillan, 1983)
McCarthy, C., *The Somme. The Day by Day Account* (Arms & Armour Press, 1993)
Middlebrook, M., *The First Day on the Somme* (Penguin, 1984)
Middlebrook, M., *The Kaiser's Battle* (Penguin, 1983)
Neillands, R., *The Great War Generals on the Western Front 1914-18* (Robinson, 1999)
Nicholls, J., *Cheerful Sacrifice* (Leo Cooper, 1993)
Passingham, I., *Pillars of Fire* (Sutton Publishing, 1998)
Pidgeon, T., *The Tanks at Flers* (Fairmile Books, 1995)
Prior, R. and Wilson, T., *Command on the Western Front* (Blackwell, 1992)
Prior, R. and Wilson, T., *Passchendaele: The Untold Story* (Yale University Press, 1996)
Sheffield, G., *Forgotten Victory* (Headline, 2001)
Simkins, P., *Kitchener's Army* (Manchester University Press, 1988)
Simpson, A., *Evolution of Victory* (Donovan, 1995)
Smithers, A.J., *The Fighting Nation* (Leo Cooper, 1994)
Spicer, L.D., *Letters from France* (Robert York, 1979)
Stedman, M., *Fricourt-Mametz. Battleground Europe* (Pen & Sword, 1997)
Tattersfield, D., *A Village Goes to War* (Maxiprint, 2000)
Taylor, A.J.P., *The First World War* (Penguin, 1966)
Terraine, J., *To Win A War 1918 The Year of Victory* (Papermac, 1983)
Terraine, J., *Douglas Haig: The Educated Soldier* (Leo Cooper, 1990)
The Times Diary and Index of the War 1914-1918 (J.B. Hayward & Son, 1985)
Winter, D., *Death's Men* (Penguin, 1979)
Winter, J. and Baggett, B., *1914-18* (BBC Books, 1996)

★Edmonds's *Military Operations France and Belgium* is the *British Official History* referred to throughout the text and notes.

UNPUBLISHED DOCUMENTS:

War Diary 9th KOYLI (Public Record Office)
War Diary 64th Brigade (Public Record Office)
War Diary 21st Division (Public Record Office)
War Diary 10th KOYLI (Public Record Office)
War Diary 15th DLI (Public Record Office)
War Diary 1st East Yorks (Public Record Office)
The First World War Letters of Colonel H.E. Yeo, MBE MC 1915–1919 (Imperial War Museum
The First World War Papers of Brigadier G.F. Ellenberger MC (Imperial War Museum)
Various Documents held by the KOYLI Association, Pontefract, including *The Bugle*, journal of KOYLI and *The Snapper*, journal of the East Yorkshire Regiment.

Daily Mail
Dewsbury Reporter
Huddersfield Examiner

INDEX

If you are interested in purchasing
other books published by Tempus, or in case you have
difficulty finding any Tempus books in your local bookshop,
you can also place orders directly through our website

www.tempus-publishing.com